BEFORE THE
INDUSTRIAL
REVOLUTION

BEFORE THE INDUSTRIAL REVOLUTION

European Society and
Economy, 1000–1700

THIRD EDITION

Carlo M. Cipolla

W·W·NORTON & COMPANY
New York   London

Third Edition first printed by
W. W. Norton & Company 1994

Printed in the United States of America

Manufacturing by Courier Companies, Inc.

Library of Congress Cataloging-in-Publication Data
Cipolla, Carlo M.
[Storia economica dell'Europa pre-industriale. English]
Before the industrial revolution : European society and economy,
1000–1700 / Carlo M. Cipolla. — 3rd ed.
p.   cm.
Includes bibliographical references and index.
1. Europe—Economic conditions.   I. Title.
HC240.C49513   1994
330.94—dc20   94–2708
ISBN 0-393-31198-8
W. W. Norton & Company, Inc., 500 Fifth Avenue,
New York, N.Y. 10110
W. W. Norton & Company Ltd., 10 Coptic Street,
London WC1A 1PU

3 4 5 6 7 8 9 0

CONTENTS

Part I A static approximation

CONTENTS

Part II Toward a dynamic description

ILLUSTRATIONS, MAPS, AND FIGURES

ILLUSTRATIONS

MAPS

FIGURES

TABLES

TABLES

TABLES

PREFACE

The world in which we live and the problems we face cannot be understood without referring to that momentous upheaval known as the Industrial Revolution. Yet the Industrial Revolution was only the final phase, the coherent outcome of a historical development which took place in Europe over the first seven centuries of our now expiring millennium. The purpose of this book is to offer an up-to-date and fully documented summary of the human developments from which our world, with all its blessings and all its woes, eventually emerged.

The book is therefore intended for both students and general readers; although focused on social and economic problems, its approach is essentially interdisciplinary. This double ambivalence may help to explain some of its peculiarities.

Style and exposition have been kept at a reasonably simple level but no efforts have been spared to provide the reader with precise references, abundant statistical material and a wealth of bibliographical information. Disconcerting technicalities have been eliminated without sacrificing scholarly accuracy. At the same time the logical tools of economic and social analysis have been clearly spelled out rather than taken for granted or hidden away in the tissue of the narrative. This, it is hoped, will help the economics student to trace the connections between economic theory and economic history, while acquainting the layman with some of the basic tools of contemporary social sciences.

The book has been organized in two parts. In Part I our analysis is essentially static. It aims to clarify the way in which the society and economy of preindustrial Europe functioned, while emphasizing certain constant characteristics of that society and that economy. Part II illustrates the changes which took place within that framework and which gradually transformed Europe from a primitive, uninteresting and underdeveloped corner of the world, under constant threat from its more powerful neighbors, into a dynamic, highly developed and creative society which came to establish undisputed political, cultural, and economic predominance all over the globe.

Quite naturally, the nature of our inquiry is molded by values, mentalities, and beliefs which are peculiar to our own age and society. When another society is under scrutiny, questions which bear little or no relation to the philosophy, values, and beliefs of that society inevitably pose difficulties. It may be that we are interested in the size of the population, the patterns of consumption or the level of production of, let us say, the province of Reims in France at the beginning of this millennium. What the documents relating to that area give us, however, is detailed information on miracles performed by St Gibrian. Because the documentation left by the past reflects the interests and the values of the past, many of the problems raised in the following pages can receive only tentative or approximate answers. The answers become more precise for centuries closer to our own, as people began to ask the same questions that we ask.

This new edition has given me the opportunity to include findings not available when this book was first published and to revise material based on the suggestions of readers and reviewers. The principal changes are in the discussions of demography and agricultural economics and include the introduction of new material on the history of the northern Netherlands and on Italian manufacturing and trading.

Professor Marcella Kooy and Miss Alide Kooy translated the original Italian text into English. Mr Robert E. Kehoe carefully edited the book and checked on its progress. All additional material included in this third English edition has been translated by Christopher Woodall.

Berkeley, California

Part I

A STATIC
APPROXIMATION

1

DEMAND

TYPE OF ANALYSIS

The functioning of any economic system can be looked at from two points of view, that of demand and that of supply. The two perspectives are intimately linked and reflect the same reality. When one describes them, however, the need to analyze first one and then the other tends arbitrarily to accentuate the distinction between them.

POPULATION

From the point of view of demand, the first point to consider is population. If there were no people there would be no human wants. And if there were no human wants there would be no demand.

The study of population presupposes the collection of demographic data. Venice took censuses of its population as long ago as 1509. In the Grand Duchy of Tuscany censuses covering the whole state were taken in 1552, 1562, 1622, 1632, 1642, and several times thereafter. However, at national levels, reasonably accurate figures about the size as well as the structure of a population are not available before the nineteenth century, with the exception of Scandinavia, for which accurate data are available for the eighteenth century. In Spain a national census was completed in 1789 and was particularly excellent: technically a model of its kind. It found the population of the entire country to number 10,409,879 inhabitants. Other nationwide censuses soon followed: in the United States (1790), in England (1801) and in France (1801) but they were all qualitatively inferior to the Spanish census of 1789.

For the period before 1800, demographic historians have tried to overcome the dearth of data by estimating population on the basis of indirect and heterogeneous information from fields as disparate as archaeology, botany, and toponymy, as well as from written records of the most diverse kind, such as inventories of manors, lists of men liable for military service, and accounts of hearth taxes or poll taxes. Table 1.1 shows estimates of total population for the major areas of Europe. Such figures can be taken only as rough approximations.

The figures for the columns relating to the eleventh and fourteenth centuries are the product of rough hypotheses. Their margin of error is fairly high, not less than 20 percent and perhaps higher. Although the figures in the last two columns are more reliable, they also must not be taken as precise. More reliable figures are available for selected cities (see Appendix Table A.1), but they too are affected by large margins of error and must be taken only as estimates.

However rough, all the figures in Table 1.1 do consistently indicate that up until the eighteenth century the population of Europe remained relatively small. For long periods it did not grow at all, and when it did, the rate of increase was always very low. Few cities ever numbered more than one hundred thousand inhabitants (see Appendix Table A.1). Any city of fifty thousand inhabitants or more was considered a metropolis. The pre-industrial world remained a world of numerically small societies.

If a population does not increase or increases only slightly, in the absence of sizable migratory movements, the reason lies either in low fertility or high mortality or both. In preindustrial Europe fertility varied from period to period and from area to area, so that any generalization must be taken with more than a pinch of salt. Celibacy was always fairly widespread, and when people married they generally did so at a relatively advanced age. These facts tended to reduce fertility; however, prevailing birth rates were still very high, always above the 30-per-thousand level (see Appendix Table A.2). While fertility rarely reached the biological maximum, it was nearer to this maximum than to levels prevailing in developed countries of the twentieth century. If the population of preindustrial Europe remained relatively small, the reason lay less in low fertility than in high mortality. We shall return to this point below, in Chapter 5.

Table 1.1 Approximate population of the major European countries, 1000–1700 (in millions)

	c. 1000	c. 1300	c. 1500	c. 1600	c. 1700
Balkans	—	—	7	8	8
Low Countries	—	—	2	3	3
British Isles	2	5	5	7	9
Danubian countries	—	—	6	7	9
France	5	15	16	18	19
Germany	3	12	13	16	15
Italy	5	10	11	13	13
Poland	—	—	4	5	6
Russia	—	—	10	15	18
Scandinavian countries	—	—	—	2	3
Spain and Portugal	—	—	9	11	10
Switzerland	—	0.8	0.8	1.1	1.2

It is worth distinguishing between normal and catastrophic mortality. The distinction is arbitrary and somewhat artificial, but it has the merit of facilitating description. We can broadly define *normal mortality* as the mortality prevailing in normal years – that is, years free from calamities like wars, famines, epidemics. As a rule normal mortality was below current fertility. *Catastrophic mortality* is the mortality of calamitous years and as a rule far exceeded current fertility. In years of normal mortality, the natural balance of the population (namely, the difference between the number of births and the number of deaths) was generally positive. In years of catastrophic mortality, the natural balance of population was always highly negative. Owing to recurrent ravages of catastrophic mortality linked to famines, wars, and plagues, the populations of the various areas of pre-industrial Europe were constantly subject to drastic fluctuations which, in their turn, were a source of instability for the economic system severely affecting both supply and demand.

NEEDS, WANTS, AND EFFECTIVE DEMAND

All members of a society have "needs." The quantity and quality of these needs vary enormously in relation to numerous circumstances. Even those needs which seem most inelastic, like the physiological need for nourishment, vary considerably from person to person according to gender, age, climate, and type of work. In general, one can say that the quantity and quality of a society's needs depend on:

a. population size
b. the structure of the population by age, gender, and occupation
c. geographical and physical factors
d. sociocultural factors

The first point requires no comment. As to the second, it seems unnecessary to explain that old people and children do not have exactly the same needs, nor do men and women. As for the third, it should be obvious that a man living in Sweden or Siberia has many needs that are totally different from those of a man living in Sicily or Portugal. The relationship between needs and sociocultural conditions is more subtle.

In preindustrial England people were convinced that vegetables "ingender ylle humours and be oftetymes the cause of putrified fevers," melancholy, and flatulence. As a consequence of these ideas there was little demand for fruit and vegetables and the population lived in a prescorbutic state.[1] On the other hand, while many people refused to drink fresh cow's milk, many well-off adults paid wet nurses for the opportunity to suckle milk directly at their breasts. Old Dr Caius maintained that his character changed according to the character of the wet nurse who breast-fed him. Whether his changes of disposition depended primarily on the quality of the

5

milk or on his own hormonal secretions is not a question which should concern us here. The point is that there was a sustained demand for wet nurses not only to feed infants.

Other cultural factors can have an equally determining influence on needs, their nature, and their structure. For centuries Catholics made it a duty to eat fish on Fridays, while the men of the Solomon Islands forbade their women to eat certain types of fish. The Muslim religion forbids its followers to drink wine, while the Catholic religion created in all religious communities a need for wine to celebrate Mass. Extravagant ideas also contributed to the formation of needs held to be indispensable. The Galenic theory of humours created for centuries a widespread need for leeches.

These last examples have actually been chosen to prove that economists have good reason for distrusting the word *needs*. The word implies "lack of substitutes," and is thus seriously misleading in economic analysis. One must also consider that the line of demarcation between the necessary and the superfluous is difficult to define. While daily bread clearly seems necessary and a trip to the Bahamas superfluous, between bread and a trip to the Bahamas there is a vast number of goods and services whose classification is problematic. Obviously the definition of need cannot be limited to the minimum amount of food required to sustain life. But as soon as the criterion is extended beyond that limit to include other items, it is difficult to say where the line between the necessary and the superfluous should fall. Is one steak per week a need? Or is only one steak a month really necessary? We feel we need bathtubs, central heating, and handkerchiefs, but three hundred years ago in Europe these things were luxuries that no one would have dreamed of describing as needs. Someone once wrote that we regard as necessary what we consume and as superfluous what other people consume.

As long as a person is free to demand what he wants, what counts on the market are not real needs but wants. A man may need vitamins but may want cigarettes instead. The distinction is important, not only from the point of view of the individual, but also from the point of view of the society. A society may need more hospitals and more schools, but the members of that society may want more swimming pools, more theaters, or more freeways. There may also be dictators who impose or feed specific wants for military conquest, political prestige, or religious exaltation. For the market, what counts is not the objective need – which in any case no one can define except at minimum levels of subsistence – but the want as it is expressed by both the individual and the society.

In practice our wants are unlimited. Unfortunately, both as individuals and as a society, we only have limited resources at our disposal. As a result, we are continually forced to make choices, imposing on our wants an order of priorities that we derive from a battery of economic as well as political, religious, ethical, and social considerations.

Wants are one thing, effective demand is another. To count on the market, wants must be backed by purchasing power. A starving individual may want food with excruciating intensity, but if he has no purchasing power to back up his want, the market will simply ignore both him and his want. Only when expressed in terms of purchasing power do wants become effective demand, registered by the market.

Since purchasing power depends on income, it follows that, given a certain mass of wants, both private and public, and given a certain scale of priorities, the level and the structure of effective demand are determined by:

a. level of income
b. the distribution of income (among individuals as well as institutions, and between the public and private sectors)[2]
c. level and structure of prices

INCOME AND ITS DISTRIBUTION

The mass of incomes can be divided into three broad categories:

a. wages
b. profits
c. interest and rents

These different kinds of income correspond to different ways of participating in the productive process. Income gives individuals as well as institutions the power to express their wants on the market in the form of effective demand. Obviously the person who earns and receives income spends it not only on himself but also on those he supports. In other words, the head of the family, who works and receives a wage, spends it to maintain not only himself or herself but also a spouse, children, and perhaps also an old mother or father. The earner of income, therefore, translates into effective demand not only his own personal wants, but also those of his own dependants. In other words, the income of the "active population" converts to effective demand the wants of the total population (active population plus dependent population).

Over the centuries, for the mass of the people, income was represented by wages (and in the agricultural sector by shares of the crops). Up to the Industrial Revolution one can say that, given the low productivity of labor (see below) and other institutional factors, wages were extremely low in relation to prices; that is, real wages were extremely low. Turning this on its head, we can say that current prices of goods were too high for current wages. In practical terms we would be saying the same thing, but we would be emphasizing that the basic problem was scarcity.

European society was fundamentally poor, but in every corner of Europe there were gradations of poverty and wealth. There were poor and very

7

poor, and alongside them there were some rich and some very rich. Among the poorest, the peasants were overrepresented, yet even among them one would have found the very poor, the poor, and the not so poor. Differences were not only clearly visible at single places or within well-defined areas but also broadly across the borders. Early in the seventeenth century, a well-informed English traveler recorded:

> As for the poore *paisant* [in France], he fareth very hardly and feedeth most upon bread and fruits, but yet he may comfort himselfe with this, and though his fare be nothing so good as the ploughmans and poore artificers in England, yet it is much better than that of the *villano* in Italy.[3]

As to craftsmen, many shared the fate of the seventeenth-century artisans of the parish of Saint-Reim in Bordeaux who, according to the local parson, survived only because they received from time to time the charity of the *dames de charité*.[4] The artisans of more developed cities like Florence or Nuremberg, however, managed to lead a life which, if not comfortable, was at least not completely wretched. It was not unusual for an artisan in Nuremberg in the sixteenth century to have meat on his table more than once a week.[5] Several Florentine artisans were able to put aside small savings or to accumulate dowries for their daughters.[6] As always, reality can not be painted in black and white. However, it is undeniable that one of the main characteristics of preindustrial Europe, as with all traditional agricultural societies, was a striking contrast between the abject misery of the mass and the affluence and magnificence of a limited number of very rich people. If with the aid of slides one could display the golden mosaics of the monastery of Monreale (Sicily) alongside the hovel of a Sicilian peasant of the time, no words would be needed to describe the phenomenon. While it is worth keeping this image in mind, one has to go further and supplement that picture with a few measurements. Unfortunately, there is little available data and what there is is not very reliable. According to the fiscal assessments of the time in Florence (Italy) in 1427 and in Lyon (France) in 1545, estimated wealth was distributed as shown in Tables 1.2 and 1.3 respectively. If the assessments were correct, 10 percent of the population controlled more than 50 percent of the wealth assessed. Fiscal documents available for other cities suggest similar conclusions.[7]

Fiscal assessments are rarely reliable, and those of medieval and Renaissance times are particularly open to doubt. One may turn to other evidence. Frequently, the city authorities inquired about reserves of grain stored in private homes. Bags of grain were difficult to hide, and the quantity of grain stored was a function of the income as well as the size of the family. In a city in Lombardy at the middle of the sixteenth century the distribution of private grain reserves was as shown in Table 1.4. Thus 2 percent of the families held 45 percent of the reserves, while 60 percent held no reserves at all.

Table 1.2 Distribution of wealth in Florence (Italy), 1427

Percent population	Percent of wealth			
	Real property	Movables	Bonds	Total wealth
10	53	71	86	68
30	39	23	13	27
60	8	6	1	5
100	100	100	100	100

Source: Herlihy, "Family and Property," p. 8.

Table 1.3 Distribution of wealth in Lyon (France), 1545

% Population	% Wealth
10	53
30	26
60	21
100	100

Source: Gascon, *Grand commerce,* vol. 1, p. 370.

Table 1.4 Distribution of grain reserves in Pavia (Italy), 1555

Size of reserves of grain per family	% Families	% Reserves
More than 20 bags	2	45
Between 2 and 20 bags	18	45
Up to 2 bags	20	10
None at all	60	—
	100	100

Source: Zanetti, *Problemi alimentari,* p. 71.

In general it is extremely difficult to evaluate the distortions caused by inaccurate assessments, fiscal evasion, and so forth. Occasionally some individual of the time, on the basis of direct experience, tried to do what we cannot do. If that person was competent and had talent, his conclusions are invaluable. In 1698 Vauban classified the French population as follows:

rich: 10 percent
fort malaisé (very poor): 50 percent
near beggars: 30 percent
beggars: 10 percent

This estimate was no more than an educated guess.[8] Ten years earlier in England a man of genius, Gregory King, made more accurate calculations of national income, trade, and distribution of wealth, putting to good use all the material he had available in addition to his personal observations. The calculations he made are summarized in Table 1.5. If King's estimates are correct, in the England of 1688 about 5 percent of the population (classes A and B) controlled 28 percent of income, while the lower classes, which made up 62 percent of the population, received 21 percent of income. In Figure 1.1 King's data are contrasted graphically with income distribution data for England in 1962.

Although completely different in nature and origins and therefore hardly comparable, the above five estimates all point to an extremely inequitable distribution of both wealth and income.[9] However, they also suggest that, contrary to Pareto's statement, the distribution of wealth and income was

Table 1.5 Distribution of income in England in 1688 according to the calculations of Gregory King

Socioeconomic class	Number of families (thousands)	Total income in thousands of pounds sterling	% Families	% Income
A (temporal and spiritual lords; baronets; knights; esquires; gentlemen; persons in offices, sciences, and liberal arts)	53	9.816	4	23
B (merchants and traders by sea)	10	2.400	1	5
C (freeholders and farmers)	330	16.960	24	39
D (shopkeepers, tradesmen, artisans, and craftsmen)	100	4.200	7	10
E (naval and military officers and clergymen)	19	1.120	2	2
F (common seamen, laboring people and outservants, cottagers and paupers, common soldiers)	849	9.010	62	21
Total	1.361	43.506	100	100

Source: King, "Natural and Political Observations," p. 31.

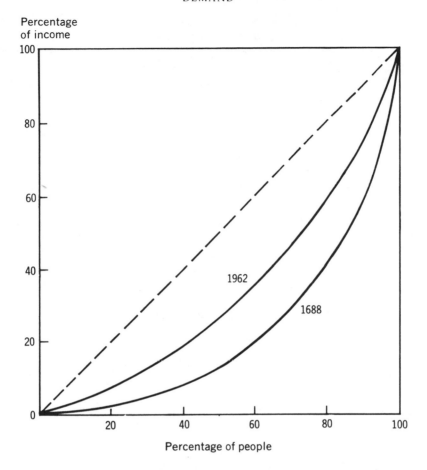

Figure 1.1 Income distribution in Great Britain in 1688 and 1962.

Source: L. Soltow, "Long-run changes in British income inequality," p. 20.

not a constant.[10] In his report on Spain at the beginning of the sixteenth century, Francesco Guicciardini noted that "except for a few Grandees of the Kingdom who live with great sumptuousness, one gathers that the others live in great poverty."[11] The tone of this comment suggests that even a contemporary observer could not fail to notice that the distribution of income and wealth varied greatly from country to country. Wealth and income were inequitably distributed everywhere, but in some countries and/ or at certain times they were much more inequitably distributed than in other countries and/or at other times.

The fundamental poverty of preindustrial societies and the unequal

11

distribution of wealth and income were reflected in the presence of a considerable number of "poor" and "beggars" (the two terms being then used as synonyms). Alongside the great mass of people who received minimal incomes there was a group of people who, because of lack of employment opportunities, incapacity, ignorance, poor health, or laziness, did not take part in the productive process and therefore did not enjoy any income at all. There is no chronicle or hagiography of medieval or Renaissance Europe which does not mention the beggars. Miniatures and paintings devote a good deal of space to these wretched characters. Travelers and writers make frequent reference to them. In England, as late as 1738, Joshua Gee remarked that

> notwithstanding we [in England] have so many excellent Laws, great Numbers of sturdy Beggars, loose and vagrant Persons, infest the nation but no place more than the City of London and Parts adjacent. If any person is born with any Defect or Deformity, or maimed by Fire or any other Casualty or by any inveterate Distemper, which renders them miserable objects, their way is open to London where they have free Liberty of showing their nauseous Sights to terrify People and force them to give money to get rid of them.[12]

In 1601, Fanucci wrote, "In Rome one sees only beggars, and they are so numerous that it is impossible to walk the streets without having them around." In Venice the beggars were so numerous as to worry the government, and measures were taken not only against the beggars themselves, but also against the boatmen who ferried them from the mainland. Such evidence easily creates the impression that the beggars were "many." But how many?

The existence of such a large number of destitute people was so troublesome that attempts were made to count them – if only to find, as in Florence in 1630 that "the number of poor was greater than had been believed."

As we have already seen, Vauban estimated that beggars in France at the end of the seventeenth century accounted for about 10 percent of the population. This does not sound far-fetched. A variety of surveys relating to different countries show that the "poor," the "beggars," and the "wretched" represented a proportion that normally ranged from 10 to 20 percent of the total population of the cities (see Table 1.6). Poor people gravitated toward the cities because that was where the rich lived and where alms were more readily available. However, even if one examines whole areas and not just the cities, one still finds that the poor accounted for a significant segment of society.

At the end of the seventeenth century in Alsace, in the Alençon area, of a total population of 410,000 inhabitants, 48,051 were beggars, that is, about 12 percent. In Brittany, of a population of 1,655,000, there were 149,325 beggars, or about 9 percent.[13] At the beginning of the eighteenth century the

Table 1.6 The poor as percentage of the total population in selected European cities, fifteenth to seventeenth centuries

City	Years	% of total population
Louvain[a]	End of 15th century	18
Antwerp[a]	End of 15th century	12
Hamburg[b]	End of 15th century	20
Cremona[c]	*c.* 1550	6
Cremona[c]	*c.* 1610	15
Modena[d]	1621	11
Siena[e]	1766	11
Venice[f]	1780	14

Sources: a Mols, *Introduction*, vol. 2, pp. 37–39.
       b Bücher, *Bevölkerung*, p. 27.
       c Meroni, *Cremona fedelissima*, vol. 2, p. 6.
       d Basini, *L'uomo e il pane*, p. 81.
       e Parenti, *La popolazione della Toscana*, p. 8.
       f Beltrami, *Storia della popolazione di Venezia*, p. 204.

Duke of Savoy could consider himself fortunate that in his states, of a total of 1.5 million inhabitants, only 35,492 or 2.5 percent were classified in the census as beggars.[14] In England the percentage of the poor was high enough to preoccupy the English monarchs from Henry VIII onwards, and to provoke specific custodial legislation which has gone down in history under the name of the Poor Laws. Of the end of the seventeenth century, Charles Wilson wrote:[15]

> We need look no further than Gregory King's statistics for striking evidence of the magnitude of this problem at the end of the seventeenth century. Out of his total population of 5.5 million, 1.3 million – nearly a quarter – are described baldly as "cottagers and paupers." Another 30,000 were "vagrants or gypsies, thieves, beggars, etc: ..." At a conservative estimate, a quarter of the population would be regarded as permanently in a state of poverty and underemployment, if not of total unemployment. This was the chronic condition. But when bouts of economic depression descended, the proportion might rise to something nearer a half of the population.

As implied at the end of the above quotation, the number of the poor fluctuated wildly. Most people lived at subsistence level. They had no savings and no social security to help them in distress. If they remained without work, their only hope of survival was charity. We look in vain in the language of the time for the term *unemployed*. The unemployed were confused with the poor, the poor person was identified with the beggar, and the confusion of

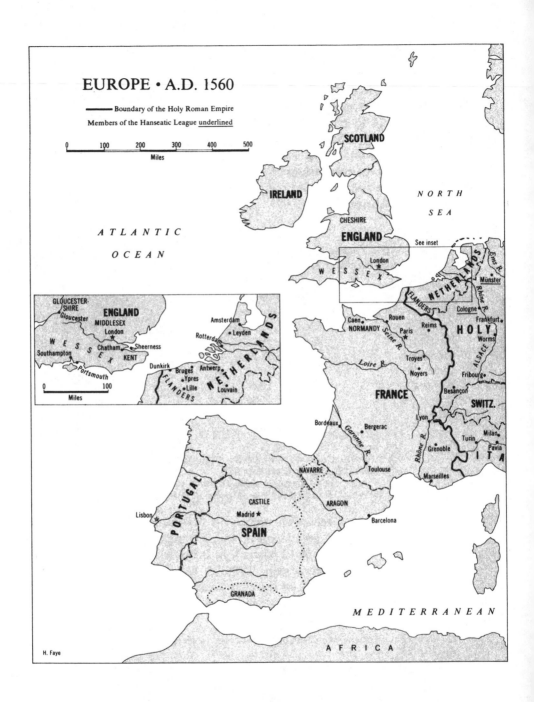

EUROPE • A.D. 1560

—— Boundary of the Holy Roman Empire
Members of the Hanseatic League underlined

0   100   200   300   400   500
Miles

SCOTLAND

IRELAND

NORTH
SEA

CHESHIRE

ENGLAND

See inset

ATLANTIC

OCEAN

W E S S E X

London ★

Ems R.

Münster

NETHERLANDS

FLANDERS

Cologne

Rhine R.

Caen
NORMANDY

Rouen

Reims

Frankfurt

Paris ★

HOLY

Seine R.

Worms

Troyes

ALSACE

Loire R.

Noyers

Fribourg

FRANCE

Besançon

SWITZ.

Bordeaux

Bergerac

Garonne R.

Lyon

Grenoble

Rhône R.

Turin

Milan

Pavia

I T A

NAVARRE

Toulouse

Marseilles

PORTUGAL

CASTILE

ARAGON

Lisbon ✦

Madrid ★

Barcelona

SPAIN

GRANADA

MEDITERRANEAN

AFRICA

H. Faye

Inset:

GLOUCESTER-
SHIRE

ENGLAND

Gloucester

MIDDLESEX

London

Amsterdam

W   E   S   S   E   X

Chatham
Sheerness
KENT

Rotterdam

Leyden

NETHERLANDS

Southampton

Portsmouth

Dunkirk

Antwerp

Bruges
Ypres
Lille

Louvain

FLANDERS

0   100
Miles

the terms reflected the grim reality of the times. In a year of bad harvest or of economic stagnation, the number of destitute people grew conspicuously. We are accustomed to fluctuations in unemployment figures. The people of preindustrial times were inured to drastic fluctuations in the number of beggars. Especially in the cities the number of the poor soared in years of famine because starving peasants fled the depleted countryside and swarmed to the urban centers, where charity was more easily available and hopefully the houses of the wealthy had food in storage. Dr Tadino reported that in Milan (Italy) during the famine of 1629 in a few months the number of beggars grew from 3,554 to 9,715.[16] Gascon found that in Lyon (France) "in normal years the poor accounted for 6 to 8 percent of the population; in years of famine their number rose to 15 or 20 percent."[17]

The fundamental characteristic of the poor was that they had no independent income. If they managed to survive, it was because income was voluntarily transferred to them through charity. Income is generated by the participation of labor and capital in the productive process. Income, however, can be transferred as well as earned, and the transfer of income is not necessarily linked with productive activity. In every society there are many different kinds of income (or wealth) transfer. To simplify matters, we can speak of two broad categories: voluntary transfers and compulsory transfers. Charity and gifts are common forms of voluntary transfer of income (or wealth). Taxation is one common form of compulsory transfer.

In the contemporary world we are accustomed above all to transfers that take the form of taxes. As a modern economist has bluntly observed, "Charity and gifts are outside the logic of the system." This, however, was not the case in preindustrial Europe. At that time charity and gifts were very much within "the logic of the system." Chronicles and documents continually refer to voluntary transfers of income or wealth by princes as well as by the ordinary people. The tradition of charity was strong and the act of charity an everyday affair. Certain events accentuated the phenomenon.

When death knocked at the door, people opened their purses more freely, for fear of the devil or for more reasonable sentiments. The chronicler Giovanni Villani relates that

> in the month of September 1330, one of our citizens died in Florence who had neither a son nor a daughter ... and among the other legacies he made, he ordered that all the poor of Florence who begged for alms would be given six pennies each.... And giving to each poor man six pennies, this came to 430 pounds in farthings, and they were in number more than 17,000 persons.[18]

When Francesco di Marco Datini, the great "Merchant of Prato," died in 1410, he left 100,000 gold florins to establish a charitable foundation and 1,000 florins to the hospital of Santa Maria Nuova in Florence for the construction of an orphanage. In Venice in 1501 the patrician Filippo Dron left rich legacies to the hospitals and other institutions of Venice, as well as a legacy with which to build one hundred small houses to give "for the love of God to the poor sailors."[19]

Disasters also served to accentuate the phenomenon of charity. In times of plague or famine, to appease God and the saints or from a natural spirit of solidarity, people donated more freely. In the eight years between the Easter of 1340 and June 1348, the parish of Saint Germain l'Auxerrois in Paris received 78 bequests. Then came the plague and in only eight months bequests reached the record figure of 419.[20] During the same plague of 1348 the hospital of Santa Maria Nuova in Florence received donations totalling 25,000 gold florins, and the Compagnia della Misericordia received bequests worth 35,000 gold florins.[21] The donors did not come only from the ranks of the rich. An antiquarian who patiently compiled the list of benefactors of the Hospital of Santa Maria Nuova in Florence noted that "the list shows that every social class can boast generous souls full of charity for their brothers," among the donors one finds "the humble maidservant" leaving the few florins she has accumulated with the sweat and savings of many years, as well as powerful and rich citizens, owners of large estates, like Giovanni Pico della Mirandola.[22]

Apart from private largesse, there were the donations of princes and public administrations. In the plague epidemic of 1580 the Commune of Genoa spent, taking charity and health expenditure together, about 200,000 ecus.[23] Very often food, and occasionally articles of clothing, were given to the poor. Henry III of England had a mania for distributing footwear.

Feasts were also suitable occasions for charity. In Venice the Doges made large donations to the poor at election time; in 1618, Antonio Priuli distributed two thousand ducats in small coins and a hundred in gold coins. In Rome at the election of a pope and subsequent anniversaries,

> a half giulio was given to anyone who came to ask for it and the gift increased for each child; pregnant women counted as two. People lent or hired each other their children, and pillows multiplied the pregnancies. The more opportunistic managed to present themselves more than once and to collect a good amount of money.[24]

In Venice, epidemics and famines in 1528 and 1576 caused the state to levy general poor-rates, hence on those occasions the poor were helped not by voluntary acts of charity but by compulsory transfer payments levied by public authorities.[25] In England, the Elizabethan administrators and their seventeenth- and eighteenth-century successors repeatedly tried to enact a system of public relief based on the levy of poor-rates on the propertied classes.[26] No matter how commendable and modern in their conception, however, these efforts remained isolated and their effectiveness limited: even in Venice and in England, private philanthropy continued to play by far the major role in alleviating the dire poverty of a large segment of society.

The preceding observations are interesting, but they still leave the basic macroeconomic question unanswered: what order of magnitude did charity represent in relation to income?

Various family budgets of the rich and the well-off in the sixteenth and seventeenth centuries show "ordinary charity" in the order of 1 to 5 percent of consumption expenditure, but, in addition to these gifts private individuals left to charity part of their wealth at death. Business enterprises regularly gave to charity; in the books of the Florentine mercantile companies, charity outlays are normally recorded in a special account under the heading "*conto di messer Domineddio*" (literally, "account of Milord God"). Much of the "charity," however, was actually a transfer of wealth to the Church.[27] In its turn, the Church gave to the poor only a very small part of what it received. Churches in our own time still spend much more on new construction and on congregational expenses than on charity.[28] At the end of the Middle Ages, in normal times, the immensely rich English monasteries gave less than 3 percent of their income to the poor.[29] In fact, documents show that the monks sometimes embezzled money which had been left to them as charity trustees.[30] However, if one adds together charity from private individuals and companies, from the public powers, and from the Church, one is led to believe that transfer payments to the poor must have amounted to much more than 1 percent of the gross national product. (According to Kohler, in the United States, in about 1970, voluntary interfamily transfer involved altogether only "a tiny fraction of one percent of GNP".)

The part played by charity in satisfying the wants of a large segment of the population is indicated not only by the amount of funds involved but also by the broad spectrum of wants to which the said funds were destined. During the five-year period between 1561 and 1565, the *Scuola di San Rocco* at Venice – a religious society for the laity – dispensed charity to the tune of 13,027 ducats, the equivalent of 70,290 days' wages of a worker. This broke down as follows:[31]

    58 percent in alms
    23 percent to provide dowries to poor girls
    15 percent to hospitals
    4 percent in medicinals

Until recent times hospitals, houses for abandoned children, and foundations for the distribution of dowries to poor girls operated in Europe with the income accumulated over the years from private donations. Also, schools were often subsidized by private donations and, especially in Protestant countries, after the Reformation, charity was increasingly directed to the instruction of the poor in useful skills.[32]

The gift is, like charity, a transfer of income or of wealth, but its motivation is not (or not necessarily) the poverty of the recipient. Like charity, the gift

18

has not completely disappeared in industrial societies, but its economic importance has decreased considerably: all commodities and services have a price, and buying with money on the market is by far the most common way to acquire desired commodities and services. In preindustrial Europe the situation was different and the further back one goes, the more important the role of the gift becomes in the system of exchanges. Often the motive behind the gift was not generosity, but either the compulsion to show off the donor's social status or the expectation of receiving in exchange another gift or the favors of someone in power. Traces of this tradition recur in industrial societies on the occasion of events like weddings or holidays like Christmas.

Gifts and charity do not exhaust the possible forms of voluntary transfers of wealth. In preindustrial Europe dowries and gambling had considerable importance. Although such transfers had no connection with productive activity, they could nevertheless affect it. As in all underdeveloped societies, people thought of dowries and of gambling as means of financing business. Goro di Stagio Dati, for example, recorded:

> On 31 March 1393, I was betrothed to Betta, the daughter of Mari di Lorenzo Vilanuzzi and on Easter Monday, 7 April, I gave her the ring ... I received a payment of 800 gold florins from the Bank of Giacomino di Goggio and Company. This was part of the dowry. I invested in the shop of Buonaccorso Berardi and his partners.

Betta died in October 1402. In the trading accounts of 1403, Goro recorded:

> When the partnership with Michele di Ser Parente expired, I set up a shop on my own.... My partners are Piero and Jacopo di Tommaso Lana who contribute 3,000 florins while I contribute 2,000. This is how I propose to raise them: 1,370 florins are still due to me from my old partnership with Michele di Ser Parente. The rest I expect to obtain if I marry again this year, when I hope to find a woman with a dowry as large as God be pleased to grant me.[33]

Buonaccorso Pitti tells in his *Cronica* how gambling brought him the necessary capital for (quite literally) some horse-trading:

> they began to play and I with them and at the end I brought home from this twenty golden florins in winnings. The next day I returned and I won about eleven florins and so for about fifteen days, so that I won about twelve hundred florins. And having Michele Marucci continually in my ears begging me not to play again, and saying, "Buy some horses and go to Florence." I, in fact, listened to his advice and I bought six good horses."[34]

So far we have discussed voluntary transfers of income and/or wealth, but

19

as mentioned above there were also compulsory transfers. When we think of compulsory transfers we think mostly of taxation, but plundering raids, highway robbery, and theft in the narrow sense belong to the same category. In medieval Europe some political theorists saw only a fine line between taxation and robbery. As for distinctions between war, plunder, and robbery, they were very tenuous indeed. There is a curious clause in the laws of the Ine of Wessex which seeks to define the various types of forcible attack to which a householder and his property might be subjected: if fewer than seven men are involved, they are thieves; if between seven and thirty-five, they form a gang; if more than thirty-five, they are a military expedition.[35]

The relative importance of taxation on the one hand and plunder and theft on the other cannot be quantitatively assessed, but there is no doubt that the earlier the period in question the greater the importance of plunder and theft relative to taxation.

We shall discuss below the incidence of taxation in preindustrial Europe. Here it is worth devoting a few words to plunder and theft. Much has been written about theft from the legal and judicial points of view, but little from the statistical. We know, however, that it was a very frequent event – which is not surprising if one considers the great proportion of poor in the total population, the inequality in income distribution, the frequency of famine, and the limited capacity of preindustrial powers to control people and their movements. All this helps to explain the frequency of theft and robbery on the part of common and low-class people. However, the noble and the wealthy also did their share, especially in the earlier centuries of the Middle Ages. In 1150 the Abbey of St Victor of Marseille complained to Raymond Beranger, Count of Barcelona and Marquis of Provence, that Guillaume de Signes and his sons had stolen over the years 5,600 sheep and goats, 200 oxen, 200 pigs, 100 horses, donkeys and mules from the various possessions of the abbey. In 1314 a great quantity of timber was stolen from a royal possession in the Craus valley (Haute-Provence, France). An inquiry showed that the robbery had been perpetrated by the men of the Count of Beuil, under his orders: the count traded in timber.[36] As for war-plunder, one may mention that at the beginning of the fifteenth century the sire d'Albret admitted to a Breton knight that "Dieu mercy" war paid him and his men well, but that it had paid still better when he fought on the side of the King of England, because then "riding à l'aventure," he could often "get his hands on the rich traders of Toulouse, Condon, La Réole or Bergerac."[37] The leader of the *lansquenets*, Sebastian Schertlin, who fought in Italy from 1526 to 1529 and took part in the sack of Rome, returned to Germany with a booty of money, jewels, and clothing valued at approximately 15,000 florins. A few years later, the good Sebastian bought himself an estate which included a country house, furniture, and cattle at a price of 17,000 florins. Among the Swedish commanders who participated in the Thirty Years'

War, Kraft von Hohenlohe amassed war spoils of about 117,000 thalers, Colonel A. Ramsay about 900,000 thalers in cash and valuables, and Johan G. Baner, a fortune estimated at something between 200,000 and a million thalers which he deposited in the bank of Hamburg.[38]

Ransom is one form of plunder. We are best informed on large-scale ransoms paid by princes and high dignitaries for their release. When Isaac Comnenus, duke of Antioch, was captured by the Seljuqs in the reign of Michael VII, the sum of 20,000 gold besants had to be paid for his release.[39] In 1530 King Francis I of France had to pay the enormous ransom of 1.2 million gold ducats to Emperor Charles V for the liberation of his two children.[40] Individuals of lesser importance were worth a great deal less. But the total amount of ransoms paid by travelers captured by pirates, soldiers and citizens captured in war, and towns captured by the enemy, represented at all times a continuous large transfer of wealth.

We have absolutely no way to measure the relative importance of unilateral transfers (including charity, gifts and dowries, as well as plunder, ransom, and theft) on the one hand and exchanges on the other. But it appears that the earlier the period under examination, the greater is the relative importance of transfers compared to that of exchanges. Indeed, for the Dark Ages Grierson has asserted that "the alternatives to trade (gift and theft) were more important than trade itself."[41] Another authority has aptly observed, "Savage society was dominated by the habit of plundering and the need for giving. To rob and to give: these two complementary acts covered a very large portion of exchanges."[42] Such was the logic, as it were, of *that* system.

As there was as yet little trade (whether in the form of barter or involving money), weekly markets or fairs were more than able to satisfy the needs of the population. These weekly markets were held in the vicinity of the manorhouse or the abbey or in a village. In some localities, particularly blessed by geographical or political conditions, there developed monthly or yearly fairs in addition to the weekly market. On such occasions people would come from further afield and sometimes merchants arrived bearing exotic goods.

As time progressed and civilization developed, after the end of the tenth century, trade expanded and began quite naturally to concentrate in the cities that were then developing partly as a cause and partly as an effect of the growth in trade. As the division of labour proceeded, people in the cities became increasingly less self-sufficient and more and more dependent on trade. To contemporaries, cities therefore looked like permanent fairs. This was beautifully expressed by the troubadour Chretien de Troyes at the end of the twelfth century:

> Et l'on eut pu dire et croire
> Qu'en ville ce fu toujours foire

(And one might have said and believed/That in town there was always a fair).

The system therefore changed slowly but the world where trade predominates and unilateral transfers are reduced to a minimum only emerged in the last few centuries.

The transfer of income or wealth, whether voluntary or compulsory, entails redistribution. In general, charity works in favor of a more equal distribution. Through charity, income or wealth is transferred from the rich to the poor. In Europe, however, during the Middle Ages and the Renaissance, every donation to the Church was regarded as charity. To the extent to which charity to the Church was kept by the Church and not redistributed among the poor, it favored the concentration of wealth (in this case in the hands of the Church) rather than a more equitable distribution of it.

Similarly, taxation could be ambivalent. Inasmuch as tax revenues were used to maintain hospitals, to pay communal teachers or community doctors, or to finance free distributions of food, taxation meant a more equitable distribution of income. If, however, taxation was used to concentrate a larger share of available resources in the hands of the prince, the imbalance in the distribution of wealth was made worse, especially when the burden of taxation fell proportionately more heavily on the lower orders.

TYPES OF DEMAND

Total effective demand can be divided into

a.   demand for consumption goods
b.   demand for services
c.   demand for capital goods

This division intersects with another, inasmuch as demand can also be divided into

a.   private internal demand
b.   public internal demand
c.   foreign demand

Each section a, b, c, can be subdivided into subsections 1, 2, and 3 and vice versa.

PRIVATE DEMAND

Let us begin with internal demand for consumer goods and services in the private sector. The lower the disposable income is, the higher the proportion spent on food. The reason for this phenomenon – in technical terms – is that the demand for food has an income elasticity lower than unity. It sounds forbidding, but all it means is that people cannot easily cut down on food expenditure when their income diminishes, and they cannot expand their food intake beyond a certain point when their income grows.[43]

In 1950 expenditures on food made up 22 percent of total consumption expenditure in the United States, 31 percent in the United Kingdom and 46 percent in Italy. Clearly, the poorer the country the greater the proportion of available income its inhabitants have to spend on food. An analogous argument applies to the relation between expenditure on bread and total expenditure for nourishment. The lower the income, the higher will be the percentage spent on "poor" items such as bread and other starchy foods.[44]

In sixteenth-century Lombardy a memorial on the cost of labor and the cost of living stressed that:

> the peasants live on wheat, ... and it seems to us that we can disregard their other expenses because it is the shortage of wheat that induces the laborers to raise their claims; their expenses for clothing and other needs are practically non-existent.[45]

Peasants were relegated to the lowest income groups in preindustrial Europe. The mass of the urban population was better off, but whenever extant documents allow some tentative estimates on the structure of expenditure, one generally finds that, in normal years, even in the towns, 60 to 80 percent of the expenditure of the mass of the population went on food (see Table 1.7).

Though ordinary people spent about 60 to 80 percent of their income on food, this does not mean that they ate and drank well and plentifully. On the contrary, the masses ate little and poorly, but the average man's income was so low that even a poor diet swallowed up 60 to 80 percent of that income – this in good times. Untroubled years, however, were not the norm in preindustrial Europe. Plants were not selected, people did not know how to fight pests, fertilizers were scarce. As a result, crop failures were exceedingly frequent. In addition, a relatively primitive system of transportation made any long-distance supply of foodstuffs impossible, unless by sea. Consequently, the prices of foodstuffs fluctuated wildly, reflecting both the inelasticity of demand and man's limited control over the adverse forces of nature. Between 1396 and 1596, in a port such as Antwerp, easily supplied by sea, the price of rye registered yearly increases of the order of 100–200 percent in eleven years and in nine other years made yearly jumps of more than 200 percent.[46] As has been observed, "the buying power of the working classes depended essentially on climatic conditions."[47] When there was a poor harvest and prices of foodstuffs soared, even the expenditure of 100 percent of a worker's income could hardly feed him and his family. Then there was famine, and people died of hunger.

The lower orders lived in a chronic state of undernourishment and under the constant threat of starvation. This explains the symbolic value that food acquired in preindustrial Europe. One of the traits which distinguished the

Table 1.7 Estimated breakdown of private expenditure of the mass of the population in selected areas, fifteenth to eighteenth centuries

Percent of expenditure

	England (15th century)	Lyon, France (c. 1550)	Antwerp – Low Countries (1596–1600)	Holland (middle 17th century)	Northern France (before 1700)	Milan, Italy (about 1600)	England – non-agricultural labor (1794)
Food	≈80	≈80	≈79	≈60	≈80		74
Bread (percent of food)	(≈20)	(≈50)	(≈49)		(≈25)	(≈30)	
Clothing and textiles		≈5	≈10		≈12		5
Heating, light, and rent	≈8	≈15	≈11		≈8		11
Various							10

Sources: Phelps Brown and Hopkins, "Wage-rates and Prices," p. 293; Phelps Brown and Hopkins, "Seven Centuries of Building Wages," p. 180; Gascon, Grand commerce, vol. 2, p. 544; Schollier, De Levensstandard in de 15 en 16 Eeuw te Antwerpen, p. 174; Eden, The State of the Poor; Posthumus, Geschiedenis der Leidsche Lakenindustrie.

A Country Wedding. A painting by Pieter Brueghel the Elder, about 1565. In this glimpse of peasant life a wedding takes place in a barn sparsely furnished with rough stick furniture and crude clay blowls, and jugs. Kunsthistorisches Museum, Vienna.

rich from the poor was that the rich could eat their fill. The banquet was what distinguished a festive occasion – a village fair, a wedding – from the daily routine. The generous offer of food was the sign of hospitality as well as a token of respect: university students had to give a lavish dinner for their professors on the day of their graduation; a visiting prince or a foreign emissary was always greeted with sumptuous banquets. On these occasions, as a reaction to the hunger that everyone feared and saw on the emaciated faces of the populace, people indulged in pantagruelic excesses. The degree of hospitality, the importance of a feast, the respect toward a superior – all were measured in terms of the abundance of the fare and of the gastronomic excesses which resulted from it.

Having bought their food, the mass of the people had little left for their wants, no matter how elementary they were. In preindustrial Europe, the purchase of a garment or of the cloth for a garment remained a luxury the common people could only afford a few times in their lives. One of the main preoccupations of hospital administration was to ensure that the clothes of the deceased "should not be usurped but should be given to lawful inheritors."[48] During epidemics of plague, the town authorities had to struggle to confiscate the clothes of the dead and to burn them: people waited for others to die so as to take over their clothes – which generally had the effect

25

of spreading the epidemic. In Prato (Tuscany) during the plague of 1631 a surgeon lived and served in the pest house for about eight months lancing bubos and treating sores, catching the plague and recovering from it. He wore the same clothing throughout. In the end, he petitioned the town authorities for a gratuity with which to buy himself new apparel: it cost fifteen ducats, which was as much as his monthly salary.[49]

Among the ordinary people, lucky was he who had a decent coat to wear on the holy days. Peasants were always clothed in rags. All this led to a status symbolization process. As Louis IX of France used to say, "It is just right that a man should dress according to his station." Since the price of cloth was high in relation to current incomes, the very "length of the coat depended to a large extent on social position."[50] Nobles and rich men were noticeable because they could afford long garments. In order to save, the common people wore garments which reached only to their knees. As the length of the coat acquired symbolic value it became institutionalized. In Paris, surgeons were divided into two groups, the highly trained surgeons, who had the right to wear long tunics, and the low-class barber-surgeons, who did not have the right to wear a tunic below the knee.

Having spent most of their income on food and clothing, the lower orders had little left to spend on rent and heating. In the large towns rents were exceedingly high in relation to wages. In Venice in the second half of the seventeenth century, the rent for one or two miserable rooms amounted to more than 12 percent of the wage of a skilled worker.[51] Thus housing often consisted of a hovel shared by many, a condition that favored the spread of germs in times of epidemics. Commenting on the high death rates which prevailed among the lower classes during the plague of 1631 in Florence, Rondinelli recorded that

> when the counting of the population took place, it was found that 72 people lived crowded together in an old ugly tower in the courtyard of de' Donati, 94 were crowded in a house on Via dell'Acqua and about 100 in a house on Via San Zanobi. If by mischance only one had fallen prey to the disease, all would probably have been infected.[52]

The physician G.F. Fiochetto, in his report on the 1630 epidemic in Turin, recorded that one of the first cases of infection was that of Francesco Lupo, shoemaker, who stayed in a house "where sixty-five people, men and women, all artisans, were living."[53] In Milan during the plague epidemic of 1576, in the poorer sections of the city 1,563 homes were regarded as infected. In these homes containing 8,956 rooms lived 4,066 families.[54] This gives an average of six rooms per house and two rooms per family. The Milanese Public Health Board issued an ordinance in 1597 to the effect that

> no matter how poor and how low their status, people are not allowed

to keep more than two beds in one room and no more than two or three people should sleep in one bed. Those who claim that they have rooms large enough to contain conveniently more than two beds, must notify the Health Board which will send an inspector to check.[55]

This was wise, but poverty stood in the way of wisdom. When the plague hit Milan in 1630, a clergyman reported that

the poor are worst hit by the plague because of the confined living conditions in houses vulgarly called stables, where every room is filled with large families and where stench and contagion prevail.[56]

In Genoa, during the epidemic of 1656–57 a nun reported that

a very great number of poor people live in crowded conditions. There are ten to twelve families per house and most frequently one finds eight or more people sharing one room and having neither water nor any other facility available.[57]

Of course not all laborers lived in such appalling conditions. As already noted, there were differences within the lower orders. Also, in the smaller centers the situation was not as bad as in the larger cities. In the small town of Prato in 1630 there were on average three to four persons per house, and rarely more than five or six.[58] In the countryside, however, most peasants lived in crowded conditions very similar to those prevailing in the poorest quarters of the larger cities. As life at home was so unpleasant, whenever possible the men moved to the tavern.

As indicated above, the well-off and the rich ate adequately. In fact, in reaction to the hunger that surrounded them, they ate too much, as a result of which they suffered from gout and had to have recourse to the barber-surgeons for frequent blood-letting. The estimate of the food consumption in the homes of the rich is complicated by the continuous presence of domestic staff and the frequent presence of guests. A further difficulty in estimating food consumption is the fact that the rich and the well-off were usually land owners: at least part of the food they consumed was grown on their lands and often does not appear in their bookkeeping.

Precise calculations are often impossible, but on the basis of existing family accounts one can hazard rough estimates. For the sixteenth and seventeenth centuries, one is inclined to believe that the rich spent 15 to 35 percent of their total consumption on food and the well-to-do 35 to 50 percent (see Table 1.8a). These percentages, however, are not comparable to the 70 to 80 percent that has been calculated for the budget of the lower orders. Whereas for the bulk of the population income and consumption practically coincided (saving being a negligible amount), in the case of the rich income far outstripped consumption by an amount difficult to define and which, in any case, would have little meaning in terms of averages.

Table 1.8a Structure of expenditure on consumer goods and services of three families of middle-class and princely rank in the sixteenth and seventeenth centuries

	% of expenditure		
	I (Well-to-do middle class)	II (Wealthy middle class)	III (Princely)
(a) Food[1]	47	36	34
(b) Clothing	19	27	8
(c) Housing	11	3	27
Subtotal: a + b + c	[77]	[66]	[69]
(d) Wages of servants	1		10
(e) Hygiene and medicines	2	1	3
(f) Entertainment	6	5	
(g) Purchases of jewelry and works of art	2.5	27	
(h) Taxes	1		Exempt
(i) Charities	0.5		6
(j) Various	10	1	12

Sources: I – Expenses of the notary Folognino of Verona in 1653–57 from Tagliaferri, Consumi di una famiglia borghese del Seicento.
II – Expenses of the middle-class burgher Williband Imhof of Nuremberg, about 1560, from Strauss, Nuremberg, p. 207.
III – Expenses of the Odescalchi family in 1576–77, from Mira, Vicende economiche di una famiglia italiana, Chapter 5.

1 In the expense accounts of the noble English families of the sixteenth and seventeenth centuries collected by L. Stone, food accounted for 10 to 25 percent of consumption expenditure. Expense on food of the wealthy Cornelis de Jonge van Ellemeet of Amsterdam, at the end of the seventeenth century, amounted to about 35 percent of total annual expenditure (excluding taxes). Account must be taken of the fact that for the well-to-do, expenditure on food included food for the servants and that abundantly offered to many guests.

When compared to total income rather than to consumption, expenditure on food by the rich and well-to-do would thus represent a lower percentage than the 15 to 35 percent mentioned above.

The same psychological force that induced the rich to overeat drove them to excessive display in their dress. Public authorities had to intervene with sumptuary laws to restrain wealthy citizens from overostentation and prevent them from squandering wealth on conspicuous clothing. The acquisition of jewelry was partly exhibitionism, but also a form of hoarding. Expenditure on clothes and jewelry, however, could often not be separated, and one can conjecture that in the sixteenth and seventeenth centuries this type of expenditure absorbed, depending on circumstances, from 10 to 30 percent of consumption of the rich and the well-to-do (see Table 1.8a). At the end of the fifteenth century, the expenditure of the king of France on

Table 1.8b Some examples of expenditure by aristocratic and institutional consumers in England

Thomas de Berkeley 1345–46			Sir Gilbert Talbot 1417–18		
Food	£742	(57%)	Food	£176	(71%)
Food and bedding of horses	£148	(11%)	Food and purchase of horses	£ 16	(7%)
Horses and falcons	£ 26	(2%)	Wax and candles	£ 1	(0%)
Clothing	£142	(11%)	Fees and wages	£ 22	(9%)
Household cloth and silver	£ 45	(3%)	Cloth	£ 20	(8%)
Wax	£ 22	(2%)	Travel	£ 3	(1%)
Legal expenses	£ 11	(1%)	Letters	£ 6	(2%)
Pensions & gifts to relatives	£ 65	(5%)	Miscellaneous	£ 4	(2%)
Building	£ 21	(2%)	Total	£248	(100%)
Miscellaneous (including alms, boots, shoes, wages etc.)	£ 86	(6%)			

St John's Hospital Cambridge 1484–85

Total	£1308	(100%)	Food	£32	(45%)
			Wages	£13	(18%)
John Catesby 1392–93			Rent	£ 2	(3%)
			Buildings	£12	(17%)
			Fuel	£ 5	(7%)
Food	£13	(12%)	Clothing	£ 1	(1%)
Horses	£ 1	(1%)	Wax	£ 1	(1%)
Payments to servants	£15	(13%)	Miscellaneous	£ 6	(8%)
Clothing	£18	(16%)			
Building	£14	(13%)	Total	£72	(100%)
Agriculture	£17	(15%)			
Education	£ 2	(2%)	An esquire 1471–72		
Kitchen equipment	£ 2	(2%)			
Rents	£23	(21%)	Food and fuel	£24	(48%)
Tithes and taxes	£ 3	(3%)	Clothes and alms	£ 4	(8%)
Miscellaneous (including alms and entertainment)	£ 2	(2%)	Buildings	£ 5	(10%)
			Horses, food for horses	£ 5	(10%)
			Servants' wages	£ 9	(18%)
			Robes	£ 3	(6%)
Total	£110	(100%)	Total	£50	(100%)

Source: Dyer, *Standards of Living*, p. 70.

jewelry and clothing amounted to no less than 5 to 10 percent of all royal revenues.[59]

Then there was household expenditure on heating, candles, furniture, gardening, and so on. When a person overspent on one category he naturally saved on another. On the whole, food, clothing, and household expenses usually involved a good 60 to 80 percent of the expenditure on current consumption of the rich and the well-to-do.

The combination of pronounced inequality of income distribution and a low level of real wages favored the demand for domestic services. This demand was highly elastic in relation to income as the number of servants was a symbol of opulence. Even at the end of the eighteenth century, a girl like Mary Berry, who belonged to a well-off but not very rich English family, in planning with her fiancé the balance sheet of their future household, came to the conclusion that provision had to be made to cover "the wages of four women servants – a housekeeper, a cook under her, a housemaid and a lady's maid – three men servants and the coachman."[60]

As we shall see later, the number of servants in relation to population was very high and, of course, domestics were concentrated in the houses of the rich and the well-to-do (see Table 2.9). Nevertheless, given the low average level of wages, servants' pay did not generally represent more than 1 to 2 percent of the consumption expenditure of moneyed families, although in exceptional cases it could reach 10 percent. One should add, however, that the money wages actually paid to servants did not represent the total effective expenditure on them. In order to evaluate this expenditure, one should take into account the costs of food, lodging, heating, and other items provided for servants by their employers. Toward the end of the seventeenth century, the very wealthy Cornelis de Jonge van Ellemeet of Amsterdam spent about forty florins a year to clothe each one of his ten servants. In addition Van Ellemeet spent on each servant about seventeen florins for meat, eighteen florins for butter, and unspecified amounts for drinks, heating, accommodation, and other facilities. The average individual wage of the servants was some seventy florins a year.[61] Clearly wages represented only a minor part of expenditure on servants. The situation was not appreciably different in the homes of the less wealthy. If the maid of the Florentine craftsman Bartolomeo Masi was able to save fourteen florins in five years, it was because her food, accommodation, and probably some clothing were provided by her employer's family.

It would be a serious mistake to believe that the demand for services by the wealthy classes was limited to the demand for domestic servants. The variety of service personnel in demand included lawyers and notaries; teachers for children; persons performing religious ministrations; various workers and artists who maintained and embellished the living quarters; in the case of the nobility, various types of entertainers, such as musicians, poets, dwarfs and jesters, falconers, and stable boys; and last, but not least, doctors, in connection with which, early in the eighteenth century, the famous physician, Dr Bernardino Ramazzini, commented,

> If the laborer does not recover rapidly he returns to the workshop still ailing and he neglects the doctor's prescriptions, if they stretch over a long period. Certain things can only be done for the rich who can afford to be ill.[62]

The consumption of the wealthy, even when it had overtones of extravagance, never showed much variety. The economic system and the state of the arts did not offer the consumer the great variety of products and services which characterize industrial societies. Food, clothing, and housing were by far the major items of expenditure of the rich. The difference between the rich and the poor was that the rich spent extravagantly on all three items, while the poor often did not have enough to buy food. Moreover, the mass of the populace had no opportunity to save, while the rich, although indulging in conspicuous consumption, did.

Not all income received is necessarily spent on consumer goods and services. Income not spent on such goods and services is naturally saved: this self-evident proposition derives from the definition of saving. Another self-evident proposition is that neither all individuals nor all societies save to the same extent. Saving is a function of

a. psychological and sociocultural factors
b. the level of income
c. income distribution

There is no need to expend many words to illustrate point (a). It is obvious that some individuals are more inclined to spend while others are more inclined to save. It is worth mentioning, however, that on a macroeconomic level, sociocultural factors powerfully influence people's propensity to consume or, conversely, to save. Even in the absence of organized publicity, factors such as fashion, emulation, ostentation, or the prevailing conditions of security or insecurity affect the amount of current income spent on consumption. About point (b) it is obvious that when income is high there are possibilities of saving that do not exist when income is low. This is true for individuals as well as for societies. In the long run the relationship between income and consumption is not as stable as in the short run: changes in institutions, morals, and fashions greatly affect the so-called "consumption function." Still, again in the long run, it remains true that the lower the income, the slighter the possibility for saving – and vice versa.

In Turin in 1630, when because of the plague all the people were quarantined within their houses, the Town Council noted that the bulk of the workers "lived from day to day,"[63] that is, they had no savings to fall back on and therefore, when restricted to their houses, had to be subsidized by the city. As we have repeatedly pointed out, however, even among the lower orders there were gradations of poverty, and if there were those who "lived from day to day," there were also those who, by tightening their belts and limiting their wants, managed to set aside a few coins.

If for the majority the saving of small sums implied heroic sacrifice, income for some was sufficiently high easily to allow a substantial accumulation of wealth. According to Hilton, in the fourteenth and fifteenth centuries in certain years, the Dukes of Cornwall succeeded in saving and

31

investing up to 50 percent of their income. In 1575–78, in Rome, the princely Odescalchi family, which enjoyed a very high standard of living, spent, on average, some three thousand lire of the time annually on current consumption. A remarkable figure, but the family's average income was about thirteen thousand lire, out of which a saving of ten thousand lire per annum was possible – that is, 80 percent of their income.[64] In the second half of the sixteenth century Ambrogio di Negro, a banker in Genoa and doge of the same city during the years 1585–87, managed to save and invest on average more than 70 percent of his annual income, in spite of his high and costly standard of living. In the early decades of the seventeenth century the Riccardi family of Florence saved and invested about 75 percent of its annual income. Cornelis de Jonge van Ellemeet, one of the five or six richest people in Amsterdam at the end of the seventeenth century, saved, on average, from 50 to 70 percent of his annual income.[65] In a predominantly poor society lacking corrective means (taxation and/or rationing), a high concentration of wealth is an indispensable condition to the formation of saving. Let us refer briefly to Gregory King's estimates for England in 1688. The reliability of the figures themselves is irrelevant to the matter under discussion. Even if they were pure invention, they would still serve as a hypothetical example. The total annual income of England was estimated at £43.5 million. The fact that 28 percent of this income was concentrated in the hands of only 5 percent of families (see above, Table 1.5) meant that these families had an average annual income of £185 and therefore a distinct possibility of saving. In fact, Gregory King estimated that these families saved 13 percent of their annual income. Their total saving of £1.3 million represented 72 percent of national saving (£1.8 million). If the national income of £43.5 million had been subdivided in a perfectly egalitarian way among the 1.36 million families which made up the English population, each family would have received an income of £32. At that level, no family would have been in a position to save, and national saving would have been reduced practically to zero.

According to Gregory King, national saving in England at the end of the seventeenth century amounted to less than 5 percent of national income. England at this time was one of the richest preindustrial societies that ever existed, but it was not characterized by a particularly high concentration of income; quite the contrary. A poorer economy with a higher concentration of income could have saved well above the 5-percent level.[66]

Imposing cathedrals, splendid abbeys, sumptuous residences, and huge fortifications are there to testify that a sizable surplus must have been available for substantial investments. The generally low level of incomes impeded the accumulation of savings, but the concentration of income facilitated it. The proportion of income saved was the result of these two opposing forces. Taking all factors into consideration, one can assume that, according to locally prevailing conditions, European preindustrial societies could in "normal" years save between 2 and 15 percent of income. An industrial society in "normal" years saves from 3 to 20 percent of its income. The substantial difference, however, is that an industrial society can attain such levels of saving while still providing the masses with a high level of consumption, while the preindustrial societies were in a position to save only if they succeeded in imposing miserably low standards of living on a large proportion of the population. Moreover, "normal" years are the standard for industrial societies, but the word "normal" acquires an ironic flavor when applied to preindustrial Europe. In those days life was hard: tears followed laughter, tragedies followed feasts with great frequency and intensity. The violent fluctuations in human mortality were a reflection on this general variability. Years of fat cattle, during which it was possible to save, were followed by years of lean cattle, during which saving took on negative value. Averaging would make little sense, because it would cancel out one of the main characteristics of the period, namely, the violent contrasts from one year to the next.

Income is spent on the acquisition of goods and services. In turn, expenditure creates new income in the form of wages, profits, interest, and rents. Thus the flow of monetary income becomes circular. The flow, however, has a critical point at which various mechanisms must insure its continuity. The mechanisms in question must insure that the monetary income which is not spent on consumption will not lay idle but will instead be borrowed by people who will spend it on capital goods – in other words, that saving will be converted into investment.

If the money saved or part of it remains unspent, the volume of the flow is correspondingly reduced and the economy becomes subjected to deflationary pressures. If the process continues, the contraction of the flow can actually reach a level at which no further saving is possible.

In a modern economy monetary savings reach the money market and the main problem is to ensure that there are enough people and/or institutions willing to borrow it for investment purposes. In preindustrial Europe, however, large amounts of monetary savings were often hoarded, that is, they did not reach the financial market (which existed only in primitive forms) and remained idle under mattresses or in pots or strong boxes. The trap of hoarding was, in fact, very effective. Archeological evidence in this regard is overwhelming. It is enough to open at random a journal of numismatics and one encounters an endless list of hoards discovered accidentally. Take for example the 1962 issue of the French *Revue numismatique*; it reported the following findings which had come to notice that year:

early in 1954, at Courcelles-Frémoy, while repairing a well a mason found a copper vase containing more than 13,000 coins dating from the thirteenth century, an equivalent of approximately 13 kilograms of silver;

in January 1960, during the demolition of the church of St Hilaire at Poitiers, workers found a bag containing more than 490 gold coins of the sixteenth and seventeenth centuries, each coin weighing approximately 3.5 grams;

at Easter 1960, while leveling the border of a country road, a worker discovered a pot containing 280 coins of vellon, dating from the thirteenth and fourteenth centuries;

early in 1961, while demolishing a wall at a farm in Chappes, a farmer uncovered a pot containing 640 coins dating from the twelfth and thirteenth centuries;

in October 1961, at Vancé (Mayenne), while bulldozing a wall, a farmer uncovered three pots containing 5 silver coins, 12 coins of vellon and 4,483 copper coins, all dating from the sixteenth and seventeenth centuries;

in March 1962, while excavating land to make foundations for a new building at Montargis, construction workers found 132 gold coins dating from the period 1445–1587.

Most of the hoards contain between 50 and 500 coins but much larger finds are not uncommon. During repairs to a house in the rue d'Assaut in Paris in 1908, workers found a hoard of over 140,000 silver pennies dating from the thirteenth century. At Košice in Czechoslovakia in 1935 workers found a hoard of just under 3,000 gold coins of the sixteenth and seventeenth centuries.

The reasons for the high propensity to hoard are not difficult to detect. Conditions varied greatly from place to place and from period to period, but it is safe to say that in general people lived in constant fear of bandits and soldiers (occupations which were hardly distinguishable in those days) and robbery and plunder were regarded as a permanent menace. Hoarding coins was the easiest way to conceal and protect wealth. "Emergency hoards" were particularly frequent in areas and periods suffering from political and military turmoil, but hoarding was common also in areas and times of peace and stability. To understand this fact one has to consider that money in circulation consisted of pieces of metal. Gold and silver always had a special fascination for man, and the temptation to hoard gleaming pieces of gold and silver is stronger than the temptation to hoard printed paper. More important than that, institutions to collect savings and to direct them to productive uses were either lacking or inadequate. In this regard, as we shall see (Part II, Chapter 7), momentous changes took place after the tenth century. By the fourteenth century a common man, Paolo di Messere Pace da Certaldo in Tuscany, strongly advised "people who have cash not to keep it idle at home."[67] But commercial and credit developments took place mostly in the major cities. In the minor cities or in the countryside, hoarding remained the preferred form of saving. When Pasino degli Eustachi, a rich merchant and at the same time an official in the administration of the Duke of Milan, died in Pavia (Lombardy) in 1445, his estate included:[68]

	Value in golden ducats	Percentage of wealth
Cash	92,500	77.6
Jewels	2,225	1.9
Provisions	150	0.1
Clothing	1,495	1.3
Furniture and household goods	483	0.4
Buildings	5,000	4.2
Land	12,300	10.3
Capitalized value of rents	5,000	4.2
	119,153	100.0

Coins represented in relative terms about 78 percent of the value of the estate. As the golden ducat weighed 3.53 grams, in absolute terms the coins hoarded amounted to about 720 pounds of gold – and in those days, the purchasing power of gold was much higher than it is today. Admittedly, Pasino was an extreme case because as a government official he enjoyed an extraordinarily high income and Pavia, the small town in which he lived, did not offer great opportunities for investment.

In the large cities where credit and commercial institutions had developed and were continuously developing, things were different. However, even in such major centers people easily resorted to hoarding. A good example is provided by Samuel Pepys. He was an extremely capable administrator and lived in the bustling, mercantile London of the seventeenth century. On the night of 12 June 1667, when news came that the Dutch had broken the chain in the Medway and burnt *The Royal Charles*, Samuel Pepys discussed with his wife and father what to do with "the little that I have in money by me." Next morning he sent the pair off by coach with £1,300 in gold, and instructions to conceal the money safely at his country estate in Huntingdonshire. Later in the day he dispatched his clerk with another thousand guineas to the same destination, while he himself acquired a belt in which, very uncomfortably, he could conceal £300 in gold on his person. Not until four months later was Pepys able to recover what had been buried, digging at night in his garden with the help of a lantern, under extremely exasperating conditions: the exact place of the hoard could not be found, his arguments with his father were hampered by the fact that the latter was deaf, and Pepys dared not shout for fear of attracting the attention of neighbors.

I find the story rather humorous, but the reason why I report it at length is that it shows that even in bustling seventeenth-century London, a man like Samuel Pepys, who was comfortably off but not rich, kept nearly £3,000 in gold coins in his house and could refer to it, apparently without affectation, as "the little that I have in money by me."[69]

Of course, if there were people who hoarded wealth, there were others who dis-hoarded it. At the beginning of the eleventh century the Archbishop of Cologne used up all the treasure accumulated by his predecessors to help the poor in time of famine. When Bishop Burkard of Worms died in 1025, he left behind some books and three pennies, having lavished on the poor all the treasure he had inherited. In accordance with the mystical spirit of the age, deliberate dis-hoarding on the part of an ecclesiastical dignitary was often presented as the result of miraculous divine activity. Thus when the Bishop of Orleans spent all his treasure on the construction of the new cathedral, Raoul Glaber recounted the story in the following terms:

> While the Bishop and all his associates were busily pressing on with the work that had been started, he was visibly blessed with Divine encouragement. One day, when masons were testing the firmness of the ground to select a site for the basilica's foundations, they came across a considerable quantity of gold. They estimated that there would certainly be enough to carry out all the work of restoration on the basilica, despite its size. They picked up the gold discovered and conveyed it to the Bishop. He gave thanks to Almighty God for the gift, took it and consigned it to those in charge of the work, telling them to spend it all on building the church.[70]

The sacking and robberies of armed bands served by turns to build up treasures and to put them back in circulation. When Charlemagne succeeded in penetrating the intricate fortifications of the Avars, he found there riches accumulated over centuries. Fifteen big wagons, each drawn by four oxen, were needed to carry the gold, silver and gems back to Aachen.

From a macroeconomic point of view the relevant point is whether, during a given period, the total amount of hoarding was greater, equal or smaller than the total amount of dis-hoarding. Historically there have been periods when hoarding clearly prevailed, and periods of net dis-hoarding. In Italy in the tenth and eleventh centuries, bishops and monasteries emptied their treasuries during their struggle against the German emperors.[71] The bishops across the Alps did the same for the benefit of various reform movements.[72] Throughout Europe the feverish activity in religious building which characterized the eleventh and twelfth centuries was seemingly financed through a massive process of dis-hoarding.[73] When wealth is hoarded it is not available for investment. On the other hand, hoarding may occur because investment is not attractive.[74] Conversely, dis-hoarding was generally related to periods of investment euphoria and all the reclamations of land which were accomplished, the cathedrals, the castles, the palaces which were built, the canals which were excavated, the ships which were launched, clearly show that periods of investment euphoria were not so rare in preindustrial Europe.

PUBLIC DEMAND

So far we have dealt with private demand. Let us now consider public demand.

It is necessary to state in advance that, before the eighteenth century, public and private sectors are difficult to distinguish, and the earlier the period in question, the more artificial and antihistorical the distinction becomes. The fact is that in the feudal world of the eighth to eleventh centuries there was no distinction between public and private. With the emergence of the city-states and then the absolute states, the distinction between public and private re-emerged, but these two concepts asserted themselves very slowly and not contemporaneously in the various sectors. As far as government finance is concerned, until recent times European monarchs made no distinction between their private patrimonies and the treasuries of the states. In fourteenth- and fifteenth-century France, even the seigneurs of the kingdom thought "that they had rights to the financial resources of the state and that it was legitimate for them to get hold of a large part of such resources."[75] As for seventeenth-century England, "in every sense it is probably more illuminating to speak of royal rather than public finance since far from distinguishing between the financial problems of the Crown and those of the private individual, contemporaries show a remarkable fondness for the analogy between the position of the King and that of the private landowners."[76]

Another factor that helped to obscure the distinction between the private and public domains was the powerful presence of the Church as a patrimonial and economic entity. Was the Church a private entity, or was it, rather, a public body? Any answer would be arbitrary, for although we raise this question today, it did not exist in the minds of the people at that time. In the following pages, we shall consider the Church as distinct from both the private and the public sectors. This distinction is also arbitrary; but as stated above, any alternative solution would be equally arbitrary.

The level and the structure of public demand depends on

a.   the income of the public power
b.   the "wants" of those in power and of the community which they control or represent
c.   the price structure

Point (a) needs some comment. While in the case of private people, income, in a sense, is given, public powers have the potential to increase taxes so that up to a certain point their income is also a function of their "wants." "Up to a

37

certain point" only, because beyond that point fiscal pressure can dry up the sources of income; in other words, you cannot eat the cow and then hope for milk.

Fundamentally, public authorities might derive income from (1) the forced transfer of income from the private sector via taxation; (2) the transfer of income and/or wealth through public loans which, as we shall see, were also often forced; (3) from the economic exploitation of what we would nowadays refer to as state property; and (4) from "seigniorage" or "gain of the mint."

As regards public debt, one should recall that this form of income or wealth transfer was unknown in either ancient Rome or ancient Greece. Public debt was an invention of the Italian city-states of the Middle Ages. These so-called "loanings" were in fact moneys lent to the state by private citizens: but mostly they were "forced" loans. A citizen might, in other words, be forced to lend the Commune a sum of money, calculated by officials of the Commune on the basis of the economic resources of the citizen in question. The citizen would receive interest on the sum lent and if the loan was not consolidated the citizen might hope that the sum would eventually be paid back. Very often, however, citizens forced to loan money to the Commune later found themselves short of cash, having invested their wealth in property or in merchandise. They might then be prepared to waive their credit to the Commune to another citizen for an amount of money smaller than the sum originally lent. They would thereby incur a straight loss, whereas citizens who had plenty of ready cash could indulge in lucrative speculation.

Public debt was developed furthest in Genoa, Venice, and Florence. In Florence, because of the wars the city fought with ever more costly companies of mercenaries and with artillery, the public debt rose from around 50,000 gold florins in 1300 to around 450,000 gold florins in 1338, and topped 600,000 by 1343. In Genoa public debt titles were known as *luoghi* (shares) and were managed by the Banco di San Giorgio which was the state's creditors' consortium. The *luoghi* issued by the San Giorgio bank each had a face value of 100 lire but were bought and sold by citizens and foreigners just like present-day stocks and shares, their market price rising and falling freely above and below their face value, reflecting fluctuations in supply and demand. The Genoese *luoghi* provided a variable income, based on the income of the Republic's taxes (managed by the Bank). In this they were different from the fixed income public debt titles issued by Venice.

In Spain, between 1550 and 1650, the Genoese, who had by this time amassed several centuries of expertise in managing public debt, exploited the opportunity provided by the hopelessly indebted Spanish state to establish a busy and complex traffic in public debt titles know as "juros." In France, public debt was introduced under Francis I in 1522 when the French king borrowed 200,000 *livres tournois* at 12½ percent interest from Paris merchants. In 1560 Caterina de Medici, Charles IX's regent, informed the nobility that the Crown debt stood at 42 million lire. By 1642 the debt had swollen to 600 million lire and the interest payments swallowed up more than half of the state's income. In England public debt was initiated in 1689 and because of costly warfare had risen by 1697 to £21.5 million. The War of the Spanish succession pushed the debt to £54 million and by the end of the War of the Austrian succession in 1748 it totalled £78 million.

The protests and complaints of taxpayers are the most frequently encountered items in the documents of every age and country. In the Middle Ages, the chorus of protestations was joined by the moralists and the political theorists (the two groups being scarcely distinguishable), who never missed an opportunity to point out that any prince who fleeced his subjects so that he might live in pomp or wage a war was committing a deadly sin. If one were to take the content of all these documents and texts literally, one would conclude that people were constantly being bled to death by greedy and bloody rulers.

There is no doubt that throughout the late Middle Ages and the Renaissance the public powers managed to broaden the tax base, to eliminate the constitutional obstacles to taxation, and to raise the rate of taxation. They also constantly devised new and ingenious fiscal expedients. In France after 1522 the Crown's efforts to increase the number of fiscal windfalls and to search out additional expedients was institutionalized in the form of a fiscal bureau with the superbly well-chosen name of the office of *parties casuelles*. All this reflected the emergence of the modern state from the ruins of the feudal world, and the progressive enlargement of its functions. The revenues of the republic of Siena at the beginning of the thirteenth century were about 1,000 lire a month in tributes and loans; by mid-century they were about 20,000 lire a month, and at the end of the century about 50,000 lire.[77] The total revenues of the Republic of Venice increased from about 250,000 ducats around 1340 to about 1.15 million ducats around 1500, to about 2.45 million ducats around 1600.[78] The income of the Pope rose from 170,000 ducats of "spiritual revenues" and 120,000 ducats of "temporal revenues" in 1480 to 202,000 ducats of "spiritual revenues" and 220,000 ducats of "temporal revenues" in 1525.[79] In Spain the income drawn with two taxes, the *alcabala* and the *millones*, increased by more than 500 percent between 1504 and 1596. Moreover, while in 1504 the revenue from the *alcabala* represented 85 percent of the state's revenues, in 1596 it represented only 25 percent.[80] In England the revenues of the Crown grew from about £140,000 a year around 1510 to about £860,000 a year around 1640.[81] In France the revenues of the Crown rose from about 4 million livres around 1500 to about 31 million around 1610.[82]

Information of this kind strikes the imagination, but we must beware of misleading appearances: the figures quoted above have to be seen against the background of rising prices, growing population, and increased wealth. Similarly, the hue and cry of the moralists and the political theorists must be interpreted in the light of the view that a well-ordered state should be funded without taxation.[83]

The fact of the matter was that the fiscal pressure from the public administration was always met with resistance, often strong and sometimes insuperable. The preindustrial state did not have at its disposal the techniques and the means of investigation available to the industrial state, and the concealment of wealth was relatively easy. Moreover, the nobles and the clergy normally enjoyed fiscal immunity. As late as 1659 in the territory of Ravenna (Italy), clergy, nobility, and foreigners were exempt from paying taxes, and they held 35, 42, and 15 percent of the land, respectively.[84] Some professional groups, such as university professors in Renaissance Italy and lawyers and doctors in fourteenth-century France, were also normally excused from paying taxes. Such privileges did not, like a talisman, protect the recipients for evermore. In the course of time both the Church and the nobility lost ground in their effort to evade taxes, and at times exceptionally energetic rules brushed aside existing privileges. Still, over most of Europe for most of the time, fiscal privileges were a reality that created delays, reduced receipts, and complicated the tax-raising process. Worst of all, fiscal privileges also forced the public power to turn to indirect taxation, which fell heavily on the consumption of necessities. Consequently the fiscal burden hit the poor proportionally harder, which in turn explains the complaints, protests, and lamentations mentioned above.

All in all, one must admit that the portion of income drawn by the public sector most certainly increased from the eleventh century onwards all over Europe, but it is difficult to imagine that, apart from particular times and places, the public power ever managed to draw more than 5 to 8 percent of national income.[85]

As has been said above, given the size of public revenues and the structure of pricing, the level and structure of public demand depend on the wants of the public powers and the community they control or represent. In preindustrial Europe the wants that counted were, of course, the wants of those in power. These wants were generally related to war and defense, civil administration, court life, and festivities.

Publicly organized feasts had both a practical purpose and a symbolic value. They amused the populace, pacifying it with diversions and charity.[86] At the same time, they were intended to represent symbolically a certain sharing of interests and sentiments between the people and the prince – thus the festive celebrations after a military victory, the birth of an heir, the recovery of a prince, and the end of an epidemic. Some of these celebrations cost enormous fortunes.

To facilitate description, we have distinguished between expenditures on festivities and those on administration, but the people of the time would have wondered at this distinction. The administrative tasks of the state were very few and simple, and the organization of public festivities was regarded as one of them. A major item of expenditure was embassies and other forms of representation. Part of this money was spent, again, on pomp, banqueting, and festivities, and part went on informers and spies. For the rest, little was spent. It is true that from the twelfth century onward bureaucrats became progressively more numerous, but many administrative tasks continued to be performed by noblemen who – in deference to the principle of *noblesse oblige* – received no salary for their activity, though they often found other and not always reputable ways to obtain some compensation.

One type of public demand deserves special consideration, although it did not represent a large figure in the budgets. Given the low level of income, the mass of the population could hardly satisfy the most elementary wants for food, shelter, and clothing. A series of other wants, especially for medical and education services, while strongly felt, could not be satisfied because people did not have the income necessary to translate them into effective demand. In the communes of Italy and Flanders, it was speedily recognized that some of these wants qualified as necessities with an ethical and social value that could not be ignored. Thus a system of paying doctors, surgeons, and teachers with "public money" was devised so that any sick person, even if he was poor, could be treated, and the children of common people could go to school. In 1288, Milan (Italy), with approximately 60,000 people, had three surgeons "receiving salary from the community" who had to treat "all the poor who needed care." In 1324 Venice, with a population of about 100,000, had thirteen physicians and eighteen surgeons who were on the payroll of the community to serve the poor. In 1630 in the smaller centers in the provinces of Florence and Pisa, thirty physicians out of fifty-five and twenty-four surgeons out of sixty-two were "municipal." Outside Italy, there were municipal doctors in Bruges in the thirteenth century; in Lille, Ypres, and Dunkirk in the fourteenth; and later in Bordeaux, Freibourg, Basel, Colmar, Paris, Lyon, and other cities.[87] In education also, public demand acquired progressively more importance. In the early Middle Ages the very few who received an education received it in convents or from private teachers. With the emergence of the communes, the practice of paying teachers with public money spread. Private teaching never disappeared completely and until recently continued to play an important role, particularly in the education of the children of the upper class. But public teachers and schools spread fairly rapidly after the eleventh century. It is worth recalling the wise words with which the administrators of a modest Tuscan community – Casteldelpiano – decided in 1571 to allocate part of the modest funds of the community to the employment of a schoolteacher:

That for no other reason nor occasion could they make as convenient and lawful use of the funds of their community to the benefit of the community and the citizens as in this, namely, in hiring a school-teacher.

Education may be viewed not as consumption but as investment in human capital. As to public investment of a more conventional type one must mention military construction like city walls (see Table 1.9), fortifications, castles, and so on. Other kinds of public construction included communal buildings, hospitals, and bridges. Finally, there was construction of a conspicuous type, such as the royal palaces. In Renaissance Italy, the more illustrious princes invested considerable resources also in the embellishment of the cities. Guns and warships are an unattractive form of capital, but they are capital goods, and from the middle of the fifteenth century they absorbed rapidly increasing amounts of public expenditure.

We shall see below that in the private sector part of the available resources were always used to build up and maintain food reserves. The same is true of the public sector. The public authorities were doubly interested in the problem of food supplies: first, for humanitarian reasons and for good administration; second, for reasons of political stability, because hunger was the most frequent cause of popular revolts and insurrections. In 1549 the Venetian officer Bernardo Navagero wrote to the Venetian senate: "I do not esteem that there is anything more important in the government of cities than this, namely the stocking of grains, because fortresses cannot be held if there are no victuals and because most revolts and seditions originate from hunger." Florence, Pisa, Lucca, Siena, and other cities established "*Uffici dell' Abbondanza*" (Offices of Abundance) between the end of the twelfth and the beginning of the thirteenth centuries. These *Uffici* were entrusted with the task of overseeing food supply and building up public stores for distribution in time of scarcity. Grain purchases on the part of the Commune of Florence *pro annona publica* are mentioned in documents as early as 1139.[88] Another case of acquisition of grain on the

Table 1.9 Dates of construction and length of city walls in relation to population in selected cities

	Date of construction	Length (in kilometers)	Population (in thousands)
Avignon	1355–1377	5	30
Tours	1355–1360	4.5	10
Ghent	13th–14th cent.	12.7	60
Orleans	1466–1486	6	12
Reims	1337–1360	6.5	14
Louvain	1357–1379	7	15
Brussels	1357–1379	7	13

part of the Commune of Florence for the building up of public reserves is recorded in a document of May 1258.[89] By the beginning of the fifteenth century the municipality of Frankfurt-am-Main (Germany) had an elaborate system of reserves fed by taxes in kind. Occasionally the community resorted to market operations as in 1437 when it purchased up to 28,380 bushels of grain to be stored.[90] At Bassano (Italy) in the second half of the fifteenth century, the town administration built a *fondaco* (depot) in which it stored grain against future needs.[91] At Modena (Italy), there was a public body for the establishment and maintenance of food reserves. Besides the public body, however, in 1501 a *Santo Monte della Farina* (Holy Mountain of Flour) was set up on the initiative of Father Girolamo da Verona. It was designed to store grain, but it was administered by the guilds of the city.[92] Obviously, faith in state bureaucracy was shaky.

Where enlightened administrations held power, public investment of a more productive nature was also undertaken. Between 1168 and 1191, Philippe d'Alsace, Count of Flanders, opened canals linking the valley of the Escaut with the coast and created the new harbors of Gravelines, Nieuport, and Damme. About the same time the Bishops of Bremen and Hamburg organized the reclamation of the marshy lands called *Stauffen*. In 1230–31 the Commune of Bologna spent considerable sums on the purchase of machinery which was freely given to immigrant craftsmen for the development of woollen and silk manufactures. In Florence during the depression that accompanied the plague of 1631,

> The Grand Duke made eighteen-month interest-free loans for a total amount of 150,000 *scudi* to the wool and silk workshops, so that they could continue to work and thus support the labor force of these principal crafts in the city. He also ordered the start of construction of the façade of Santa Maria del Fiore and the completion of the Pitti Palace. All this was done to support more craftsmen and laborers. And since the farm laborers are the backbone of the state, he also provided for them by making them dig ditches and canals to draw plenty of water for the use and beautification of the city.[93]

The relative importance of the various kinds of public expenditure varied noticeably from place to place and from time to time, so that any attempt to reconstruct the patterns of a typical budget would have little or no meaning. One should also distinguish between the demand of the central administrations and the demand of the local administrations.

However, whether one considers the north or the south of Europe, bad or good times, local or central administrations, one finds that the largest portion of public expenditure was always devoted to payments of interest and above all to military affairs. The fact that so many developments of a technological nature, from the casting of iron to the emergence of schools of veterinary science and engineering, had military beginnings clearly indicates the sector favored by public spending.

Commenting on the budget of the Venetian republic, Fabio Besta concluded that public spending on public works was "not high" (with the exception of outlays for the defense of the lagoon against the damage done by the sea and the rivers), interest paid on public loans "appears in all the budgets to be high," spending on embassies and representatives "was always considerable," and military expenditure "surpassed by far all the other expenditures and at times reached extraordinary levels."[94] It has been estimated that at the end of the sixteenth century in Venice expenditures on the fleet and the arsenal alone amounted to 25 to 30 percent of revenues,[95] to which must be added the expenditure for the land army. This was in time of peace. In time of war the standard revenues were not sufficient, and it was necessary to resort to voluntary and/or forced loans and/or to the depreciation of the currency to pay for military expenditures. Early in the sixteenth century, military affairs absorbed about 60 percent of the public expenditure provided by the budget of the Duchy of Milan.[96] In England, Henry V spent about two-thirds of his budget plus nearly all of the revenues from his French possessions for military purposes. Three-quarters of the public expenditures in the last five years of the reign of Elizabeth I were for war or war-related activities. In the first years of the reign of James I the proportion was cut to one-third, but it rose later in his reign.[97] Things have not changed much since those days. Today military expenditure may represent a smaller share of public expenditure, but public expenditure accounts for a higher percentage of national income.[98]

What has been said so far in regard to public expenditure can be usefully complemented with the presentation of a few selected public budgets. Table 1.10 summarizes the annual average public expenditure of Perugia (Italy) in the first half of the fourteenth century. Perugia was then a free commune, that is, a city-state: military expenditure accounted for one-third of the

Table 1.10 Annual average expenditure provided in the budgets of the Commune of Perugia in the first decade of the fourteenth century

Type of expenditure	Lire	Percent of budget
Wages	21,299	34
Military	21,022	33
Embassies	2,420	4
Public works	5,050	8
Charity	3,600	6
Miscellaneous	10,184	15
	63,575	100

Source: Mira, "Le entrate patrimoniali di Perugia," p. 21.

Table 1.11 Expenditure provided in the budget of the Kingdom of Naples, 1591–92

Type of expenditure	Ducats	Percent
Dues to the Apostolic See	12,632	1
Honorarium to the Viceroy	10,000	1
Court expenditure	10,021	1
Embassies and secret expenditure	187,690	9
Wages and salaries	66,696	3
University	2,256	—
Head Physician (health)	145	—
Mail and couriers	22,000	1
Police	38,557	2
Charity	2,556	—
Army and navy	1,091,299	55
Outstanding interests	485,172	25
Miscellaneous	48,752	2
Total	1,977,776	100

Source: Amodeo, A proposito di un antico bilancio; compare also Coniglio, Il viceregno di Napoli, pp. 123 et seq.

budget. Table 1.11 summarizes the budget of the Kingdom of Naples for the 1591–92 fiscal year. As the figures show, military expenditure amounted to 55 percent of the total.

In assessing the expenditure of the central administrations of the states of preindustrial Europe, one must bear in mind that the central authority at that time was infinitely less encroaching and pervasive than in the industrial state. Several activities were left to the competence of the local administrations which also contributed, with their expenditure, to public demand. In general, in the budgets of the local authorities, administrative outlays made up a bigger share of the whole, but not much bigger. In the budgets of the local administrations, especially in the case of French, German and Italian towns, military spending often weighed excessively, in the form of troop billeting, contributions toward the purchase of arms, and repairs of city walls. In this respect, for totally different reasons, English and Swiss towns fared much better.

DEMAND OF THE CHURCH

One can hardly overestimate the importance of the Church as an economic entity in preindustrial Europe. The Church was always ready to condemn those who pursued Mammon, but it never applied to itself the advice it preached to others.

The Church acquired most of its properties through donations from people seeking a passport to Paradise. In this regard the Golden Age for the Christian Church was in the centuries which preceded the eleventh. At the time the barbarian kings, heirs to the vast latifundia bequeathed by the Roman emperors, had at their disposal a well-nigh inexhaustible store of wealth in the form of land, mostly depopulated, which they were quite unable to manage themselves. Counts and barons were in a similar position and their propensity to donate to the Church was proportionate to their fondness for robbery and plunder. Especially the monasteries amassed extraordinary fortunes. The Abbey of St Bertin owned some 25,000 acres in the ninth century. The nucleus of estates of the Lorsch Abbey comprised half the surface of what later would become the Palatinate of the Rhine. The land held by the Abbey of St Germain des Prés in the ninth century consisted of some 35 to 38 square kilometers.[99] It is hard for the modern observer to visualize the magnitude of such estates.

In the following centuries, the process of cumulation continued at a slower pace but accelerated in times of disaster and catastrophe. When the Black Death devastated the Iberian Peninsula in 1347–51, the nobles and the wealthy of Castile outdid themselves in donating lands and buildings to the Church. At the end of the epidemic, the dislocation of wealth was such that in 1351 King Pedro I (possibly entreated by those survivors to whom, ex post, the price paid for the help of Providence must have seemed excessive) ordered the Church to return at least part of the donations it had received.

Donations were supplemented by acquisitions and for one reason or another the wealth of the Church kept increasing (see Table 1.12). Throughout the sixteenth and seventeenth centuries the growing size of the ecclesiastical land holdings was a source of constant concern to the Republic of Venice. In Tuscany, by the end of the sixteenth century, the Church had come to own such a large proportion of the houses and the land in the city and territory of Pistoia that the local people petitioned the Pope to prohibit both churches and monasteries from acquiring or inheriting additional holdings. In the province of Ravenna the clergy held about 27 percent of the land in 1569; it held 30 percent by 1612–14, 35 percent by 1659, and 36 percent by 1731. By the middle of the eighteenth century, the Church owned between 50 and 65 percent of the land in the Kingdom of the Two Sicilies.[100]

Every now and then, however, the Church fell upon hard times, times in which bad administration or individual cunning unfavorably affected its property. Before the eighteenth century, the worst period was perhaps the Reformation. The dissolution of the English monasteries by Henry VIII in the first half of the sixteenth century is deservedly famous. About 1430 the English monasteries owned about 15 percent of the English land while the rest of the Church owned another 10 percent and the Crown only 6 percent. In 1530 there were about 825 monasteries in England with about 9,300 monks and nuns. The total annual net income of the religious orders amounted to about £175,000, or nearly three-quarters as much again as the

Table 1.12 Size of the ecclesiastical property in selected areas of the Florentine Territory in the fifteenth and sixteenth centuries

Territory	Size of the territory in acres	Percentage of lands owned by the Church		
		1427	*1498*	*1508–12*
Acone (Valdisieve)	319	14	13	27
Gaville (Valdarno)	1,986	10	23	24
Macioli (Valli del Mugnone and della Carza)	3,684	7	15	15
Monteceraia (Mugello)	2,249	2	7	7
Montulivi (Valdipesa)	907	2	24	
Mosciano (Florence)	385	9	33	36
Panzano (Valdigreve and Valdipesa)	2,852	19	21	19
Passignano (Valdipesa)	1,804	46	60	64
Paterno (Florence)	692	6	31	27
Pulica (Valdipesa)	1,124	15	26	28
Le Rose (Florence)	504	23	18	16
Rostolena (Mugello)	3,197	8	6	6

Source: Conti, *La formazione della struttura agraria*, vol. 3, part 2, pp. 26ff.

average annual income of the Crown at the same date.[101] By 1550 nothing was left of the English monasteries and their immense estates. Not only were their lands confiscated and sold, but their furniture, silver, libraries, jewels, and other holdings were also dispersed. In Yorkshire alone, the revenues to the Crown from this despoliation were as follows:[102]

Year of account	Value of jewels and plate and proceeds from sale of goods (£)	Income from rents (£)	Total income (£)
1536	3,102	186	3,288
1538–39	1,639	3,200	4,839
1541–42	158	11,061	11,219
1544–45	149	8,837	8,986

In Sweden, Gustav Vasa was no less formidable than Henry VIII was in England. Between 1500 and 1550 ecclesiastical property in Sweden was literally liquidated for the benefit of the Crown (Table 1.13).

What the Reformation did in these areas was done in Lombardy by bad administration, nepotism, and the policies of the dukes. In fact, in Lombardy the ruin of the ecclesiastical estate began well before it began in the countries affected by the Reformation. The erosion became evident in the

Table 1.13 Percentage distribution of land ownership in Sweden between 1500 and 1700

	Year		
	1500	*1560*	*1700*
Crown	5	28	36
Church	21	—	—
Nobles	22	22	33
Peasants	52	50	31
	100	100	100

Source: Hecksher, *An Economic History of Sweden*, pp. 67 and 126.

second half of the fourteenth century and progressively accelerated during the fifteenth century and the first half of the sixteenth. By 1555, in the State of Milan, the Church held only about 15 percent of the land.[103] We do not know precisely what it held one and a half centuries earlier, but we have reason to believe that its property was much greater. The State of Milan was not unique. In the Duchy of Parma and Piacenza as well as in the Duchy of Mantua, by the end of the sixteenth century, the Church was left with only about 9 percent of the land.[104] Elsewhere, however, as in the Grand Duchy of Tuscany, the Kingdom of the Two Sicilies, and in Spain, ecclesiastical property continued to grow throughout the sixteenth and seventeenth centuries. In 1592, the grand duke of Tuscany declared to the cardinal of Florence that "there are very many people and the territory is cramped and ecclesiastic bodies own a great part of it" and that due to the institution of the dead hand "in sixty or seventy years the nuns will have swallowed up everything." The following year in Pistoia, considering that the Church owned "four fifths and more of the possessions of their city and surrounding countryside," the citizenry asked that "no holdings of whatever sort" should be further enlarged.[105]

As indicated, the current income of the Church did not come only from revenues from its estates, but also from transfers of income. Such transfers were in part voluntary (charity, donations, and such) and in part forced (tithes). The Reformation cut into this source as well. In Geneva, for example, in 1544 alone, 12,000 florins in papal tithes were appropriated by the Commune, which spent 4,000 for the Protestant pastors and 1,500 for the hospital.[106]

For a long time, the Church State resisted the temptation to resort to public credit because of the scruples that discouraged it from paying the interest rates it denounced from the pulpit. But in 1526, under pressure from exceptional financial troubles, Pope Clement VII (a Medici from Florence and accordingly very skilled in the handling of public loans and interest rates) took the heroic decision to launch a public loan for the sum of 200,000 gold ducats at a rate of 10 percent. By 1592 the debt had reached 5.6 million scudos, by 1604 roughly 9 million, by 1616 15 million and by 1657 28 million. In 1599 the payment of interest on this debt accounted for 35 percent of total State expenditure.

It is easy and in a sense justifiable to speak of the Church, but the Church was an abstraction. The reality was represented by a vast array of economic units endowed with vastly different amounts of wealth and income. There were the pope, the cardinals, the bishops, the wealthy monasteries whose economic condition was in all respects comparable to that of the richest nobles.[107] And there were also country priests and the mendicant orders, and they shared the fate of the humblest and poorest classes.

The distribution of wealth within the Church reflected the unequal distribution of wealth in society as a whole. Conti has highlighted the ruin of the lower and middle clergy, and the enrichment of the monasteries, in the territory of Florence in the eleventh and twelfth centuries.[108] In the seventeenth century in the district of Ravenna, according to G. Porisini, 70 percent of the Church's enormous property was held by the four wealthy abbeys of Ravenna, while the remaining 30 percent was divided among many parishes, chapters, and secular clergy.[109] In the Duchy of Urbino, three abbeys which represented only 9 percent of ecclesiastical proprietors controlled about 70 percent of ecclesiastical property.[110] In the region northeast of Paris in 1639, out of thirty-five parishes, some had property valued between 140 and 200 livres, while one had property to the tune of about 20,000 livres.[111] In the territory of Cannes (France) in 1772, the Church held about 10 percent of the landed property, but most of this property was concentrated in the hands of the abbey of Lerins; the other priests of the area had a very small share.[112]

The aggregate effective demand of the Church was the sum of a vast range of different schedules of demand. The demand of the poorer units was directed above all to food and clothing, their demand schedule closely resembling that of family units in the poorer classes. The demand of the bishops, cardinals, and monasteries on the other hand, paralleled the structure of demand of the upper classes. At the apex of this imposing structure, the demand of the papal court had all the characteristics of the conspicuous demand of a lavishly rich princely court.

FOREIGN DEMAND

So far we have dealt with internal demand. Every economic system has, however, a network of exchanges with other economic systems. These exchanges include exchanges of goods and services, transfers of wealth, and movements of capital and precious metals.

The foreign trade of a given country consists of its imports and exports. Exports are the response to foreign demand, while imports are determined by internal demand.

As indicated above, the demand of the mass of the populace was largely centered on food, and the consumption expenditure of the wealthy was largely – and conspicuously – directed toward food, clothing, and housing. In view of this fact, it is not surprising that the great bulk of foreign trade consisted of foodstuffs and textiles. As late as the end of the sixteenth century, cloth accounted for about 80 percent of the total exports of England while textile materials, groceries, timber, and wine were the four main categories on the imports side. Owing to high transportation costs, especially during the Middle Ages, foreign trade was largely – though by no means exclusively – concerned with high-quality products; hence the large share of spices and expensive wines in the international exchange of primary products and the large share of luxury cloths in the international exchange of textiles. It also followed that the mass of the people generally had to content itself with local products and that only the well-to-do could afford exotic produce. The ability of the average man in the street to walk into a shop in Milan or in London to buy something produced in Hong Kong or Tangier is a recent development made possible by the Industrial Revolution.

To measure foreign trade, one can add together the values of imports and exports and compare the total to the Gross National Product. The result is influenced by the volume and the value of imports and exports, but also by other factors, such as the physical size of the country and the size of its population which are relevant in determining the size of the Gross National Product. A country like the United States might have considerable foreign trade, but given the vastness of the country, the greater part of economic activity exhausts itself within its boundaries, where a wide variety of resources is found. For a little country like Luxembourg, on the other hand, nearly every exchange is an international exchange, and, therefore, in relation to the Gross National Product, the value of foreign trade represents a much higher percentage. In recent years, the ratio was about 10 percent for the United States and about 160 percent for Luxembourg.

The number of studies devoted to international trade in medieval and Renaissance Europe defies imagination, but the focus has been almost exclusively on commercial techniques and the behavior and fortunes of individual firms. The lack of statistical material worthy of the name has perpetuated the lack of interest in certain macroeconomic relationships. England is perhaps the country for which the best statistics on foreign trade exist for the preindustrial era (see Table 1.14).

One can estimate that at the beginning of the reign of Henry VII English imports and exports were balanced at the level of about £300,000 a year; by the end of the seventeenth century, exports (of locally produced goods) had increased to about £4.5 million a year and imports to about £4.7 million a

Table 1.14 Approximate value of English imports and exports, 1500–1700

	(million of current pounds)			
	Exports	*Re-exports*	*Total exports*	*Net imports*
c. 1490	0.3			0.3
c. 1600	1.0			
c. 1640	2.3	0.5	2.8	2.2
c. 1660	3.0	0.9	3.9	3.1
1700–09	4.5	1.7	6.2	4.7

Sources: Davis, *Commercial Revolution*; Minchinton, *English Overseas Trade*, pp. 9–15; Schumpeter, *English Overseas Statistics*; Gould, *Economic Growth*, p. 221n; Coleman, *The Economy of England*, p. 133. Between 1500 and 1700 the general level of prices rose about 400 percent.

year. This increase reflected in part a rise in prices but was mostly due to a remarkable increase in the volume of foreign trade.

At the end of the seventeenth century, exports of domestic goods alone must have come to 10 percent of the national product.

For states territorially much smaller than England, such as the Communes of Florence and Genoa or the Republic of Venice, in the thirteenth and fourteenth centuries the ratio of foreign trade to the national product must have been nearer to the level of Luxembourg today than to that of England at the end of the seventeenth century. As for other countries, it is difficult to say. Moreover, while it makes some sense to consider England as a whole, since the country was fairly well integrated economically, it would be stretching history too much to consider, for example, fourteenth-century France or sixteenth-century Germany as economic units.

From a general point of view, there is no doubt that the development of international trade brought positive overall net effects. But from the point of view of single regions, or even of single states or nations, the problem is not so simple.[113] The idea of trade as an "engine of growth" is a gross oversimplification. For any given society, the long-run consequences of foreign trade depend largely on the qualitative structure of that trade and the effects of foreign demand on both patterns of employment and capital formation in the society in question.

The economic development of the Italian communes was largely related to the development of foreign trade. But examples to the contrary are not difficult to find, even without turning to the cases of colonies or of certain countries in Latin America today. The strong Dutch demand for grain on the Polish market in the sixteenth and seventeenth centuries; the Dutch,

English, and French demand for oil and silk on the Italian market in the seventeenth century, favored the involution of the economies of Poland and Italy along feudal-agricultural lines and created the preconditions for long-term stagnation in these countries. In Portugal, about half a century after the Methuen Treaty of 1703, the Marquis of Pombal could justifiably complain that "two-thirds of our necessities are now supplied by England. The English produce, sell, and resell everything which is needed in our country. The ancient manufactures of Portugal have been destroyed." Port wine and the gold of Brazil paid for the imports, and the pressure of foreign demand kept Portugal's human and physical resources strictly tied to the agricultural and mining sectors.

2

THE FACTORS OF PRODUCTION

CLASSES OF "INPUTS"

A productive system can be fancifully described as a huge box: certain things flow in one side and other things flow out the other side. What flows in, we call *input*, and what flows out, we call *output*.

Input is made up of heterogeneous elements called *factors of production*. Traditionally economists group the innumerable and heterogeneous factors of production under three broad headings, called, respectively, *labor, capital*, and *natural resources* (the last category including land as well as water supply, iron ore, coal deposits, and so forth). Like most classifications, the tripartition is arbitrary and oversimplifies matters, but as it has proven useful for analytical purposes, we adopt it in the historical analysis below. However, it is essential to sound a warning.

One of the major difficulties in historical reconstruction is that, in order to express ourselves, we must make use of the current language. Unfortunately, the words we use daily evoke in our minds pictures of the contemporary world. Expressions such as *labor* and *capital* automatically evoke in our minds the picture of the factory, with its high concentration of managers, wage laborers, and complex machinery. An effort of the imagination is required to recapture, behind the modern spoken expression, the very different reality of the past. In this attempt, one must be careful not to go to the other extreme, to fall victim to stereotyped, fanciful typologies.

The factory in the modern sense did not exist; instead there was the small workshop. The equivalent of the modern businessman was the merchant, but he was not what we now mean by the word *merchant*. Specialization had not yet developed to the degree that characterizes industrial societies, and a merchant was very often the head of a manufacturing enterprise, a money lender, and a trader, all at the same time. As a trader he generally dealt in a variety of products, in cloths as well as spices, cereals as well as metals. Even the distinction between wholesale and retail trade did not exist. The one recognizable difference among merchants was that some operated on an international scale with substantial capital, while others were petty, local merchants of limited means and horizons.

Similarly, for the term *labor* we must try to recapture a different reality from that which we associate with the term today. Wage labor did exist in preindustrial Europe, but it was not as preponderant as in the modern world. In agriculture, sharecropping was quite common and in most parts of Europe it was the predominant form of compensating agricultural labor. As for the manufacturing sector, all textbooks emphasize that, before the Industrial Revolution, the artisan was the most common type of worker. This is true, but the artisan was far from being a stereotype. There were many craftsmen who worked with the help of an apprentice. There were workshops with a number of artisans joined in a company. And there were even more complex units in which craftsmen actually employed both wage-earners and apprentices and, we can now see, functioned as proto-capitalists.

LABOR

All members of a population are consumers, but not all of them are producers. Apart from parasites and the infirm, the youngest and oldest members of a population consume but do not produce. In any society, once population totals have been established, it is important to identify (a) the economically active population (those who produce and consume), (b) the dependent population (those who consume but do not produce), and (c) the relation between the two (dependency ratio).[1]

Prevailing birth and death rates and, in cases of significant migratory movements, immigration and emigration, determine the age structure of a given population. Preindustrial European societies were characterized by high fertility and high mortality rates. Consequently, the so-called age pyramid of European preindustrial populations normally presents a relatively wide base as against an acutely angled apex (see Figure 2.1). Consider the structure of two populations when both were at a preindustrial stage, namely, the Swedish population in the second half of the eighteenth century and the Italian population soon after the middle of the nineteenth century – the one Nordic and Protestant, the other Mediterranean and Catholic. The percentage distribution of the two populations divided into broad age groups is shown in Table 2.1.

Despite wide differences in latitude, climate, color of eyes and hair, food, religion, and culture, in both cases the population in the fifteen to sixty-four age group represented little more than 60 percent of the total while the group under age fifteen made up almost a third. Before the nineteenth century, national censuses were not taken in Italy but data available on the population of various Italian cities confirm that the population under fifteen years of age always made up a third or more of the total population (see Table 2.2).

Before proceeding, it may be useful to make a comparison with the

54

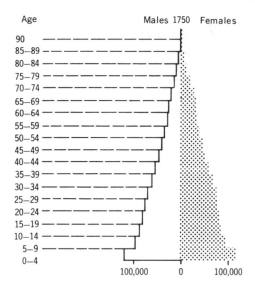

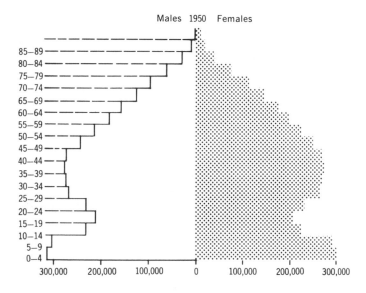

Figure 2.1 Age and sex structure of the population of Sweden in 1750 and 1950.

Source: *Historisk Statistik för Sverige*, Stockholm, 1955, vol. 1, Appendix fig. 4 (1750) and fig. 5 (1950).

Table 2.1 Percentage age distribution of two preindustrial populations,
Sweden (1750) and Italy (1861)

Age groups	Sweden 1750 %	Italy 1861 %
65 and over	6	4
15–64	61	62
0–14	33	34
Total	100	100

Table 2.2 Adolescents as percentage of total population in selected Italian areas,
1427–1642

City	Year	Age group	Percent of total population
Arezzo and surrounding countryside	1427–29	0–14	32
Pistoia and surrounding countryside	1427–29	0–14	37
Parma (city)	1545	0–14	32
Parma (countryside)	1545	0–14	41
Brescia	1579	0–18	40
Siena	1580	0–10	23
Vicenza	1585	0–15	42
Milan	1610	0–9	24
Carmagnola	1621	0–15	41
Padua	1634	0–15	30
Venice	1642	0–18	46

structure of industrial populations. Table 2.3 contains data relating to the Swedish and English populations in 1950–51. As one can see, in an industrialized society, the population in the fifteen to sixty-four age group represents about two-thirds of the total population, that is, little more than in the preindustrial society. The most striking difference between the societies of preindustrial Europe and those of contemporary Europe lies in the composition of the dependent population. While in modern Europe children of zero to fourteen years make up from 65 to 70 percent of the dependent population, in preindustrial Europe they represented about 90 percent. In other words, the burden of dependence in preindustrial Europe was almost totally represented by children. The gravity of the problem is measured by the number of abandoned children.

In Venice in the sixteenth century, the *Ospedale della Pietà* usually cared for an average of 1,300 foundlings, which, out of a total population of

Table 2.3 Percentage age distribution of two industrial populations,
Sweden (1950) and England (1951)

Age groups	Sweden 1950 %	England 1951 %
65 and over	10	11
15–64	66	67
0–14	24	22
Total	100	100

130,000 to 160,000, represented almost 1 percent.[2] In Florence in 1552, in the *Ospedale degli Innocenti* there were 1,200 foundlings; out of a total population of about 60,000 the foundlings made up 2 percent. In Prato (Italy) in 1630 the *Ospedale della Misericordia* cared for 128 young girls, 54 boys, and 98 babies, a total of 280 foundlings. Prato then had a population of approximately 17,000, and the foundlings were, therefore, about 1.6 percent of the total population.[3] It must be noted that values of the order of 1 or 2 percent of total population meant, in a preindustrial society, some 3 to 7 percent of the children in the age group zero to fourteen. It must also be remembered that the figures above refer in large measure to the number of foundlings who survived. According to a Venetian estimate in the sixteenth century, 80 to 90 percent of the foundlings died in their first year of life.[4] If one relates the number of those "admitted to the Ospedale della Pietà" to the number of births in the city, one finds that in Venice, in the second half of the eighteenth century, foundlings represented 8 to 10 percent of all births (see Table 2.4). In Milan at the end of the seventeenth century the number of foundlings was on average 450 per year (Table 2.5), and this figure represented more than 12 percent of the estimated births in the city.[5]

Such high percentages must be viewed with caution. We know from various sources that those who wished to rid themselves of newly born babies often came from far away to abandon them in the city. The number of foundlings, therefore, ought to be related to a larger population than the local one. This would lower the percentages mentioned above, but even so, it would be difficult to deny that the practice of abandoning newborn babies was tragically widespread.

In our industrial societies, we consider as economically active the population in the age group fifteen to sixty-four. It is an arbitrary assumption based on the rationales that (a) in many countries compulsory education for the young continues to the age of fifteen and (b) the age of sixty-five is, in many professions, the limit for retirement. In reality, however, there are individuals who start working long after their fifteenth year of age and others who start earlier. There are people who retire before sixty-five and

Table 2.4 Foundlings in Venice, 1756–87

Year	Foundlings			No. births	% foundlings over births
	M	F	MF		
1756	199	210	409	5246	7.8
1759	204	201	405	5172	7.8
1765	192	233	425	5090	8.3
1776	230	248	478	5243	9.1
1782	229	238	467	5166	9.0
1783	235	244	479	5077	9.4
1785	228	233	461	5074	9.1
1787	231	250	481	5220	9.2

Source: Beltrami, Popolazione di Venezia, p. 143, n. 18.

Table 2.5 Foundlings in Milan, 1660–1729

Decade	M	F	MF
1660–69	1967	2090	4057
1670–79	1802	1913	3715
1680–89	1774	1816	3590
1690–99	2616	2699	5315
1700–09	2697	2610	5307
1710–19	2479	2625	5104
1720–29	2250	2172	4422

Source: Buffini, Ospizio dei Trovatelli, vol. 1, Appendix, tables 1 and 2.

others who are still working at a later age. There are adults who have never worked and there are people who collect a regular salary but whose inclusion among the active population is the result of gentle violence wrought by statistics upon reality. To consider as active all those in an industrial society who fall in the fifteen to sixty-five age group and as dependent all the remainder, probably overestimates the percentage population which is effectively productive and thus underestimates the real dependency ratio. Productivity in industrial societies is so high that it is not difficult for such societies to afford dependency ratios of 50 to 65 percent. In fact, it is high industrial productivity that has allowed the introduction of compulsory education up to fifteen years, allows many to continue their education until the age of twenty-five or twenty-eight, allows most people to retire at sixty-five, and allows many to figure in statistics of active population while doing nothing more than keep their chairs warm.

The conditions prevailing in preindustrial Europe were vastly different. Those who were economically "active" worked from dawn to dusk, but given the low average of productivity they could not support many dependants. It followed that normally the few old people had to work until the end of their days (which, incidentally, was psychologically good for them), and the young people had to be set to work long before the age of fifteen.

In general, child labor is described as a ghastly by-product of the Industrial Revolution. The truth is that in preindustrial society, children were as widely employed as at the time of the Industrial Revolution. An English royal statute of 1388 mentions the boys and the girls who "use to labor at the plough and cart or other labour or service of husbandry till they be of the age of twelve years." There was a difference, however. In preindustrial society, the mass of children was employed in the fields and, therefore, only during the summer months (hence the tradition of long school holidays during summer). With the development of the factory system, the children were employed instead the whole year around. Life in the fields was perhaps not so unhealthy as in the factories of the early Industrial Revolution, but the hardships to which children were subjected were not more tolerable. A Lombard ordinance of the late sixteenth century pointed out:

> At the time when the weeds are pulled from the rice patches, or other work is performed in the rice fields, some individuals called "foremen of the rice workers" manage in various ways to bring together a large number of children and adolescents against whom they practice barbarous cruelties. Having brought the children with promises and inducements to the chosen place, the foremen then treat them very badly, do not pay them, do not provide these poor creatures with the necessary food, and make them labor as slaves by beating them and treating them more harshly than galley slaves are treated, so that many of the children, although originally healthy, die miserably in the farms or in the neighboring fields. As His Excellency the Governor does not want these foremen of the rice workers to act in the future as they did in the past or to continue to slaughter children, he orders this traffic to be stopped.[6]

In the eighteenth century the Austrian physician J. P. Frank wrote that:

> In many villages the dung has to be carried on human backs up high mountains and the soil has to be scraped in a crouching position; this is the reason why most of the young people are deformed and misshapen.[7]

Preindustrial Europe also made widespread use of female labor in areas other than domestic service. First of all, women produced many commodities at home which today are produced industrially and exchanged on the market (bread, pasta, woollens, socks, and so on). Miniatures of the

59

fourteenth, fifteenth, and sixteenth centuries show us, however, that women were also regularly employed in agricultural work, and documents show that, in the major manufacturing centers, women were widely employed in spinning and weaving in the workshops. In Florence, among wool weavers, women workers made up 62 percent of the labor force in 1604 and 83 percent in 1627.[8]

Textile manufactures were often organized on the basis of the putting-out system; that is, a merchant gave out raw wool, for example, to workers who worked in their own homes, and later collected the product from them for sale or for further processing. This system facilitated the employment of women who, between one task and another at home, busied themselves with work for the merchants. In 1631, when plague struck San Lorenzo a Campi, in Tuscany, and many houses were quarantined, a health inspector reported that he had "found a greater amount [of wool] than anticipated" and provided his superiors with a list of twelve houses in each of which a woman was working wool for some merchant.[9]

Women were also employed in work which we usually consider to be the preserve of men. In Toulouse, between 1365 and 1371, in the building yard of the Périgord College, men and women were employed in almost equal numbers, and the women carried stones and bricks in baskets, which they placed on their heads.[10] The French miniature reproduced opposite depicts women employed in metallurgical works. In Venice women were largely employed in the arsenal in the manufacturing of sails.[11]

For a correct evaluation of female employment in the preindustrial era, one must also take into account wet nurses. The wet nurse is a person who, for a monetary reward, sells food (mother's milk) and a service (care of the infant). The economic and social importance of wet nurses in pre-industrial Europe compares with the importance of the baby-food industry in our contemporary society.

The "active" population can be usefully analyzed in relation to its distribution by productive activity.

Generally speaking, statisticians and economists like to distinguish between three broad categories of occupations, corresponding to the three sectors of activity respectively termed primary, secondary, and tertiary. The primary sector normally includes agricultural activities and forestry. Sometimes fishing and mining are also included. The secondary sector consists of manufacturing. The tertiary sector includes the "remainder." Like all residual categories, this one is a source of ambiguity and confusion. In industrialized societies, the tertiary sector is mainly represented by the production of services such as transport, banking, insurance, the liberal professions, advertising, and the like. Some years ago, an Australian economist, Colin Clark, put forward the theory of a highly positive correlation between the general level of development of an economy and the relative size of the

A French metallurgical works. This sixteenth-century French miniature shows that women were employed also in metallurgical works where the skills they practiced in the kitchen were put to use in operating small furnaces.

tertiary sector. But other economists with firsthand knowledge of certain primitive societies have shown that in a preindustrial society, the tertiary, or "residual" group, is also fairly large, with the difference that, instead of including bankers and insurance agents, it includes a picturesque variety of

61

people with trades ranging from dealers in stolen goods to gatherers of used items.

Because of the lack of statistical data, no one will ever know with any degree of accuracy what percentage of the European population was employed in the primary sector at various times before the eighteenth century. Only for the middle of the eighteenth century are there some reasonable estimates relating to England, France, Sweden, and the Republic of Venice (see Table 2.6). They are still far from precise, but they can be taken as broad indications.

On this basis it does not seem far-fetched to maintain that in the centuries preceding 1700, in every European society, the percentage of the population actively employed in agriculture varied, as a rule, between 65 and 90 percent, reaching minima of 55 to 65 percent only in exceptional cases. The reason for this concentration lay in the low productivity of agriculture.

Seven or eight peasants succeeded with difficulty in producing (over and above what was necessary to maintain themselves and their families) the surplus necessary to maintain two or three other people. In particularly favorable circumstances, especially when water routes made the supply of cereals from abroad economical, a country could reduce the percentage of population actively employed in agriculture to below traditional levels. A typical case is that of Venice, which regularly imported grain from Lombardy, southern Italy, and the Black Sea, while the local population was engaged in everything but agriculture. A document dating from the end of the tenth century described the Venetians with amazement: *et illa gens non arat, non seminat, non vindemiat* (that nation does not plow, sow, or gather vintage). Venice's case was exceptional, but between 1400 and 1700, marked developments in maritime transport made it possible for some countries with favorable geographical positions to depend considerably on the supply of grain from abroad. This was certainly the case with seventeenth-century Holland, which imported large quantities of cereals from eastern Europe via the Baltic–Sund–North Sea, not only for her own consumption, but also for re-export. Undoubtedly seventeenth-century Holland employed a much

Table 2.6 Estimates of population employed in agriculture as percentage of total labor force, about 1750

Country	Percent
England	65
France	76
Sweden	75
Republic of Venice	75

lower percentage of its population in agriculture than other European countries did, but even in the case of the Dutch Republic it is doubtful that the percentage ever fell below 50 percent. On the other hand, if the imports of the Dutch contributed to reduce the fraction of those employed in the primary sector in certain areas of western Europe, they favored an increase of the same fraction in the countries of eastern Europe. For every ten who ate bread, seven or eight had to produce wheat, and if these seven or eight were not all in one geographical area, they had to be in another.

The large percentage of the population employed in the primary sector can easily lead one to overestimate the percentage of effective labor put into this sector. For a more precise assessment of the labor input, one has to take into account the fact that, for climatic reasons, during long periods of the year the peasant did not work; he was there, but he was not active, while most handicraftsmen were active all months of the year. Furthermore, peasants' wives, normally regarded as being employed in agriculture, in addition to their agricultural activities generally contributed to the manufacturing sector (especially in weaving) and to the services sector (as domestic servants or as wet nurses) during the winter months.

It would be a mistake to imagine that the rural population coincided with the population employed in agriculture. Country villages were home not only to peasants, but to tailors, blacksmiths, carpenters, cobblers, and sometimes barber-surgeons and schoolteachers. Borrowing Louis Malassis's classification, in the rural world we can distinguish between the *agricultural sub-set*, consisting of farmers, the *agro-food sub-set*, consisting of agricultural workers, a manufacturing and trading superstructure that processed and distributed farm products, and lastly the *rural sub-set*, covering all other activities of whatever type performed in the countryside or in country villages. In the middle of the sixteenth century, in the completely rural parish of Myddle in Shropshire which had a population of about 350 souls, roughly 11 percent of the adult male population were craftsmen – smiths, carpenters, tailors, cobblers, and coopers.[12]

Table 2.7 shows the occupational distribution of the population in selected European cities. The first thing to emphasize is the correlation between what emerges from these figures and what has been said in the preceding chapter about the structure of demand. The bulk of demand was concentrated on food, clothing, and housing. The structure of demand influences the price structure, which, in turn, determines the structure of production. It is, therefore, not at all surprising that in Table 2.7 the three sectors – food, textiles, and construction – account for the greater part of the active population under consideration – that is, broadly, from 55 to 65 percent. Those employed in the food sector represent a relatively small percentage because the data refer to urban populations, and the bulk of those employed in the production of food lived in the country. For Gloucestershire, in 1608, a census is available that includes not only three

Table 2.7 Occupational distribution of the population of selected European cities, fifteenth to seventeenth centuries

	Verona 1409	Como 1439	Frankfurt 1440	Monza 1541	Florence 1552	Venice 1660
a. Food distribution and agriculture	23	21	21	39	13	17
b. Textiles and clothing	37	30	30	25	41	43
c. Building	2	4	8	1	6	4
Subtotal: a + b + c	[62]	[55]	[59]	[65]	[60]	[64]
d. Metalwork	5	8	8	10	7	5
e. Woodwork	5	4	5	2	2	8
f. Leather	10	7	4		7	7
g. Transport	2	3	} 22	{ 1	1	9
h. Miscellaneous	6	17		21.5	21	2
i. Liberal professions	10	6	2	0.5	2	5
	100	100	100	100	100	100

Sources: For Verona: Tagliaferri, *Economia Veronese*; for Como: Mira, *Aspetti dell'Economia Comasca*; for Frankfurt: Bucher, *Die Bevölkerung von Frankfurt*; for Monza: Cipolla, *Per la Storia della Popolazione Lombarda*; for Florence: Battara, *Popolazione di Firenze*; for Venice: Beltrami, *Composizione Economica e Professionale*. Domestic servants were not always included in the censuses on which the table is based.

major cities (Gloucester, Tewkesbury, and Cirencester), but also the surrounding rural areas.[13] Putting together both townsmen and country dwellers, one sees (Table 2.8) that those employed in the production and distribution of food represented by far the largest group (46 percent) and that the combined group of those employed in the three sectors of food, clothing, and construction represented about 73 percent of the working male population. However high the subtotals, a + b + c in Table 2.8 and a + b + c + d in Table 2.9, they still underestimate the relative importance of the mixed food-clothing-construction group, because, for example, many of those included in the category "leather" produced shoes and sandals and therefore should be added to the "clothing" sector, and many of those in the category "woodwork" produced goods and services connected with housing and therefore should be added to the "building" sector.

In the discussion of the level and structure of demand, it was mentioned that the great disparity between the wealth of a few and the low average level of wages logically stimulated demand for domestic services. Kings were not the only ones to have a retinue of servants. In England in the thirteenth century the household of the Earl and Countess of Leicester counted sixty servants. The household of a minor baron like the Lord of

Table 2.8 Occupational distribution of males, aged 20–60, in Gloucestershire, by percentages, 1608

	Cities	Countryside	Cities and countryside together
a. Agriculture	4	50	46
b. Food and drink	7	2	2
c. Textiles and clothing	26	23	23
d. Building	2	2	2
Subtotal: a + b + c + d	[39]	[77]	[73]
e. Metalwork	6	3	3
f. Woodwork	6	4	4
g. Leather	5	1	1
h. Transport	3	2	2
i. Professionals and gentry	6	3	3
j. Servants	3	7	7
k. Miscellaneous	32	3	7
	100	100	100

Source: Tawney, "An Occupational Census," p. 36.

Eresby included a steward, a wardrober, a wardrober's deputy, a chaplain, an almoner, two friars, a chief buyer, a marshal, two pantrymen and butlers, two cooks and larderers, a saucer, a poulterer, two ushers and chandlers, a baker, a brewer, a potter and two farriers, and each had their own boy helpers. In the monastery of Evesham, in England in 1096, there were fifty-two servants for sixty-six monks and the former figure did not include gardeners, a blacksmith, a mason and other laborers of various kinds. In the monastery of Meaux (England) in 1393, twenty-six monks were served by forty domestics. Domestic service was abundantly available also to the middle and lower-middle classes. A Florentine census of 1551 shows that only 54 percent of the families of Florence were without domestic servants living with them (see Table 2.9).

Domestic personnel are not always easily pinpointed in the demographic and fiscal records of the time, because either the listings in the documents were limited to heads of families, or the service staff was mixed in with members of the family. In some urban censuses, however, domestic servants were listed separately. Whenever the available figures allow some calculations, the result is that in the European cities of the fifteenth, sixteenth, and seventeenth centuries domestic servants represent about 10 percent of the total population, which means about 17 percent of the population in the age group fifteen to sixty-five (see Table 2.10).

Table 2.9 Percentage distribution of families in Florence (Italy) according to number of servants, 1551

	% families
With more than 5 servants	5
With 2 to 5 servants	18
With 1 servant	23
Without servants	54

Source: Battara, *La Popolazione di Firenze*, p. 70.

Table 2.10 Domestic servants as a percentage of total population in selected European cities, 1448–1696

City	Year	%
Freiburg	1448	10
Bern	1448	9
Nuremberg	1449	19
Basel	1497	18
Ypres	1506	10
Parma	1545	16
Florence	1551	17
Venice	1581	7
Bologna	1581	11
Rostock	1594	19
Bologna	1624	10
Florence	1642	9
Venice	1642	9
Münster	1685	15
Lille	1688	4
Ypres	1689	7
London (40 parishes)	1695	20
Dunkirk	1696	6

Devoutness and superstition strengthened each other in creating and supporting the demand for religious services. On the other hand, widespread devoutness led many individuals of both sexes into the ranks of the clergy. Other factors also favored the increase in the ecclesiastical population. The institution of the dowry was an incubus for most families and a danger to the integrity of the family inheritance. In Europe to solve the problem the well-to-do frequently confined their daughters to a convent.

Table 2.11 provides some data on the ecclesiastical population in selected European cities from the fifteenth to the seventeenth centuries. Viewing a region as a whole, one finds that in 1745 the Great Duchy of Tuscany had 890,605 inhabitants, including

Clerics: 3,955
Priests: 8,095
Monks: 5,482
Hermits: 168
Nuns: 9,736

The 27,436 ecclesiastics represented about 3 percent of the total population.[14] Beloch has estimated that, at the middle of the eighteenth century, in all of Italy the ecclesiastical population represented about 2 percent of the total population.[15] In 1591, Spain, with a total population of about 8.5 million people, had about 41,000 priests, 25,000 friars, and 25,000 nuns.[16] Thus the clergy represented about 1.1 percent of the total population. About France we know that in Alsace and the area of Alençon, at the end of the seventeenth century, of a total of 409,822 inhabitants the clerical population numbered 4,609 individuals, or about 1.1 percent. In Brittany in 1696, the ecclesiastical population amounted to 18,889 in a total population of 1,654,699 – again about 1.1 percent. In the area of Caen, out of 609,203 inhabitants, the clergy totaled 5,225 – that is, nearly 1 percent.[17] In England and Wales in 1377 the priests numbered about 24,900 and the monks and nuns about 10,600. In a total population of some 2.2 million people the clergy represented about 1.5 percent. In the first decades of the sixteenth century in England and Wales there were about 9,300 monks and nuns in a population of approximately 3.5 million inhabitants.[18] In Poland around 1500 there were about 6,900 monks and nuns and about 15,000 priests. The population of Poland numbered about 4.5 million, thus the clergy represented about 0.5 percent.[19] In considering these figures one has to bear in mind that, given the age composition of preindustrial populations, 1 or 2 percent of the total population meant respectively 1.5 or 3 percent of the population above age fifteen.

From an economic point of view the clergy can be seen as producers of a particular type of service, and, inasmuch as there is a demand for this service (a demand which, like all other producers, the clergy does its best to stimulate) the clergy have the right to be considered part of the economically active population. In most respects the contribution of the clergy to a community is not different from that of psychiatrists in modern societies, and it has been observed that in countries where people have no recourse to the confessor, they end up by having recourse to the psychiatrist (with the disadvantage that individually they pay much more for the service). In addition, in preindustrial Europe, and especially in rural areas, the parish priest often also performed those functions which we now regard as belonging to the schoolteacher and the doctor.

Table 2.11 Ecclesiastical population in selected European cities, 1400–1700

City	Date	Total population (thousands) (a)	No. of priests (b)	No. of monks & nuns (c)	Total no. of priests, monks & nuns (d)	Clergy as % of total population		
						$\frac{b}{a} \times 100$	$\frac{c}{a} \times 100$	$\frac{d}{a} \times 100$
Toulouse	c. 1400	c. 23			c. 1,000			4.3
Frankfurt	1440	10			225			2.3
Nuremberg	1449	20			250			1.3
Bologna	1570	62			3,310			5.3
Venice	1581	135	586	3,553	4,139	0.4	2.6	3.1
Naples	1599	233		5,702			2.4	
Besançon	c. 1600	11			600			5.5
Rome	1603	105	1241	4,512	5,753	1.2	4.3	5.5
Cremona	1621	40	150	1,852	2,002	0.4	4.6	5.0
Florence	1622	66		4,917			7.5	
Pisa	1622	15		951			6.3	
Bologna	1624	62	138	3,431	3,569	0.2	5.5	5.7
Venice	1642	120	735	4,171	4,906	0.6	3.5	4.1
Siena	1670	16		1,755			10.9	
Pistoia	1672	8		726			9.1	
Besançon	1709	17	275	571	846	1.6	3.4	5.0

One of the major drawbacks of traditional textbooks is that they identify the active population of preindustrial Europe with *merchants, craftsmen, landlords,* and *peasants* and they neglect professionals, in particular notaries, lawyers, and physicians. There was considerable demand from the private sector as well as from the public sector for the services of professionals, and this aspect of the problem has been discussed above in Chapter 1. Tables 2.12 and 2.13 provide some data relating to the size of the major professions in selected European cities. The Italian cities of the thirteenth and fourteenth centuries stand out for the size of the professional group and especially for the size of the notarial profession. Between the tenth and the fourteenth centuries the notaries constituted the bulk of the bureaucracy of the Italian cities. Table 2.13 shows also that the number of physicians was generally relatively higher in Italian cities than in other European towns, at least until the end of the seventeenth century. Whether this was beneficial to people's health is another matter altogether. Most likely it was harmful,[20] but if people were prepared to pay for doctors' services, the supply of such services satisfied psychological needs, and, therefore, the availability of doctors, regardless of what they were able to do, must be put on the same plane as that of priests and hermits.

From the economic and social points of view, the importance of notaries,

Table 2.12 Number of notaries, lawyers, and physicians in relation to total population in selected Italian cities, 1268–1675

City	Year	Per 10,000 inhabitants		
		Notaries	Lawyers	Physicians
Verona	1268	124		
Bologna	1283	212		
Milan	1288	250	20	5
Prato	1298	278		
Florence	1338	55	9	
Verona	1409	70	6	3
Pisa	1428	90		
Como	1439	17	12	2
Verona	1456	54	4	9
Verona	1502	40	6	5
Verona	1545	26	7	5
Verona	1605	8	17	4
Carmagnola	1621	21	14	3
Florence	1630			5
Pisa	1630			9
Rome	1656			12
Rome	1675			13

Source: Cipolla, "The Professions," p. 43.

Table 2.13 Number of physicians in relation to total population in selected European cities, 1575–1641

City	Year	Physicians	Population (thousands)	Doctors per 10,000 inhabitants
Palermo	1575	22	70	3.1
Florence	1630	33	80	4.1
Pisa	1630	12	13	9.2
Pistoia	1630	5	9	5.5
Rome	1656	140	120	11.6
Rome	1675	164	130	12.6
Antwerp	1585	18	80	2.2
Rouen	1605	16	80	2.0
Lyons	1620	20	90	2.2
Paris	1626	85	300	2.1
Amsterdam	1641	50	135	3.7

Source: Cipolla, *Public Health*, Chapter 2.

lawyers, and doctors can hardly be exaggerated and most certainly it was far out of proportion to their numbers. To begin with, members of the medical, legal, and notarial professions usually belonged to the small circle of the well-to-do, many of them aś affluent as the rich merchants. Enjoying high incomes, physicians, lawyers, and notaries originated a demand for distinctive clothing, beautiful houses, and land, as well as for books, entertainment, and educational services for their children. Moreover, physicians, lawyers, and notaries gave the middle class a strength, respectability, and prestige that affluence alone could never have procured.[21]

Economic history, if it is to make sense, must include social history, taking account of values and factors which cannot be measured in solely economic terms. The history of the professions is an essential part of the story of "intangible" values. Scholarly prestige, restrictive practices through the enforcement of licensing, relatively high personal income – all these factors individually reinforced each other and in combination made possible the social ascent of the professionals. In this respect medieval and Renaissance Europe stands out as a unique example in world history. In other parts of the world, such as China, the providers of medical and legal services never succeeded in asserting themselves socially as well as economically. In certain other societies they did, but as members of a priestly caste. Only in western Europe, during the Middle Ages, did the professionals clearly separate themselves from the clergy and still move to the higher steps of the social ladder. The preeminence acquired in medieval western Europe by the professionals is at the origin of many institutions and characteristics of our industrial societies.

Obsessed with merchants, craftsmen, landowners, and peasants, economic historians have usually ignored the representatives of "the oldest profession in the world." Medieval canonists were more realistic: Thomas de Chobham had no doubts – the prostitutes work, he maintained, even if their work is ignominious. A distinction must obviously be made between general prostitution and legalized prostitution. As regards the first, one cannot hope to have adequate information, but as regards the second, enough is known to justify the statement that, squalid though it may be, this sector always had great economic relevance. Moreover, it is easy to show that there is some positive correlation between the economic development of a given center and the presence of women of easy virtue. The fairs that were held in the province of Scania (southern Sweden) between August 15 and November 9 in the thirteenth and fourteenth centuries (the famous *nundinae Schanienses*) were well known not only for the number of merchants and fishermen who met there, but also for the number of *fahrende Frauen*.[22]

In the sixteenth and seventeenth centuries, the two major centers of prostitution in Europe were Venice and Rome, a primacy which, with the Industrial Revolution, was to be taken over by London and Paris. The gamesome ladies of Venice, called courtesans, were famous for their refinement and culture and, as Thomas Coryat wrote, "the name of a Cortezan of Venice is famous all over the Christendome."[23] In the sixteenth century, Montaigne, who was a great gossip as well as a great mind, relates that the Cardinal d'Este regularly traveled to Abano for the baths, but even more to visit the "lovelies" of the Serenissima.[24] In fact, the courtesans were one of Venice's main attractions for tourists and traders, and the English travelers of the early seventeenth century have left valuable information on the subject.

To establish numbers of prostitutes is a difficult task. First of all, the occupation does not lend itself to an exact definition, because between the two extremes of "honest woman" and "common prostitute" there is a vast range of intermediate conditions with blurred outlines. Second, anyone wishing to make a survey of the subject inevitably finds himself faced with reticence of every possible kind. Finally, the topic is such as to lend itself easily to the most fanciful tales. In Florence in the sixteenth century it was held that "about 8,000 courtesans" plied their trade,[25] but the 1551 census recorded only three.[26] The first figure is certainly an exaggeration, but the second does not reflect the truth, as witnessed by a poem of 1533 that lists forty women of easy virtue, describing them by name, surname, and noting their various qualities.[27] In sixteenth-century Venice, those interested in "all that the brigand apple brought" could buy at little expense a booklet containing the "tariff of all prostitutes in which one finds the price and the qualities of all courtesans of Venice." According to two chroniclers of the early sixteenth century, there were then in Venice about 12,000 official prostitutes, but the figure is probably an exaggeration.[28]

71

In Rome, in the sixteenth and seventeenth centuries, it was said that there were 10,000 to 40,000 prostitutes.[29] Possibly this figure too was an exaggeration. Official figures are of course, as Table 2.14 indicates, much lower, ranging from 7 to 9 per thousand of total population. In assessing such figures, however, one has to bear in mind that in Rome, with its exceptional preponderance of priests, monks, and cardinals, women were underrepresented. In 1600, out of 109,729 inhabitants, there were only 46,596 females, and the women in the fifteen to sixty-five age group must have numbered approximately 30,000; thus the 604 women of easy virtue listed in the census of that year represented about 2 percent of the adult female population of Rome. For a holy city, the percentage looks high, especially if one considers that the figures refer only to those prostitutes who were officially recognized as such.

The economic importance of this social group was more than proportional to its numerical size. Thomas Coryat, at the beginning of the seventeenth century, wrote of Venice:

> Some of them [the courtesans] having scraped together so much pelfe by their sordid facultie as doth maintaine them well in their old age: for many of them are as rich as ever was Rhadope in Egypt, Flora in Rome or Lais in Corinth. One example whereof is Margarita Aemiliana that built a faire monastery of Augustinian monkes.[30]

About the same time, Fynes Moryson wrote:

> Each cortizan hath commonly her lover whom she mantaynes, her *balordo* or gull who principally mantaynes her, besydes her customers at large, and her *bravo* to fight the quarrels. The richer sorte dwell in fayre hired howses and have their owne servants but the common sorte lodge with bandes called ruffians, to whome in Venice they pay of their gayne the fifth parte, as foure shillings in twenty, paying

Table 2.14 Number of officially recognized prostitutes in relation to total population of Rome, 1598–1675

Year	Total population	Prostitutes	Prostitutes per 1,000 inhabitants
1598	97,743	760	8
1600	109,729	604	6
1625	115,444	940	8
1650	126,192	1,148	9
1675	131,912	889	7

Source: Schiavoni, "Demografia di Roma."

besydes for their beds, linnen and feasting, and when they are past gayning much, they are turned out to begg or turne bandes or servants.

Since official prostitutes were taxed for their trade, in the larger towns they represented an important source of income for the public finances. According to Robert Dallington, at the end of the sixteenth century the Grand Duke of Tuscany "hath an income out of the brothel stewes which is thought at the least thirty thousand crownes a yeare in Florence onely."[31] In Rome, the attempt made by Pius V in 1566 to expel prostitutes from the Holy City failed because, in the words of the Venetian ambassador, Paolo Tiepolo,

> to send them away would be too big a thing, considering that, between them and others who for various reasons would follow them, more than 25,000 people would leave this city; and tax-farmers in Rome let it be understood that (if the prostitutes were expelled) they would either renounce their contracts or ask for a compensation amounting to 20,000 ducats a year.[32]

Italy has always been the country of the oddest compromises. We have already seen in the passage by Coryat that a monastery of the Augustinians in Venice was built with funds provided by a prostitute. In Rome, prostitutes were under obligation to bequeath part of their possessions to the Monastery of the Converted. When Pius V dedicated himself to the building and beautifying of the Civitas Pia, one of the expedients to which he had recourse in order to raise funds was to release the prostitutes from the obligation to bequeath part of their possessions to the monastery as long as they contributed at least 500 scudi toward his holy building.[33]

As has already been said, it would be wrong to identify the rural population wholly with the agricultural population, and the urban population entirely with the active population in the secondary and tertiary sectors. In the suburbs of the cities lived laborers who grew vegetables or performed other essentially agricultural activities. On the other hand, one encountered artisans and a few professional people also in small rural and semi-rural communities. As Christopher Dyer pointed out, the frequent finds of spindle whorls in excavations on village sites show that spinning yarn with a distaff was an almost universal practice among peasant women. Large-scale industrial employment was often localized, like the tin-mining and smelting which occupied as many as one in ten of the population of Cornwall. The woods themselves provided an environment for a wide range of crafts, for potters, glass-makers, coopers, turners, wheelers, cartwrights, arrow-makers, bow-makers, and charcoal burners. In the village of Lomello (Lombardy) around 1435, out of a population of about 500 or 600, there were at least two tailors, one weaver, a schoolteacher, and other artisans.[34] In 1541 in the area of Monza (Lombardy), in the rural centers numbering fewer than 200 inhabitants each, those engaged in agriculture made up about 75 percent of the population; the remaining 25 percent consisted of craftsmen, traders, cart drivers, boatmen, and the like.[35] In the wholly rural Shropshire parish of Myddle (England) with a total population of around 350 in the mid-sixteenth century, about 11 percent of its adult male population were craftsmen – blacksmiths, carpenters, coopers, tailors, shoemakers, though, as was normal, many such men were small husbandmen as well.[36] In the small rural parish of Ealing in Middlesex (England) in 1599, out of 426 inhabitants there were three tailors, one smith, one carpenter, one wheelwright, and four clerks.[37] In France in 1691 in the small rural parish of Laguiole, among 990 people were found one lawyer, six barber-surgeons, one schoolteacher, five master cobblers and eight journeyman cobblers, four master tailors and three journeyman tailors, one architect, three master masons and three journeyman masons, two carpenters, eight weavers, one glazier, three locksmiths, one wool-draper, and other craftsmen.[38]

The presence of skilled labor both in the cities and in the countryside was a decisive factor for the success of manufacturing activity. Current economic analysis tends to stress the importance of human capital, but this is not a modern discovery. If anything, it is a rediscovery. In the Middle Ages and in the Renaissance, the relevance of human capital to economic prosperity was taken for granted. Governments and princes were active in trying to attract artisans and technicians and in preventing their emigration. We shall return to this point in Part II, when dealing with the spread of technology. Here, however, it is worth mentioning a significant example.

In 1230, the Commune of Bologna launched a definite policy of economic development. The idea was to encourage the setting up and development of textile manufactures, particularly wool and silk. To achieve its aim, the Commune announced that those artisans who would move to Bologna and start an enterprise would enjoy the following advantages:

a. they would receive free, from the city, a *tiratorium* (or the equivalent value of 4 lire) and two looms (or the equivalent value of 2 lire each)
b. a loan of 50 lire for five years free of interest, to cover the expenses for the initial installation, the cost of raw materials, upkeep of the family, and so forth
c. exemption from all taxes for fifteen years
d. immediate grant of citizenship

In the two years 1230–31, 150 artisans with their families and their assistants settled in Bologna. (At that time Bologna numbered at most 25,000 inhabitants.) In its undertaking, the Commune of Bologna freely distributed some nine thousand lire of the time, a very large sum.[39] The operation was repeated in 1385 and between 1385 and 1389 more than 200 craftsmen (not counting their relatives) migrated to Bologna.

Bologna's case is particularly interesting because of the early period in which it took place, because of the size of the operation in both human and monetary terms, and for the excellent documentation which has survived but, as we shall see in Chapter 6, one encounters many similar cases in the following centuries. They show that everywhere in Europe public powers were very much aware of how important the availability of skilled labor was to economic progress.

The number employed in a particular sector of the economy tells us something, but not everything, about the effective quantity and quality of the labor in that sector, both in an absolute sense and in relation to labor inputs in other sectors. A lot depends on the number of working days actually put in, the number of working hours per working day, the physical and psychological condition of the workers, and the workers' level of education and technical training.

A Lombard document dated 1595 recorded that

> the year consists of 365 days, but 96 are holy days, and thus one is left with 269. Of these, a great many are lost, mostly in wintertime and even at other times, because of rain and snow. Another part of the year is lost because everyone does not always find work, except in the three months of June, July and August.[40]

The document in question refers to agricultural labor and points out that religious festivities and climatic and seasonal conditions had a marked effect on the amount of labor actually put into productive activities. The holidays were traditionally numerous. The above document cites a total of ninety-six a year in Lombardy. They numbered eighty to ninety a year in sixteenth-century Venice, eighty-seven in sixteenth-century Florence, and one hundred and forty in Prato.[41] In Protestant Europe the Reformation noticeably reduced their number.[42]

Climatic conditions and seasonal fluctuations in demand hit agricultural and building activities especially hard. Consequently, the percentages of those employed in agriculture and construction tend to overestimate the proportion of labor inputs in these sectors in relation to labor inputs in other sectors of the economy.[43]

We know very little about the physical and psychological conditions of the labor force before the Industrial Revolution. We do know that the mass lived in a state of undernourishment. This gave rise, among other things, to serious forms of avitaminosis. Widespread filth was also the cause of troublesome and painful skin diseases. To this must be added in certain areas the endemic presence of malaria, or the deleterious effects of a restricted matrimonial selection, which gave rise to cretinism. As late as

1835 L. R. Villermé wrote that in France out of 343 recruits from the lower orders, only 100 were fit for military service.[44] To all this one should add the effects of occupational diseases due to the appallingly unhealthy conditions under which certain trades were conducted and to the handling of toxic substances.

Separately or together, these factors had a negative influence on the quantity and quality of effective labor inputs. On the other hand, the beauty and perfection of many products of European preindustrial craftsmanship give the inescapable impression that the craftsman of the time found in his work a satisfaction and a sense of dignity which are, alas, foreign to the alienating assembly lines of the modern industrial complex.

Little or nothing is known of the level of education of the masses before the Industrial Revolution. The urban revolution of the eleventh and twelfth centuries ushered in a new era with the introduction of public schools, and many a city witnessed a noticeable development of elementary education. In Florence, around 1330, Giovanni Villani recorded: "There are from 8,000 to 10,000 boys and girls who are at school learning how to read and from 1,000 to 1,200 boys who learn abacus and arithmetic" in the schools.[45] We know from other sources that Florentine youths went to school to learn reading and writing at the age of five or six. At the age of eleven, those who were both willing and able continued their education in one of the six schools of arithmetic where they remained for two to three more years. About 1338, Florence had a population of roughly 90,000 inhabitants. Given the age structure of populations in those days, the age group between five and fourteen must have consisted of about 23,000 children. If Villani's data are correct, more than 40 percent went to school. A document dated 1313 shows that in Florence it was taken for granted that an artisan should be able to "write, read, and keep accounts," and it is known that a good many humble Florentine artisans wrote extremely readable, and, for us, instructive, family histories.[46]

Florence was in the vanguard of Europe in the fourteenth century. During the fifteenth and sixteenth centuries, one city after another followed her example, but the spread of elementary education among the masses long remained a typically urban characteristic. In the Protestant countries the Reformation succeeded in spreading the rudiments of reading and writing among the rural population, but in Catholic countries the bulk of the peasants remained illiterate until the modern era. About the middle of the seventeenth century, less than 50 percent of the adult population of the major western European cities were illiterate; elsewhere, the figure ranged from 50 to 95 percent.[47]

These observations lead us to discuss education and professional training in an economic context.

To raise and educate a child costs money. If the young person is of working age and is instead sent to school, the person also costs the economy what he does not produce. That which the young person could produce if he were sent to work and does not because he is at school is income forgone for the economy and represents an opportunity cost.

These costs are borne by the family and the society, in expectation of future incomes. What is spent in raising and educating a person is a form of investment, which is directly comparable to the building of a factory. While it is being built, the factory, too, does not produce and the cost of construction is borne in expectation of future incomes. In the training of a person, as in the building of a factory, the investment can be a good one or a bad one. A student who studies little and badly during his school years is the equivalent of a factory which is badly built: the defects will become evident when production starts.

The poverty of preindustrial societies did not allow for large investment in human capital. A few years at school were a luxury that not many could afford, especially in the country. Apprenticeship offered the advantage that the young people produced while they learned; thus the opportunity cost of their education was practically eliminated. In fact, all professional and technical training was given by way of apprenticeship.

In Venice, at the beginning of the seventeenth century, the ages for acceptance into apprenticeship in certain trades varied from ten to twelve years (see Table 2.15). The average duration of apprenticeship varied according to trades; for instance:

victualling and sale of products of the soil: 5 years
production of clothing or personal services: 3 years
other trades: 5 years

Table 2.15 Age limits for acceptance into apprenticeship in selected trades in seventeenth-century Venice

	Age limit	
Trade	Minimum	Maximum
Tinkers		16
Dyers		20
Weavers	12	17
Stonecutters	11	13
Caulkers	10	20
Painters	14	16
Goldsmiths	7	18
Sausage makers	16	18

Source: Beltrami, *Popolazione di Venezia*, pp. 198–99.

The guilds regulated professional education in every detail, and in some cases, to the benefit of the children of their own members, they even organized school courses to teach the rudiments of reading and writing.[48]

Originally, training for the higher professions – jurisprudence, medicine, and notarial art – also took place through various forms of apprenticeship. But from the end of the twelfth century, and more decidedly in the thirteenth century, special schools were created, from which the universities emerged.

The main trouble with employment statistics is that they encourage us to regard people as if they were potatoes. Taking account of a worker's education and his psychological and physical conditions is a step in the right direction, but a very small one. In any statistics on employment, Michelangelo would figure as "sculptor: 1." Or if the statistics were fairly advanced, he might be slotted into the category of "artisans (or artists) with more than 10 years' education." And that would be the end of it. The statistics we possess leave out the most important feature of work, i.e. the human element, the most profound meaning of which cannot be measured in quantitative terms – or, if it can, we have not yet found out how. Michelangelo is an extreme case but there is a world of difference between work that is prepared and executed with care and efficiency and work that is slapdash and aimless. We take *work* to cover not just unskilled laboring but any and every kind of productive activity. Anyone who has had the opportunity to compare developed and underdeveloped societies will readily acknowledge that the difference between the two lies in the value of "human capital" in both the upper and the lower classes. The trouble that besets an underdeveloped country is not so much the lack of capital or the backwardness of technological knowledge as the poor quality of the human component: an underdeveloped country has entrepreneurs who are of little value, workers worth even less, teachers who are incompetent, students who laze around, rulers who don't know how to rule, and citizens devoid of any civic sense. This is why a country remains underdeveloped. A country's shortage of capital and its technological and administrative backwardness are more a consequence than a cause of its underdevelopment.

Education plays an important part in any upgrading of human capital. But education is not enough. For a society to function properly, psychological and ethical qualities are also essential: a spirit of co-operation, a sense of honesty, tolerance, self-sacrifice, initiative, perseverance, intellectual curiosity, a willingness to experiment, etc. The analysis of these factors is one of the most difficult and neglected areas in the social sciences. Econometric techniques are particularly ill-suited to this kind of investigation. And other types of analysis tend to be terribly vague and inconclusive.

One of the fundamental characteristics of the urban societies of preindustrial Europe was the tendency toward association, which manifested itself increasingly from the end of the twelfth century. If in the preceding centuries men had sought protection and the safeguard of their own interests in a relationship of subordination to the powerful (feudalism), with the emergence of urban societies the safeguard of personal interests was sought mainly in associations among equals. This was the essence of the urban revolution. The commune was initially nothing more than the sworn association of citizens – the super-association, above and beyond the particular associations which took the name of Arti, guilds, companies, confraternities, societies, or universities.

Class and group conflicts played a fundamental part in determining who could and who could not form a guild, and the dominance or decline of a group signified the opportunity (or lack of it) for rival groups to unite in a legally recognized guild. Within the guilds, a definite order of precedence faithfully reflected the distribution of power. For the whole of the thirteenth century, merchant guilds remained unchallenged in dominating the European scene. In the ensuing centuries, various occupational categories gradually acquired the right to constitute themselves into autonomous associations, and the craft guilds became increasingly influential.

The guilds satisfied a number of requirements. Among the various tasks of the guilds, there was usually that of collective organization of religious ceremonies, charity, and mutual assistance. These tasks were not a smokescreen. For a craftsman of the time, participation by his own guild in the town's procession in honor of the patron saint or the Virgin Mary was as important as, if not more important than, a discussion of wages and production. And the guilds played an important role in providing social assistance to their own members and education for their members' children as well as in setting and enforcing quality controls in production.

All these functions should not be underestimated. But neither should one underestimate the fact that one of the fundamental aims of all guilds was to regulate and reduce competition among their own members. With regard to the supply of labor, a guild aimed at exercising strict control over the admission of new members and their entry into the labor market. On the other hand, when competition among employers was in question, the corporate body always served to control and strictly regulate competition among its members as far as demand for labor was concerned. Consequently, in any study of the level and structure of employment and wages in centuries preceding the eighteenth, the action of the guilds must occupy a salient position.

CAPITAL

Physical capital is represented by goods which are produced by people and are not consumed, being either used as productive inputs for further production or stored for future consumption. Capital can be usefully divided into *fixed capital* and *working capital.*

Fixed capital consists of those economic goods produced by people which are repeatedly used in the course of a number of productive cycles. Machine tools are the classical type of fixed capital, but the shovel, the plow, and the barrel, as well as the ship, the cart, and the bridge are also fixed capital.

Sir John Hicks wrote a few years ago:

> What is the essential mark by which we are to distinguish modern industry from the handicraft industry? ... This is a clue to the distinction between the two kinds of industry for which we are looking.
>
> The capital of a merchant is, mainly, working or circulating capital – capital that is turned over. A particular merchant may indeed employ some fixed capital, an office, a warehouse, a shop or a ship; but these are no more than containers for the stock of goods on which his business centres. Any fixed capital that he uses is essentially peripheral.
>
> As long as industry remained at the handicraft stage the position of the craftsman or artizan was not so very different. He did indeed have tools, but the tools which he used were not usually very valuable; the turnover of his material was the centre of his business. It is at the point when fixed capital moves, or begins to move, into the central position that the revolution occurs. In the days before modern industry, the only fixed capital goods that were being used, and which absorbed in their production any considerable quantity of resources, were buildings and vehicles (especially ships).[49]

The thesis that fixed capital acquired a degree of importance only with the Industrial Revolution and, even then, only in the final stages of the Revolution, has never been questioned and has, indeed, been reasserted emphatically by a number of scholars.[50] However, even as a first and rough approximation, the statement needs qualifications.

Fixed capital was admittedly of negligible importance before the eleventh century when all forms of capital were in any case in painfully short supply. Documents of the eighth century clearly suggest that large estates suffered from a shortage of livestock.[51] In the ninth century, of the twenty-nine farms of the Abbey of St Germain des Prés outside Paris, only eight had water mills (though these totaled fifty-nine); and at the beginning of the tenth century, the records of the Abbey of St Bertin referred to the construction of a mill as an exceptional and admirable event.[52]

From the eleventh century onward, however, things changed considerably. Water mills and windmills proliferated and became a common feature of the rural landscape. Toward the end of the eleventh century in England, more than 5,600 mills were in operation and in some areas, such as Surrey, there was a mill for every thirty-five recorded families.[53] In 1350, in the territory of Pistoia (Italy), there was approximately one mill for every twenty-five recorded families.[54] In the course of time, not only did the number of mills continue to increase, but their average power per unit also increased. Toward the end of the eighteenth century, more than half a million water mills operated in western Europe, and many of them had more than one wheel.

Besides water mills and windmills, other buildings related to agriculture grew both in number and in size in the centuries following the year 1000. Barns deserve special mention because many of them not only represented a sizeable investment (see Table 2.16) but were built so beautifully that they are no less relevant to the history of architecture than castles and cathedrals.[55]

As buildings grew in number and in size, tools were improved and were produced in larger quantities.[56] Most important of all, livestock became more abundant. Horses, cattle, and sheep were a special kind of fixed capital. (I call it "a special kind of capital" because livestock can be consumed as food whenever necessary or convenient.) On nine Ramsey Abbey manors in eastern England, draft animals increased by 20 to 30 percent between the end of the eleventh and the mid-twelfth century.[57] At the end of the thirteenth century in the territory of Chieri (Piedmont) over an area of about 20,000 acres, there were four cattle and six sheep for every 100 acres.[58] In 1336 on about 1,900 acres owned by Merton College (England), of which about two-thirds were arable land, there were four horses, twelve cattle, and sixty sheep for 100 acres.[59] In 1530 six country parishes in Brianza, north of Milan (Italy), there were 11,058 persons above seven years of age, 762 children below seven years of age, and 1,823 animals. For every 100 persons older than seven, there were, therefore, about seven children and sixteen animals.[60] In 1574 on property belonging to the Hospital at Imola (Italy), there were 96 persons. Of these, 33 were workingmen who made use of fifty-one head of cattle and thirty-seven sheep, with a ratio of cattle to laborers of about 1.5 to one.[61] An inquiry made in 1471 in the regions of Grasse, Castellane, Guillaume, and

Table 2.16 Volume of selected barns built in the thirteenth century

	cubic ft
Cholsey (Berkshire)	482,680
Beaulieu-St Leonard (Hampshire)	526,590
Vaulerand (France)	869,980

Source: Horn and Born, The Barns, p. 41.

Saint-Paul-de-Vence in Haute-Provence (France) yielded the following results:[62]

	No. of localities	No. of households	No. of donkeys, mules, and horses	No. of sheep and goats	Head of cattle
Totals	70	3,167	2,494	114,837	5,498
Averages:					
Per locality		45	36	1,641	78
Per household			0.8	36	2

For the period 1560–1600, the following estimates have been calculated for various parts of England:[63]

	Percentage of peasant laborers possessing		No. of cattle per 100 laborers
	cows, calves, heifers	other cattle	
Northern Lowlands	74	26	227
Northern Highlands	84	16	197
Eastern England	82	18	122
Midland Forest Area	92	8	142

As one can see from the figures quoted above, the ratios of animals to land, of animals to laborers, and of animals to population varied greatly from one area to another and from one period to another. But always and everywhere, animals were a form of fixed capital which was far from being "peripheral" to the productive system. Toward the end of the seventeenth century, William Petty calculated that, if the value of all agricultural land in England could be estimated at about £144 million, the animals could be valued at a quarter of that sum, that is, at about £36 million.[64] In many areas, livestock was much more abundant in the Middle Ages and the Renaissance than in modern times. For six of the seventy localities in Haute-Provence covered by the aforementioned inquiry of 1471, the following comparison has been made:[65]

	No. of households	No. of sheep and goats	Head of cattle
in 1471	863	25,050	1,451
in 1956	12,834	471	407

Horses, cattle, and sheep were capital not only for agriculture. Sheep provided the raw material for the woollens industry. Horses and oxen were indispensable for transport. Also, the military sector relied heavily on this sort of capital. From the fifteenth century onward, armies tended to move with greater speed as horses and mules gradually replaced oxen as a means of transport in military operations. As late as the second half of the nineteenth century in several European countries, the census tabulations included not only people, but also horses and mules; and the object of the enumeration was essentially military. Toward 1845, the number of horses and mules available in the major European nations was estimated as shown in Table 2.17.

As mentioned above livestock as a form of capital has the advantage that when necessary or advisable it can be killed and consumed as food: its cost is not all sunk cost. On the other hand, livestock as a form of capital had the disadvantage of being highly vulnerable. In medieval and Renaissance Europe, epizootic diseases were no less frequent or disastrous than epidemics.[66] At times, these diseases assumed international political significance, as when in Pannonia, in 791, nine-tenths of Charlemagne's horses died and the Frankish king found himself in great military difficulties.[67] More often, an epizooty was of purely local significance, but not infrequently it brought tragedy to entire regions. In 1275, "A rich man of France brought into Northumberland a Spanish ewe, as big as a calfe of two yeares, which ewe being rotten infected so the country that it spread over all the realme; this plague of murrain continued for 28 years."[68] Between 1713 and 1769 in Frisia, major epizootics caused the following losses:[69]

December 1713–February 1715: 66,000 head of cattle
November 1744–August 1745: 135,000 head of cattle
November 1747–April 1748: 23,000 head of cattle
May 1769–December 1769: 98,000 head of cattle

When cattle died, the consequences for the economy of the time were comparable with the consequences of large fires which would destroy machines and power stations in a modern industrial economy. Moreover, replacement was made difficult by the fact that among horses, cattle, and

Table 2.17 Number of horses and mules in selected European countries, about 1845

Country	Horses and mules
Austria (Empire)	2.7 million
France	2.7 million
England	2.3 million
Italy	1.0 million
Prussia	1.5 million
Russia	8.0 million

Source: Balbi, L'Austria, p. 165 and Annuario Statistico Italiano, 1857, p. 554.

sheep, sterility was very widespread. For the territory of Montaldeo (Italy), a survey of forty-nine cows during the period 1594–1601 shows an index of sterility of about 50 percent, with only twenty-five calves born; the sterility of sheep in Montaldeo was even higher, about 70 to 75 percent.[70]

Despite being small, hungry, and often sterile, horses, oxen, and sheep were an extremely valuable form of capital. Supply was limited and demand was high. In Montaldeo in the seventeenth century, one had to accumulate the wages of 100 ten-to-twelve-hour work days to buy one cow. At the beginning of the eighteenth century, it was necessary to sell over 50 liters of wine to buy one small pig.[71]

The value of this form of capital was a temptation to the mass of the poor. Fernand Braudel wrote that "... in England at the beginning of the nineteenth century, thieves and horse-thieves were a class of their own."[72] The fact is that cattle thieves were a thriving and numerous class not only in England, but in all European countries.

Contrary to what one would expect, fixed capital was not peripheral, even in areas of the tertiary sector. A study of fifteenth-century Lombard pharmacies shows that their working capital amounted to only 30–35 percent of the investment; fixed capital in the form of furniture, vases, pestles and mortars, glasses, distillers, condensers and the like amounted to 65–70 percent.[73]

In the transport sector, one must distinguish between waterborne transport and overland transport, and for the latter between long-distance and local transport. In waterborne transport, boats and ships were fixed capital. In long-distance overland transportation until the sixteenth century, horses and mules were the predominant form of fixed capital employed – not until the second half of the sixteenth century were there enough roads to allow the extensive use of carts and carriages for long-distance travel. On the other hand, carts were used very early for local overland transport, especially for agricultural products. From whatever point of view one looks at things, fixed capital, in the form of draft animals, beasts of burden, ships, boats, carts and carriages, was not peripheral in transport services.

The thesis that fixed capital had a purely peripheral importance in the productive process before the Industrial Revolution is most valid for the manufacturing sector. As discussed above, when, in 1230–31 the Commune of Bologna invited a number of foreign artisans to set up manufactures of silk and wool, the city administration provided each artisan with a *tiratorium* worth 4 Bologna lire of the time and two looms worth 2 lire each. The fixed capital considered necessary for a productive unit was, therefore, valued at 8 lire. At the same time, the Commune loaned each artisan 50 lire for the expense of setting up and starting the plant, for raw materials and for the upkeep of his family. The artisans undertook to repay the 50-lire loan over a

The Great Crane at Bruges. This machine is a typical example of fixed capital in preindustrial Europe. As one readily notices, the main problem was the power source; the crane had to be operated with human energy. Bayerische Staatsbibliothek.

period of five years. This fact suggests that, under normal conditions, the fixed capital necessary to an enterprise, valued as we have seen at 8 lire, could be amortized in less than a year. Other examples of this kind can be easily assembled, but only with some qualifications. In the case of the textile manufactures of Bologna, the productive process was not entirely completed in the houses of the artisans. From an early date, mills were used for the fulling of cloth, and they represented a considerable investment in fixed capital. Over the centuries in Bologna itself, special mills were built for the manufacture of silk. By the seventeenth century these mills had reached an exceptional level of mechanical sophistication and represented an important investment. The mill set up in early eighteenth-century England by Sir Thomas Lombe in imitation of the Bologna silk mills consisted of 25,586 wheels and 97,746 pieces and could produce 73,726 yards of silk yarn for every revolution of the enormous driving wheel.[74] In the mining sector, machines were needed for pumping water and for lifting and carrying ore; during the fifteenth and sixteenth centuries, this machinery often attained notable dimensions. In a lead mine in Poland about one hundred horses were employed to operate a pumping contraption, and in the second half of the sixteenth century 32 kilometers of galleries for drainage were excavated when the cost of excavating one kilometer equalled the price of about fifteen homes in the center of the mining town of Olkusz. In the shipbuilding sector, basins, docks, workshops, implements, and cranes represented considerable fixed capital. The Arsenal of Venice was deservedly famous throughout the later Middle Ages and the early modern periods for its size, its installations, and its stocks of materials. In England at the end of the seventeenth century, the fixed assets of Kentish shipyards at Chatham, Deptford, Woolwich, and Sheerness, were valued at about £76,000 (Table 2.18). If we accept Gregory King's estimates of the English national income for 1688 (£43.5 million, according to Table 1.5) the sum of £76,000 was equivalent to almost 0.2 percent of the annual English national income.

There is no doubt, however, that apart from specific industries, normally in the manufacturing sector, fixed capital was of limited size. Moreover, since machinery and equipment were relatively simple, the greatest part of

Table 2.18 Fixed plants in four major English naval shipyards, 1688

	Docks	Work-shops	Depots	Workers' houses	Cranes	Value of plant (£)
Chatham	5	24	10	10	4	44,940
Deptford	1	17	2	7	2	15,760
Woolwich	2	5	1	7	2	9,669
Sheerness	1	3	1	8	12	5,393

the fixed capital sunk in most manufactures was represented by buildings. In five factories operating in the Republic of Genoa (Italy) near the end of the eighteenth century, the composition of fixed capital was as follows:[75]

	Value of building (%)	Value of equipment (%)	Total
Silk-throwing factory	87	13	100
Paper mill	87	13	100
Paper mill	85	15	100
Paper mill	85	15	100
Furnace	100	—	100

One important form of fixed capital was represented by weaponry. The armament of a preindustrial state may seem ridiculously small in comparison to the weaponry of a modern industrial state, but in relation to the Gross National Product of the time it represented quite an investment. Moreover, while in a modern state the armory in the hands of private individuals is practically insignificant when compared to the weaponry controlled by the public powers, in preindustrial Europe the situation was totally different. Troyes is a medium-sized city in France which in October 1474 counted some 2,300 households. An official inspection of all homes showed that at the time the citizens owned 208 jacks, 51 complete suits of armor, 109 breastplates and overshirts, 199 shirts of mail and coats of mail, 73 surcoats, 49 brigandines and underskirts, 785 sallets and armets, 151 barbutes and basinets, 271 crossbows, 547 muskets, with both automatic recoil and manual, 4 cannons, one serpentine, 389 lances, 855 hatchets and hammers, 1,047 spears, 201 javelins, double-hooked lances, and pikes, 37 bows, 657 two-headed hammers of lead, copper, and iron. Moreover, in the shops of the town merchants there were for sale: 69 jacks, 6 complete suits of armor, one decorated breastplate, 5 overshirts, 14 brigandines, 6 shirts of mail, 79 lances, 110 sallets, 16 steel crossbows, 8 hammers, 56 swords, 17 pairs of gauntlets.[76] Admittedly that was a turbulent period for France, and in particular the citizens of Troyes feared the consequences of the war between Louis XI and Charles le Téméraire. Still, even for calmer periods and quieter areas, if one combines the armory in the hands of private citizens and the weaponry owned by the public powers, one always finds that that particular form of capital represented quite a sizable amount of wealth.

There are no reliable statistics to evaluate precisely the relative importance of the various kinds of fixed capital in preindustrial Europe. The only data available are the educated guesses of Gregory King for England in 1688 (see Table 2.19), but they seem to confirm the general impression one obtains from the scanty and casual information provided by the surviving

Table 2.19 Gregory King's estimate of English capital in 1688

		Million pounds
Fixed capital	Buildings	54
	Livestock	25
Working capital	Plants, tools, and machinery	33
	Stocks and inventories	
	Total	112

Source: Deane, "Capital Formation," p. 96.

records – namely, that the most important form of fixed reproducible capital was buildings, followed by livestock, with plants, tools, and machinery ranking in third place.

If one were to distinguish between the various uses to which fixed capital was put, one would notice that churches and monasteries abounded. A medium-sized city such as Pavia (Italy) in the fifteenth century, with about 16,000 inhabitants, had over one hundred churches, and this was in no way exceptional. Hospital beds, on the other hand, were so scarce that, until well into the nineteenth century, it was common practice in every part of Europe to place two or three patients in one bed. Bridges were few and roads inadequate, but castles were abundant.

The distribution of capital among various forms and uses is influenced by technological as well as economic and cultural factors. The building of magnificent cathedrals at a time when hospital beds were so scarce that the sick had to be piled up two or more to a bed reflects the unequal distribution of wealth as well as a peculiar set of preferences. If wonderful private mansions were built while bridges were few and roads inadequate, this imbalance is related to the fact that, all things considered, public agencies were able to draw on only a limited part of available resources. But the explanation does not end there. The same hospitals which lacked beds were adorned with costly works of art. The state which did not build bridges sank considerable resources into military expenditure. The direction of investment was and is determined by the structure of demand – that is, by tastes and standards of value.

Working capital essentially consists of *stocks and inventories*, which can conveniently be subdivided into

a. stocks of raw materials
b. stocks of semi-finished goods
c. stocks of finished goods

There is no doubt that in preindustrial Europe the ratio of working to fixed capital was much higher than it is nowadays. The reason for this difference may be explained as follows. The maximum possible consumption of a given society at a given time is determined by the volume of stocks plus the volume of current production. Therefore, the significance of stocks is a function of both the intensity of fluctuations in current production, and the inelasticity of demand. Economic life in preindustrial Europe was characterized by violent fluctuations in harvests, insecurity of transportation and, therefore, irregularity of supplies, both of foodstuffs and of raw materials. Transportation was expensive, which made long-distance transport of low-priced commodities an uneconomical proposition. As a result, people usually built up stocks of foodstuffs wherever they could, and businessmen normally built up ample stocks of raw materials and/or finished goods. Stocks of food were particularly important. We saw previously, in Chapter 1, that public authorities spared no efforts to build up and maintain stocks of victuals. The same attitude prevailed at the household level, as the specter of famine and hunger continually loomed over the consciousness of the people. It was investment prompted by fear. Pavia, a small city of northern Italy, at the middle of the sixteenth century numbered about 12,000 inhabitants. In one year this community obtained from its surrounding territory about 28,000 bags of wheat (almost 100,000 bushels) for current consumption. In 1555 it was found that people held in their homes about 3,700 bags.[77] It was already May, and one-tenth, at most, of the stock was destined for the year's consumption until the harvest. The remaining 3,330 bags were, therefore, long-term reserves.

The reader will have noted that this discussion of food reserves has been couched in the context of investment. It may seem strange to some that wheat and bread should be treated as capital. In fact, when they are consumed, bread and wheat are consumption goods. But when they are spared from consumption and kept in storage, even goods like bread and wheat become by definition part of the stock of wealth which we call capital. Capital formation is future oriented, and the supply of capital is determined by how much consumption it promises for the future and by how much consumption it takes away in the present.

Creating and maintaining stocks generates costs. There are costs related to warehousing and to the possible deterioration of all or part of the product. If the businessman finances the building up of stocks with borrowed money, costs also include the rate of interest paid. If the businessman finances the building up of stocks with his own means, he incurs an opportunity cost.

Because stocks cost money, one tends to keep them to a minimum, and since the industrial world does not operate under as heavy a burden of insecurity and high costs of transportation as preindustrial Europe did, the ratio of working capital to fixed capital is today noticeably reduced. However, even today when fears of international complications and conflicts arise, stocks of strategic materials and basic necessities increase markedly, reflecting conditions reminiscent of those which prevailed in preindustrial Europe.

So far we have referred only to monetary costs. In preindustrial Europe, however, stocks of foodstuffs implied also a high externality cost, of which the people of the time were not aware. The storing of large quantities of grain was the source of a large and prosperous rat population, which, in turn, was the source of frequent plague and typhus epidemics.

Stocks represent working capital, and in comparison with fixed capital they have a much higher degree of volatility. Fixed capital is *sunk*; it is embodied in a particular form (a building, a machine, a ship) from which it can only gradually, at best, be released. It is hard to disinvest once the investment has been sunk in fixed capital. Working capital, on the contrary, is continually *turned over*; it is continually coming back for reinvestment. When investment is in the form of working capital, disinvestment is easier: one sells existing stocks (if one can) and refrains from replenishing them.

This means that when stocks and inventories make up a large fraction of

The storage of foodstuffs. The conditions which existed in preindustrial Europe drove families to keep as large a reserve of foodstuffs as possible. The reserves were stored in attics and roofs with special openings for ventilation. This picture shows the roof of a house in Strasbourg, France. Commission Régionale d'Inventaire d'Alsace, Strasbourg.

the existing capital, disinvestment can be more massive and drastic than if a large fraction of investment is sunk in fixed capital. Big recessions are not an exclusive trait of contemporary capitalism. Preindustrial slumps could also be very severe, and one of the reasons was the relative size and the volatility of working capital. The severe recessions of 1619–21 and 1630–32 in northern and central Italy are classic examples of crises which resulted in and were magnified by dramatic reductions in the volume of stocks and inventories.

For the reasons that have just been illustrated, much of the accumulated capital took the form of stocks. Stocks were a stabilizing kind of capital rather than a kind that promoted development. Further, the very fact that savings resulted from a high concentration of wealth meant that such savings tended to be channeled into military investment (towers, ramparts, castles), religious investment (cathedrals, churches, monasteries) and luxury (palaces, works of art) rather than into more productive forms of investment. It should also be remembered that as long as most available energy was derived from either animal or vegetable sources, the marginal return on capital invested in production was bound to fall very sharply. As for medieval agriculture, Professor Postan has written that the reasons why investment was so limited was not so much "the poor potential for saving" but rather the fact that "opportunities for productive investment were extremely limited." In my view, this comment holds good not only for medieval agriculture but also for other sectors of the European preindustrial economy. Taken together these factors help to explain the low levels of production of preindustrial societies and the vicious circle of poverty to which they were condemned.

NATURAL RESOURCES

The third factor of production consists of *natural resources*. The term is used to mean land as well as other resources. Today it is fashionable to refer to these resources as *nonreproducible capital* in order to emphasize the fact that when, for example, a coal deposit is exhausted, it is beyond human power to reconstitute it. And, if it is true that reclamation can increase the quantity of available arable land, it is also true that the amount of land on the earth is finite.

In preindustrial Europe, the natural resource *par excellence* was *land*. In Malthus's and Ricardo's time, land was still the factor which, in the last analysis, "set limits to population growth and determined the distribution of the population."[78] As has been rightly observed:

It is natural to ascribe a large importance to the *per capita* supply of land in a dominantly agricultural society where levels of technology are low and little capital is employed. Agricultural techniques may improve or nonagricultural pursuits develop, but too slowly to offset the depressive effect of a falling supply of land per head when the population rises.... The ratio of cultivable land to population has been the chief determinant of the level of real income of pre-industrial societies.... It is tempting to relate the great secular fluctuations [of real wages] of the first five and a half centuries *primarily* to changes in the ratio of population to land.[79]

By "land," one meant, above all, arable land. The resources of the subsoil, however, were not ignored. Among the natural resources exploited in Europe prior to the eighteenth century, of particular importance were mineral deposits of silver, mercury, alum, tin, sulfur, copper, and iron. Pit-coal was already in use in the Middle Ages, but medieval people were very suspicious of this type of fuel, vaguely but strongly feeling that its use "poisoned the air." Albeit with overtones of superstition, medieval people were more conscious of possible pollution damage than people at the time of the Industrial Revolution.

Forests must be considered separately. From a theoretical point of view, forests cannot be treated as nonproducible capital because trees can be, and are, planted by man; forests are, therefore, reproducible capital. In fact, during the Middle Ages and the Renaissance, trees were planted and attention was paid to the problem of forest preservation. In mountain districts, the felling of trees in communal woods was regulated, from an early date, by precise rules. In 1281, the English Cistercians established enclosures of five years to protect the seedlings in their forests. In the same period the Statutes of the Commune of Montaguloto dell'Ardinghesea, in the district of Siena, laid down that every member of the commune inheriting a hide had to plant ten trees a year. In France from the end of the thirteenth century public concern about the fate of the forests gave rise to a series of royal as well as local provisions. In 1346 King Philip IV issued an ordinance regulating the cutting of trees and the consumption of timber. In 1669 the great minister Colbert inspired the formulation of an organic law for the protection of the forests. In the Hapsburg territories, Emperor Ferdinand I issued a general ordinance on the matter of forestry in 1557 and instituted the position of *Königlich-Kaiserlich Förstmeister* (Royal and Imperial Master of the Forests) for all hereditary territories of the Crown. One perceives the same kind of concern at the level of the local agricultural units. In the seventeenth-century accounts of the Medicean farm of *Cafaggioli*, it is clearly specified that "the trees are cut in the woods only once every ten years." Ordinances, statutes, decrees, and individual provisions, however, did not prove very effective. When population pressure grew and/or the demand for wood increased, the knell of the forest was rung.

Throughout the Middle Ages and the Renaissance, the Europeans behaved toward the trees in an eminently parasitic and extremely wasteful way. The *maquis* of southern France, the barren lands of central Spain, are a sad testimonial to what Europeans increasingly did to their forests after the end of the tenth century. Italy exhausted her forest reserves very early, which explains the extensive use of brick and marble in Italian architecture. In Lombardy the area covered with trees was reduced to less than 9 percent of the whole rural territory by 1555.[80] The forested area represented about 33 percent of the French territory around 1500 and only 25 percent around 1650; in the meantime, also, the quality of the forests had noticeably deteriorated.[81] For reasons that we shall analyze below, in the sixteenth and seventeenth centuries England provided the worst example of massive destruction of forests. At the beginning of the nineteenth century, the European forested area was reduced to the levels shown in Table 2.20.

The main bottleneck of preindustrial economies was the strictly limited supply of energy. The main sources of energy other than man's muscular work were plants and animals, and this fact set a limit to the possible expansion of any given agricultural society. The limiting factor was again the supply of land on which plants are grown and animals bred.

Since earliest antiquity the sailing ship had enabled man to master the energy of the wind on water, and this fact accounts for the fortunes of peoples who, like the Greeks and the Phoenicians, had open access to easily navigable seas. As we shall see below, the people of medieval and Renaissance Europe learned to harness the energy of water and wind to a remarkable extent for land-based activities. The mills of European design could do the work for which other societies needed gangs of slaves, and the medieval and Renaissance men feverishly built mills wherever and whenever they could. Availability of steady winds and the presence of waterfalls and streams must thus be counted among the natural resources of preindustrial Europe. They were to the people of the time what coal, oil, and uranium are to an industrialized society. The difference is that while the energy potentially embodied in coal, oil, and uranium can be transported, the energy of wind and water has to be used on the spot. This fact dictated the location of most manufactures of preindustrial Europe: they were normally located where mills could be built.

Table 2.20 Forested area in Europe in about the middle of the nineteenth century

	Thousand acres
Russia	429,868
Austro-Hungary	36,546
Germany	34,977
France	21,992
Italy	12,417
Spain	11,737

ORGANIZATION

In order to result in any production, labor, capital, and natural resources must be combined in organizational forms which vary according to technology, the size of markets, and the types of production. Within any given society, at a given level of technology, and for the same kind of production, greatly different forms of organization can coexist. In a modern metropolis, for instance, the giant supermarket coexists with the little grocery shop run as a family business. The following generalizations must therefore be taken with more than a pinch of salt and allowance must be made for an infinite number of variations and exceptions.

When our millennium started, in the agricultural sector the prevalent (although, by no means the exclusive) form of organization of labor, capital, and land was represented by the manorial system. Manors were large concentrations of landed property. Within a manor the land was generally divided into several farms. One farm was very large and was managed directly by the lord himself (the *demesne* or *mansus indominicatus*). The other farms, variable in number, were unequal in size but much smaller than the central farm; they were scattered at some distance and were granted out to peasant households. The fundamental role of these satellite farms was to be subsidiary to the *demesne*: specifically they had to provide the lord with periodic tributes and above all with contributions in labor (*corvées*) for the needs of the central farm. Fundamentally the classical manor around the year 1000 was an economic microcosm, centrally planned, largely self-sufficient, within which both the division of labor and monetary exchange played minimal and irrelevant roles.

By the middle of the twelfth century, the manorial system was beginning to disintegrate: first in Italy, then in France, and finally in Germany and England. Italian developments seem to have been a whole century ahead of those of France and the latter almost a century ahead of those of England.

Large-scale demesne farming operations gradually ceased, the land hitherto managed directly by the lord was let to peasant farmers and the labor services due from customary holdings were commuted to monetary rents or shares of the crops. The story of western European agriculture in the thirteenth and fourteenth centuries is completely dominated by the disintegration of the manorial organization. What emerged in its place was an extraordinary variety of organizational forms suited to local economic and geophysical conditions. In Tuscany *mezzadria* (sharecropping) prevailed; the Lombard plain in the fifteenth century saw the flourishing of proto-capitalistic *fermiers* who acted as intermediaries between absentee landowners and tenant sharecroppers; in sixteenth-century England enclosing and engrossing were the prevailing trends. The detailed description of these and similar local forms of agricultural organization would be of great interest and significance but would occupy a space too large for the present book.

94

Let us turn to the manufacturing sector. We are accustomed today to the idea of the factory. In preindustrial Europe, however, from the beginning of our millennium to the Industrial Revolution, the prevailing technical unit of manufacturing production was and remained the workshop. The industrial factory is characterized by a high concentration of wage-labor and machines. In the workshop, the concentration of labor and capital was minimal and wage-labor was almost unknown.

The wage worker of the modern factory operates with capital not his own, is subject to a strict work discipline, and performs a series of highly specialized and routine operations which contribute to a limited part of the final product. The craftsman of the preindustrial workshop often, if not always, owned the capital or at least part of it, worked longer hours than the industrial worker, but was not subject to the hard discipline of the factory, and in some manufacturing sectors had the pleasure and pride of seeing the final product emerge from his own hands. These are the human aspects. But in order to understand the preindustrial workshop, it is necessary to delve into more technical aspects, in particular the relation between craftsmen and merchant-entrepreneurs.

In the more highly developed trades, the artisan did not normally produce for the market. With his limited financial resources, he could not undertake the risks connected with such production. He normally worked on commission. The man who gave him the orders was the "merchant," who often advanced to the craftsman the necessary working capital (raw materials) and sometimes also lent him the fixed capital (looms, for example). The economic dimension of the craftsman's business was thus determined by the economic dimension of the business of the merchant, who gave the work order, provided the raw materials, undertook the distribution of the products, developed the markets, determined the type of product, and exercised quality control over the activities of the worker.

The merchant produced for the market and, as one can still see in Florence and Venice, the mansions of the merchants included in their structure large rooms intended solely for the storage of the raw materials and the finished goods.

The organization of production thus revolved around these two poles, the craftsman's workshop and the warehouse of the merchant. In the first, work was done to order. In the second, production was for the market and the merchants concerned themselves with both the supply of raw materials and the marketing of finished goods.

These are the broad lines of the picture but there were countless gradations and exceptions, and especially in the course of the sixteenth and seventeenth centuries, some enterprises assumed more modern characteristics in relation to both size and organization. Mining and shipbuilding were the typical sectors in which "bigness" prevailed at an early stage. By the sixteenth century the arsenal of Venice was more the prototype of a modern factory than the appendix of the old artisan yards. In seventeenth-century England, "in all dockyard centers and especially at Portsmouth and in the Medway towns there was a clear picture of substantial concentration of workers laboring under conditions very different from those surrounding the domestic system."[82] At Chatham in 1665, 800 workers were assembled in the local dockyard. Outside the mining and shipbuilding sectors, the units of manufacturing production usually remained small, although there were exceptions. In the 1550s Gilbert van Schoonbeke built in Antwerp an integrated system of breweries that involved the enormous investment of 271,000 florins.[83] In seventeenth-century Amsterdam a manufacturer of crystal and fine glass possibly employed 80 workmen.[84] In northern Italy, in the second half of the seventeenth century, some silk thread manufacturers employed as many as 150 and 200 workers.[85]

These large units of manufacturing production were dwarfed, however, by the giants which, in the course of the seventeenth century, emerged in the tertiary sector, and specifically in overseas trade. The Dutch East India Company employed directly some 12,000 men toward the end of the seventeenth century.

The "big ones," whether in manufacturing or in trading sectors, formed the vanguard of modern capitalism. But no matter how important, for the volume of business they carried or for the example of organization they set, they remained exceptions. Between them and the traditional workshops there was a wide spectrum of intermediate forms such as that represented by the glass and earthenware business of Giovan Pietro *moyollario* in the small town of Pavia (Italy). We have an inventory of this business dated 1546. At the head of the enterprise was Giovan Pietro. One part of the business included the workers (*magistri*), a furnace, and the utensils (*fornax et instrumenta*). Another part included the sales shop and special salesmen (*venditores*) who divided their time between attending to customers in the shop and wandering around in the city with special baskets (*cavagnolle longhe a venditoribus*) to sell the product. The house of the master included the furnace and the shop, but also an office (*studieto*), a room for the workers (*camera magistrorum*) with three beds and two tables, and a room for the salesmen (*camera venditorum*) with one bed. That is, the workers and salesmen lived and slept in the factory, which was, at the same time, the house of the master.[86]

History is seldom schematic or simple: hybrid, transitional forms prevail, such as the productive unit of Giovan Pietro, which was no longer a work-shop but not yet a factory.

3

PRODUCTIVITY AND PRODUCTION

CHOICE AND PRODUCTIVITY

The level and structure of effective demand result from a twofold set of choices – a choice between how much to spend and how much not to spend and a choice between an infinite number of possible types of expenditure. These choices are like votes: by purchasing product A and not purchasing product B, one pushes up the price of product A while depressing that of product B.

On the supply side, in a market economy, economic operators decide when, what, and how much to produce on the basis of price indications. Once they have decided what to produce, these operators must then choose the best possible combination of factors of production.

The whole economic process is therefore a matter of choices – on the part of the consumers and on the part of the producers. In the last analysis, choices are necessary because resources are much more limited than wants. Production is the outcome of all these individual and social choices acting on both the demand and the supply side.

THE DETERMINANTS OF PRODUCTION

Put simply, production is a function of capital, labor, and natural resources. Some twenty-five years ago, economists were content to stop at this point in macroeconomic analysis, but since the 1950s they have taken to splitting hairs.

The factors of production – labor, capital, and natural resources – are the *inputs* of a productive system. From their combination emerges *output* – that is, production. Any single mixture of *inputs* can produce different *outputs* – different in quality and/or quantity. Physical productivity is the factor which determines the quantity and quality of the product, given the quantity and quality of the inputs.

Economists have lately discovered that, during the last century, output (as measured by Gross National Product) has consistently grown faster than can be accounted for by the increase of the inputs of labor, capital, and natural resources. This discovery led economists on a hunt for another factor which might explain the difference between "how much has been produced" and "how much would have been produced if the factors at play had been only labor, capital, and natural resources."

However, "how much would have been produced . . ." represents an arbitrary estimate which depends on a series of hypothetical assumptions made by those who undertake research of this kind. Even if some agreement could be reached about the *size* of the residual (the difference between "how much was produced" and "how much would have been produced if . . ."), the *source* of the residual remains in question. The following factors are generally quoted:

a. increase in division of labor between different economies, through the development of trade
b. economies of scale
c. more efficient allocation of factors of production
d. technological development
e. better education

Classifications of this type are useful for logical-anatomic analysis, but they are artificial. In reality, there are no separate streams; everything flows together. For example, "technological development" is in no way separate or "exogenous" to the economic system. Economists often classify it as "exogenous" because it suits their analysis to do so. But it is a trick. As R.O.C. Matthews and C.H. Feinstein have written, "exogeneity is a label applied for conceptual reasons and in no sense an intrinsic attribute of the factors in question." On the contrary, technological development springs from the brains of the people – that is, labor – and is incorporated in the machines and tools that they use – that is, in capital. It seems unlikely, in any case, that any list can ever be regarded as complete. In 1947, long before Aukrust, Dennison, Solow, and the other "residualists" appeared, J. Schumpeter wrote that "only in very rare cases" can economic development be explained in terms of "causal factors such as an increase in population or the supply of capital." An economy or a firm often succeeds in doing "something more," and according to Schumpeter this "something more" "from the standpoint of the observer who is in full possession of all relevant facts . . . can be understood *ex post* but it can never be understood *ex ante*; that is to say, it cannot be predicted by applying the ordinary rules of inference from the preexisting facts."[1] Schumpeter identified this "something more" as the "creative response of history." Schumpeter had a profound intuition but, wishing to reduce the intangible to the tangible, the very complex to the very simple, made the mistake of reducing the whole to a part – in this specific case, to entrepreneurial activity.

Entrepreneurial activity is a necessary ingredient, but not a sufficient one.

It is the human vitality of a whole society which, given the opportunity, comes into play and sets loose the "creative response of history."

When a society shows vitality it does so at all levels, not only the economic, and it succeeds better than other societies which seemingly have the same amounts of resources at their disposal. It is not by chance that, when Italian merchants greatly contributed to European economic development, Dante was writing the *Divine Comedy*, Giotto was introducing innovations in painting, and St Francis was starting his religious movement. In the seventeenth century, when the Low Countries became the prime movers in international trade while producing great entrepreneurs and merchants such as De Geer or the Tripps, they also produced jurists like Grotius, experimentalists such as Huyghens and Leeuwenhoek, and painters such as Rembrandt. Economists who try to split the product of this human vitality, arbitrarily attributing parts of it to this factor and parts to that, bring to mind a fellow who, confronted with one of Giotto's paintings, would try to measure how much of the beauty of the painting was due to the type of brush used, how much to the chemistry of the colors, and how much to the time taken by the artist. In order to understand what happened in certain societies, it is necessary to understand an atmosphere of collective enthusiasm, of exaltation and of cooperation. When the Cathedral of Chartres was being built "people pulled carts loaded with stones and with wood, and with everything necessary for the construction of the church...."[2] "Silence and humility" dominated, wrote Ugo[3] and another chronicler commented, "He who has not seen these facts will never see the same again." When in 1066 the Abbot Desiderio started the construction of a basilica at the top of Monte Cassino, the first great marble column was borne to the summit on the shoulders of people filled with mystical fervor.[4]

In other cases, political ideology operated; in yet others, enthusiasm for new lands, the spirit of the frontier, the feeling of liberation from restrictions imposed by scarcity of resources or by ossified social and political institutions. When one admires certain exquisite works of art by humble craftsmen of the past, knowing how inadequate the economic incentives were, one cannot but conclude that intangible and nonmeasurable factors, such as the creative urge, love of one's work, pride in one's own ability and self-respect, where they exist, make miracles possible; and that the absence of these factors depresses production both quantitatively and qualitatively. Sociologists, analyzing these facts, have coined numerous and varied terms, such as "motivation," "collective enthusiasm," "cooperation," or, in the opposite sense, "alienation." There is no lack of words; what is lacking is the ability to analyze these things in a functional way, to understand them *ex ante* as causal elements rather than *ex post* as a residual which – whether positive or negative – remains largely mysterious.

MEDIEVAL AND RENAISSANCE PRODUCTIVITY LEVELS

As we shall see later, in the centuries of the Middle Ages and the Renaissance there was marked technological progress. Undoubtedly, the levels of productivity prevailing in Europe at the end of the sixteenth century were considerably higher than they had been six hundred years earlier. But by our standards they were still abysmally low. After all, Europe started her ascent from an extremely primitive stage at the turn of our millennium; and until the seventeenth century, the lack of a systematic criterion of experimentation and research made every innovation dependent upon wearisome and rough empiricism. The productivity of labor was adversely affected by the poverty and scarcity of the equipment and by the low educational levels of the labor force itself. The productivity of capital remained depressed because of the low technological levels and by the limited availability of sources of energy, which were essentially still of animal and vegetable nature.[3] Land was by far the most important available natural resource, and its yield was limited.

All this is interesting but extremely vague. Adjectives such as *low, reduced, limited,* are like mist: they leave too much to the imagination. Let us try to emerge from the fog with a few figures, beginning with agriculture.

A pioneer in the quantitative study of agricultural history is Slicher van Bath. Having gathered data on yield–seed ratios from various European countries, van Bath calculated synthetic averages for wheat, rye, barley, and oats. The results are summarized in Table 3.1.[6]

Figures of this kind must be taken with more than a simple grain of salt.[7] J.Z. Titlow, who patiently collected a vast amount of data on agricultural returns in medieval England, has shown that, by extending the sample, one obtains results which differ noticeably from those of van Bath (Table 3.2). At any rate, in both Tables 3.1 and 3.2, averages for the various countries are not based on comprehensive data but on scattered information derived from a relatively small number of cases.

Table 3.4 contains analogous data for selected areas of Italy, from the fertile plain of the Po Valley (Imola), to the Tuscan farms, to the poor soils of the Ligurian Appenines (Montaldeo). Table 3.5 is based on an exceptionally comprehensive statistic regarding the whole territory of Siena, which was by far the most important grain-producing area of the Grand Duchy of Tuscany.

A cursory glance at the figures in the following tables is enough to show that agricultural yields varied greatly from one year to the next and from one area to another, owing to the very poor control of man over the forces of nature. Consequently, in the presence of these massive fluctuations, statistical averages have little meaning. Moreover even when one takes the most fertile areas and the most propitious periods, one still finds miserably low yields. The yield ratio for wheat reached the level of 6

Table 3.1 Average gross yields per seed for wheat, rye, barley, and oats in selected European countries, 1200–1699

| Period | Grains yielded per seed planted | | |
	England	France	Germany
1200–1249	3.7		
1250–1499	4.7	4.3	
1500–1699	7.0	6.3	4.2

Source: Slicher van Bath, "Yield Ratios," p. 15.

Table 3.2 Average yields per unit of wheat seed in England, 1200–1349

	According to Slicher van Bath	According to Titow
1200–49	2.9	3.8
1250–99	4.2	3.8
1300–49	3.9	3.9

Source: Titow, *Winchester Yields*, p. 4.

Table 3.3 Mean yield ratios on the estate of the bishopric of Winchester, 1209–1453

Date	Wheat	Barley	Oats
1209–70	3.85	4.32	2.63
1271–99	3.79	3.36	2.21
1300–24	3.90	3.57	2.21
1325–49	3.96	3.74	2.25
1349–80	3.66	3.53	2.43
1381–1410	3.88	4.13	2.93
1411–53	3.66	3.64	3.03

Source: D.L. Farmer, "Grain yields on the Winchester manors in the later middle ages," *Ec.H.R.*, 2nd ser., 30 (1977), p. 560.

only in the best years, while today in the American wheat belt it normally reaches the level of above 30.

In the territory of Bologna (Italy) in the second half of the fifteenth century 2.5 acres of vineyard produced on average fifty gallons of wine per year. Today in the same region production is seven times greater and of much better quality.[8] The land produced little because seeds were not selected, crop rotation and implements were primitive, pesticides were

Table 3.4 Average yields per unit of wheat seed in selected areas of Italy,
1300–1600

Area	Year	Yield	Area	Year	Yield
Arezzo[1]	1386	5.3		1625–34	5.6
	1387	11		1635–44	5.7
	1390	6.5		1645–54	4.9
Parma[2]	1510–19	2.4–5.6		1655–64	5.5
	1520–29	2.6–6.0		1665–74	6.6
	1530–39	2.5–5.7		1675–84	6.0
	1540–49	2.6–6.3		1685–94	6.6
	1550–59	0.2–5.3		1695–1704	5.8
	1560–69	1.7–5.8	Montaldeo[5]	1560	1
Florence[3]	1611–20	9.4		1649	<1
	1621–30	7.6		1650	<1
	1631–40	7.4		1664	3
	1641–44	7.5		1672	2.3
	1656–60	6.7		1673	1.3
	1661–70	6.1		1674	2.9
	1671–80	5.9		1677	1.3
	1681–90	6.7		1678	3.5
	1691–1700	6.0		1681	1.8
				1683	4
Imola[4]	1515–24	7.3		1686	2.5
	1525–34	6.3		1687	3
	1535–44	6.7		1688	3.3
	1545–54	6.3		1692	1.9
	1555–64	5.2		1693	2.5
	1565–74	6.0		1694	2.6
	1585–94	5.6		1695	1
	1595–1604	5.1		1697	1
	1605–14	6.4		1699	2
	1615–24	5.4		1700	1.5

Sources: 1. Cherubini, "Proprietà fondiaria," p. 40. 2. Romani, Nella spirale di una crisi, p. 137. 3. Conti, Formazione della Struttura Agraria, vol. 1, p. 359. 4. Rotelli, "Rendimenti." 5. Doria, Uomini e Terre, p. 29.

unknown, and last, but not least, manure, the only known fertilizer, was always in very short supply; on the landed property of the abbey of Staffelsee in the Dark Ages the manure available was barely sufficient for 0.5 percent of the land, and in the thirteenth century in the regions around Paris, certainly one of the more advanced areas of the time, fields were fertilized with manure only once in every nine years.[9]

The animals, like the land, performed rather poorly, because they were not adequately fed and there was no adequate selective breeding. Cows' milk production was meager. It is estimated that milk production per cow in

Table 3.5 Quantity of grain sown and harvested and yield ratios in the territory of Siena, 1593–1609

Year	Quantity of grain (in moggia)		
	Sown	*Harvested*	*Yield*
1593–94	18,063	78,914	4.4
1594–95	16,230	98,893	6.1
1595–96	17,231	67,933	3.9
1596–97	18,727	102,717	5.5
1598–99	21,540	89,294	4.1
1599–1600	20,048	92,010	4.6
1600–01	18,048	76,545	4.2
1602–03	17,500	90,327	5.2
1603–04	17,630	70,089	4.0
1606–07	16,281	74,741	4.6
1607–08	15,888	94,983	6.0
1608–09	16,297	74,151	4.5

Source: Diaz, *Il Granducato di Toscana*, p. 339. A *moggio* was equivalent to 583 litres.

fourteenth-century England was about 500 liters per year, with a low butterfat content.[10] In the late 1960s in the United States, though state averages varied noticeably, the overall national average was almost 3,000 liters per year, with a high (about 4 percent) butterfat content.

Since the animals were small, they produced little meat. Table 3.6 shows data comparing seventeenth-century cattle weights in the Montaldeo area (Italy) with weights of cattle of similar age today. The disparity is striking. Data available on northern Europe in the seventeenth century fail to paint a rosier picture: even on pastures which were richer than in Montaldeo, oxen

Table 3.6 Deadweight of male cattle in the district of Montaldeo (Italy), seventeenth century

Year	Age of animal	Weight in pounds	
		17th century	*20th century*
1684	5 months	72	245
1690	1 year	130	540
1686	2 years	240	880
1675	3 years	320	1,100
1675	4 years	480	1,310
1675	5 years	560	1,550

Source: Doria, *Uomini e Terre*, p. 57.

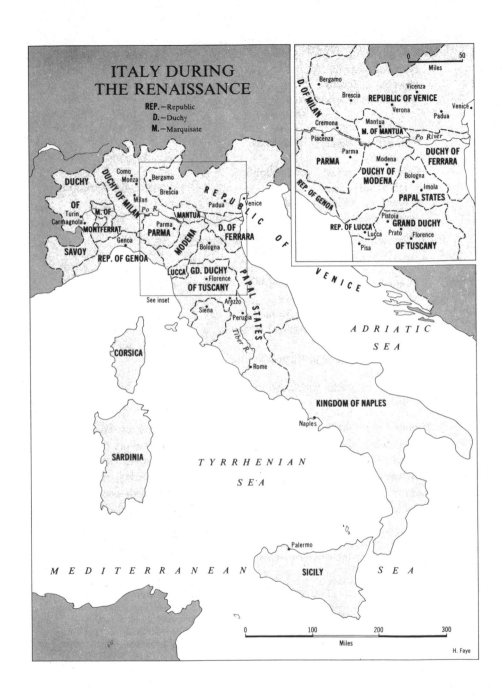

ITALY DURING
THE RENAISSANCE

REP. —Republic
D. —Duchy
M. —Marquisate

DUCHY OF MILAN
Como
Monza
Bergamo
Milan
Brescia
Po R.
Padua
Venice

DUCHY OF
Turin
Carmagnola
M. OF MONTFERRAT
Genoa
PARMA
Parma
MANTUA
MODENA
Bologna
D. OF FERRARA

SAVOY

REP. OF GENOA

REPUBLIC OF VENICE

LUCCA
GD. DUCHY OF TUSCANY
Florence
Siena
Arezzo
Perugia

PAPAL STATES

See inset

Tiber R.

CORSICA

Rome

ADRIATIC SEA

KINGDOM OF NAPLES
Naples

SARDINIA

TYRRHENIAN SEA

MEDITERRANEAN

Palermo

SICILY

SEA

Inset map

0   50
Miles

D. OF MILAN
Bergamo
Vicenza
Brescia
REPUBLIC OF VENICE
Verona
Venice
Padua
Cremona
Mantua
M. OF MANTUA
Piacenza
Po River
PARMA
Parma
Modena
DUCHY OF FERRARA
DUCHY OF MODENA
Bologna
Imola
REP. OF GENOA
PAPAL STATES
Pistoia
REP. OF LUCCA
GRAND DUCHY
Lucca
Prato
Florence
Pisa
OF TUSCANY

0   100   200   300
Miles

H. Faye

weighed only between 400 and 500 pounds and cows about 220 pounds.[11]

For the nonagricultural sectors information is much poorer. However, much of the available data suggests that productivity in these areas was hardly more encouraging than in the agricultural sectors. We know, for instance, that at the beginning of the seventeenth century, the situation of the woollen manufacturers in Florence was as follows:[12]

	1604	1627
Number of firms	120	52
Number of looms	1,420	782
Number of weavers: males	878	268
females	1,457	1,315
Total	2,335[13]	1,583
Number of pieces[14] produced annually	14,000	7,998
Value of annual production (in *scudi*)	>900,000	430,000
Percent of wages on value of production	55	

From the above data one derives the following ratios:[15]

	1604	1627
Number of weavers per firm[16]	19	30
Number of looms per firm	12	15
Number of weavers per loom	1.6	2
Number of pieces produced annually per firm	117	154
Number of pieces produced annually per loom	10	10
Number of pieces produced annually per weaver	6	5

In Florence, during the 1458–62 period, a weaver would take 4 to 5 weeks to produce roughly 30 metres of taffeta, 6 to 10 weeks to produce the same length of satin, about 8 weeks for damask and 10–14 weeks for velvet.[17] In Genoa, at the end of the sixteenth century, a weaver produced on average slightly more than 16 inches (28 inches wide) of velvet per day.[18] In Milan at the beginning of the seventeenth century, a weaver produced, on average, little more than half a yard of velvet per work day.[19] In Venice, also at the beginning of the seventeenth century, the average daily production of a silk-loom varied between a minimum of 0.4 yards for the *gold velvets* to a maximum of 1.5 yards for satin and damask, and with a general average for all the various types of silk materials of about 1.2 yards.[20] In Yorkshire in the 1580s it took about fifteen persons one week to make a short broadcloth measuring 12 yards by 1.75 yards.[21] In the fifteenth century in England a miner could extract a maximum of 30–40 pounds of lead mineral.[22] In the Dean (England) four furnaces built by 1613 produced a minimum of about 250 tons and a maximum of 700 of cast iron per furnace per year.[23] In 1621, John Browne claimed that in the foundry at Brenchley (England), he could cast two hundred iron cannon in 200 days; in all likelihood, 200 was the number of working days in a year at the furnace. At about the same time in Sweden, a foundry produced between 100 and 150 tons a year of cast-iron cannons.[24] In Italy, again in the seventeenth century, most of the paper mills possessed only one or two vats and the average daily production of one vat did not exceed a maximum of 4,500 sheets – in this instance, approximately 110 pounds of paper.[25]

Low labor productivity obviously meant that production processes were labor-intensive. When the population of London numbered only about 35,000 people, the building of Beaumaris Castle provided employment for 400 masons, 30 smiths and carpenters, 1,000 unskilled workers and 200 carters.

The building industry is most definitely one in which little if any improvement was accomplished as far as labor productivity is concerned until very recent times. In a number of other sectors, however, noticeable improvements were achieved in the course of the Middle Ages and the Renaissance. In iron production in England, for instance, between 1350 and 1550, productivity allegedly increased seven or eightfold.[26] Although, in regard to book production, it would be absurd from an esthetic point of view to compare a handwritten book with a printed one, it is not absurd from the point of view of the diffusion of ideas, to compare the number of manuscripts a copyist could prepare in one year with the number of volumes a printer could print within the same period. After Gutenberg's invention, a continuous series of technical improvements progressively increased printers' productivity. The first printers succeeded in printing (in the language of the trade, "pulling") about 300 pages a day. By the end of the fifteenth century, the average had risen to over 400. At the beginning of the eighteenth century, two printers could pull about 200 pages an hour, that is, given the high number of working hours per day in those times, about 2,500 pages a day. In the shipping sector, the ratio of crew to cargo improved even if defense requirements slowed down this progress. About the year 1400 the crew-to-cargo ratio averaged one sailor for every 5 or 6 tons. By the middle of the sixteenth century, the ratio was one man per 7 or 8 tons. When peace and a decrease in piracy reduced the needs for defense, the ratio dropped to one man per 10 tons. Of course these gains in the crew-to-cargo ratio must also be considered in the light of the notable gains in the speed and safety of ships and in the rate of their utilization.

The main reason for productivity gains was technological progress, and we shall discuss this in Chapter 6. The gains which were achieved in western Europe in the course of the Middle Ages and the Renaissance were conspicuous when compared to the productivity levels typical of the traditional agricultural societies. But the highest productivity levels reached by pre-industrial Europe still look abysmally low when compared with the productivity levels of an industrial society.

Once the foregoing facts about preindustrial European productivity have been established, one important qualification remains to be made. The data which allow us to measure productivity in the past refer exclusively to quantity and leave aside quality. Now, it is simply not true that all the products of the preindustrial era were of better quality than those of the industrial era. Our maps, even if less artistic, are qualitatively better than those of the preindustrial era, and so are our telescopes, our microscopes, and perhaps also our fruit and vegetables. But if one simply states that the average production of a weaver consisted of so many yards of cloth a day, that the average production of a cabinetmaker consisted of so many pieces of furniture a year, or that of the locksmith so many locks a month, one ignores the fact that some of those pieces of cloth, many of those pieces of furniture and many of those locks were exquisite works of art, infinitely more beautiful and better than analogous, contemporary products. If one could adequately take into consideration the qualitative element, then the productivity of the craftsmen of the preindustrial age would appear under a different light.

POSITIVE PRODUCTION

The combination of the available factors of production results in production. Production as a whole is made up of the most extraordinary variety of goods and services. It includes the apple and the ship, the needle and the plough, the services of a chambermaid and those of a surgeon. To analyze such a complex of different things one must have recourse to broad categories. Oversimplifying an otherwise very complex matter, one may say that in response to the structure of demand as defined above in Chapter 1, the greatest part of production in preindustrial Europe took the form of food-stuffs, textiles, buildings, and domestic services. By the end of the seventeenth century England was no longer a typical preindustrial country. The extraordinary development of her foreign trade had given her economy characteristics of an altogether peculiar nature. Yet about 1688 in England and Wales agriculture still accounted for some 50 percent or more of the national product, the textile manufactures for some 8 percent, building for more than 5 percent, and domestic services for some 10 percent.

If most of the production was centered on a few basic sectors, from a geographical point of view production was extremely scattered. A few products were manufactured in some specialized places – until the fourteenth century the production of silk textiles in the west was concentrated in Lucca (Tuscany), the production of paper in Fabriano (Marche, Italy), and until the end of the fifteenth century Venice maintained a virtual monopoly in the production of high-quality soap and glass. But for most necessities of life there was little geographical division of labor. We saw above, when discussing labor as a factor of production, that the rural population was far from being totally occupied with agricultural pursuits. Not only every town but almost every village had its weavers, spinners, drapers, shoemakers, carpenters, coopers, blacksmiths, armorers, and the like. Interregional and international trade grew immeasurably after the tenth century, but in most communities a large number of manufactures continued to be produced locally. In agriculture, monocultures were scarcely known and farmers strove to produce on their individual farms as wide a variety of grains, vegetables, and fruit as possible – of course, at the expense of productivity.

NEGATIVE PRODUCTION

When textbooks refer to production they generally mean *positive production*, but human societies, by combining labor, capital, and natural resources, also give rise to *negative production*. There are essentially two types of *negative production*:

a.   the deliberate destruction of men and wealth
b.   pollution and the destruction of the environment.

Let us analyze these two types of negative production separately. In all human societies there are perverse people who destroy human lives and wealth, for one reason or another. Some of these persons place their acts in the framework of political ideology or religious doctrine, but in essence they are nevertheless agents of destruction. The assassin is "labor" which by the use of "capital" (say, a gun) brings about a negative production by destroying human capital. The arsonist is "labor" which, in combination with "capital" (often, a match and a gasoline can) destroys physical capital. The bomb-thrower is "labor" which, making use of "capital" (dynamite), destroys human and physical capital at the same time. The mass of those who, with one excuse or another, or without any excuse whatever, destroy instead of build varies from society to society and from period to period. Their potential number is, however, always higher than their actual number because society defends itself, devoting resources – labor and capital – in an effort to control the phenomenon.

At a macroscopic level, the negative production of major significance is war. The first victim of every war is truth. There is no war that has not been cloaked in lies and specious arguments designed to convince people of its timeliness or necessity, in the same way as there is no bomb-thrower who does not try to convince himself and others of the need or worth of his criminal action. In the course of human history, men have been massacred and riches have been destroyed continually, and the most absurd and cruel crimes have been committed, always in the name of some remote ideal, at times religious, at times political, at times social and economic. Whatever the ultimate motivation, war remains essentially the organization of "labor" (the military) and "capital" (weaponry) with the avowed intention of destroying the maximum quantity and quality of the labor and capital of the so-called enemy. In the animal world, only man and the ant have developed mass organization for the destruction of their own kind.

We have seen that man's productive capacity is a function of the quality and quantity of labor and capital, of the state of the arts, and of a certain collective psychological climate. The same can be said of man's destructive capacity. Capital, technology, and the organizational skills which assist him in his productive activities also help him in his destructive activities. Consequently, a criminal in an industrial society has a destructive potential infinitely superior to that of his counterpart in a preindustrial society. In the same way, an industrial-era army has a destructive power infinitely greater than that of an army in preindustrial times. A battalion of any contemporary Central American republic would destroy the armies of imperial Rome in the course of a few hours.

These considerations must be borne in mind when one speaks of wars of the past. It has been written that "some thousand fighters, some hundred dead" was the balance sheet of most conflicts of the preindustrial era. Nevertheless, if the wars of bygone days were hardly murderous in a direct sense, they could cause serious destruction of physical capital and could cause high mortality via famine and disease. Armies on the move killed or confiscated livestock, burned or confiscated food reserves, and destroyed houses, mills, barns, and other agricultural buildings. Since the armies of the past inflicted the worst damage on rural areas, the predominantly agricultural societies in question were struck at the very foundation of their economic structure. From a purely economic point of view, war was a much greater evil than the plague, and all the more evil as the societies in question suffered from a relative scarcity of capital in relation to existing population. Plague destroyed men, but not capital, and those who survived the onslaught of the disease usually found themselves in more favorable economic conditions. War, on the other hand, hit capital above all, and those who survived found themselves in conditions of the most abject misery. In the chronicles and documents of the time, descriptions abound of countrysides and towns reduced to flaming wastes and of children who, crying and begging for bread, died of hunger in the streets. Phrases such as "the whole area was turned into a desert" or "where men lived there are now only savage animals" recur frequently in the documents of those times.[27] They were not rhetorical exaggerations. The historian often can replace the prose with figures and confirm the dismal, anguished accounts of the time with factual data. In Cheshire (England) out of a total of 264 villages, 52 were wholly or partly devastated in the Norman invasion in 1066. By 1070, as a result of William's campaign of 1069–70, this figure had increased to 162.[28] About the middle of the fourteenth century, the armies engaged in the Hundred Years' War ravaged, among innumerable others, the possessions of the Abbey du Lys (near Melun, France). In 1384, fifteen years after the most recent pillage, the estate was in the following condition.

> forest: 460 *arpents* of which 300 were burned
> vineyards: 32 *arpents* of which 22 were destroyed
> arable land: 190 *arpents* of which 90 were laid waste.[29]

In the early fifteenth century, at la Bastide des Jourdans in Haute-Provence (France), 336 of the 346 acres of good arable land belonging to the Order of Saint John of Jerusalem were laid waste, and a vineyard of 178 acres was completely destroyed. Near Grambois, a vineyard of 74 acres was destroyed, and most of the 618 acres of arable land were abandoned. At Montegut, "where there used to be a beautiful farm there is now neither a man, nor a woman, nor a chicken."[30] The effects of the various campaigns of the Hundred Years' War (1337–1453) on the volume of trade in northern France are reflected in the dramatic fluctuations of the revenues from the toll at the Port de Neuilly, in the valley of Paris:[31]

> 1301: 250 livres
> 1340: 200
> 1376: 248
> 1409: 320
> 1425: 36
> 1428: 80
> 1444: 26

In the territory of Saarburg (Germany) during the Thirty Years' War (1618–48), the livestock was drastically depleted as shown in Table 3.7. Such destructions were particularly disastrous because the available resources and productivity normally ruled out rapid recovery.

Human perversity is the source of certain forms of negative production. Ignorance and individual selfishness are sources of other ills. In this respect one must distinguish between (a) destruction of natural resources, (b) pol-

Table 3.7 Livestock losses in Saarburg territory (Germany) during the Thirty Years' War

Livestock	Number of head	
	Before the war	After the war
Horses	2,651	116
Oxen	5,077	36
Hogs	5,927	10
Sheep	18,267	
Goats	2,749	

Source: Franz, *Dreissigjährige Krieg*, p. 45.

lution of the environment with the waste products of consumption, (c) pollution of the environment with undesirable by-products of productive activities, (d) damage to the health of those engaged in production.

From all these points of view, the capacity for negative production of European preindustrial societies was infinitely lower than that of industrial societies. First of all, the population was small and per-capita production limited. Moreover, pervasive poverty compelled people to reduce waste to a minimum, and durable goods were continually re-used. Lastly, there was no widespread use of many products such as petroleum and coal, which are largely responsible for pollution of the environment in the contemporary world.

Considerations of this kind recently led an economic historian to assert:

> Pollution, loss of natural environment, traffic congestion and accidents have clearly resulted from industrialization and modern technology and have no obviously important analogues in preindustrial societies. Moreover, the more work that is done on traditional peasant societies the clearer does it become that these societies have often achieved an almost miraculous accommodation with nature, balancing present use and preservation for the future with a degree of success which the modern economic machine has rarely approached.[32]

Unfortunately, however, things were not so rosy in preindustrial Europe. Undoubtedly the capacity of preindustrial societies for disturbing ecological equilibria was infinitely smaller than that of industrial societies. But, this limitation aside, even preindustrial societies managed to mismanage. The following story, reported by Dr Ramazzini in his celebrated book, published in 1713, is good evidence that certain evils which afflict industrial societies were well known, though on a smaller scale, in preindustrial Europe:

> A few years ago a violent dispute arose between a citizen of Finale, a town in the dominion of Modena, northern Italy, and a certain business man who owned a huge laboratory at Finale where he manufactured sublimate. The citizen of Finale brought a lawsuit against the manufacturer and demanded that he should move his workshop outside the town or to some other place, on the ground that he poisoned the whole neighborhood whenever his workmen roasted vitriol in the furnace to make sublimate. To prove the truth of his accusation the citizen produced the sworn testimony of the doctor of Finale and also the parish register of deaths, from which it appeared that many more persons died annually in that quarter and in the immediate neighborhood of the laboratory than in other localities. Moreover, the doctor gave evidence that the residents of that neighborhood usually died of wasting disease and diseases of the chest; this he ascribed to the fumes given off by the vitriol, which so tainted the

111

air near by that it was rendered unhealthy and dangerous for the lungs.[33]

Another common example of shortsighted behavior was the destruction of forests. It meant not only the direct destruction of rich capital, but also the deterioration of the environment in the plains below, facilitating floods and the accumulation of stagnant waters, which became the breeding grounds of malaria.

Within the city walls, one ought not to be dazzled by the presence of magnificent structures, such as the cathedrals, the large *palazzi* of the rich, or the palace of the Commune. As Robert Dallington wrote about Tuscany at the beginning of the seventeenth century:

> All is not gold in Italy, though many travellers gazing onelly at the beautie of their cities and the painted surface of their houses, thinke it the only Paradise of Europe.[34]

In order to remain within the shelter of the walls, people crowded into relatively small areas, creating dangerously high population densities. Water wells were unsafe. The almost complete lack of hygienic facilities created serious problems in relation to the disposal of human wastes. People used streets and squares as public latrines and threw everything out of the window without care for passersby.

In the middle of the seventeenth century, the mother of the Regent of France wrote:

> Paris is a horrible place and ill smelling. The streets are so mephitic that one cannot linger there because of the stench of rotting meat and fish and because of a crowd of people who urinate in the streets.

At the end of the eighteenth century, the English diplomat John Barrow remarked that Peking "enjoys one important advantage, which is rarely found in capitals out of England: no kind of filth or nastiness, creating offensive smells, is thrown out into the streets."[35]

To human was added animal refuse. Automobile exhaust fumes are toxic. The dung of numerous horses in the narrow and airless streets of pre-industrial towns was, perhaps, not as harmful to health, but it was no more pleasant.

From the thirteenth century onward, town administrations made numerous provisions to deal with such inconveniences. How effective these measures were is hard to say, but the fact that prohibitions and threats were continually repeated makes one suspect that people took little notice of the ordinances and that penalties were not enforced strictly enough. On occasion the municipal authorities took positive measures. In Siena, toward the end of the thirteenth century, the town administration was concerned with the garbage and filth accumulating daily in the Piazza del Campo. So it entrusted the cleaning of the square to Giovannino di Ventura, who kept a sow and four piglets in the Piazza to eat the abundant supply of refuse.[36]

Even traffic congestion is not an altogether new problem. Early in the fourteenth century, traffic had become so congested in Florence that the statutes of the *Capitano del Popolo* of 1322–25 (lib. V, rub. XXII, c. 86) prohibited the circulation of carts carrying timber in the center of the city on Saturdays.

With the sixteenth century, the increased use of coal in England, first for domestic and then for industrial purposes, opened the doors to the Industrial Revolution but also to our pollution problems. By the seventeenth century, that eminent physician, Thomas Sydenham (1624–89), advised living in the country because "the town air is full of vapors." In 1661 John Evelyn wrote his famous pamphlet *Fumifugium* in which, among other things, one reads:

> in London we see people walk and converse pursued and haunted by that infernal smoake. The inhabitants breathe nothing but an impure and thick mist, accompanied by a fuliginous and filthy vapour, which renders them obnoxious to a thousand inconveniences, corrupting the lungs and disordering the entire habit of their bodies, so that catharrs, phtisicks, coughs and consumption rage more in that one City than in the whole Earth besides.

Many activities damaged not only the environment, but also the health of the men who took part in them. The founder of industrial medicine was Bernardino Ramazzini of Bologna, professor of practical medicine at the University of Modena from 1682 to 1700 and at the University of Padua from 1700 to 1714. It is sufficient to open at random his masterpiece *De Morbis Artificum Diatriba* to find innumerable examples of the fatal consequences of many activities:[37]

> *miners*: they come up into the untainted open air looking as ghastly as the retinue of the god of the underworld because of their stay in those foul dark places. Whatever metal they mine, they invite dreadful diseases which too often mock at every remedy.... But it is from mercury mines that there issues the most cruel bane of all that deal death and destruction to miners.... In the mines of Meissen where black pompholyx is found, the hands and legs of the miners are eaten away to the bone.

> *gilders*: we all know what terrible maladies are contracted from mercury by goldsmiths, especially by those employed in gilding silver and copper objects. This work cannot be done without the use of amalgam, and when they later drive off the mercury by fire they cannot avoid receiving the poisonous fumes into their mouth, even though they turn away their faces. Hence craftsmen of this sort very

113

soon become subject to vertigo, asthma, and paralysis. Very few of them reach old age, and even when they do not die young their health is so terribly undermined that they pray for death.

potters: they need roasted or calcined lead for glazing their pots ... their mouths, nostrils, and the whole body take in the lead poison, hence they are soon attacked by grievous maladies. First their hands become palsied, then they become paralytic, splenetic, lethargic, cachectic, and toothless, so that one rarely sees a potter whose face is not cadaverous and the color of lead.

sulfur workers: among the minerals that are in daily use, sulfur is employed for many purposes and does serious harm to those who roast and liquefy it or use it in their manufactures. Those who deal with burning or liquefied sulfur contract coughs, dyspnoea, hoarseness, and sore eyes.

tanners: they steep the hides of animals in pits with lime and gall-nuts, tread them with their feet, wash and clean them, and smear them with tallow for various purposes; I mean that they are distressed in the same way by the incessant stink and foul exhalations; one can see them with cadaverous complexions, swollen bodies, ghastly looks, and oppressed breathing; they are nearly all splenic. I have observed many cases of dropsy in workers who follow this trade.

glass-workers: during the process of making glass vessels the men stand continually half-naked in freezing winter weather near very hot furnaces ... they are liable to diseases of the chest.... Pleurisy, asthma, and a chronic cough are the natural result. But a far worse fate awaits those who make colored glass for bracelets and other ornaments for women. In order to color the crystal, they use calcinated borax, antimony, and a certain amount of gold; these they pound together to an impalpable powder and mix it with glass to make the paste needed for this process, and however much they cover and avert their faces while they do this they cannot help breathing in the noxious fumes. Hence it often happens that some of them fall senseless, and sometimes they are suffocated; or in the course of time they suffer from ulcers in the mouth, oesophagus, and trachea. In the end they join the ranks of consumptives, since their lungs become ulcerated, as has been clearly shown by the dissection of their corpses.

More than two centuries were to pass before Dr Ramazzini's concern for the working condition of labor became public concern and found expression in preventive legislation.

Part II

TOWARD A DYNAMIC DESCRIPTION

4

THE URBAN REVOLUTION:
THE COMMUNES

The rise of the cities in Europe in the tenth and twelfth centuries marked a turning point in the history of the West – and, for that matter, of the whole world.

Towns had prospered and proliferated in the Greco-Roman world, but the decline of the Empire brought with it their ruin. In a letter dated AD381 Ambrose, bishop of Milan, described the towns of central Italy as *"semi-rutarum urbium cadavera"* – remains of half-ruined cities. If some urban centers survived, their role was simply that of headquarters of religious and/ or military administrations. In the primitive world of the Dark Ages, the city was an anachronism.

The areas of Europe which had been part of the Roman Empire most certainly experienced a process of economic decline which became more obvious and severe during the fifth century of our era. Outside the Empire, in the northern part of Europe, there had been nothing in the way of towns and little in the way of industry and commerce; after the fall of the Empire, the north slowly but surely improved its relative position, partly because of more active contacts with the south. Consequently, the startling contrast which had sharply divided the north and the south in Roman times diminished. On the other hand, the Muslim invasion loosened the ties which had linked southern Europe with North Africa and the Near East. In Roman times, there had been two separate worlds: the Mediterranean world and the northern world. In the seventh century, the Mediterranean world split in two, and the impoverished European half tied itself more closely to the northern part of the subcontinent. Bound by a common religious creed, Europe emerged in embryo.

It was a poor and primitive Europe, a Europe made up of countless rural microcosms – the largely self-sufficient manors, whose autarchy was part cause and part consequence of the decline in trade. Society was dominated by a spirit of resignation, suspicion, and fear of the outside world. People withdrew into the economic isolation of the manors just as they sought spiritual isolation in the monasteries.

The arts, education, trade, production, and the division of labor shrank and withered. The use of money almost completely disappeared. The population was small, production meager, and poverty extreme. Social structures were primitive. There were those who prayed, those who fought, and those who labored. Prevailing values reflected a brutal and superstitious society – fighting and praying were the only respectable activities, and those who fought did so in order to rob, and those who prayed did so superstitiously. Laborers were regarded as despicable serfs. The encroaching forests were inhabited by wild animals and, according to popular imagination, by gnomes, fairies, witches, and goblins. In this depressed and depressing world, the rise of cities between the eleventh and thirteenth centuries represented a new development which changed the course of history.

More than forty years ago, the Belgian historian Henri Pirenne formulated a general theory to explain the rise of cities in the various parts of Europe.[1] Pirenne attempted to accommodate very different developments within a single model, and no one can deny that the model is both ingenious and thought-provoking. Yet Pirenne failed, and he did so essentially because he focused on the outward form of the phenomenon instead of examining its inner nature. The theory of the *portus*, which spread out, absorbed the original fortified feudal nucleus, and eventually gave birth to the new urban unit, is valid for the Low Countries and northern France, but does not fit the facts for other parts of western Europe.

According to Edith Ennen, three areas must be distinguished in western Europe: (a) Italy, Spain, and southern France, where towns, however impoverished, continued to exist throughout the Dark Ages; (b) England, northern France, the Low Countries, Switzerland, the Rhinelands, southern Germany, and Austria, all regions in which Roman urban life substantially disappeared with the fall of the Empire but in which, nevertheless, medieval towns bear the stamp of Roman activity; and (c) northern Germany and Scandinavia, where the Roman urban tradition had no significant impact whatsoever.[2]

The trouble with subdivisions of this kind is that they can be endlessly multiplied. In southern Europe, which Ennen considered a unit, distinctions could be made between northern and southern Italy. Significant differences can easily be identified between northern Italy and Spain: in northern Italy, the lesser nobility played an essential part in the urban movement;[3] in Spain, the urban movement cannot be understood apart from the movement of *Reconquista* and the Arab tradition.

These differences, however, do not undermine the unity of a sociocultural and economic movement which had common roots, whether it took the form of a revival of an ancient Roman town or of the formation of a new town around a fort, a monastery, or an imperial palace. Such unity cannot be sought in forms which are bound to vary from place to place: it must be sought in the substance of the development.

At the root of urban growth was a massive migratory movement. Towns grew because their populations grew. But the urban population did not grow naturally. Fertility in urban centers was never appreciably higher than mortality: urban population grew because of an influx of people from rural areas.

People migrate for two sets of reasons, which are not necessarily alternative: reasons of repulsion (*push* forces) and reasons of attraction (*pull* forces). Between the tenth and thirteenth centuries, the economic trend was upward in rural Europe, partly because of technological innovations, partly because of investments, and partly because of reorganization of property. But although economic conditions were generally improving, life remained essentially unpleasant for the mass of the people. Most serfs saw no means of escaping serfdom, and the lesser nobility could see no clear way of breaking the stranglehold of the establishment. It was at this point that the town came into play as an element of innovation, a place to seek one's fortune. The town was to the people of Europe from the eleventh to the thirteenth centuries what America was to Europeans in the nineteenth century. The town was the "frontier," a new and dynamic world where people felt they could break their ties with the past, where people hoped they would find opportunities for economic and social advancement, and where there would be ample reward for initiative, daring, and hard work. "Stadtluft machts frei" (Town air makes one free) it was said in German towns. It was not only that the serf, having escaped from the countryside, found legal freedom in the towns, but that the whole social atmosphere there was open to ambition and talent, whether the town-dweller was a member of the lesser feudal nobility, or a merchant, or a craftsman. In the city, labor had an intrinsic dignity and all honest callings were granted respect. This is not to say, however, that city democracy was egalitarian and total. Any claim to absolute equality would have seemed a revolt against the very order of things laid down by God himself. Concern with rank and status prevailed from the early days in the medieval city, and it later became an obsession at the time of the Renaissance.

As father Salimbene da Parma explicitly reported in his Chronicle (*Cronaca*, ed. G. Scalia, Bari, 1966, pp. 937–38), whereas in France (and, we might add, in Germany and in England too) the nobility remained entrenched in their country castles in a position of more or less overt hostility toward the emerging cities, in northern Italy many members of the feudal nobility, perceiving the new direction in which history was moving, while not abandoning their castles in the countryside, took up residence in the cities and built palaces and towers that gave Italian cities a singularly feudal aspect – even at the physical level.

At the beginning of the urban development in the eleventh and twelfth centuries, the citizenry, in its struggle for autonomy and independence, did not feel strong enough to challenge the establishment and instead chose to seek the protection of the local bishop in whom political and administrative power were vested. In the course of time, however, as the process of economic development strengthened the business and professional classes, they found they could no longer endure the pre-eminent position enjoyed by the nobility and the bishop. There ensued a series of very complex and lengthy struggles from which the merchant and professional classes emerged victorious. The cities became the seats and centers of the power of the triumphant bourgeoisie.

Urban society grew and developed in sharp contrast with the surrounding countryside. The walls of a town had both a practical purpose and a symbolic significance: they represented the boundary between two cultures locked in conflict. It was this conflict which gave the medieval city its unmistakable character and made the urban movement of the eleventh to thirteenth centuries the turning point of world history.

Towns had existed in ancient Egypt, as in the classical world of Greece and Rome. In the Middle Ages, towns existed in China as well as in the Byzantine Empire. But the cities of medieval and Renaissance Europe were quite different from the towns of other areas and times. In the towns of the classical world, as in the towns of China and the Byzantine Empire, merchants, professionals, and craftsmen never achieved a socially prominent position. Even when they acquired wealth, they still acquiesced in an inferior social position. The rural ideals of the upper classes permeated the whole society; and as the landed gentry dominated both the countryside and the towns, socially as well as politically and culturally, powerful elements of cohesion obliterated the differences between the urban and the rural worlds. The town was not an organism in itself but rather an organ within the broader context of an urban–rural continuum.

In the Roman world, the distinction between city and country was only *de facto*, since Roman law did not distinguish between citizens on the grounds of their residence. In medieval Europe, by contrast, the town came to represent a separate entity. The medieval city was not just part of a larger organism, but an organism in itself, proudly autonomous and clearly separated from the surrounding countryside. Physically, the city was separated from the countryside by walls, moat, and gates. More important than that, the city was another world from a legal point of view, too. When a person passed through the gates of a city, he became subject to different laws, as when today we cross the border from one country to another. The contrast was as sharp in cultural as in economic terms. The merchants, the professionals, the craftsmen who lived in the towns did not acknowledge the control of the rural world or its cultural values; on the contrary, they evolved their own culture and their own values. The emergence of European towns in the eleventh to thirteenth centuries was not a spin-off of regional evolution. It was rather the expression of a cultural and social revolution which was based in the towns. The champions of the rural–feudal establishment were well aware of this, and they did not hide their indignation. *"Communio – novum ac pessimum nomen,"* commented Guibert of Nogent. And Otto of Frisingen, the uncle of Frederic Barbarossa, wrote:[4]

> In the Italian communes they do not disdain to grant the girdle of knighthood or honorable positions to young people of inferior station, and even to workers of the vile mechanical arts, whom other peoples bar like the plague from the more respectable and honorable circles.

People living in the city came to enjoy a unique, personal status. They were "burghers." In Flanders prior to 1100 the term *burgensis* is attested to in three places only (St Omer, Cambrai, and Huy). In the course of the twelfth century, this typically medieval term spread all over western Europe.

There were however striking differences between various different areas in Europe. In Italy the revolutionary character of the city was more apparent than elsewhere, not only in its dealings with baronial and ecclesiastical power but also as conflict grew with the central power of the Empire. Italian cities thus set out to attack and conquer the surrounding territory. In Germany, to further his struggle against the great feudal powers, the Emperor granted certain cities independent self-government, the right to mint their own coinage, the right to confer full citizenship on immigrants, and the right to develop their own policies. Yet German cities never dared push their privileges beyond their own walls or to launch an attack on the feudal forces that encircled them. In France the communal-citizen movement was soon tamed by the power of the monarchy. In England cities developed at a slower and less dramatic pace and assumed no or very few revolutionary characteristics. In eastern Europe, most cities arose not on the basis of their own strength but on the initiative of feudal lords in their *Drang nach Osten*. There were many instances when cities in eastern Germany made an effort to assert their independence, only to be subjugated later by the barons.

But apart from eastern Germany, the political and social triumph of the urban middle class, and of its peculiar sets of values, had revolutionary consequences at the economic level. The new set of values stimulated new kinds of wants, and the economic success of the new classes gave these wants the backing of considerable purchasing power. The fact that the history of the medieval city proved so different in its ultimate effects from the history of the Greek *polis*, the Roman *urbs*, or the Chinese city, was largely due to the structure of effective demand.

Surrounded by a hostile world, the people of the town felt the need for union and co-operation. Frontier people have to unite. In the feudal world, a vertical arrangement typically prevailed, where relations between men were dictated by concepts of fief and service; investiture and homage; lord, vassal, and serf. In the cities, a horizontal arrangement emerged, characterized by co-operation among equals. The *gild*; the *confraternity*; the *university*; and above them all, that guild of guilds, the sworn union among all burghers, the *Commune*, were the institutions created by the new outlook and which reflected the new ideals.

Thus, the city, whether emerging from a *portus* beside a feudal castle or rising again from the foundations of a Roman town, was essentially a new phenomenon: it was the core of a new society which evolved new social structures, rediscovered the state, developed a new culture and a new economy. For the surrounding rural world, the successful burgher had nothing but disdain. "*La villa fa buone bestie e cattivi uomini*" (the countryside produces good animals and bad men) wrote Paolo da Certaldo. Where the surrounding feudal world was too powerful for the town's forces, as in Germany, the city remained on the defensive, sheltering behind the protection afforded by its walls, its wealth, and its artistic and economic pride. Where, as in Italy, the town developed to the point at which it could overturn the previous balance with the surrounding feudal world, it then moved to conquer the surrounding area. The events that followed bore the mark of the urban-versus-rural cultural dichotomy. The town did not create or intend to create a regional body, but asserted instead its right of conquest. The relationship between towns and their conquered territories in the thirteenth and fourteenth centuries reminds one more of the relationship between European states and their colonies in the nineteenth century than of the relationship between a provincial capital and its province in our contemporary society.

With the appearance of the medieval city and the emergence of the urban bourgeoisie, a new Europe was born. Every sector of social and economic life was transformed. Sets of values, personal circumstances and relations, types of administration, education, production, and exchange, all underwent drastic transformation.

The urban revolution of the eleventh and twelfth centuries paved the way for the Industrial Revolution of the nineteenth century.

5

POPULATION:
TRENDS AND PLAGUES

Broadly speaking one can say that at the beginning of the new millennium Europe's population was thinly scattered across the continent: around the year AD 1000 there were probably no more than 30 to 35 million people in the whole of Europe (Russia and the Balkans included). From the tenth century until the beginning of the fourteenth century the population grew slowly but steadily.[1] During this period the populations of France, Germany, and the British Isles probably tripled, while the population of Italy probably doubled. By the 1330s and 1340s the total population of Europe must have been at least 80 million. Then in 1348 came the Black Death, which wiped out some 25 million in a matter of about two years. Wars, famines, and above all epidemics struck again and again over the following 150 years or so, and population recovery was painfully slow. At the end of the fifteenth century the total population of Europe was still around the 80-million mark. The sixteenth century saw substantial growth, and by the beginning of the seventeenth century Europe must have totaled about 100 million people. The wars and epidemics of the seventeenth century had the effect of stabilizing the population at that level, and in 1700 Europe must still have numbered around 110 million inhabitants (see Table 1.1, p. 4).

Some of the main characteristics of the population in question have already been discussed, but it may be useful to recall at least two points. First, whatever its ups and downs, the population of preindustrial Europe remained young – in other words, the age structure consistently showed a marked prevalence of younger age groups. Secondly, notwithstanding the growth of the tenth to thirteenth centuries and of the sixteenth century, the population of Europe remained relatively small. At the high point of their demographic expansion the population of the largest countries ranged from ten to eighteen million people (see Table 1.1) and very few metropolises ever reached the 100,000 mark (see Appendix Table A.1). One could offer an extremely concise and rather sweeping explanation of this by saying that the European population remained young because of high fertility and small because of high mortality. But both points deserve further comment.

It is fashionable nowadays in scholarly circles to point to several cultural factors which helped, in one way or the other, to limit fertility in pre-industrial Europe. It is commonly stated, for instance, that western Europe was characterized by a marriage pattern unique or almost unique in the world. The distinctive features of the European pattern were (a) a relatively high proportion of people never married and (b) many of those who married did so at a relatively advanced age.[2] In regard to point (a) it is emphasized that in preindustrial Europe, celibacy, far from being condemned as it was in oriental societies,[3] was generally praised. For priests, monks, and nuns, celibacy actually became a way of life. Until modern times in Europe intellectualism was inconceivable except in a state of celibacy. The tragedy of Abélard was rooted in this social convention. Until the end of the Middle Ages, the school of medicine at Paris did not allow married men to graduate. At Oxford and Cambridge, until the end of the nineteenth century, married men were not admitted among the fellows of the colleges.

Marriage was also avoided for economic reasons – to preserve a family estate from too many subdivisions or to avoid the cost of running a household. Fynes Moryson, a keen and witty English traveler who visited the continent in around 1700, observed:[4]

> In Italy marryage is indeed a yoke, and that not easy one but so grevious as brethren nowhere better agreeing yet contend among themselves to be free from marryage and he that of free will or by persuasion will take a wife to continue their posterity, shall be sure to have his wife and her honour as much respected by the rest, besyde their liberall contribution to mantayne her, so as themselves may be free to take the pleasure of women at large. By which liberty they live more happily than other nations. For in those frugall commonwealths the unmarried live at a small rate of expenses and they make small conscience of fornication, esteemed a small sinne and easily remitted by Confessors.

In more general terms, and basing his observations on the mortality bills of Breslau, Edmund Halley wrote in 1693:

> The growth and increase of Mankind is not so much stinted by anything in the nature of the species as it is from the cautious difficulty most people make to adventure on the state of marriage, from the prospect of the troubles and charge of providing for a family.

Obviously all generalizations must be taken with a grain of salt. The proportion of people who never married varied greatly not only from country to country and from time to time but also according to social class, economic condition, and place of residence (see Table 5.1).

Similarly, average age at marriage must have varied greatly from time to

Table 5.1 Percentage unmarried in selected social groups in preindustrial Europe

Born in the period	English nobility	
	Percentage unmarried at 45	
	M	F
1330–1479	9	7
1480–1679	19	6
1680–1729	30	17
	Geneva bourgeoisie	
	Percentage unmarried among the deceased of over 50	
	M	F
1550–99	9	2
1600–49	15	7
1650–99	15	26
	Milanese nobility	
	Percentage unmarried among the deceased of over 50	
	M	F
1600–49	49	75
1650–99	56	49
1700–49	51	35
	Physicians and surgeons practising in the Grand-Duchy of Tuscany in 1630	
	Percentage unmarried at 40 and over	
	M	
1550–90	20	

Sources: Hollingsworth, *British Ducal Families*, p. 364; Henry, *Familles Genevoises*, pp. 52–55; Zanetti, *Patriziato Milanese*, pp. 84–88; Cipolla, *Public Health*, p. 103.

time, from class to class, and from country to country. Moryson reported that in Germany "women are seldom marryed till they be twenty-fyve years old."[5] The tone of his remark would make one believe that in England girls married at a younger age. In the village of Colyton (England), however, over the period 1560–1646, the average age at first marriage for women was twenty-seven.[6] In any case, in medieval and Renaissance Europe girls rarely married as early as girls in ancient Rome or in Asian societies, and obviously the higher the age of a woman at marriage, the lower are her probabilities of legitimate fertility over time. Table 5.2 shows the average age at first marriage for women in selected social groups and places. The figures confirm that one must be cautious in making generalizations.

Table 5.2 Average age at first marriage for women in selected social groups and places in preindustrial Europe

Place	Period	Average age at marriage
Florence	1351–1400	18
	1401–1450	17
	1451–1475	19
England (British Peers)	1575–99	21
	1600–24	21
	1625–49	22
	1650–74	22
	1675–99	23
England (Village of Colyton)	1560–1646	27
	1647–1719	30
Amsterdam (Holland)	1626–27	25
	1676–77	27
Amiens (France)	1674–78	25
Elversele (Flanders)	1608–49	25
	1650–59	27

Sources: Herlihy and Klapish, Les Toscans et leurs familles, p. 205; Wrigley, Population and History, pp. 86–87; Hollingsworth, British Ducal Families, p. 364; Hart, "Historisch-demografische notitie"; Deyon, Amiens; Deprez, The Demographic Development of Flanders.

It has been argued that "in preindustrial Europe the chief means of social control over fertility was by prescribing the circumstances in which marriage was to be permitted." On the other hand, it would be a mistake to suppose that once marriage had taken place fertility was governed solely by physiological and nutritional factors.[7] Particular customs may have had some effect on fertility after marriage. It has been suggested that in parts of seventeenth-century France, a long breast-feeding period may have been adhered to in order to prolong amenorrhea among married women and thus increase the gap between births. E.A. Wrigley maintains that "there is strong statistical evidence pointing to the existence of family limitation in [the little village of] Colyton (England) during the late seventeenth century and coitus interruptus appears more likely to have been used than any other method."[8]

All this is interesting but it is possible that in reaction to the previous belief in unrestrained fertility, researchers now tend to overgeneralize from some limited observations and tend to exaggerate the likely results of the facts and circumstances mentioned above. It is true that a number of Europeans did not marry, but many who did so made up for the others. Average age at marriage may have been delayed, but the number of children born to any married woman was still generally very high. Long periods of breast-feeding may have been resorted to, but high infant mortality reduced the efficacy of this method. The fact of the matter is that whenever we are able to calculate some rough figures we often find crude birth rates above 35 per thousand and almost never find rates below 30 per thousand (see Appendix Tables A.2 and A.4). Fertility could have been higher – but this fact does not mean that it was low. High fertility largely explains the youthful age structure of the population. It also accounts for the survival of the European population despite very high mortality.

Mortality was very high indeed in medieval and early modern Europe. A woman who managed to reach the end of her fertile life, let us say at age forty-five, had normally witnessed the deaths of both her parents, the majority of her brothers and sisters, more than half of their children, and often she was a widow. Death was a familiar theme. And it was a grim business. With no alleviation of pain, the bitterness of death was very real.[9] To make things worse there was the cruelty of people, who had become hardened to the horror of natural death: apart from the give and take of warfare, there was the ferocity of justice, the homicidal intolerance of orthodox religion, and the lack of clemency for the weak and the captive.

As we saw in Part I, for demographic purposes it may be useful to distinguish between normal and catastrophic mortality. The distinction is arbitrary and artificial, but it has the merit of facilitating description. We have already defined *normal mortality* as that prevailing in normal years – i.e. years free from calamities such as wars, famines, and epidemics. In such years, the deaths of infants and adolescents represented a large proportion of overall deaths. In more technical terms, the major components of normal mortality were infant and adolescent mortalities.[10]

Bianca of Castilla lost four children before they reached age one and she lost three others before they reached age thirteen. Margherita of Anjou had eleven children, five of whom died before reaching the age of twenty. The death of infants and adolescents was such a common event that people scarcely took any notice of it. Of more than one hundred medical tips given by the famous physician Ugo Benzi (1376–1439) only two concern children below the age of ten. Recounting his own experience, the great Montaigne wrote "I lost two or three children as nurslings not without regret but without great grief." In Florence, after the middle of the fifteenth century, the deaths of infants and adolescents were not even recorded in the official Books of the Deceased of the city.[11] When it is possible to gather accurate and comprehensive data (see, for instance, Appendix Table A.3) one finds that in the communities of preindustrial Europe, whether large or small, for every 1,000 babies born, between 150 and 350 died before reaching one year of age, and another 100 to 200 died before reaching the age of ten.

The high mortality of the young was essentially an index of the poverty of the population, of the strained conditions in which most people lived and, in the case of the well-to-do people, of the futility of medical assistance.

These were conditions of selection which left only the strongest alive However, even those who had survived the hard apprenticeship of the first ten years did not enjoy an easy life for the rest of their days. Adults were as vulnerable as the young to the ravages of *catastrophic mortality*. The fundamental characteristic of preindustrial societies was indeed their extreme vulnerability to calamities of all sorts. The most common invocation was "*a bello, fame, et peste libera nos Domine*" (God deliver us from war, famine, and plague). War, famines, and epidemics relentlessly caused dramatic peaks to appear in the diagrams marking the course of mortality in the various communities (see Figure 5.1).

The brutality of warfare lives on in many literary descriptions as well as in many illuminations. Sieges were followed by massacres and by the torture of the defeated to make them reveal the whereabouts of their hidden treasures, and often religious differences gave a hideous sanction to the slaughter. People spoke of war with terror because the brutality, atrocities, and infamies of soldiering caught the imagination of all. But of the three calamities – war, famines, and epidemics – war was generally the least murderous. It was disastrous largely because of its indirect consequences, in that it provoked a greater frequency or intensity of the other two evils, famines and epidemics. Famines could easily result from the destruction and pillaging of harvests, herds, and agricultural implements. Epidemics were another common by-product of wars. The sanitary conditions of medieval and Renaissance armies were appalling. The Mayor of Padua wrote in 1631 that the soldiers were "extremely dirty and filthy individuals who, wherever they settle, give out intolerable fetor." Early in the eighteenth century, Dr Ramazzini wrote that "in the summer there is a stench so strong from the camps that no cavern of hell could possibly be more fetid."[12] Armies were

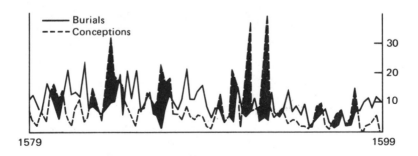

Figure 5.1 Mortality and fertility in a French village (Couffé) at the end of the sixteenth century. Data are on a quarterly basis. Black areas indicate excess of burials over conceptions.

Source: Croix, "La Démographie du pays nantais".

better at disseminating epidemics than at waging wars. A small army of some 8,000 soldiers that Cardinal Duc de Richelieu moved from La Rochelle to Monferrat in 1627–28 spread an epidemic of plague which killed more than one million people.[13] And as Hans Zinsser once wrote, "Epidemics often determined victory or defeat before the generals knew where to place the headquarter mess."[14]

It is difficult for those living in the industrialized countries of the twentieth century to imagine hunger and famine. But preindustrial Europe resembled nineteenth-century India more than it did nineteenth-century Europe. The following is a description, chosen at random, of the scene that one would witness in a period of famine. The writer was a physician and the place was the northern Italian city of Bergamo in 1630:

> The loathing and terror engendered by a maddened crowd of half-dead people who importune all comers in the streets, in the piazzas, in the churches, at street doors, so that life is intolerable, and in addition, the foul stench rising from them as well as the constant spectacle of the dying and the dead and particularly of people so maddened that it is impossible to escape their clutches without giving them alms, and if alms be given to one, a hundred will besiege the giver – this cannot be believed by anyone who has not experienced it.[15]

About the same time, a noble of Vincenza (northern Italy) wrote in a similar vein:

> Give alms to two hundred people and as many again will appear; you cannot walk down the street or stop in a square or church without multitudes surrounding you to beg for charity: you see hunger written on their faces, their eyes like gemless rings, the wretchedness of their bodies with the skins shaped only by bones.

And the diarist Sanuto reported for Venice: "You cannot hear Mass without ten paupers coming to beg for alms or open your purse to buy something without the poor asking for a farthing."[16] People literally died of hunger. In the cities it was not unusual to find men dead in the streets or under the portals. In the countryside they were found at the roadside, their mouths full of grass and their teeth sunk in the earth. During the famine of 1433 and 1434 in Poland, a witness reported on "the poor gathered in Wroclaw, having their lodgings in the square and cemeteries; they perished from hunger and cold." In Venice, in the winter of 1527, Sanuto described the scene in the following terms:

> Everything is dear and every evening in the Piazza San Marco, in the streets and at Rialto stand children crying "bread, bread, I am dying of hunger and cold" – which is a tragedy. In the morning dead have been found under the portals of the Doge's Palace.

For Bergamo in 1630, the physician M.A. Benaglio reported that "most of these poor wretches are blackened, parched, emaciated, weak and sickly ... they wander about the city and then fall dead one by one in the streets and piazzas and by the Palazzo."[17]

Apart from contributing directly to the increase in mortality, famines also contributed indirectly by encouraging the outbreak of epidemics. The abbot Segni noted at the beginning of the seventeenth century that at a time of famine "most of the poor people" were attacked by illnesses "born from grasses and from poor foods," and the good abbot explained that thus, "since the stomach cannot cook such food, nor can the liver reduce it to blood, the natural order of the body is ruined and wind, or indeed, water develops in the belly and in the legs, the skin takes on a yellow color, and people die."[18]

An anonymous chronicler from Busto Arsizio (Lombardy) noted that during the famine of 1629 people were reduced to eating things from which "there followed the most atrocious and incurable diseases, which neither physicians nor surgeons were able to identify and which lasted for 6, 8, 10, or 12 months, and a great multitude of people died of them and the population of our community was reduced from eight thousand to three thousand."[19]

Epidemics contributed most to the frequency and the intensity of catastrophic mortality.[20] Historians always mention the Black Death but generally leave the readers with the impression that no serious epidemics hit Europe before 1348 or afterwards. The fact is that until the end of the seventeenth century not a year passed without particular cities or entire regions of Europe suffering badly from some epidemic. The most frequent epidemics were those of typhoid fever, typhus, dysentery, plague, and influenza with its lethal bronchial-pulmonary complications. Of all the infectious diseases plague was by far the most tragic and lethal, with fatality rates ranging between 60 and 75 percent in the case of bubonic plague and no less than 100 percent in the case of pneumonic plague (the reason for this high fatality rate being that the parasite that causes the plague – yersinia pestis – is a parasite of rodents and not of men).

Though wars, famines, and epidemics were not unknown in the eleventh, twelfth, and thirteenth centuries, low population densities limited the devastating effects of epidemics. However, as the population grew and concentrated in the towns, the nature of the problem altered.

The population growth that took place between 1000 and 1300 did not have the intensity of demographic developments in the nineteenth and twentieth centuries, but even relatively low growth rates, if protracted over centuries, clearly result in explosive situations. At the beginning of the fourteenth century, several areas of Europe were overpopulated in relation to prevailing levels of production and technology. By 1339 the barren mountains of Oisans (France) achieved a population density not reached again until 1911.[21] In Tuscany, the population of the territory of San Gimignano reached, in 1332, a density higher than in 1951. The population density of the territory of Volterra in the 1330s was as high as it was in 1931.[22] To make things worse, people crowded into towns where water-wells were unsafe, sanitary arrangements nonexistent, and rats, fleas, and lice were overabundant. Rubbish and human and animal waste piled up on the roads and in the yards, soap was scarcely used, and personal hygiene was a little-known practice, however much physicians recommended it. The imbalance between demographic growth on the one hand and the lack of medical and public-health development on the other reached a critical point at the beginning of the fourteenth century. What happened next in Europe is a good example of how, once human action has created dangerous imbalances, equilibrium is eventually restored. It also demonstrates that famines are not the only rebalancing device in the hands of nature.

As mentioned above, between 1348 and 1351 a frightening epidemic of plague killed about 25 million people out of a total European population of about 80 million. The tragedy did not end there: the plague established itself in Europe in a more or less endemic form, and from that time onward, for

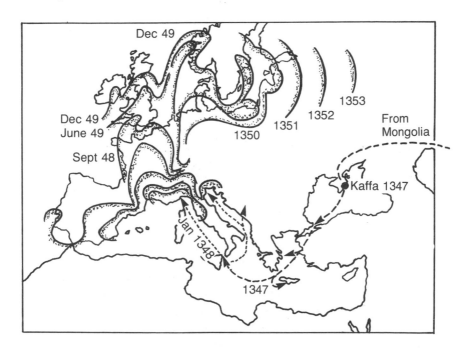

The spread of the Black Death in Europe, 1347–53.

Source: McEvedy and Jones, *Atlas*.

about three centuries, horrible epidemics flared up from time to time on a local, regional or national scale.

In England between 1351 and 1485, plague broke out in thirty different years and between 1543 and 1593 it broke out in twenty-six years. In Venice between 1348 and 1630 plague broke out in epidemic form in twenty-one years. In Florence too plague broke out in twenty-two years between 1348 and 1500. Between 1348 and 1596 Paris was hit by plague epidemics in twenty-two years. Between 1457 and 1590 Barcelona suffered from plague epidemics in seventeen years.[23]

It would be hard to estimate accurately the number of casualties from plague epidemics. In his famous *Natural and Political Observations upon the Bills of Mortality*, first published in 1662, John Graunt remarked "that the knowledge even of the numbers which dye of the plague is not sufficiently deduced from the mere report of the searchers" and that it was necessary to make "corrections upon the perhaps ignorant and careless searchers' reports."[24] Sir William Petty, who liked to indulge in all kinds of exercises of "political arithmetic," wrote in 1667 that

London within ye bills hath 696 thousand people in 108 thousand houses. In pestilential yeares, which are one in twenty, there dye one sixth of ye people of ye plague and one fifth of all diseases. The people which ye next plague of London will sweep away will be probably 120 thousand, which at £7 per head is a losse of 8,400 thousand.[25]

More accurate estimates are available for Italian towns, and Table 5.3 shows the horrible ravages caused by the epidemics of 1630–31 and 1656–57. In general, an epidemic of plague killed, in the course of a few months, from a quarter to half of the population affected.

The effects of an epidemic on a given population are determined not only by the number of people killed but also by the age distribution of mortality. Clearly, if an epidemic kills mostly young people, the consequences on the subsequent development of the population in question are more severe than if it mainly kills people past their reproductive age. Nor do data on mortality tell the whole story. In the course of a famine as well as during an epidemic, not only did more people die but fewer children were born. The diagram in Figure 5.2 illustrates the typical course of mortality and fertility during a period of crisis. The "scissors" movement of fertility and mortality normally produced a hugely negative balance in the population totals.

It would be hard to overestimate the importance of these demographic crises as a long-term device in regulating preindustrial populations. Fertility was generally higher than *normal* mortality. Under these circumstances, population grew, although relatively slowly because the gap between fertility and mortality was slight. Sooner or later, however, a peak of catastrophic mortality would cancel out the previous demographic gains and the cycle would start all over again. In this way the frequency and severity of

Table 5.3 Mortality in selected Italian cities during the plague epidemics of 1630–31 and 1656–57

Period	City	Population before the epidemic (000's)	Number of deaths during the epidemic (000's)	Deaths as a percentage of population (%)
1630–31	Bergamo	25	10	40
	Bologna	62	15	24
	Brescia	24	11	45
	Carmagnola	7.6	1.9	25
	Como	12	5	42
	Cremona	37	17	38
	Empoli	2.2	0.22	10
	Milan	130	60	47
	Modena	18	4	22
	Monza	7	4	57
	Padua	32	19	59
	Parma	30	15	50
	Pescia	2.8	1.4	50
	Prato	6	1.5	25
	Venice	140	46	33
	Verona	54	33	61
	Vicenza	32	12	38
1656–57	Genoa	75	45	60
	Naples	300	150	50
	Rome	123	23	19

the peaks of catastrophic mortality determined the population trend. Turbulent political and social conditions naturally promoted the destructive action of microbes and this explains why the period of the Hundred Years' War (1337–1453) and that of the Thirty Years' War (1618–48) were also periods of demographic stagnation and decline.

Clearly, there was a link between the frequency of epidemics on the one hand and population density and urbanization on the other. The general impression is that the cities of preindustrial Europe had a negative demographic balance and that they survived only because of a continual inflow of people from the countryside. One of the first, if not the first scholar to make this point on the basis of statistical observation was John Graunt, who wrote in 1662:

> In the said Bills of London there are far more burials than christenings. This is plain, depending only upon arithmetical computation for in forty years, from the year 1603 to the year 1644, exclusive of both years, there have been set down 363,935 burials and but 330,747

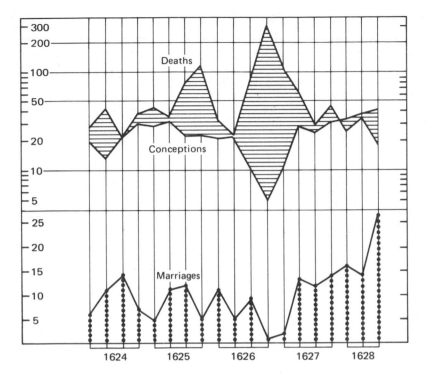

Figure 5.2 Trends in mortality, fertility, and marriage during a typical demographic crisis. The case is that of the village of Saint-Lambert-des-Levées (France).

Source: Goubert, *Beauvais et le Beauvaisis*.

christenings within the 97, 16 and 10 out parishes; those of Westminster, Lambeth, Newington, Redriff, Stepney, Hackney and Islington not being included. From this single observation it will follow that London should have decreased in its people; the contrary whereof we see by its daily increase of buildings upon new foundations, and by the turning of great palacious houses into small tenements. It is therefore certain that London is supplied with people from out the country, whereby not only to supply the overplus differences of burials above-mentioned, but likewise to increase its inhabitants according to the said increase of housing.[26]

In spite of their vitality in the economic, political, artistic, and cultural spheres, from a purely biological point of view the cities of preindustrial Europe were large graveyards.

This fact placed a limit on the process of urbanization. If more people died than were born in the cities, obviously the percentage of urban population grew, and the stronger was the brake on the growth of the total population.[27] According to Father Mols, eighteenth-century Holland, for instance, was "too much urbanized" and "the natural reserve" of the country with its positive demographic balance was not enough to fill the gaps in the negative balance of the urban population.

This brief and summary outline of the history of population in preindustrial Europe must end on a mysterious note. As M. Goubert wrote of the eighteenth century, "un monde démographique semble défunt" (certain demographic patterns died out). The great peaks of mortality due to epidemics progressively subsided. Not that epidemics had become a thing of the past: there were epidemics of influenza in London in 1685 and in 1782, and an epidemic of measles in 1670. The late 1730s and 1740s saw pandemics of influenza and typhus striking most countries in Europe. However, while death rates greatly increased in such periods, momentarily exceeding birth rates, mortality no longer assumed catastrophic proportions. Even death rates of 69 and 112 per thousand, such as were recorded in Norway and the Swedish province of Värmland respectively in 1742, are still a far cry from those experienced by some regions of Europe in previous centuries.[28] The most dramatic aspect of this phenomenon was the disappearance of plague. The great pandemic killer vanished as mysteriously as it had appeared three centuries earlier. There were no more plague epidemics in Italy after 1657, in England and France after the 1660s, or in Austria and Germany after the

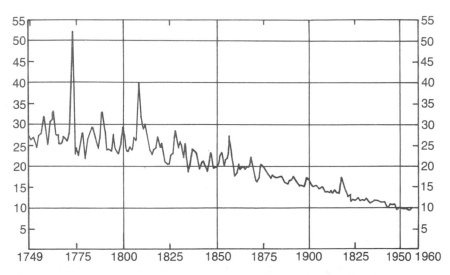

Figure 5.3 The mortality rate in Sweden, 1749–1950. This graph shows clearly how, with the advent of the contemporary age, a high level of normal mortality in Europe with frequent peaks of crisis mortality gave way to a lower level of normal mortality and the almost total disappearance of crisis peaks.

1670s. All kinds of ingenious hypotheses have been constructed to account for this mysterious disappearance – from alleged improvements in building, to better ways of burying corpses, to the story of the invasion of the gray rat and the disappearance of the black rat. But all such hypotheses have proven untenable.

Medieval and Renaissance Europe did not go the way of Asia. European development was not halted by the suffocating pressure of population. Credit for this restraint, however, must go not so much to the rationality of the Europeans (i.e. low fertility) as to the blind action of microbes (i.e. high mortality). By the end of the seventeenth century the deadliest of the microbes had ceased its nefarious activities; and again this event was not man's achievement, but the result of an obscure ecological revolution. Europe then embarked upon the initial stage of its so-called demographic revolution. The fact, however, that the ensuing demographic growth was not quickly arrested by the inexorable operation of Malthusian forces is attributable to the technological and economic achievements of western Europe.

6

TECHNOLOGY

TECHNOLOGICAL DEVELOPMENTS: 1000–1700

In the history of technology, it is often stated that, after a series of startling innovations, a phase of stagnation took hold in the western world during classical times and lasted for many centuries.

> Around 2500 BC technological advance ground almost to a stop and during the next three thousand years rather little progress took place.... When compared with the revolution that preceded them, these three millennia constitute a technological stagnation.[1]

The Greco-Roman world, and especially the Roman world, while highly creative in other fields of human activity, remained, according to this point of view, strangely inactive in the technological field.[2] As regards Rome, the classic example of the water mill and the anecdote about Vespasian are always cited. The Romans knew about the water mill, but built relatively few of them and continued to make far wider use of mills employing animal or human power.[3] And it is said that when Vespasian was offered the plans of machines which would have saved on human labor, the emperor, though awarding a prize to the inventor, prohibited the construction of the machines "to allow the populace to make their living."[4]

Starting from observations of this kind, historians have undertaken research into the possible reasons for the "failure" of the classical world, some pointing out the overabundance of slave labor, others the type of culture and prevailing sets of values. In all likelihood, the Greek and Roman technological "failure" has been exaggerated.[5] All too often we tend to identify technology with mechanics, because our civilization is essentially mechanical. Political and administrative organization, military organization, architecture and road construction, even artistic products such as frescoes, bear the marks of technology, and in none of these fields could the Greeks and Romans be considered failures.

It remains true, however, that the Dark Ages ushered in a period in which technological innovations succeeded each other at a faster pace, and with an increasing emphasis on mechanical aspects. As Samuel Lilley wrote, "It was early in the Middle Ages that men began to find a way out of the [technological] impasse."[6] Lynn White put it this way:

> The millennial span of the Middle Ages has the interest of being the period during which Europe built up the self-confidence and the technical competence which, after 1500, enabled it to invade the rest of the world, conquering, looting, trading and colonizing.[7]

Undeniably "modern technology is the extrapolation of that of the Western Middle Ages, not merely in detail but also in the spirit that infuses it."[8]

A schematic inventory of the main technological developments of the West from the sixth to the eleventh century should include:

a. from the sixth century: spread of the water mill
b. from the seventh century: spread, throughout northern Europe, of the heavy plow.
c. from the eighth century: spread of the crop rotation system
d. from the ninth century: spread of the horseshoe and of a new method for harnessing draft animals

In relation to these developments three points should be made: First, the innovations just listed were not, properly speaking, inventions. The water mill, as previously noted, was known to the Romans. The heavy plow was of Slavic origin.[9] The horseshoe seems to have been known to the Celts prior to the Roman conquests.[10] The new methods for harnessing horses originated in faraway China and doubts have recently been raised about the productivity gains achieved by adopting this technique.[11] What the Europeans displayed from the sixth to the eleventh centuries was not so much inventive ingenuity as a remarkable capacity for assimilation. They knew how to seize on good ideas and apply them to large-scale productive activity. Perhaps this attitude was influenced by the fresh outlook of the German invaders: the pride which drove the Romans and the Chinese to describe as barbarians all those who did not belong to their empires made them unreceptive to foreign ideas. Second, the innovations mentioned above were all linked to agricultural activity and, in combination, strengthened each other. As Lynn White noted,

> The heavy plow, the open fields, the new integration of agriculture and herding, three field rotation, modern horse harness, nailed horseshoes and the whipple tree had combined into a total system of agrarian exploitation by the year 1100 to provide a zone of peasant prosperity stretching across Northern Europe from the Atlantic to the Dnieper.[12]

Finally, some of these innovations allowed for a more effective use of horsepower. The horseshoe increased the efficiency and therefore the value of the horse. At the end of the eleventh century, a road toll in the Angers region of France taxed a horse without horseshoes at one penny and a horse with horseshoes at two pennies. At the same time, throughout Europe the breeding of horses increased markedly, and efforts were made to improve breeds by importing horses from the Muslim countries. Increasingly, oxen were replaced with horses. In Picardy (France), from about 1160 onward, references to plowing with horses become more common and by the early thirteenth century references to plow-oxen had all but disappeared from the documents. On one manor belonging to Ramsey Abbey (England) the number of oxen halved while that of draft horses quadrupled between 1125 and 1160. "The horse costs more than the ox," wrote Walter of Henley in his thirteenth-century treatise on practical husbandry. But the horse is stronger and faster than the ox and it can do more work than an ox before tiring, and in less time. Essentially the substitution of the horse for the ox meant the substitution of a more expensive but more efficient form of capital for a less expensive but less efficient one. The story of the horse was paralleled by that of iron. The amount of iron in agricultural equipment seems to have been extremely limited before the eleventh century. With the twelfth century, the more expensive but more efficient iron implements are mentioned more and more frequently in the documents.

In the barbarous West, it was certainly with an eye to greater effectiveness in battle that the technical innovations in iron working and horse breeding had been first promoted. Eventually, in the course of the twelfth century, both the use of the horse and that of iron were handed down from the squires to the peasants. It was in the twelfth century that the plow was improved, at least in the most thriving parts of Europe. Pieces of iron were added to the wood from which it was wholly constructed in Carolingian times, thus enhancing its ability to penetrate the soil.

The use of more efficient capital led to gains in productivity. In turn, progress in productivity made it possible to adopt more costly but more efficient types of capital. At the same time there were developments in human capital with the emergence of technicians trained in the new technologies. Studies have been made of the spread of the village blacksmith in Picardy. Until the early twelfth century, no trace is found. Then thirty blacksmiths appear at random in the sources between 1125 and 1180. By the end of the twelfth century there was a smith at work in ten of the thirty villages belonging to the priory of Hesdin.[13]

To maintain the fertility of the land despite the severe scarcity of fertilizers, the people of the Middle Ages and of the Renaissance resorted to a very primitive form of rotation. Until modern times between a third and a half of all arable land of Europe lay fallow – a constraint which was particularly severe if one considers that the fields that were under cultivation did not yield more than three to six times the seed sown. Fitting new crops into the rotation was the technical innovation which made it possible to reduce or abandon the fallow year. When and where the innovation was first put into practice we do not know. When Philippe de Commines arrived in Lombardy with the French army of Charles VIII at the end of the fifteenth century, he remarked that some of the land he saw "never rests." A common rotation was publicized by Richard Weston, an English traveler in Flanders in 1652; it consisted of rotating grain, turnips, and clover. These practices, however, spread only very slowly and throughout the preindustrial period land remained largely under-exploited. The Europeans of the Middle Ages and of the Renaissance proved much more innovative and successful in other fields.

Until the tenth century, mills were used in the West for milling grain. In contrast, early information on water mills in China suggests they were used not for turning simple millstones, but for the more complicated job of blowing bellows in metal work. The difference should not surprise us: in the Dark Ages the West was essentially agrarian and was both poorer and less developed than China. But as cities, trade, and manufacturing expanded in Europe from the tenth century onward, motive power derived from hydraulic energy was applied to an increasing variety of productive processes (Table 6.1). Water mills became more complicated and powerful. Perhaps as early as 822, and certainly by 1088 in Picardy and Normandy, water mills were used to prepare the malt necessary for the manufacture of beer. The adaptation of the mill to this and other types of operation involved the introduction of new mechanisms, in particular a series of vertical hammers set in motion by cams inserted on one of the axes of the mill.

Between about 950 and about 1050, water mills were applied to cloth fulling in Parma, Milan, and Florence. By the end of the eleventh century, the new technology had reached Grenoble and Lérin and would soon reach the rest of France and arrive in England and Germany also. Water mills were used for fulling cloth in 1161 in Sköna (Sweden), at least since 1185 in England, in 1223 and 1246 respectively at Spier and Trier in Germany. The adoption of the new process revolutionized the textile industry of the time to such an extent that Carus-Wilson, describing these developments in England, labeled them "An Industrial Revolution of the Thirteenth Century." In France the adoption of the mills sparked off violent protests among workers who maintained that the new technology was detrimental not only to the quality of the product but also to employment. These were the earliest instances of protest by labor against the adoption of labor-saving mechanical devices. In England the new technology caused the manufactures to relocate. Until the thirteenth century they had been mainly concentrated in the southeastern areas of the country; then they moved into the northwestern areas, where the availability of adequate flows of water made it possible to construct mills.[14]

Table 6.1 Emergence of new industrial applications of the vertical water wheel to *c.* 1550

Type of mill	Date of first occurrence	Location
Beer	861	N.W. France
Hemp	990	S.E. France
Fulling	962	Italy
	820?	Switzerland?
Iron	1025?	S. Germany
	1197	S. Sweden
Oil	*c.* 1100	S.E. France
Ore-stamping	1135	N. Italy
Tanning	1138	N.W. France
Sugar	1176?	Sicily?
Cutlery (grinding and polishing)	1204	N.W. France
Saw	1204	N.W. France
Mechanical bellows	1214	Styria
Mustard	*c.* 1250	S.E. France
Poppy	1251	N.W. France
Paper	1276	N. Italy
Mine-pumping (chain type)	1315	Moravia
Mortar	1321	S. Germany
Turning (lathes)	1347	S.E. France
Pigment (paint)	1348	N.W. France
Blast furnace	1384	Belgium
Pipe-boring	*c.* 1480	S. Germany
Rolling and slitting	1443	Cent. France
Wire	1351?	S. Germany
	1489	S. Germany
Gem-polishing	1534	N.W. France

Source: Bradford B. Blaine, "The Application of Water-Power to Industry during the Middle Ages" (Ph.D dissertation, University of California, Los Angeles, 1966).

There is evidence of the use of water mills in the production of iron in Styria in 1135, in Normandy in 1204, in Southern Sweden in 1197, and in Moravia in 1269. In Normandy, in 1204, a mill was used to drive wood saws. Mills were used in the manufacture of paper at Fabriano in 1276, at Troyes in 1338, and at Nuremberg in 1390. By the late fifteenth century any large western European city could be pictured much as a mid-sixteenth-century traveler described Bologna (Italy). He told of a sluice from the river Reno that provided water power

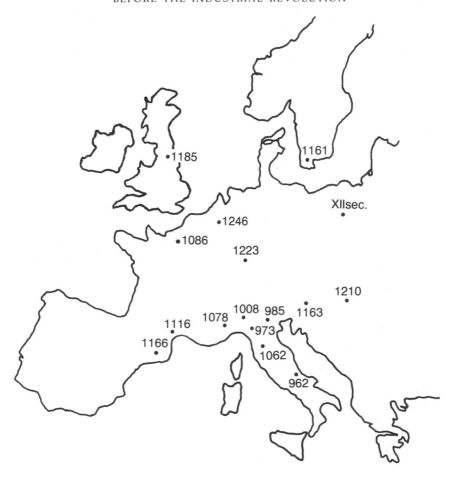

The spread of the fulling mill in various regions of Europe. Paolo Malanima.

Source: The Economist, London.

to turn various machines to grind grain, to make copper pots and weapons of war, to pound herbs as well as oakgalls [for dyeing], to spin silk, polish arms, sharpen various instruments, saw planks.[15]

By the thirteenth century water mills in the West had wheels 1 to 3.5 meters in diameter with a corresponding 1 to 3.5 horsepower. By the seventeenth century it was possible to make wheels 10 meters in diameter. The Italian water mills used in the production of silk thread were not only extremely complicated but also monstrously large pieces of machinery. However, the majority of the mills were still built with wheels 2 to 4 meters in diameter.

Builders preferred to increase the number of wheels rather than deal with all the complicated technological problems involved in the concentration of energy on one single wheel.

The story of the water mill runs parallel to that of the windmill. When the windmill first appeared in Persia, possibly in the seventh century AD, it was mounted on a vertical axle and appears to have been used mostly for irrigation purposes. The Chinese became acquainted with the Persian mill in the course of the thirteenth century AD and soon adopted it. As far as we know, the windmill first appeared in Europe at the end of the twelfth century in Normandy and in England. Windmills are mentioned in 1204 in Picardy, in 1237 in Tuscany, in 1269 in Burgundy, in 1259 in Denmark, in 1274 in Holland. The tradition persists that the windmill was brought back to Europe by the Crusaders. The European windmill, however, displays some originality. While the oriental mill had sails mounted on a vertical axis, the European mill had sails mounted on a horizontal one. It appears that someone brought back from the Middle East not a description of the local windmills, but the idea of harnessing wind energy and that the European craftsmen then devised a totally new contraption. Originally the western windmill was mounted on a heavy post and the mill had to be turned to face

The Winged Mill. An engraving by Johannes Stradanus (1523–1605). The caption reads "The winged mill which now wants to be driven by the winds is said to have been unknown to the Romans." In this Flemish setting are shown both types of windmills, the post mills and the tower mills. New York Public Library.

into the wind. This limited the size of the mills. By the fourteenth century, however, the tower mill had been developed; in this type of mill the building and the machinery remain stationary; only the top rotates to face the sails into the wind. This innovation allowed the erection of much larger and more powerful units. The sails had to be turned into the wind manually, but this job was later made easier by the introduction of cranks and gears. Finally, in 1745, Edmund Lee invented the fantail, a device which held the sails into the wind automatically, probably the earliest example of automatic control in machinery.

Many tower mills could generate as much as 20 or 30 horsepower. Thus the windmill was a more powerful motor than the water mill. But its spread was severely restricted by geography and climate. This explains why, although windmills became characteristic landmarks in some areas, they never became as numerous or as widespread as water mills. But like water mills, windmills, originally built for grinding grains, were later employed in an increasing variety of productive processes. In Amsterdam in 1578, there were windmills used in throwing silk, printing ribbons, fulling and calendering cloth, dressing leather, extracting oil, making gunpowder, and rolling copper plates.[16]

The proliferation and increasing power of water mills and windmills, like the increased use of horses, made available more energy for productive uses. Unlike horses, however, the mills supplied inanimate energy. Their widespread use marked the beginning of the breakdown of the traditional world in which man had to depend for power on animal or vegetable sources of energy.[17] It was the distant announcement of the Industrial Revolution.

The use of the mill in manufacturing signalled a new trend: thus far innovations had occurred only in the agricultural sector; now they increasingly began to occur in the manufacturing and service sectors. This trend was both a consequence and evidence of the expansion of these two sectors.

About the middle of the eleventh century the vertical loom was introduced in Flanders, and possibly in Champagne. In comparison with the traditional horizontal loom, it was claimed that the new loom increased labour productivity by three to five times and also made possible substantial improvements in the quality of production.

A Chinese reference to a magnetic pointer floating in a bowl of water dates from about AD 1040. In the late twelfth century an English Augustinian monk described a magnetized needle which he said sailors used for locating the North Star in bad weather. Somewhere in the Mediterranean region, in about 1300, the transition was made from the primitive needle-and-bowl to a self-contained instrument, the compass. The perfecting of the gyroscopic compass, the adoption of the waterclock for measuring the movement of the ship, the drawing up of naval charts with related instructions, the compilation of trigonometric tables for navigation, and the adoption of the stern rudder on the central line of the ship, made possible instrumental or mathematical navigation, which in turn made possible a greater utilization of the ship as capital. Frederic C. Lane has shown that during the thirteenth century the idle period of ships in winter was gradually shortened and that, by the last quarter of the century, a ship could complete two round trips a year throughout the Mediterranean, traveling even in winter.[18]

The contemporaries of Dante (1265–1321) felt that they lived in a period of great technological change. In 1267 Theodoric, Bishop of Bitonto, wrote that *"quotidie instrumentum novum et modus novus solertia et ingenio medici invenitur"* ("owing to the laboriousness and ingenuity of the physicians, every day a new instrument and a new technology are invented"). In a sermon delivered in Florence in 1306, Father Giordano da Pisa declared "Every day new arts are discovered." Among the innovations of the period one should mention the spinning wheel and spectacles. About the latter, in the sermon mentioned above, Father Giordano had the following to say:

> It is not twenty years since there was discovered the art of making spectacles which help you to see well, and which is one of the best and most necessary in the world. I myself saw the man who discovered and practiced it, and I talked with him.[19]

At the beginning of the fourteenth century came the first clocks and the first firearms. The fourteenth century also saw the invention of canal locks.

The shipwrights of ancient Greece, of ancient Rome, and of the Vikings would build a hull by attaching each plank laboriously to the plank below it; only after the shell was complete were ribbing and braces inserted. By the later Middle Ages, European shipwrights were building ships skeleton-first, making a vast saving in both time and labor. Exactly when and where the transition first took place we do not know. It was, in any case, just the first in a remarkable series of technological innovations. In the course of the fifteenth century the full-rigged ship was developed. This type of ship combined the best of both the northern and the southern European traditions. The hull was carvel-built, but the greatest innovation was in the rigging. By the ninth century the problem of shifting the sail spar over the mast during tacking, which had prevented the Romans from building larger ships using fore-and-aft rigging, had been solved, and larger merchant ships were fitted with lateen sails. Thus equipped, a ship could sail 60–65 degrees off the wind. This marked a major advance in ship performance. A full-rigged ship carried three masts, the fore- and mainmasts with square sails and the mizzenmast with a lateen (triangular) sail. With this combination, the square sails could be made large, while the lateen sail made sailing close to the wind possible. As time went on, more sails were added, and the big, bulging mainsail which was characteristic of the early caracks was divided into several smaller square sails – a change that made the canvas stand flatter and the ship better able to beat to windward. To understand fully the

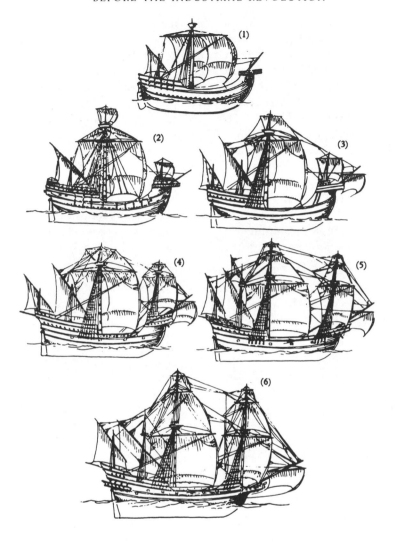

The development of ships' rigging, 1430–1600. (1) *c.* 1430, (2) *c.* 1450, (3) *c.* 1500, (4) *c.* 1530, (5) *c.* 1560, (6) *c.* 1600.

Source: Unger, *The Ship in the Medieval Economy.*

importance of these developments, one must see them against the background of the chronic shortage of energy which thwarted the activity of preindustrial people. The full-rigged ship enabled the Europeans to harness the energy of the wind over the seas to an extent inconceivable in previous times.

146

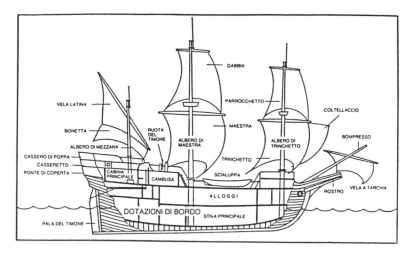

Eighteenth-century English merchant vessel. This type of ship generally ranged in size from 150 to 250 tons: the crew would vary from 15 to 25 men, plus the captain. The ships might be armed with anything from 15 to 20 cannon. This was the most common type of vessel in the merchant navies of seventeenth-century Europe.

vela latina: lateen sail	*gabbia*: topsail
bonetta: stun-sail	*maestra*: mainsail
albero di mezzana: mizzenmast	*parrocchetto*: fore-topsail
cassero di poppa: poop deck	*trinchetto*: foresail
casseretto: deck cabin	*scialuppa*: lifeboat
ponte di coperta: upper deck	*alloggi*: quarters
pala del timone: rudder blade	*stiva principale*: main hold
cabina principale: main cabin	*albero di trinchetto*: foremast
ruota del timone: helm	*coltellaccio*: studding sail
cambusa: galley	*bompresso*: bowsprit
DOTAZIONI DI BORDO: SHIP'S OUTFIT	*vela a tarchia*: spritsail
albero di maestra: mainmast	*rostro*: cutwater

The economic consequences were immediately felt. Full-rigged ships no longer had to wait for only the most favorable breeze, and consequently the elapsed time of voyages diminished. Since the sail area could be increased and more energy exploited, the size of vessels grew and their carrying capacity rose until the middle of the sixteenth century,[20] and costs were correspondingly reduced. Eventually the development of the Dutch *fluyt* (see p. 258) brought to a stop the growth in size of cargo ships, well below the technically feasible maximum of over 2,000 tons. The *fluyt* showed that the optimum tonnage for intra-European and for many extra-European trades in the seventeenth and eighteenth centuries was in the range of 300 to 500 tons. Ships in Europe did not grow much above that tonnage until after 1800.

While naval construction was progressing, more sophisticated techniques of open-seas navigation were being developed. By 1434, the Portuguese, who had succeeded in rounding the formidable and feared Cape Bojador on the west coast of Africa, had developed systematic knowledge of the winds in the Atlantic. Before 1480 they learned to calculate latitude by converting, with the help of declination tables, the heights of the sun or the North Star over the horizon. The quadrant for measuring latitude must have come into use in about 1450, and by 1480 the astrolabe was also in use.

Navigation was anything but a peaceful occupation in those days, and ships carried ordnance for both defensive and offensive purposes. Traditionally, naval guns were made of bronze, and in the course of the sixteenth and seventeenth centuries noticeable progress was made in the casting of bronze. Beginning in the middle of the sixteenth century, however, England first, and then Holland and Sweden, developed the technique of casting iron guns, which were much less expensive than bronze cannon. Thus it became possible to put more guns aboard ships at lower expense.

The combination of innovations and progress in the techniques of naval construction, navigation, and armament production provided a basis for Europe's expansion overseas. And that changed the course of world history. As Lynn White put it: "The bursting of Europe's oceanic boundaries at the end of the fifteenth century is one of the central events in history. It was made possible by a long and ingenious series of Medieval and Renaissance improvements in shipbuilding and the nautical arts which were entirely empirical. The majestic result is the measure of the effectiveness of such empiricism."[21]

Another revolutionary technological innovation of the fifteenth century was heralded by Gutenberg's printing of the Bible with movable characters. Before that event books were so expensive that only a few wealthy people could afford to own them. In Spain in around 800, a book cost about as much as two cows. In Lombardy between the end of the fourteenth and the end of the fifteenth century the average price of a medical book equaled the living costs of an average person for about three months, and a law book cost as much as such a person's maintenance for one year and four months.[22] This helps to explain why in 1392 the Countess of Blois, wife of the Baron of Castellane, on bequeathing to her daughter a parchment manuscript of the *Corpus Juris*, expressly stipulated that the daughter should marry a jurist so that the valuable treasure would come into the right hands. As long as books remained so outrageously expensive it was unlikely that literacy would become widespread. The introduction of movable type marked a new era. As the full-rigged ship opened up vast new geographical horizons to the Europeans, so the press with movable characters opened up vast new horizons and opportunities in the fields of knowledge and education. The new invention spread rapidly through Europe and beyond (see map opposite).

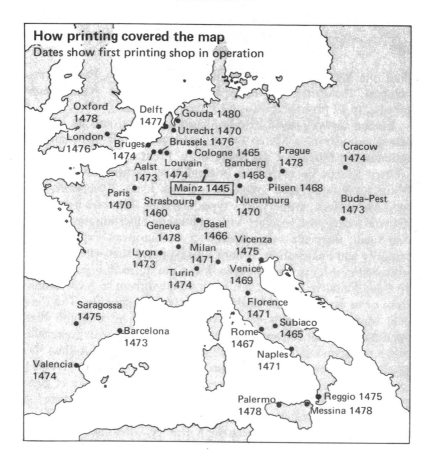

How printing covered the map
Dates show first printing shop in operation

Oxford 1478
Delft 1477
Gouda 1480
Utrecht 1470
London 1476
Bruges 1474
Brussels 1476
Cologne 1465
Prague 1478
Cracow 1474
Aalst 1473
Louvain 1474
Bamberg 1458
Paris 1470
Mainz 1445
Pilsen 1468
Strasbourg 1460
Nuremburg 1470
Buda-Pest 1473
Geneva 1478
Basel 1466
Vicenza 1475
Lyon 1473
Milan 1471
Turin 1474
Venice 1469
Saragossa 1475
Florence 1471
Subiaco 1465
Barcelona 1473
Rome 1467
Naples 1471
Valencia 1474
Palermo 1478
Reggio 1475
Messina 1478

Source: *The Economist*, London.

The spinning wheel was known in China as early as the eleventh century. In Europe it appeared in the course of the twelfth century. The spinning wheel is the earliest known application of belt-driven transmission. Its use in the production of cloth in western Europe raised productivity by a factor of two or possibly three.

These were a few of the innovations that emerged during the Middle Ages and the Renaissance. They formed part of a broader process of innovation. More often than not the process of innovation advanced in small steps and through numerous minor experiments, by the gradual accumulation of small improvements rather than by sudden eruptions of invention. The approach was always empirical and unsystematic. It was only after the Industrial Revolution, with the emergence of modern science and the controlled experiment, that the essential character of this process changed.

Many innovations were interrelated. For instance, the success of Gutenberg's invention can be understood only in the context of the availability and spread of the optical glass, the water-powered mills for pulping rags for paper, and a system of schooling. Similarly, the development of ocean navigation techniques can be understood only in the context of improved shipbuilding technology, advances in the production of naval ordnance, and the spread of literacy among sea captains.

As noted above, many of the innovations which occurred in Europe after the eleventh century were adaptations of ideas developed elsewhere. In all likelihood the windmill was a Persian invention; the spinning wheel, a Chinese invention; the Europeans learned how to use the compass from the Arabs; gunpowder, in all probability, was a Chinese invention.

Europe always proved extraordinarily receptive, and the enthusiastic curiosity of a Marco Polo is evidence of this open-minded attitude. But this is not the whole story. From the twelfth century onward, western Europe developed an original inventiveness which manifested itself in a rapid crescendo of new ideas. Spectacles, the mechanical clock, artillery, new types of sailing ships and new navigational techniques, together with a thousand other innovations big and small, were the original product of European experimental curiosity and imagination. It must also be noted that when Europe absorbed new ideas from outside, it did not do so in a purely passive and imitative manner, but often adapted them to local conditions or to new uses with distinct elements of originality. The Persian windmill was built with a vertical axis. The windmill that spread throughout Europe, the type we know today, with great sails and a horizontal axis, was a much more efficient machine than the original conceived by the Persians. Though the Chinese invented gunpowder, they used it mostly for fireworks. The adoption of gunpowder by Europeans was accompanied by the manufacture of firearms, the construction of which rapidly improved, so much so that, at the beginning of the sixteenth century, when the Europeans arrived in China aboard their galleons, the Chinese were astounded and terrified by western guns. Paper was invented in China, and its manufacture spread to the Muslim Empire in the course of the eighth century, probably after the Arabs conquered the city of Samarkand in AD 753. In about AD 793 the first paper factory was set up in Baghdad and by AD 1000 bound books made of paper circulated widely in different parts of the Muslim Empire. The Byzantines, typically conservative, never learned how to manufacture paper. The Europeans learned the technique during the thirteenth century. The appearance of the first paper factories at Xátiva and at Fabriano represented the transplantation into Europe of an idea born elsewhere. But while the production of paper outside Europe remained at the level of manual production, it is typical that, in the West, the pulp was processed by machines driven by water mills. Printing was invented by the Chinese, but by the end of the twelfth century the Europeans had turned it into an extremely efficient mass production process.

One of the original features of western technological development after the twelfth century was the increasing emphasis placed on the mechanical aspects of technology. There was a real passion for the mechanization of all productive processes. In the Forez by 1251, there existed a mill to grind mustard, and by the end of the Middle Ages mechanical clockwork had been successfully applied to the roasting of meats. The basic reason for this attitude is not easy to grasp. One may argue that the shortage of labor brought about by repeated epidemics favored the adoption of labor-saving devices, but a phenomenon by its nature so complex can scarcely be reduced to naïve and simplistic determinism.

Necessity explains nothing; the crucial question is why some groups respond in a particular way to needs or wants which in other groups remain unformulated and unfilled. The case of the mechanical clock is particularly instructive.

From earliest antiquity man had created a variety of devices to solve the problem of measuring time. The sundial was the first solution, followed by the *clepsydra*, or water clock. Occasional use was also made of sticks of combustible material (incense or wax), properly calibrated, which marked the passage of time while burning. The Europe of the Dark Ages inherited these techniques without adding new ones. But at least from the thirteenth century onward, there were people in Europe who sought a mechanical solution to the problem. In 1271, Robertus Anglicus reported such efforts but acknowledged that the solution had not yet been found. A few decades later, however, mechanical clocks rang the hours on the bell towers of St Eustorgio and St Gottardo in Milan, and of the Cathedral of Beauvais. About the middle of the fourteenth century Giovanni De' Dondi produced a mechanical masterpiece which marked the passing of the days, the months, the years, and the revolutions of the planets.

It is very likely that the mechanical solution to the problem of how to measure time was discovered in northern Italy. It has been argued that the invention of the mechanical clock came in response to the European climate because in winter the water in the clepsydras froze and overcast skies often rendered sundials useless. Such an explanation exemplifies the kind of simplistic determinism criticized above. The earliest mechanical clocks kept time so imperfectly that they had to be continually adjusted, the corrections being made by "clock governors" who turned the hour hand (the minute hand appeared only a good deal later) backward or forward precisely on the basis of sundials and water clocks. The first mechanical clocks cannot there-fore be regarded as substitutes for sundials and water clocks.

Why Europeans produced the mechanical clock is much more subtle. Some years ago P.G. Walker wrote:

Because we see the machine reshaping society and changing man's habits and ways of life, we are apt to conclude that the machine is, so to speak, an autonomous force that determines the social super-structure. In fact, things happened the other way around.... The reason why the machine originated in Europe is to be found in human terms. Before men could evolve and apply the machine as a social phenomenon they had to become mechanics.[23]

The men of the thirteenth century thought of measuring time in mechanical terms because they had developed a mechanical outlook of which mills and bell ringing mechanisms were clear evidence. Clocks spread rapidly throughout Europe, but production was not limited to clock faces, hands, and motors. On public buildings, as in Basel and Bologna, or inside churches, as in Strasbourg and Lund, extremely complicated clocks were constructed. Often, telling the time was almost incidental, accompanied as it was by the revolutions of the stars, and by the movements and pirouettes of angels, saints, and Madonnas. These contraptions were both the result and the evidence of an irrepressible taste for mechanical achievements. This taste took extreme forms during the Renaissance and had practical results. Efforts were directed at replacing factors of production (e.g. labour) that were in short supply while at the same time increasing productivity. In 1402 the managers of the *Fabbrica del Duomo* in Milan studied proposals for a stone-cutting machine which, with the help of a horse (costing 3 shillings a day), would do work for which four men (at a wage of 13½ shillings per man per day) would otherwise be needed. A few years later, the same managers studied the plans for another machine – to transport marble – which was also designed to reduce the labor force normally required.[24]

The constant and generalized preoccupation with machines and mechanical solutions had a duel series of consequences. On the one hand, clear productivity gains were achieved in a number of productive sectors. On the other hand, a cumulative process was set in motion whereby the more the machine was studied the more it reinforced people's mechanical outlook. Books on mechanics proliferated in the course of the sixteenth and seventeenth centuries. More significant than that, a mechanical outlook began to pervade such improbable fields as art and philosophy. While the artists of the Far East delighted in painting flowers, fish, and horses, Leonardo da Vinci and Francesco di Giorgio Martini were obsessed with machinery. Philosophers came to regard the universe as a great piece of clockwork, the human body as a piece of machinery, and God as an outstanding "clockmaker."

If, at the time of the Scientific Revolution, the leading branch of learning was mechanics, if the very characteristic of the Scientific Revolution was, as has been said, the "mechanization of the world view," all this was not a new development unrelated to previous events; on the contrary, it was the logical consequence of a mental outlook which had taken centuries to develop. And we, with our obsession for computers, mechanical gadgetry and mathematical models, represent the final outcome of a centuries-long development.

The dominant theme of the Greco-Roman and the oriental conceptions of the world was that of harmony between man and nature – a relationship that presupposed the existence of irresistible forces in nature to which man was compelled inevitably to submit. The myths of Daedalus, Prometheus, and the Tower of Babel clearly indicated the fate of those who attempted to reverse the man–nature relationship by asserting man's predominance. When the inhabitants of Cnidus asked the oracle of Delphi for its opinion on the timeliness of digging a canal bisecting the isthmus of their peninsula, the oracle replied: "Jove would have created an island instead of a peninsula if that had been his wish." Technological progress was thought likely to bring more or less dubious material benefits but it was also feared as a possible source of dangerous disturbances to existing political, social, and natural equilibria. It might be a force for good but it might equally well turn out to be a force for evil. The position of the Greeks and Romans was to favor the defensive use of *technai* in relation to *technai* itself. This involved caution, restrictions, and fear, and it made the bearers of *techne* socially vulnerable.

The medieval world somehow managed to break with this tradition. Still too technically backward to dominate nature to any appreciable degree, the Europeans of the Middle Ages found refuge in the world of dreams. The "animism" of the ancients and of the orientals was replaced by the cult of the Saints. The saints were not devils or demons; they were men – men in the grace of God, but still men whose features everyone could see on the portals of, or inside, the churches. Their features were like those of all other men. The saints did not recline in the hieratic immobility of oriental holymen, nor did they find amusement like the Greek gods in punishing men for their audacity. On the contrary, they were always at work to overcome the adverse forces of nature: they conquered diseases, calmed stormy seas, saved harvests from storms and locusts, softened the fall for anyone who leapt into a ravine, put out fires, buoyed up the drowning, and guided ships in danger. The saints practiced what the commoners dreamed of: they harnessed nature and, far from being condemned for doing so, they lived pleasantly in Paradise in the company of God. Harnessing nature was not regarded as a sin; it was a miracle. A belief in miracles is the first step toward making them possible. Inadvertently, medieval man moved in the direction of making miracles less the result of the action of saints and more the result of his own actions.

Easy explanations of complex historic phenomena charm people, precisely because they are easy and, therefore, reassuring. The explanation pleases, the problem irritates. And yet the explanation is often unattainable, while the problem remains the only valid thing.

It is tempting to say that the Greco-Roman world failed to develop technologically because there were too many slaves, and that medieval and Renaissance Europe produced notable technological developments in re-action to the scarcity of labor caused by epidemics. But the factors at play were much more numerous and complex. What has been mentioned here, albeit briefly, regarding mental attitudes and aspirations should serve to warn against easy explanations, though it does not pretend to offer alterna-tive solutions. Europe's receptive attitude, the substitution of the cult of the Saints and the faith in miracles for animism, the rise and spread of a mechan-ical outlook – these and similar things are not explanations but only problems in a wider and more intricate context. Why *was* western Europe so receptive and favorable to change? Why did medieval Europe obsessively dream of mastering nature? Why was it looking for mechanical solutions? We do not know.

THE SPREAD OF TECHNOLOGY

So far we have referred to western Europe as a single entity, but at various periods some areas were more innovative than others. From the twelfth to the fifteenth century the Italians were in the forefront not only of economic development but also of technological progress. In the sixteenth and seven-teenth centuries this primacy passed to the English and the Dutch. A key focus for analysis, then, is the diffusion of technological innovations from their area of origin to other areas, and the migrations of technicians.[25]

In 1607 Vittorio Zonca published in Padua his *Nuovo Teatro di Machine et Edificii*, which included, among numerous engravings of various contrap-tions, the description of an intricate water-powered machine for throwing silk in a large factory. Zonca's book went into a second edition in 1621 and a third in 1656, and still the details of the mill were considered a state secret. In Piedmont (Italy), where silk production played a major economic role, law regarded "the disclosing or attempting to discover" anything relating to the making of the said engines a crime punishable by death. G.N. Clark has shown that a copy of the first edition of Zonca's book had been on the open-access shelves of the Bodleian Library from at least as early as 1620. Yet it was not until nearly one hundred years later that the English succeeded in building a mill for the throwing of silk, and then only after John Lombe, during two years of industrial espionage in Italy, "found means to see this engine so often that he made himself master of the whole invention and of all the different parts and motions."[26] Critics of this story have pointed out that John Lombe's journey was really unnecessary because the silk-throwing machines could have been constructed with the help of Zonca's

154

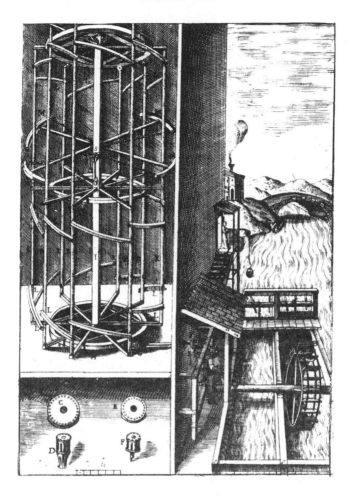

A water-powered throwing mill. Engraving from Vittorio Zonca's *Nuovo Teatro di Machine et Edificii* published in 1607. The machine was used to twist filaments of raw silk into long threads that were strong enough to weave. Master throwers owned the machine, employed eight to ten journeymen, and worked for silk merchants on a piece-rate basis.

book. They are perfectly right when they point out that Zonca's engravings are in fact more revealing than Lombe's own patent specification. But they miss the point. The point is, as Oakeshott wrote:[27]

> It might be supposed that an ignorant man, some edible materials and a cookery book compose together the necessities of a self-moved activity called cooking. But nothing is further from the truth. The

155

cookery book is not an independently generated beginning from which cooking can spring; it is nothing more than an abstract of somebody's knowledge of how to cook: it is the stepchild, not the parent of the activity. The book, in its turn, may help to set a man on to dressing a dinner, but if it were his sole guide he could never, in fact, begin: the book speaks only to those who know already the kind of thing to expect from it and consequently how to interpret it.

Even today, blueprints are considered inadequate to transmit full information, and when a firm buys new and elaborate machinery it sends some of its workers to acquire, directly from the manufacturers, the knowledge of how to operate it. Through the ages, the main channel for the diffusion of innovations has been the migration of people. The diffusion of technology has been mostly the product of migrations of human capital.

Cases of individuals who migrated temporarily in order to acquire information about innovations and to bring it back to their own countries were not unheard of before the Industrial Revolution. Nicolaes Witsen, in a passage quoted below, mentions people who went to Holland to study "economical building in the dockyards." In 1657, John Fromanteel of London went to Holland to learn the art of making pendulum clocks as recently invented by Huygens and made by Coster: on Fromanteel's return his family firm was the first to make pendulum clocks in England.[28] In the second half of the seventeenth century, Dionigi Comollo, from Como, according to his own words, "spent many a year in Amsterdam and other main towns of Holland where, at [his] expense and with great care [he] learned how to make woollens in the way the Dutch had newly developed."[29] In 1684 the Republic of Venice sent Sigismondo Alberghetti, Jr, gunsmith, to England in order to learn the new English technique of casting ordnance.[30] However, there were obstacles to this type of transmission of skills. Especially in fields where economic interests were at stake, communities and guilds were intractably jealous of their technologies and usually sought to prevent their secrets from being divulged.

Innovations spread chiefly through the migration of skilled craftsmen who settled in foreign countries. For the sixteenth and seventeenth centuries there is plenty of literature about the French Huguenots and the Flemish Protestants who brought advanced technologies to England, Sweden, and other parts of Europe and set up new trades. The dramatic story of the religious refugee has such an appeal that one is often inclined to forget that not all migrations of skilled workers and innovations in the sixteenth and seventeenth centuries can be ascribed to religious intolerance. A number of the Walloons who took to Sweden the new techniques of casting iron cannon in the first part of the seventeenth century were Catholic, and they were for a time allowed to retain their faith as well as maintain priests in their communities.[31] Although most of the French clockmakers who moved to London in the course of the seventeenth century were Huguenots, John Goddard, of Portsoken Ward, was known as a "papist."[32] The Swedish and Flemish craftsmen who moved to Russia in the seventeenth century and introduced the technique of casting iron guns were certainly not motivated by religious preoccupations.[33] Paul Roumieu, who reintroduced the art of watchmaking into Scotland, was traditionally supposed to have been one of the refugees driven out of France as a consequence of the Edict of Nantes. It has now been established that he had moved to Edinburgh at least eight years before the persecution of 1685.[34]

This brings us to the question of the forces behind the mobility of skilled labor in preindustrial Europe. As is customary in such cases, one can distinguish between "push" forces and "pull" forces. On the "push" side there was the long, grim list of misfortunes that made life unbearable for the preindustrial craftsman: famines, plagues, wars, taxes, job shortages, and political and religious intolerance. For the average worker life was pretty miserable at best. A small extra dose of misfortune was more than enough to make it unendurable. The attachment of preindustrial workers to a given place was directly proportionate to the quality of their living conditions.

Governments and administrators were perfectly aware of the situation and knew that the loss of able craftsmen had grave consequences for the economy. Decrees forbidding the emigration of skilled workers were quite common in the late Middle Ages as well as in the sixteenth and seventeenth centuries. Special attention was given to certain categories of workers whose activity was considered either essential for the safety of the state or particularly important for the economy. The Venetian government, for instance, strictly prohibited the emigration of caulkers, and from a document of 1460 we learn that a caulker who left Venice risked six years in prison and a 200-lire fine if apprehended.[35] In those days, however, the effectiveness of governmental control was, of necessity, rather tenuous. The repetitious insistence with which the governments issued decrees threatening penalties for workers who fled the country and refused to return provides conspicuous evidence of the inefficiency of control over emigration. Typically enough, impotence bred ferocity. In 1545 and 1559 the Grand Duke of Florence decreed that workers in the brocade trade who had left the town should return to it. Special favors were announced for those who would comply with the order, and penalties were threatened for those who did not. But in all likelihood the results were unsatisfactory: in 1575 the Grand Duke authorized "any person to kill with impunity any of the above-mentioned expatriates" and posted a reward of 200 scudi for each expatriate craftsman who could be brought back "dead or alive."[36]

The circumstances which "pulled" craftsmen into a given area ranged from employment opportunities to political peace or religious tolerance. Quite often there was also a conscious policy on the part of governments.

Administrators not only threatened emigrants but also devised ways to attract foreign craftsmen, especially those who could bring them new industries or new techniques. In the twelfth and thirteenth centuries the champions of the *Drang nach Osten* attracted Dutch peasants into eastern Europe with generous grants of good virgin land. As mentioned above,[37] in 1230–31 the Commune of Bologna (Italy) attracted 150 artisans with their families and assistants, granting them all kinds of privileges and aid in order to develop the woollens and silk industries. In 1442 the Duke Filippo Maria Visconti brought to Milan (Italy) a Florentine craftsman who was supposed to start "some special work of silk." The Duke paid a monthly subsidy, exempted the craftsman and all his employees from tax and waived import duties on all raw materials required by the enterprise.[38] Colbert was generous in granting privileges, land, and titles to Abraham and Hubert (Jr) De Beche, when he invited them to France to set up an iron industry on the model of that of Sweden.[39] On occasion, it was considered legitimate to resort to force, and craftsmen were literally kidnapped. An inquiry by the Bergskollegium in the 1660s into the emigration of Swedish iron masters revealed that a number of workers sailed from Nyköping believing that they were being taken to some other part of Sweden. Instead they were brought to Lübeck, from there to Hamburg, and finally to France, where Colbert was determined to start an iron industry on the Swedish model. A few workers escaped; one of them, Anders Sigfersson, returned to Sweden in 1675.[40]

Of course, it is one thing to lead a horse to water; it is quite another to make it drink. The fact that a person or group of persons with knowledge about an innovation moves into a geographic area does not ensure that the innovation will actually take root in the new environment. It depends on a number of circumstances. The personality of the migrants has to be taken into account as well as their number in relation to the size of the host society. No less important is the nature of the host environment. Many Italian technicians moved to Turkey in the course of the fifteenth, sixteenth, and seventeenth centuries, taking techniques and ideas with them. Yet no appreciable innovations took root in Turkey. The refugees who moved to England, on the other hand, found extremely fertile ground. The Huguenot clockmakers who taught the English the art of clock- and watchmaking, the refugees from the Low Countries who brought the techniques of the "new drapery" to Norwich, the French glassmakers who established the manufacture of window glass in England[41] soon encountered ingenious local imitators who, by pursuing their ideas along original lines, further developed the foreign techniques and opened the way to more innovations. What makes an environment responsive or not is difficult to determine. At first sight the problem of transplanting an innovation into an alien environment might appear to be merely one of introducing new methods of production and the instruments, tools, or machines appropriate to them. But what is really involved is a particular and more profound condition which can be understood and assessed only in human and social terms.[42] This notion was glimpsed centuries ago by the Dutchman Nicolaes Witsen, who wrote in his great treatise on shipping, published in Amsterdam in 1671:

> It is surprising that foreigners, though they may have studied economical building in the dockyards of this country, can never practice it in their own land.... And this in my opinion proceeds from the fact that they are then working in an alien environment and with alien artisans. From which it follows that even if a foreigner had all the building rules in his head, they would not serve him, unless he had learned everything here in this country by experience, and still that would not help him, unless he should find a way to inculcate in his workmen the thrifty and neat disposition of the Hollander, which is impossible.[43]

As good old Nicolaes Witsen observed, it all depends on *disposition*. And this allows one to end this chapter, for a change, on a cheerful note. Down the centuries, those countries where intolerance and fanaticism prevailed lost to more tolerant countries that most precious of all possible forms of wealth: good human minds. The qualities that make people tolerant also make them receptive to new ideas. The influx of good minds and a receptiveness to new ideas were among the main sources of the success stories of England, Holland, Sweden, and Switzerland in the sixteenth and seventeenth centuries.

7

ENTERPRISE, CREDIT, AND MONEY

ENTERPRISE AND CREDIT

Progress in organization and business was an essential component of technological advancement. The *Société du Bazacle*, a stock company formed in the twelfth century in Toulouse for the operation of the mills on the Garonne River, illustrates the close relationship between developments in mechanics and in organization.

From the eleventh century onward there was remarkable development in business techniques. The list of innovations is long: one need only consider the organization of the fairs, the appearance and spread of trading manuals, the evolution of new techniques of accounting, the check, the endorsement, insurance, and so on.[1] From the eleventh to the sixteenth century Italy was the birthplace of most of these innovations. Even the monks took an interest in business: Father Luca Pacioli sent to press in 1494 a famous treatise on accounting, and Father Bernardino da Feltre thought up and organized the *Monti di Pietà*, later to become important credit institutions. After the middle of the sixteenth century, the Dutch and the English took over and further developed business techniques with the establishment of the great trading companies, the first joint stock companies, the stock exchange, and the Central Bank.

I shall not discuss all these innovations in detail, not because they are unimportant, but to avoid boring the reader. I will examine instead the importance of just some of them, especially in regard to saving.

In Europe from the fifth to the eleventh century there were practically no financial mechanisms to facilitate the transformation of saving into investment. Those who saved either invested directly or hoarded, and most loans were for consumption purposes. The economy thus suffered from the deflationary effects of hoarding and from a lack of productive investment. With the growth of cities, credit developed very rapidly in the shape of deferred payments for goods sold – sale credit – which boosted consumption as well as investment (especially with the formation of stocks of raw materials and merchants' inventories).[2] However, a whole series of more sophisticated innovations were introduced to make it easier both to save and to transform saving into productive investment. A typical example is the introduction in the tenth century and the subsequent spread of the *contratto di commenda*.

In the *commenda*, known in Venice as the *collegantia*, Tom gave Dick a sum which Dick then used in business, usually in foreign trade. When Dick came back from his business trip he gave an account of the results to Tom. If there were losses, these were charged against Tom. If there was profit, three-quarters went to Tom and one-quarter to Dick. If Dick had also contributed part of the capital, the profits were divided according to the proportions of capital put up. While Dick was traveling and doing business, Tom stayed at home and did not concern himself with business until Dick's return. Moreover, Tom was not responsible for what Dick did. For every business trip Dick could also collect cash funds from other investors, entering into new relationships similar to that which he had with Tom. The more partners he found the more he could increase his business turnover and, therefore, the greater the potential for profit, which was reaped not only by him but also by his partners.

Jurists have discussed at length whether the *commenda* was a form of partnership or rather a kind of loan. These questions are of no interest here. More interesting are the consequences of the spread of such contracts. To understand these, it is worth examining the environment in which such contracts were drawn up.

Picture a maritime city of the twelfth, thirteenth, or fourteenth century. When the season is set fair the merchants prepare for a voyage. They need financial means to buy the goods which they will try to sell in far-off markets, and they need other financial means to use abroad, combined with revenue from their sales, to buy goods to bring back home. There is, therefore, a strong demand for liquid funds. Generally the merchants have their own funds available, but if they manage to increase their liquid assets they can increase the volume of their business, with obvious advantages; moreover, if they manage to involve other individuals in the enterprise, they can spread the risks. At this point the merchants advertise their business trip. In the square, or near the harbor, there are notaries. Anyone who holds savings and does not want to leave them lying under the bed can contact the merchants and draw up a *contratto di commenda*.

The important point to make about this arrangement is that it enabled not only institutional dealers but also ordinary members of society – with cash funds – to play a role in the process of production. In a number of respects the spread of the *commenda* had the same effects as the establishment of a stock exchange. Small as well as large savings could be put to use – the few shillings of the widow and the craftsman as well as the bags of gold and silver coins of the rich man. The following contract was drawn up in Genoa

(Italy) on 22 December 1198 between two merchants and a number of humble people who were prepared to invest their savings in a trading expedition:

> We, Embrone of Sozziglia and Master Alberto, acknowledge that we carry in *accomandatio* for the purpose of trading £142 Genoese to the port of Bonifacio and through or in Corsica and Sardinia; and from there we are to come [back]. And of this [sum], £25 Genoese belong to you, Giordano Clerico; and £10 to you, Oberto Croce. And to you, Vassallo Rapallino [belong] £10; and to you, Bonsignore Torre, £10. And £5 [belong] to Pietro Bonfante; and to you Michele, tanner [belong] £5; and to you, Giovanni del Pero, £5; and to Ara Dolce, £6; and to Ansaldo Mirto, £5; and to Martino, hemp-seller, £5; and to Ansaldo Fanti, £8; and to you, Lanfranco of Crosa, £20; and to Josbert, nephew of Charles of Besançon, £10. And £6 belong to me, Embrone; and £2 to me, Alberto. And all the pounds mentioned above are to be profitably employed and invested, and they are to draw by the pound. And we promise to send [back] the capital and the profit which God shall have granted from this *accomandatio* [to be placed] in the power of the aforesaid persons to whom they belong. And after deduction of the capital we are to have one fourth of the profit; but the [entire] profit which comes to our [own] pounds is to be ours.[3]

A telling example of the lure and opportunities provided by the *commenda* is offered by the peculiar story of two clergymen in the early years of the four-teenth century. Giovanni Mauro di Carignano, rector of a church near the main pier in Genoa's harbor, leased to merchants part of his church as well as the adjacent graveyard, where they stored sails, riggings, and other shipping tackle. When Porchetto Spinola, Genoa's archbishop, arrived on 21 November 1314, to investigate this peculiar use of church premises, he was lured into a *commenda* contract with a Genoese merchant heading for France.[4]

By the fourteenth century, things were beginning to change. Trade was becoming a routine activity and the traditional itinerant merchant was giving way to the sedentary businessman operating through agents. As a result, the *commenda* soon became an outdated form of partnership. As Professor Kedar has shown, the vast collection of surviving Genoese notarial documents clearly demonstrate that the decline of the *commenda* in Genoa began in the latter part of the thirteenth century and accelerated during the second half of the fourteenth. By the fifteenth century the *commenda* was quite a rare arrangement.[5] In its place the *compagnia* emerged as the most frequent form of partnership.

In maritime cities, the *compagnia* sometimes represented a stage in the development of the general partnership company. By the early part of the twelfth century, Venice already counted several such companies. Yet this form of association never really took hold in coastal cities. André Sayous has accounted for this by emphasizing the risk factor: there was limited appeal in staking all one's assets on the voyage of a ship that might fall into the hands of pirates or capsize and sink. It made more sense to risk a limited amount of money or merchandise through a negotiator. Conditions were different inland where strong links quickly formed between commerce and manufacturing. Business had to be organized over a longer time frame – longer in any case than a ship's voyage out and back. So it was in inland areas that companies grew best, often grafted on to that other still sound institution – the family. At first, companies consisted of family members living under the same roof who pooled their assets, i.e. family capital. In these circumstances, limitless liability was the rule, given that the father was answerable for the son, the son for the father, and the brothers for one another. Things got more complicated when it came to dividing out inherited assets and when the volume of business expanded. The means required soared beyond the reach of any single family.

The response to this problem was to extend access to the company first to more distant family members, then to outsiders, and finally even to shareholders. As Professor Sapori has written,[6] the involvement of shareholders unrelated to the original family marked the end of the first phase in the history of the company. It was a development that coincided with a general loosening of family ties. As long as companies had operated with nothing but family capital, they had concentrated on trading activities. But once they were operating increasingly with deposit capital, their activities broadened out to cover a mix of banking, commerce, and manufacturing that inevitably exposed them to greater risks and to major insolvencies. This trend was compounded by the spread of bills of exchange, in theory a mechanism for transferring money from one market to another. In practice, however, bills of exchange became the preferred means of money-lending and speculation,[7] helping to make capital highly liquid and internationally mobile.

Thus far we have concentrated on developments in the Mediterranean region. But during the Middle Ages, the Hanseatics in the north also made considerable progress in business techniques. The story of their forms of partnership – the *sendeve*, the *vera societas*, the *contrapositio*, and the *complete partnership* – parallels southern European developments.[8] A great step forward was made toward the end of the thirteenth century by the institution of business registers whose entries were publicly authenticated. The recording by merchants of their debts and contracts with a municipal guarantee was a decisive factor in the development of credit and commerce in northern Europe during the fourteenth and fifteenth centuries. The Hanseatics, however, lagged behind the Italians in their degree of sophistication in business administration. Double-entry bookkeeping remained unknown in the north until the sixteenth century and the Hanseatics became familiar with the bill of exchange only through Italians operating in

Flanders and England. To the north of the Alps no other country attained the sophistication of the Italians in business techniques and company accounting. In the first half of the sixteenth century Matthäus Schwarz, head of accounting at the mighty Fugger company, wrote: "book-keeping . . . was invented by the Italians. But this art is little appreciated by us Germans and especially by those who think they can make do without it."

The extraordinary growth of overseas trade and the related expansion in the demand for capital during the course of the sixteenth and seventeenth centuries favored the emergence in England, Holland, and France of a network of trading companies to which a monopoly was granted by their respective national authorities in their specific areas of operation. In England, the Muscovy Company, founded in 1553, was followed by the Spanish Company in 1577, the Eastland Company in 1579, the Levant Company in 1581, and many others. The East India Company was created in 1600 with the subscription of £30,000 to finance the initial sailings and it was destined to become the most famous of all. Most of the companies took the form of joint-stock companies, thus creating the beginnings of a market for stocks and shares.

Economic development depends on the creation of an economic surplus as well as on the transfer of such surplus from "savers" to "producers" when and where the latter could invest such resources most productively. Moreover, in societies suffering from chronic shortages of capital, the availability to the producers of even marginal amounts of savings is of utmost importance. The appearance and dissemination of the business techniques mentioned above has to be seen in this light. The basic fact in the economic history of Europe from the eleventh century onward was that savings were activated for productive purposes to a degree inconceivable in previous centuries.

The story had an ethical aspect also. The development and spread of the *contratto di commenda,* as that of other partnership contracts, would not have been possible without the precondition of a spirit of mutual trust and a sense of honesty in business. The merchant to whom others entrusted their savings could easily have disappeared with the capital or cheated in business conducted in far-off markets where none of his associates had any control. But if the trader showed himself to be dishonest, after a while no one would entrust their savings to him. It was this widespread sense of honesty, strengthened by the sense of belonging to an integrated community, quite apart from clearcut legal provisions, which made possible the participation of all kinds of people with their savings in the productive process. The development of civil and criminal legislation regarding commercial activities should also be considered from this point of view and should be included among the institutional factors which encouraged development.

MONETARY TRENDS

At the start of the eleventh century, as the economy developed so did the monetary system.

Medieval and Renaissance Europe only had metal coinage. The Chinese – as Marco Polo enthusiastically noted – had paper money as early as the thirteenth century. Yet, unlike many other Chinese inventions, this particular innovation was not exported to contemporary Europe.

Metal money is valued in relation to two parameters: weight and fineness. Weight was determined prior to each new coinage by monetary authorities who would specify how many coin pieces were to be struck from a given weight of metal which, depending on the area in question, might be a pound or a mark. In the case of gold coins, fineness was measured in carats. Twenty-four carat gold was absolutely pure, i.e. 24/24. The gold *ecu* of King Francis I of France, struck in July 1519, was 23 carat, that is to say twenty-three parts gold to one part copper. Silver fineness was defined in several parts of Europe in terms of *denari* (weight) and grains (weight) per ounce (weight). By definition, there were 12 *denari* in an ounce and 24 grains in a *denarius*. An eleven *denari* fineness meant, in modern terms, a fineness of 916.66 thousandths (11:12 = $\times$:1000).

By multiplying weight by fineness one obtains the fine content of the metal coin. Thus a silver coin weighing 1.76 grams at a fineness of 950/1000 would have a content of $1.76 \times 950/1000 = 1.67$ grams of pure silver.

The content of pure precious metal determines the intrinsic value of a coin. The extrinsic value is the nominal value of the coin, i.e. the exchange value that is attributed to it. The nominal value and the intrinsic value did not usually coincide and the difference was accounted for by the production costs and by "seigniorage," i.e. the tax levied on coinage.

During the Middle Ages and Renaissance, the monetary system progressed considerably.

Between 781 and 795 Charlemagne had managed to introduce throughout his vast empire a monetary reform that his father Pippin had launched and that King Ethelbert of Kent and then King Offa of Mercia had extended to their kingdoms in the British Isles. In its final stage the reform replaced all other coins with a single legal tender, the silver *denarius*. This coin had to be of almost pure silver, i.e. 950/1000 fineness. The weight of the coins was determined as follows: 240 pennies were struck from one pound weight of silver at a fineness of 950/1000. In terms of our modern decimal system, this meant that each coin had in theory to weigh 1.76 grams (see Table 7.1) and have a content of pure silver of 1.64 grams ($= 1.76 \times 950/1000$).

Obviously such a monetary system, relying on only one coin, with no multiples or fractions, was very primitive. One only has to imagine what it would be like if today there were nothing but one-dollar notes in circulation

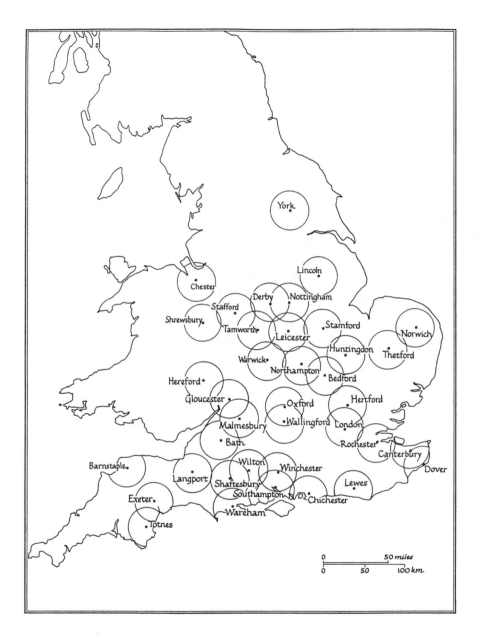

English mints, Athelstan to 973. The circles are of 15-mile radius (24 kilometers) to show the areas within market distance of a mint.

Source: Spufford, *Money and Its Use*, p. 88.

English mints, 973–1066.

Source: Spufford, *Money and Its Use*, p. 89.

A mint at work during the Middle Ages. The person in the center of the picture is beating a sheet of metal to reduce it to roughly the desired thickness. The person on the left is using a large pair of scissors to cut the sheet into small disks of roughly the desired size. The person on the right has placed one of these metal disks between two minting dies (one held in the hand, the other sunk in the block of wood). He is about to bring his hammer down on the upper die in order to produce a coin bearing the desired picture. As can be seen, minting was a very primitive process. It was not until the sixteenth century that the Germans invented a way to mechanize the process involving water-driven mills.

in the US. The situation could be tolerated in early medieval times because transactions were few and far between, most of them took the form of barter, and there were many goods (gems, horses, weapons, wheat, clogs) that were used in the place of cash.

From the second half of the tenth century onward, in response to a growing demand for money, the situation became increasingly unsatisfactory. New mints were built all over Europe. In England, every mint in the

Barter and the exchange of money were often combined. The miniature reproduced
here portrays two peasants who are trading a pair of shoes for a pigeon. The shoes,
however, were clearly worth more than the pigeon and the peasant who wants the
shoes is about to hand over a coin as well as a pigeon.

kingdom struck coins in accordance with standards (fineness and weight)
stipulated by the king or by his officers. So although many new mints were
founded, this did not result in a plethora of competing currencies. Things
turned out differently on the continent. In Italy and Germany, where the
central (imperial) power was conspicuously feeble, each individual town or

prince that possessed the legal right to strike coins proceeded to do so, with the result that both countries were quickly swamped with money of all possible weights and alloys. The situation in France was midway between these two extremes. When Hugh Capet ascended the throne (987), French monarchs, like other feudal barons, still struck coins of only local value and circulation. King Philip Augustus (1180–1223) managed to change this situation. While allowing local barons and cities to continue striking their own coin, Philip introduced two overarching monetary systems under royal control: the system of the *parisis denarius* for the eastern part of the kingdom and the system of the *tournois denarius* for the western part. King Louis IX (1266–70) then proclaimed the principle that "the baron's coin might circulate exclusively within the borders of the barony whereas the king's coin shall circulate throughout the entire Kingdom."

Mints had to comply with the standards of weight and fineness stipulated by the authorities to which they were accountable (king, city, or baron) but the volume of coin struck was determined by the market, i.e. by the amount of metal that private citizens chose to bring to the mint. A private citizen (normally a moneychanger, a banker, or a merchant) would bring metal to the mint. The mint would then strike money from this metal, following weight and alloy standards currently in force. From the amount of coin struck, the mint would take a cut to cover its own working expenses and another cut by way of "seigniorage" or tax. The remaining money would then be handed over to the citizen who had brought the metal to the mint. To express this mathematically:

$$M = P + (C + S)$$

where M is the entire amount of money coined from the metal brought to the mint, P is the amount of money handed over to the person who brought the metal to the mint, C is the amount of money taken to cover the mint's costs of production and S is "seigniorage." Self-evidently, P was also the market price for metal.

As time passed, money was gradually debased, with each denomination of coin tending to contain a steadily diminishing amount of noble metal. The exception to this rule was provided by gold coins, such as the gold florin from Florence and the gold ducat from Venice, both of which served as international means of payment. There were two main reasons for debasing the currency: (a) to increase the state's revenue from taxation on coinage; (b) to respond to monetary requirements. The latter could vary in nature. The authorities might for example decide on devaluation in order to cope with changes in the market ratio between gold and silver or in an attempt to offset a balance of payments deficit. But most often the objective was to increase the amount of money in circulation.

At first sight, all that was needed to increase revenues from taxing coinage was to increase S (seigniorage). But if S was increased while leaving

C and M unchanged, P would be squeezed. A drop in P, the price paid to whoever brought metal to the mint, would soon restrict the flow of metal to the mint and result in a fall in S rather than an increase. If monetary authorities wished to increase the tax revenue from S, they therefore had to find a way of increasing P. Since C (production costs) could not be significantly reduced, the only way to increase both S and P was to increase M, the amount of coins struck from a fixed amount of metal. In other words, they had to devalue the currency.

But devaluations could also have monetary causes. It should be borne in mind that throughout the Middle Ages, western Europe suffered from an inadequate supply of precious metals. This shortage is vividly illustrated by the fact that medieval coins were always wafer-thin discs of metal. If the monetary authorities wished to increase the amount of money in circulation, they had to find a way of attracting citizens to bring metal to their mint rather than to a competing one. The way to do this was to increase P, the price paid for the metal. Unless S was to be proportionally cut (a course rarely chosen), and since C could not be substantially reduced, any increase in P necessarily entailed an increase in M – more coins from the same amount of metal – devaluation once again.

Devaluation might also be, as it were, involuntary. Even without any help from coin-clipping fraudsters, metal coins in circulation wore down at a rate of between 0.1 and 1 percent a year. This confronted monetary authorities with a tricky problem. If they continued to strike coins without altering either their weight or their fineness, before long the new coins would vanish from circulation, following Gresham's law that bad money (the coins in circulation) chases out good (the newly minted coins). They might of course withdraw worn coins from circulation and replace them with new ones, though this would be hard to do and very costly. The solution adopted most frequently was to bring newly minted coins into line with already circulating coinage by issuing debased coins.

Of all western European countries, England distinguished itself by the relative stability of its coinage. English mints (the most important of which was at the Tower of London) remained under the strict control of the Crown. English monarchs, on the other hand, were strongly conditioned by the feudal barons who, since they did not manage the mints themselves, had everything to lose and nothing to gain from any debasement of the coinage. Around AD 800, the English pound was worth approximately 330 grams of pure silver. By the mid-thirteenth century, its value had only fallen to 324 grams. By 1500 it had dropped gradually to 170 grams. The real collapse of the coinage occurred between 1542 and 1551 and was a result of Henry VIII's imperious and extravagant ways.

In France the monetary system introduced by King Louis IX (1266–70) gained a place in French memories as "la bonne monnaie de Monsieur Sainct Loys." And indeed the system inaugurated by "St Louis" survived intact for several decades. It was in the time of Philip the Fair (1285–1314) or, to be precise, in the 1290s that the French currency became unstable. From then on, it was subject to a whole series of frantic and drastic devaluations and revaluations. The main reason for this instability was the Hundred Years' War. The most calamitous periods occurred during the reigns of Philip VI of Valois (1328–50), John the Bountiful (1350–64), and Charles VII (1422–61). During John the Bountiful's reign, monetary changes came so thick and fast that one noted numismatist (Jean Lafaurie), when he came to publish his classic survey of coinage under the kings of France, decided against any attempt at reconstructing the helter-skelter series of mintings during that reign. It was in 1395, in the middle of that monetary storm, that Nicola Oresme published his treatise on coinage. Oresme advanced the thesis – then quite revolutionary – that a country's coinage did not belong to the king and that it was improper for the rulers to resort to monetary juggling as a means of taxing the people.

In 1266 the *tournois* had a par value of about 80 grams of fine silver. By 1450 this had fallen to 30 grams and to about 20 grams by 1500. Although interesting, these figures hide more than they reveal. The fact is that between 1290 and 1438 the history of French currency was, as was mentioned above, one of frequent indeed often feverish devaluations followed by equally drastic revaluations. To give a rough idea of the prevailing state of chaos, one has only to mention that between 1350 and 1360 the *tournois* underwent no less than 71 alterations in both directions (devaluation and revaluation) and between 1422 and 1438 it underwent 52 such changes. For many years any average of the par value of the *tournois* would be almost meaningless, so fast and furious were the alterations to which it was subjected. The placid and gentle course traced by the English currency decade after decade offered a dramatic contrast to the leaping and diving of the French coin. It is hard to say why the French stubbornly insisted on pushing through such drastic revaluations after unsettling the market with as many drastic devaluations: what is certain is that the economy suffered not a little from this spate of alternating inflationary and deflationary shocks (analogous to the stop and go of modern monetary policies).

The monetary situation in Italy was quite different from that in either England or France. In the long run, the Italian currency was debased just as much if not more than the French one: but the downward curve in Italy was gentler, free of the convulsive surging and plunging of the French currency. Table 7.1 gives an overall picture of the long-term devaluation in the four major Italian city states.

Many historians hold stubbornly to the conviction that currency devaluations in medieval and Renaissance Europe were unqualified disasters and the source of economic distress and disorder (e.g. ch. 13, "The scourge of debasement," in P. Spufford, *Money and its Uses*). This is worse than simplistic: it is wrong. As indicated above, a distinction has to be drawn between

Table 7.1 Equivalent of the local monetary unit (lira) in terms of pure silver in four major Italian city states

Year	Florence	Genoa	Milan	Venice
800			390	
950			279	
1200				20
1250	35.0	70.0		
1300	19.0			
1350	11.1			
1400	9.0	21.2	22.4	8.6
1408	9.0		19.3	8.3
1425	8.8			7.6
1452	8.8		12.0	6.6
1474	6.9		9.6	6.9
1493	6.6		8.9	6.2

devaluations for tax purposes, designed to increase treasury revenue, and devaluations designed to increase the amount of money in circulation. Yet this distinction is not always quite so clearcut. In some cases a decision to devalue would be taken under the combined pressure of fiscal and monetary considerations. Besides, given the institutional environment and the economic conditions in which mints had to operate, the maintenance of monetary stability was by no means always the best recipe for sustaining productive activity. The consequence of measures taken to protect the stability of silver and petty coinages was to discourage any further minting for considerable periods. This in its turn starved the domestic market of means of payment.

The Carolingian system, as has been mentioned, involved only one denomination, the *denarius*. This might work well in a primitive economy and society where there was very little trading activity and where barter was very widespread. By the eleventh century, however, the European economy was growing in complexity and a monetary system restricted to a single denomination became increasingly cumbersome. To make matters worse, the coinage was steadily debased. In thirteenth-century Venice, the *denarius* withered to a wretched little disk barely a centimeter in diameter and weighing only 0.08 grams. It was so light it would float and so thin and fragile that if you weren't careful it would break in your fingers. It is not clear why the Venetian *denarius* had so quickly fallen into such a sorry state. The Venetians had probably sought to attract to their city the metal produced in the silver mines of central Europe by increasing the price they paid for metal and, as has already been emphasized, this entailed a debasement of the currency. Venice badly needed silver in order to buy oriental products in the markets of the Middle East and if that meant debasing their currency, Venice was ready to do that. Venice, however, seems to have been an extreme case, even if matters were not much better elsewhere. In Genoa, by the year 1200, the *denarius* had been whittled down to a flimsy disk weighing a mere 0.28 grams. It was at this point that the first major reform of the system was introduced. It seems that the crusaders who had arrived in northern Italy to take part in the fourth Crusade brought with them considerable amounts of silver for the purchase of ships, victuals, and the hiring of mariners. Be that as it may, around the year 1200 in Genoa and Venice, multiples of the *denarius* were struck. These were silver coins called *grossi* ("big ones"), whose fine content recalled Charlemagne's *denari*. The Genoese *grosso* weighed 1.7 grams and was worth 6 of the old local *denari*, now known as *piccioli* ("small ones"). The Venetian *grosso* weighed 2.2 grams and was worth 26 of the small local *piccioli*. There must have been a pressing need for these new coins, for their popularity was immediate and mints both in Italy and abroad soon took to striking *grossi*.

The arrival on the scene of the *grossi* signaled a new phase in which multiples of the old *denarius* quickly proliferated. In quick succession there appeared the *treina* (3*d.*), the *quattrino* (4*d.*), the *sesino* (6*d.*), and the pieces of one *soldo* (12*d.*), two *soldi* (24*d.*), three *soldi* (36*d.*), and five *soldi* (50*d.*).

The magic moment, however, came in 1252 when Florence and Genoa, almost simultaneously, issued a heavy pure gold coin weighing roughly 3.5 grams. This master stroke broke the centuries-old Carolingian monometallic (silver) system and cleared the way for a bimetallic system. Florence's golden florin soon became the internationally preferred means of exchange and payment. Across Europe a series of more-or-less successful attempts were made to follow the Florentine and Genoese example by striking gold coins (see Table 7.2). Strangely enough, Venice was slow to follow the lead set by Florence and Genoa: the Venetian gold coin, the ducat, did not make its appearance until 1284. The Venetians may have been wary about creating a coin in competition with their silver *grosso* which had met with such an enthusiastic reception in the Orient. Besides, Venice was the preferred market for German silver.

Silver *grossi* and gold pieces too were very slim coins. As has already been pointed out, throughout the Middle Ages, Europe suffered from an inadequate supply of precious metals. This situation, however, began to change by the mid-fourteenth century. During their exploration of the African coast, the Portuguese had come upon regions rich in gold such as Guinea and the Gold Coast (now Ghana). Gold from these areas had traditionally been transported in caravans across the Sahara to north African ports and from there shipped to Europe. Shortly after the arrival of the Portuguese in Guinea and the Gold Coast, the trans-Saharan caravan trade was disrupted and increasing quantities of gold started to arrive in Europe aboard Portuguese caravels. It is significant that in 1457 the Portuguese

174

launched their own gold coinage by striking a coin, the *cruzado*, using gold from Guinea.

At about the same time, fresh developments were taking place in Germany. Rich deposits of silver were discovered in the Tyrol and in Saxony. The production of Tyrolean silver at Schwaz tripled between 1470 and 1490 and the output at Schneeberg in Saxony rose from a few hundred marks in 1450 to several thousand marks by 1470. A considerable proportion of this silver found its way onto the markets of Venice and Milan, with which southern Germany had particularly intense trading relations. In 1472 the mint of Venice and two and a half years later the mint of Milan struck silver coins that broke with the medieval tradition in two respects. Firstly, in terms of their artistic appearance, the new Venetian coin bore a portrait of the doge Tron and the new Milanese coin that of Duke Galeazzo Maria Sforza. In both cases, the portrait was perfectly realistic and bore the clear marks of Renaissance artistry. In more concretely monetary terms, both coins were quite different from the wafer-thin coins of the medieval period. They were chunkier, heavier, and contained more silver. The new Venetian coin weighed 6.52 grams and had a fineness of 948 thousandths. The new Milanese coin weighed 9.79 grams with a fineness of 963.5 thousandths. Such standards contrasted sharply with those of the various *grossi* then in circulation, whose weight, at most, was around 2 grams. Owing to the head-and-shoulders portraits on the head side of these coins, the coins themselves came to be known as *testoni* ("big heads"). Quick to find favour among merchants, coins of this new type soon appeared in France and the Low Countries (see Table 7.2, section 4).

The rush towards chunky and heavy coins did not stop at the *testoni*. In 1486, Archduke Sigismund of the Tyrol, elated by the discovery of silver deposits on his territory, struck a silver coin called a *guldiner* weighing about 31.9 grams. In Bohemia, from 1519 onwards, using silver from the valley of St Joachims (nowadays known as Jachymov), Stefan and his seven brothers, all of whom were counts of Sclick and, as such, owners of the mines, struck silver coins weighing roughly 28.7 grams and known as thalers.

These Portuguese and German developments were a mere foretaste of the huge Spanish-American adventure about to unfold. From the first years of the sixteenth century and at a gathering pace after the mid century, Spanish fleets brought back to the European continent fabulous amounts of gold and above all silver. It was then that there appeared a silver coin, struck in Spain or in Mexico or in Peru and known as the *Real de a ocho* (piece of eight realos), weighing 30 grams and with a fineness of roughly 930 thousandths. The *Real of Eight* (or Piece of Eight as it was often called) quickly became by far the most important coin in international trade and finance throughout the sixteenth and seventeenth centuries. We shall return to this remarkable story in Chapter 9.

Table 7.2 Equivalent of the local monetary unit (pound) in grams of pure silver

		Date (a)	Weight (b)	Fineness/ 1000 (c)	Intrinsic fineness (d) = b.c	Nominal value (e)
Section 1	Silver denari:					
	Charlemagne	800	1.76	950	1.67	1d.
	Otto	c. 970	1.40	830	1.16	1d.
	Venice	c. 1200	0.36	250	0.09	1d.
Section 2	Silver grossi:					
	Genoa	c. 1200	1.7	960	1.6	6d.
	Venice	c. 1200	2.2	965	2.1	26d.
	France (grosso tournois)	1266	4.22	958	4.04	12d. tour.
	Naples (carlino)	1278	3.3	934	3.1	
	England (groat)	1279	5.77	925	5.34	4d.
		1351	4.67	925	4.32	
	Bohemia (groschen)	1300	3.6	932	3.4	
Section 3	Gold:			fineness/24		
	Genoa (genovino)	1252	3.52	24	3.52	20s.
	Florence (florin)	1252	3.53	24	3.53	18g.
	Venice (ducat)	1284	3.56	24	3.56	
	France (ecu)	1266	4.196	24	4.196	10s. tour.

Portugal	(cruzado)	1457	3.58	23.75	3.54	225 (?) reals
Spain	(excelente)	1497	7.0	23.75	6.85	375 maravedis
England	(gold penny)	1257	3.85			
	(noble)	1344	8.97	24	8.97	80d.
	(noble)	1346	8.33	24	8.33	80d.
	(noble)	1351	7.78	24	7.78	80d.
Hungary	(florin)	1326	3.56	23.8	3.53	
Germany	(Rhenish guilders)	1386	3.54	23	3.40	

Section 4 Silver:

fineness/1000

Venice	(testone)	1472	6.5	948	6.16	20s.
Milan	(testone)	1474	9.8	964	9.43	20s.
Southern Low Countries	(testone)	1487	7.2	935	6.73	
France	(testone)	1514	9.6	938	9.00	10s.
Bohemia	(thaler)	1519	28.7			
Spain	(real de a ocho)		30.0	930	27.90	

Table 7.3 Silver outputs from various central European mines:
annual mean outputs in kilograms for years of extant data

Place	Year	Annual output in kg
GERMANY		
Lower Harz Mountains	1510	935
Rammelsberg	1526	2,105
Freiburg	1490	177
	1511–1520	933
	1526–1530	2,100
	1572	7,860
AUSTRIA		
Tyrol: Falkenstein	1486	14,812
Tyrol: other (than Schwaz)	1505	8,851
	1523	15,710
	1530	10,013
Rattenberg	1528	1,503
Carinthia	1528	283
	1550	411
Salzburg	1520	2,250
HUNGARY		
Körmocbanya	1434–1435	660
	1486–1492	3,523
	1528–1549	5,433
Nagybanya	1481–1482	1,800
BOHEMIA		
Kutna Hora (Kuttenberg)	1300–1330	± 30,000
	1330–1350	± 20,000
	1350–1420	± 10,000
	1420–1460	?
	1460–1510	4,500
	1521–1530	2,000
	1531–1540	600
	1541–1550	700
Kasperska Hora (Bergreichenstein)	1536–1543	3,297
Krumau	1520–1521	121
Pribam	1536–1538	347
Elischau-Wilhartitiz	1536–1538	1,127

Source: Munro, "The Central European Silver Mining Boom," p. 167.

Coinage remained by far the most prevalent means of exchange in Europe throughout the whole of the Middle Ages and the Renaissance: as mentioned above, unlike contemporary China, in Europe paper money was unknown. But from the twelfth century onward, in the most developed areas, coinage was increasingly supplemented by money created through

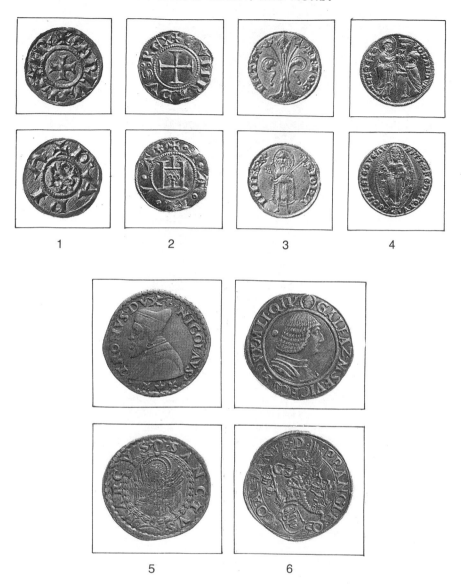

1 The silver penny of Charlemagne; 2, 3, and 4 the main gold coins of medieval Italy, respectively the *genoina* of Genoa, the florin of Florence, and the Venetian ducat; 5 the lira Tron of Venice; 6 the "testone" of Galeazzo Maria Sforza of Milan.

The coin photographs were kindly supplied by the Fitzwilliam Museum, Cambridge.

A *real de a ocho*, known in England and in the English colonies in America under the name of piece of eight. This one was minted at Segovia by Philip IV in 1633. The mint is indicated by the aqueduct on the left of the shield, the value by the figure 8 to the right. The *real de a ocho* was the means of payment *par excellence* in the international trade and financial transactions of the sixteenth and seventeenth centuries. Photograph kindly supplied by Professor P. Grierson and the Fitzwilliam Museum, Cambridge.

banking activity, i.e. by what, in today's economic statistics, appears under the heading of "deposits." For those unversed in economics, the term "deposits" may be somewhat misleading. It might be mistakenly imagined that the term refers to real amounts of cash actually stored at banks. Yet only a fraction of the money defined as "deposits" is physically kept in banks. The bulk of "deposits" is intangible, existing only in bank entries, and is created by bankers according to their willingness to take on "risk." A Florentine chronicler in the sixteenth century wittily referred to such "deposits" as "ink money."

The terms "banks" and "banker" make their first appearance in twelfth- and thirteenth-century notarial cartularies where they refer to money-changers. Given the vast range of coins in circulation at that time, money-changing was an activity of considerable importance in the major markets. Moreover, these bankers and money-changers operated as intermediaries between the public and the mints. By the end of the thirteenth century,

180

money-changers in the main trading markets were no longer willing to confine themselves to the manual exchange of different kinds of metal or to acting as intermediaries between the public and the mints. Instead they began to take deposits and to make payments on behalf of depositors. Deposits thus came to be transferred from one trader to another and these transactions were effected by means of a straightforward entry in the banker's books, thereby avoiding the transportation and handing-over of actual coins. The transfer operation was not conducted on a written order, but rather in the presence of the parties involved. In other words, if Mr Smith wished to make a payment to Mr Brown, the two men would go together to see Mr Jones, the banker with whom Mr Smith had deposited money. Mr Smith would declare to his banker Mr Jones the quantity of money that he wanted to transfer to Mr Brown. Then, in the presence of both Smith and Brown, Mr Jones the banker would enter the transaction in his book, reducing Mr Smith's deposit by the amount in question and increasing Mr Brown's deposit by the same amount. The evidence of the transaction in the banker's books was legally binding. Transfers carried out on written order (i.e. cheques) made their first appearance in Tuscany during the fifteenth century. In Venice, however, such cheques were never accepted and both parties always had to be present when any transfer was effected.

Sometimes a depositor might ask his banker to repay in cash all or part of the sum deposited, or a payee might demand to receive his payment in cash. To cover any such eventualities, bankers always had to hold a certain amount of cash. Over time, however, bankers found that it was not necessary to keep cash sufficient to cover the total value of all deposits: they only needed to have a fraction of that amount to hand and could therefore lend out the rest at interest to third parties or, alternatively, invest directly in trading activities. Bankers realized, in other words, that they could operate on a fractional reserve basis. This is the origin of bank money. Professor Reinhold C. Müller, in an excellent article on Venetian coinage, has shown that as early as 1321 bankers in Venice had created bank money by operating on such a fractional reserve system. Creating money on the basis of deposits received, the bankers increased market liquidity and helped to loosen the deflationary stranglehold that the shortage of precious metal exerted on the European economy throughout the whole of the Middle Ages. Furthermore, the bankers' activity promoted the investment of savings. In England, where monetary circulation was more homogeneous than on the continent and where the public was not confronted with too broad a spectrum of different coinages, there were not many money-changers. The developments outlined above did however occur in England too, though in England it was goldsmiths rather than bankers/money-changers who collected deposits and created money by granting loans on the basis of deposits they had received.

The creation of bank money, as has been said, was on the whole a positive development for the economy. Yet it also entailed some considerable drawbacks. The economy at that time was fragile and panic could spread fast among dealers. Shipwrecks were frequent, wars an everyday occurrence and merchants often fell victim to tricks played by foreign governments. The high risks that traders had to run rebounded on the bankers who loaned them capital. Whenever panic ran through a particular market, people would hurry to the banks to withdraw their deposits. But bankers only kept enough ready cash to cover a fraction of the deposits they had received: the money required to refund all the depositors who might come to the bank to claim their money back simply was not there. It was tied up in the investments and the loans that the bankers had made. In a similar situation today, the central bank can intervene to act as a lender of last resort. But in those days there were no central banks and panic therefore often led to bank failure. The history of banking in the Middle Ages and during the Renaissance is thus a sorry tale of continual bankruptcies. In some of the most important markets interesting attempts were made at remedying this situation. In Venice in 1356 and again in 1374 proposals were made for the establishment of a public bank that would keep reserves equal to 100 percent of its deposits.

In 1587, again in Venice, the *banco della piazza di Rialto* was founded with precisely this purpose. A bank of this kind could still carry out money transfers and assist in making payments but it would not create bank money. In Barcelona in 1401 the *Taula de Barcelona* bank was banned from making loans to private dealers and had to limit its lending activities to making loans to the state. But these were fallback solutions that did nothing to solve the fundamental problem facing banks in their role as money-creators.

8

PRODUCTION, INCOMES, AND CONSUMPTION: 1000–1500

THE GREAT EXPANSION: 1000–1300

The various developments outlined in previous chapters combined to create a vigorous phase of expansion. The spread of new technologies, the growth of towns and cities, a new sociocultural environment, a lively and widespread spirit of optimism, an increased division of labor, the monetarization of the economy, the stimuli to saving: all these factors encouraged economic expansion. What was decisive was no single factor but the particular mix achieved in the context of an altogether peculiar situation.

As already mentioned, until the nineteenth century the development of Europe, like that of any other preindustrial society, was ultimately constrained by the availability of land, because the energy which fed every biological and economic process was at least nine-tenths animal or vegetable in origin.

In the tenth century, when European development began to take off, there was plenty of land available in relation to population and this situation lasted at least until the middle of the thirteenth century. Economists are accustomed to considering situations in which, as new land is gradually brought into cultivation, diminishing returns inevitably follow. The explanation of this phenomenon is that the first areas brought under the plow are supposedly the best and that as expansion progresses, people proceed to till progressively less fertile, marginal lands. Conditions of this kind prevailed in Europe from approximately the middle of the thirteenth century but not before. In fact, paradoxically enough, the expansion of the tenth through twelfth centuries, at least in some parts of Europe, may have been characterized by increasingly marginal returns. In the anarchy of previous centuries, people had often entrenched themselves not where land was best, but where their position was most easily defensible – on the crest of a hill or at the end of a gorge. As population grew and more stable conditions prevailed, some of the new areas taken into cultivation were in fact of better quality and more fertile than those already cultivated.

Internal colonization was accompanied by external expansion. On the

southwestern frontier, the expansionist drive was expressed in the re-
conquest of the Iberian peninsula by the Christian princes. Most of the
peninsula had been taken by the Moors in the early decades of the eighth
century. With the beginning of the new millennium the tide turned.
Impeded by quarrels and dissension among the Christian princes, the
Christian *reconquista* was slow at first but nevertheless made important
progress in northeastern Spain and on the central *Meseta* toward the end of
the eleventh century. It gained momentum in the thirteenth century, when
all but the territory of Moorish Granada was reconquered (see map below).
Lisbon was recaptured by the Christians in 1147, Merida in 1228, Badajoz in
1229, Cordoba in 1236, Valencia in 1238, Murcia in 1243, Seville in 1248,
Cadiz in 1262.

On the southern frontier, between 1061 and 1091, the Normans brought
Arab domination in Sicily to an end, and on the southeastern front, from the
eleventh through the thirteenth centuries, the Crusaders launched a series
of temporarily successful attacks on Arab territories, establishing precarious
Christian potentates in the Middle East.

On the eastern border the German eastward drive (*Drang nach Osten*)
unfolded. This movement was already under way in the early tenth century,

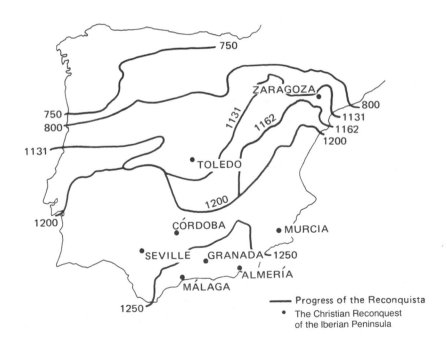

Source: C.T. Smith, *An Historical Geography of Western Europe.*

184

when the Germans conquered the Sorbenland, between the Elbe and the Saale rivers. It gained momentum towards the middle of the twelfth century and reached its height in the first half of the thirteenth century. On the Baltic, beginning in 1186, a German expedition overran Livonia and Courland. In 1231 the Order of the Teutonic Knights embarked on the systematic conquest of East Prussia. To the south of the Baltic, the Germans reached the river Oder in 1240 and over the next fifty years advanced along the Pomeranian coast. Yet further south, the Germans fought their way forward beyond the natural barrier formed by the Erzgebirge and the Sudeten mountains, and German settlement reached its outermost limit in the Oder valley. As the Germans advanced, new cities were founded. Lübeck was founded in 1143, Brandenburg around 1170, Riga in 1201, Mecklenburg around 1218, Wismar in about 1228, Berlin in about 1230, Stralsund around 1234, Danzig in about 1230, Frankfurt on the Oder in 1253.

By 1300 the movement had slowed down considerably, new expansion on a large scale being limited to eastern Pomerania and the territories of the Teutonic knights. The ravages of the Black Death (1348) further dissipated the thrust, and the eastward expansion ceased long before the German defeat at Tannenberg (1401) put an end to German aspirations in Poland for the time being.[1]

The German eastward expansion was demographic, economic, political, and religious in character. Its spirit was well expressed in the coat of arms of one of the baronial families that took part in the movement. The coat of arms showed three heads of decapitated Slavs. Its economic relevance must be seen in the light of the following circumstances. In most of the conquered territories, the Slavic economy was largely based on fishing, fowling, hunting, and stock rearing. Agriculture was poorly developed but the land was very good. In 1108 the Bishop of Bremen thundered: "The Slavs are an abominable people, but their land is rich in honey, grain and birds so that none can compare with it. Go east young men: there you can both save your souls and acquire the best land to live on." German immigrants possessed more advanced agricultural technology as well as more abundant and better capital. They moved into the new territories with the heavy, wheeled plow and with the heavy felling axes which enabled them to clear the thicker forest and cultivate the heavier soils. In this way the German eastward movement rolled back the European farming frontier. Moreover, not only German peasants but also large numbers of German miners moved eastward, and with this process of rural colonization went the founding of new towns (see map on p. 184).

The effect of this movement was felt beyond the boundaries reached by German conquest or even by German migrants. German techniques in mining, agriculture, and trade were progressively adopted in eastern Slavic territories. All these developments created the preconditions for the formation of agricultural surplus in eastern Europe, the development of the

185

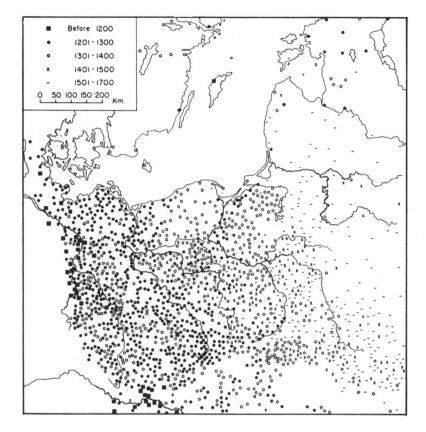

■	Before 1200
•	1201 - 1300
○	1301 - 1400
x	1401 - 1500
-	1501 - 1700

0 50 100 150 200 Km.

The foundation of towns in east central Europe.

Source: R. Kötzschke and W. Ebert, *Geschichte der ostdetschen Kolonisation Leipzig,* 1937.

Baltic trade (Brandenburg began to export grain to England and Flanders around 1250), the growth of the Hanseatic League, and the development of mining and metallurgy in central Europe.

This combination of favorable circumstances made possible a general economic expansion from which everybody in Europe appears to have benefited, though in different degrees. The information available is patchy and imprecise, but through the mist which envelops those distant centuries one can glimpse a situation in which all income levels, profits, wages, and rents, grew in real terms. Interest rates may have been the only exception, perhaps in part because the growth of income made possible greater saving, but also because a series of innovations in business techniques made saving more easily available for both consumption and production.

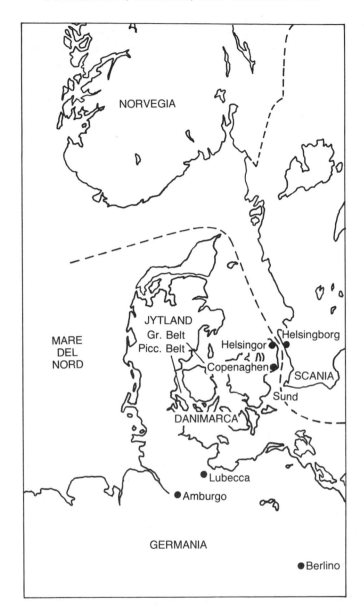

The Danish peninsula, showing the Little Belt, the Great Belt, and the Sund.

Norvegia: Norway	Berlino: Berlin
Danimarca: Denmark	Picc. Belt: Little Belt
Lubecca: Lübeck	Mare del Nord: North Sea
Amburgo: Hamburg	Germania: Germany

Until the Industrial Revolution the European economy remained fundamentally agricultural. But between 1000 and 1300 it was the cities that blazed a trail towards recovery. New towns were founded in every corner of Europe and the existing ones expanded so fast that they were forced at considerable expense to build new walls – in some cases more than once. The building of new city walls entailed a massive investment and a considerable financial sacrifice. Given the volume of public works involved, the multiplier effect must have been very considerable. After the eleventh century, the leading sectors of the economy were (a) international trade, (b) textile manufactures, and (c) building construction. The bulk of international trade, in turn, remained centered upon foodstuffs and spices, and textiles. This list reflects the basic structure of demand which, as we saw in Chapter 1, centered on food, clothing, and buildings.

As there were leading sectors, so there were leading areas. The regions of Europe in the vanguard of medieval economic development were northern Italy, the southern Low Countries and, later on, the towns of the Hansa. Italy capitalized on the Roman tradition of urban life which had been

Florence showing walls of 1173–75 and 1284–1333.

Source: Goldthwaite, *The Building of Renaissance Florence*.

humbled but not totally destroyed in the Dark Ages, and from the proximity of two empires – the Byzantine and the Arab – which, until the twelfth century, were far more highly developed than any area in Europe. The southern Low Countries capitalized on the economic development which the region had experienced during the Carolingian Renaissance. Italy and the Low Countries derived additional advantages from their respective geographical positions: Italy, as a bridge between Europe and North Africa on the one side, and between Europe and Near East on the other; the southern Low Countries as a crossroads of land and sea routes between the North Sea and the Atlantic coastlines of France and Spain, and between England and Italy.

At an early date there developed in the southern Low Countries important woollen manufactures which took advantage of the proximity of the English market where the European wool of the finest quality was produced and exported. Ghent, Bruges, Ypres, Lille, Cambrai, St Omer, Arras, Tournai, Malines, Hondschoote, and Douai were the main centres of this proto-capitalist expansion. Cities were beginning increasingly to specialize and to produce differentiated products: Lille and Douai became famous for blue fabrics, Ghent and Malines for scarlet ones, Ypres and Ghent for black cloth and Arras for lightweight material. Johannes Boinebrooke (d. 1285) was one of the most unscrupulous exponents of this expansion and, thanks to the survival of his will, we are fairly well-informed of his ruthless activities.

In northern Italy, developments were less markedly centred on manu-facturing and more evenly spread over a range of activities: trade, manufac-turing, shipping, and finance. Initially, the vanguard of development occurred in the coastal republics of Pisa, Venice, and Genoa and in a number of cities situated at important crossroads such as Asti, Piacenza, Verona, and Siena. The story of Venice was unique owing to its peculiar geographical position and to the privileged political relations linking it with Byzantium. In approximately 537 Cassiodorus, a minister of Theodoric, gave orders for certain wines, oils, and wheat from Istria to be conveyed by sea to Ravenna. Transportation was entrusted to Venetian sailors. Cassiodorus' letter contains a vivid description of the lagoonal communities and of their way of life which it said was "similar to that of aquatic birds." Until the Dogal residence and the remains of Saint Mark were transferred to Rialto, Venetians made a living principally from fishing, from collecting and milling salt, and from trade and transportation, partly by sea but to a much greater extent along the canals of the lagoon and along the rivers that flowed into it. The main axis of this activity was the river Po. From the tenth century onwards, seafaring activity was greatly extended and intensified. Under Doge Peter II Orseolo (991–1008), Venice crowned a whole series of military–naval expeditions by subjugating the cities of Zara and Trau. By imposing its supremacy on the Dalmatian coast, Venice dealt a severe blow

to the pirates who had settled there and who posed a constant threat to navigation in the Gulf of Venice. In addition to the east–west axis centered on the river Po there developed the increasingly vital north–south axis along which Venice supplied the territories of southern Germany with oriental products and the Near East with such northern products as wood, woollen fabrics, and silver.

Meanwhile other remarkable developments were proceeding apace on the other side of the Italian peninsula. Through piracy and commerce (two activities which were then inextricable), first Pisa and then Genoa developed ever closer relations with North Africa, the Middle East, and Sicily while also taking increasing advantage of opportunities provided by the development of manufacturing in the southern Low Countries. The Flemings, for their part, were searching for southern outlets for their textiles. In 1127 there appears in the documents the first mention of "Lombard" traders (Lombard, in those days, meant "Italian") in Flanders, and at the beginning of the thirteenth century mention is made of Flemish merchants in Genoa. But it did not take long to realize that it would be best to agree on an intermediate place of exchange. The enlightened policy of the counts of Champagne favored the choice of that region as the meeting ground. The fairs of Champagne were held all year round in the towns of Troyes, Bar, Provins, and Lagny. The thirteenth century was the golden century for these fairs which operated as markets and clearing-houses.

Florence was a relatively late developer. The twelfth century was drawing to a close by the time Florentine merchants made their way from Florence and Pisa to more distant markets. A variety of documents show them setting off on the road towards France: Piacenza in 1176, Monferrato in 1178, the Champagne fairs in 1209. By 1250 there were Florentine traders right throughout central and southern Italy, in the Orient, in Provence, at the Champagne fairs, in Scotland and in Ireland. It was a Pope who then declared that Florentines were the fifth element of the Universe.

There is no doubt that the axis linking the southern Low Countries to northern Italy acted as the most important trading channel in the twelfth and thirteenth centuries. This should not however make us neglect or underestimate the other trading channels that radiated from the Low Countries. The cities of Flanders exported a vast range and quantity of woollen goods to the west and especially to Gascony, in exchange for wine, some of which was then re-exported. Running eastwards was the Low Countries–Cologne axis, which was in busy use from the end of the twelfth century onwards. Silver mining in the Goslar region in the tenth century and later in Freiburg (1150–1300) and Freisach (1200–50) in central Europe gave rise to a degree of purchasing power in these areas that helped provide outlets for Flemish products. But the city of Cologne did not allow Flemish merchants to venture any further eastwards since its ambition was to become the main goods sorting centre. However, if Flemish merchants had

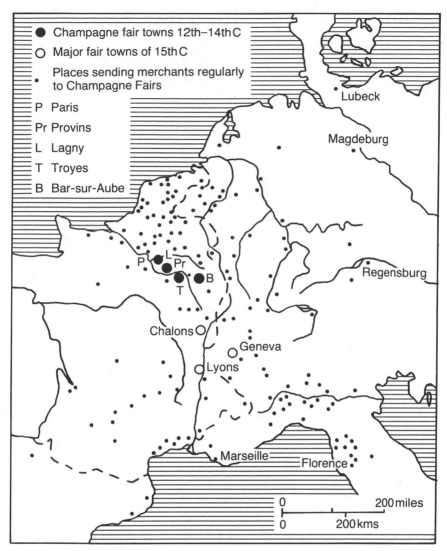

The Champagne fairs and the origins of the merchants attending them.

The fairs were held at four different localities, not far from Paris: Bar, Troyes, Provins, and Lagny. Initially, they were held only at Bar and Troyes where there is a first mention of them in 1144. In 1137–38, the fair of Provins started up and a few years later that of Lagny.

When a fair opened at one of the four localities the other three remained closed. The rotation was organized in such a way that there was always one fair in operation right throughout the year. From January to April, first Bar and then Lagny held a fair. The Provins fair operated in May. In June, the Troyes fair opened. In September, Provins opened again and in October Troyes reopened its fair.

Source: Smith, *An Historical Geography of Western Europe*.

to call a halt at Cologne, their woollens were sold right throughout central and eastern Europe thanks to the efforts of German merchants. As for the north, by the middle of the twelfth century, Flemish merchants had reached the river Weser and Flemish woollen fabrics were available on the Lübeck market. Flemish trade reached a pitch that antagonized the powerful city of Lübeck which at one point in time prohibited Flemish ships from gaining access to the Baltic sea.

Florentine merchants, on the other hand, once they had come into contact with the Flemish textile industry, were not content with buying its products for consumption or re-export. They accordingly began to import "franceschi" (i.e. Flemish) woollens in their untreated state and carried out the dyeing and other finishing processes in Florence, thus depriving the Flemings of part of the added value of the finished product.

Florentine traders in Flemish woollens and Florentine workers employed in the dyeing and finishing processes all belonged to a guild known as the Arte di Calimala. It was one of the most important guilds of Florence, if not the most important one. The woollens guild to which manufacturers of woollen cloth belonged was initially part of the circle of minor guilds. But the complete cycle of woollen production, i.e. from the raw wool stage through to the last finishing processes, developed so fast and so successfully that at a certain point the woollens guild was accepted as one of the major guilds. By about the year 1300, approximately 100,000 woollen cloths were being produced a year in Florence. Demand for raw materials was so great that at this time two hundred English and Scottish monasteries were selling wool to Florentine merchants, and this wool from England and Scotland was supplemented by wool bought by the Florentines in Spain, in southern Italy and in northern Africa. It seems that one of the reasons for the Florentines' success was not only their prevalent use of excellent quality English wool (an advantage that the Flemish manufacturers also enjoyed) but also their mechanization process using the water mill in the fulling of cloths.

The success of Florentine merchants as purchasers of high-quality wool from England must be seen in the light of the position that these merchants had gained as bankers in the British Isles. To grasp this development, one has to consider papal finances. From the second half of the thirteenth century onwards, the financial needs of the Holy See expanded enormously and papal taxes came to weigh very heavily on a huge area stretching from Scandinavia to Sicily and from Portugal to Corfu and Cyprus. Peter's pence and other taxes placed at the disposal of the Holy See sums which in those days were enormous and which had to be gathered in the furthest-flung corners of Europe and then carried back to Rome or taken to those places where the Holy See required cash funds. Nepotism, their geographical position and the fame acquired by Tuscan dealers, meant that successive popes entrusted first Sienese bankers and then above all Florentine merchants with the collection and remittance of these taxes. The Florentines, their hands full of cash, found that it was very hard to resist the temptation to launch into banking operations. Their favorite customers were princes and other such exalted dignitaries. The kind of relations that developed recall those that emerged during the 1950s: bankers in the developed country would make loans to the prince of an underdeveloped country, securing in return not only the payment of substantial interest on the loan, but also the much sought-after export licenses for raw products (in this case wool) for which there was an urgent demand for their own home market. The areas within which this web of commercial, manufacturing, and financial interests was developed furthest included England and the Kingdom of Naples, both suppliers of wool. This network of interests reached its height in the 1270–1300 period in part due to a bitter conflict between the English and the Flemings over wool exports. This was a conflict that the Florentine traders exploited with great skill.

In every corner of Europe events were taking place that tended to promote economic expansion. In the mountainous St Gothard Massif there is a plateau that makes it relatively easy to cross the Alps in that area. But the plateau is cut in two by a gorge that the river Reuss over thousands of years has dug through the rock. This gorge, though only a few meters wide, is extremely deep and absolutely sheer. For centuries the gorge made it impossible to use the plateau for crossing the Alps. Towards the middle of the thirteenth century, however, a brilliant blacksmith or group of black-smiths managed to throw an iron frame which allowed the construction of a bridge made of bricks. It was a feat which in its day was technically miracu-lous and local people, suspecting that the devil had had a hand in it, called it the "bridge of the devil." This bridge made it possible to transport goods from the Po plain to the territory of Zürich and to the Rhine towns, and it became one of the busiest trade routes in Europe. Goods were transported across the Alps by mule as far as Lucerne. At Lucerne they were loaded on to ships and dispatched onward to Zürich or to the Rhine towns.

The busy trade that developed around the St Gothard pass brought considerable benefits to the local Alpine population. At one point they even felt strong enough to rebel against the power of the Hapsburgs. In 1291 in Brunnen the cantons of Schwytz, Uri, and Unterwalden signed a mutual defense pact and this was how the Helvetian Confederation came into being. Lucerne joined the Confederation in 1332, Zürich in 1351, and Berne in 1353.

We do not have adequate data for measuring the long-run quantitative increase in production and consumption in the various regions of Europe. Only a few figures are available. It has been estimated that the value of wares imported and exported by sea and subject to duties in Genoa (Italy) increased more than fourfold between 1274 and 1293. In about 1280 Venice

193

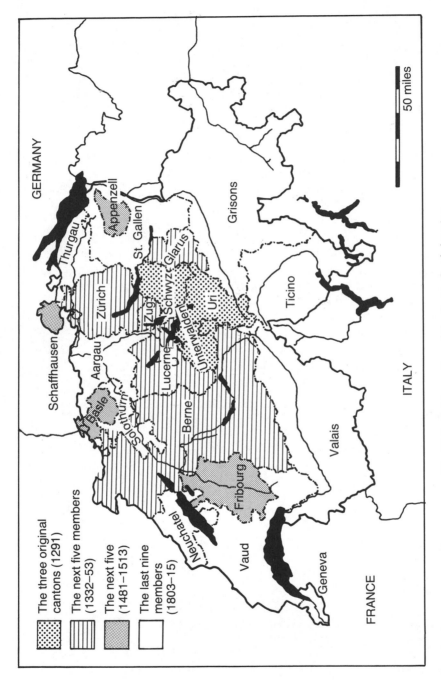

The historical formation of the Swiss Confederation.

GERMANY

Schaffhausen

Thurgau

Appenzell

St. Gallen

Zürich

Glarus

Aargau

Zug

Schwyz

Grisons

Basle

Solothurn

Lucerne

Unterwalden

Uri

Ticino

Berne

Neuchâtel

Fribourg

Valais

ITALY

Vaud

Geneva

FRANCE

50 miles

The three original cantons (1291)

The next five members (1332–53)

The next five (1481–1513)

The last nine members (1803–15)

possibly produced annually some 60,000 pieces of cotton from some 140 tons of raw cotton. Between 1280 and 1300 loanable funds became so abundant in Lübeck (Germany) that the rate of interest for money invested in bonds dropped from 10 to 5 percent. According to a Florentine chronicler, woollen production in Florence reached the level of 100,000 articles per year. The number of lead seals which Ypres (Flanders) attached as checking marks to the cloths manufactured by its weavers rose from 10,500 in 1306 to 92,500 in 1313. While it would be unwise to generalize solely from these figures, which not only refer to limited areas but also reflect short-term movements, all the evidence confirms beyond doubt that the first three centuries of our millennium witnessed remarkable expansion in all the relevant economic variables.

At the beginning of the fourteenth century Giovanni Villani, a merchant and a chronicler, wrote in glowing terms of the "greatness and magnificence" attained by Florence:[2]

We find after careful investigation that in this period (1336–38) there were in Florence about 25,000 men from the age of fifteen to seventy, fit to bear arms, all citizens.... From the amount of bread constantly needed for the city, it was estimated that in Florence there were some 90,000 mouths divided among men, women, and children and it was reckoned that in the city there were always about 1,500 foreigners, transients, and soldiers, not including in the total the citizens who were clerics and cloistered monks and nuns.... We find that the boys and girls learning to read numbered from 8,000 to 10,000, the children learning the abacus and algorism from 1,000 to 1,200 and those learning grammar and logic in four large schools from 550 to 600.

We find that the churches then in Florence and in the suburbs, including the abbeys and the churches of friars, were 110....

The workshops of the *Arte della Lana* (the gild of wool merchants) were 200 or more, and they made from 70,000 to 80,000 pieces of cloth, which were worth more than 1,200,000 gold florins. And a good third of this sum remained in the land as wages to labor, without counting the profits of the entrepreneurs. And more than 30,000 persons lived by it. To be sure, we find that some thirty years earlier there were 300 workshops or thereabouts, and they made more than 100,000 pieces of cloth yearly; but these cloths were coarser and one half less valuable, because at that time English wool was not imported and they did not know, as they did later, how to work it.

The storehouses of the *Arte di Calimala* (the gild of importers, re-finishers, and sellers of Transalpine cloth) were some 20 and they imported yearly more than 10,000 pieces of cloth, worth 300,000 gold florins. And all these were sold in Florence, without counting those which were re-exported from Florence.

The banks of money-changers were about 80. The gold coins which were struck amounted to some 350,000 gold florins and at times 400,000 yearly. And as for deniers of four pennies each, about 20,000 *liras* of them were struck yearly.

The association of the judges was composed of some 80 members; the notaries public were some 600; physicians and surgeons some 60; shops of apothecaries and dealers in spices, some 100.

Merchants and mercers were a large number; the shops of shoe-makers, slipper makers, and wooden-shoe makers were so numerous that they could not be counted. There were some 300 persons and more who went to do business out of Florence and so did many other masters in many crafts and stone and carpentry masters.

There were then in Florence 146 bakeries, and from the amount of the tax on grinding and through information furnished by the bakers we find that the city within the walls needed 140 *moggia*[3] of grain every day.... Through the amount of tax at the gates we find that some 55,000 *cogna* of wine entered Florence yearly, and in times of plenty about 10,000 *cogna* more.

Every year the city consumed about 4,000 oxen and calves, 60,000 mutton and sheep, 20,000 she-goats and he-goats, 30,000 pigs.

During the month of July 4,000 loads of melons came through Porta San Friano....

Florence within the walls was well built, with many beautiful houses and at that time people kept building with improved techniques to obtain comfort and every kind of improvement was imported.

A few decades earlier, another chronicler, Bonvesin della Riva, had written similar things about Milan (Italy), pointing to "the abundance of all goods," "the almost innumerable merchants with their variety of wares," and the ample opportunities for employment ("here any man, if he is healthy and not a good-for-nothing, may earn his living expenses and esteem according to his station").[4]

The moralists were dismayed. In his *Paradiso*, Dante countered with this ideal vision, in which[5]

> Florence within the ancient cincture sate
>   wherefrom she still hears daily tierce and nones,
>   dwelling in peace, modest and temperate.

> She wore no chain or crownet set with stones,
>   no gaudy skirt nor broidered belt, to gather
>   all eyes with more charm than the wearer owns.

> Nor yet did daughter's birth dismay the father;
>   for dowry and nuptial-age did not exceed
>   the measure, upon one side or the other.

196

There was no house too vast for household need;
  Sardanapalus was not come to show
  what wanton feats could in the chamber speed.

Nor yet could ever Montemalo crow
  your Uccellatoio, which, as it hath been
  passed in its rise, shall in its fall be so.

Bellincion Berti girdled I have seen
  with leather and bone; and from her looking glass
  his lady come with cheeks of raddle clean.

I have seen a Nerli and a Vecchio pass
  in jerkin of bare hide, and hour by hour
  their wives the flax upon the spindle mass.

Around the end of the thirteenth century and the beginning of the four-teenth, Ricobaldo da Ferrara, canon of the Cathedral of Ravenna, wrote of the dramatic improvements in living conditions in northern Italy.[6] In Milan he was echoed by Galvano Flamma, who, paraphrasing him, wrote:[7]

Life and customs were hard in Lombardy at the time of Frederic II [d. 1250]. Men covered their heads with infule made of scales of iron. Their clothes were cloaks of leather without any adornments, or clothes of rough wool with no lining. With a few pence, people felt rich. Men longed to have arms and horses. If one was noble and rich, one's ambition was to own high towers from which to admire the city and the mountains and the rivers. The women covered their chins and their temples with bands. The virgins wore tunics of "pignolato" and petticoats of linen, and on their heads they wore no ornaments at all. A normal dowry was about ten lire and at the utmost reached one hundred, because the clothes of the woman were ever so simple. There were no fireplaces in the houses.[8] Expenses were cut down to a minimum because in summer people drank little wine and wine-cellars were not kept. At table, knives were not used; husband and wife ate off the same plate, and there was one cup or two at most for the whole family. Candles were not used, and at night one dined by light of glowing torches. One ate cooked turnips, and ate meat only three times a week. Clothing was frugal. Today, instead, everything is sumptuous. Dress has become precious and rich with superfluity. Men and women bedeck themselves with gold, silver, and pearls. Foreign wines and wines from distant countries are drunk, luxurious dinners are eaten, and cooks are highly valued.

What seemed to be the height of luxury to these austere moralists would seem to us to be very primitive indeed: people were just beginning to use a knife at table but forks were still rarities. Fingers were the normal means of carrying food to one's mouth and were also used for blowing one's nose. Handkerchiefs were a "luxury" item introduced in the seventeenth and eighteenth centuries.[9] In even the wealthiest of palaces, "toilettes" were nothing but narrow passages with holes in the floor emptying directly on to the street below. But, for all these qualifications, there is no doubt that the standard of living rose appreciably between the eleventh and the thirteenth centuries and especially during the thirteenth – in some areas more than others, among some social groups more than others, but there was also an undeniable general improvement.

Though preachers and moralists found reasons for concern in the improvement in the standard of living, the greater part of the population rejoiced in it. The fourteenth century opened with the flag of optimism flying high. In the course of the thirteenth century, Siena (Italy) had erected a magnificent Duomo, a most refined and elegant demonstration of greatly increased wealth. At the beginning of the fourteenth century, the Sienese were convinced that wealth and population would continue to increase, and in 1339, L. Maitani was charged with the preparation of plans for an enormous church, of which the existing cathedral would be only the transept. The plan was made and work begun. But it was never finished. The empty arches, the unfinished walls which break away from the old cathedral bear sad witness to the fragility of men's dreams.

ECONOMIC TRENDS: 1300–1500

At the beginning of the fourteenth century, the only cause for optimism lay in the belief that in the future things would go on as they had in the past. During the thirteenth century, certain bottlenecks had begun to manifest themselves. As demographic pressure steadily increased, there eventually came into play the economic law according to which lands with diminishing marginal returns are taken into cultivation. It is by no means improbable that in the second half of the thirteenth century the frontier went beyond the optimum allowable by contemporary agricultural techniques. Various factors lead us to believe that, in several areas of Europe after 1250, the average yield-to-seed ratio began to decrease. At the same time, since population continued to increase while fertile land was becoming relatively scarce, the laws of supply and demand inevitably pushed rents up and real wages down.

On the basis of these facts, a modern economist transplanted back into the Europe of the time could have foreseen a sort of apocalypse in the shape of a series of famines. In northern Europe, one disastrous famine did in fact occur in 1317, and another occurred in southern Europe in 1346–47.[10] But the apocalypse, when it came, did not take the form of a famine but that of a terrifying epidemic of plague. We shall return to this below. What has to be stressed here is that owing to both endogenous and exogenous factors, disaster was then piled on disaster even beyond strictly demographic considerations.

At the beginning of the fourteenth century, Florence was the most important European trading and financial market and its gold florin was the preferred and most widely used means of payment both within Europe and beyond. From the 1340s onwards, Florence was shaken by a crisis of indescribable complexity and gravity. At the start of the fourteenth century the Florentine public debt had been around 50,000 gold florins but following the series of wars in which Florence became involved in the 1330s, the situation got completely out of hand. Warfare was no longer conducted so much with citizens' militias as with mercenaries and artillery, and its costs now far outstripped traditional public revenues. Florence "taxed" its citizens, forcing them to lend to the republic amounts of money in proportion to their income and wealth. At the end of the war against the Scaligers (1336–38), the city of Florence found itself indebted to its citizens to the tune of 450,000 gold florins. The following war of Lucca (1341–43) pushed the debt to over 600,000 florins. In this increasingly precarious situation, the city of Florence decided that it could no longer pay off its creditors ("non est ad presens possibile restituere predictis creditoribus ea que recipere debent"). Instead, Florence took the dramatic decision to consolidate its debt and offered its creditors a fixed maximum interest of 5 per cent per annum. Then, on 25 October 1344, Florence officially declared that the public debt titles which had hitherto been non-transferable could henceforth be negotiated. This was confirmed on 22 February 1345. This was a clever manoeuver intended to increase market liquidity, but doubts raised among tax-payers regarding the chances of recovering the money forcibly lent to the republic, and the decision of the government to pay such an artificially low interest rate, caused the value of these newly negotiable titles to slump.

It was like a present-day stockmarket crash. People in almost every social group were affected because nearly everyone, whether rich or poor, had either willingly or unwillingly "lent" the city a hand. But the great families of the Florentine financial oligarchy, owners of the major merchant-banking companies, were the worst hit. During the euphoria of the preceding decades, these companies had been quick to advance substantial sums of money to the city, believing it to be a perfectly safe investment and one that guaranteed a good return. Between 1342 and 1345 they came down to earth with a bang: not only did the returns on their supposed investment collapse but the very recoverability of their credits was put in doubt.

Under normal circumstances, most of these large companies could have toughed it out. The trouble was that circumstances were anything but normal and the bankruptcy of the city hit the companies just when most of them were already facing a serious liquidity crisis. The economic situation had started to deteriorate in the 1330s and the profits of the bigger companies had started to contract. But that was only the start of the trouble.

The Esplechin armistice of 23 September 1340 sealed the failure of the expedition with which the English had launched their war against France. It was immediately clear that the English king was in no position to pay off what he owed the Florentine bankers who had backed his venture. The Bardi and the Peruzzi, two of the biggest Florentine companies, were both involved and the Banco de' Bardi on its own had extended credits amounting to between 600,000 and 900,000 florins. Meanwhile the after-effects of Florence's own war in Lombardy had sparked off a new conflict for the possession of Lucca. In the feverish diplomatic hubbub that accompanied this new war there arose the possibility that Florence might abandon its traditional alliance with the Guelphs and switch to the Ghibelline side in support of Emperor Ludwig the Bavarian. This alarmed King Robert of Naples, his barons and the other prelates of the kingdom who had sizable amounts of capital deposited with the Florentine bankers. Fearing that their funds might be frozen, they stampeded to withdraw their money, thus placing the Florentine banks in further serious difficulty.

The triple blow of English bankruptcy, Neapolitan withdrawals, and the public debt slump was more than the economic system of Florence could bear. It spelled ruin. The entire tribe of Florentine financiers filed through the bankruptcy courts. The Acciaiuoli, the Bonaccorsi, the Cocchi, the Antellesi, the Corsini, the Da Uzzano, and the Perendoli were all ruined. And in 1343 it was the turn of the Peruzzi with the Bardi following three years later, in 1346.

It was an unmitigated disaster. The banking collapse broke over all those who held deposits. The luckiest depositors managed to retrieve only half of their savings. A mass of wealth was simply destroyed, leading Giovanni Villani to remark bitterly: "our citizens remained almost without substance."

Nor was this the end of the matter. The collapse of these companies unleashed a tidal wave that was soon rocking other sectors. This was because the companies that had gone bankrupt had been engaged not only in banking but also in trade and manufacturing, and also because their collapse led to a sudden shortage of credit. Once the crisis had broken out, a perverse upside-down multiplier mechanism came into play. The crisis fed upon itself and spread outward like an oil slick.

After 1346, Florence was never quite the same again. Yet it is interesting to observe that a crisis of the dimensions of that which overtook the main financial center of Europe between 1340 and 1346 still had no major repercussions in the other main European markets. There are many reasons for this apparently surprising fact. First, right across Europe, the bulk of gross product derived from agriculture and there is no doubt that agricultural production acted as a cushion, absorbing the leaps and plunges of the financial sector. Second, it should not be forgotten that the European economy was not yet fully integrated. A third and equally important point has been made by Professor J.I. Israel.[11] According to Fernand Braudel,

Venice first served as the hub of the European world economy. Then about 1500 the center of gravity shifted to Antwerp. The decline of Antwerp after 1585 then led to the pre-eminence of Genoa which was followed in turn, around 1600, by the rise of Amsterdam. "But Braudel's schema," comments Israel, "implies a greater degree of continuity in the form and functions of these world economic empires than is really warranted by the context." In Israel's opinion, western Europe was still in the midst of what has been termed the "late-medieval polynuclear" phase of expansion. "The markets and resources of the wider world were subject not to any one but rather to a whole cluster of western empires of commerce and navigation." The first crisis to sweep through one country after another after another right across the European continent, revealing the high degree of interdependence of the various financial markets, occurred in 1619–21.

The fourteenth and fifteenth centuries were troubled times not only for Florence but also for the other pole of European economic development, the southern Low Countries. The prosperity of this area provoked antagonism and rivalry in many quarters. Italian merchants refused access to the Mediterranean to Flemish merchants, the English barred them from England, Cologne closed the road to the Rhineland to them, and Lübeck and the Teutonic Hanse shut them out of the Baltic. The Flemings had to content themselves with an increasingly passive trading role: they could produce their woollen cloths but then had to rely on others to sell them. But their difficulties were not confined to the tertiary sector. Times were hard in manufacturing too. In the second half of the thirteenth century, England had begun to set up its own textiles industry and other nations including Italy and Germany were beginning to turn directly to the English market for their supplies of wool. Flemish manufacturing therefore encountered ever-increasing difficulties in its quest for the raw material and in the marketing of the product that had formed the basis of its success. Moreover, Flanders from the fourteenth century onwards embarked upon a series of monetary and commercial conflicts with England over wool exports from the British islands and on how these should be paid for. Difficulty was thus piled on difficulty. Within the southern Low Countries themselves, between 1280 and 1305 serious social conflicts broke out and relations were tense between the Flemish mercantile aristocracy and labor. Indeed it was in Flanders that the first case of strike action in the Middle Ages occurred at Douai in 1245. It was referred to as a "takenhans." This social strife soon led to political conflicts in which not only the counts of Flanders but also the kings of France were to play a prominent role.

In the last quarter of the thirteenth century, the Italians opened up regular sea trading lines between the Mediterranean and the North Sea. This advance was made possible by technical progress in navigation and by the need to export to England the alum that that country's burgeoning textiles industry demanded. The development of this new trading route naturally damaged the land route that had previously linked Italy and Flanders via Champagne. The conquest of the Champagne area by the kings of France, who quickly proceeded to abolish the tax privileges that had earlier been granted by local dukes, marked the completion of this process. From the end of the thirteenth century onward, the Champagne fairs fell into a slow but steady decline.

Catalonia, a region that was part of the Kingdom of Aragon but enjoyed a large measure of administrative autonomy, was remarkable during the thirteenth century for its brilliant economic and social development. In the following century, this development took the form of an unprecedented expansion in commerce and banking. It is fair to say that Catalonia, at least in the area of economic activity, reached the levels achieved by the most advanced areas in Europe. In 1381–83, however, the Catalan banking sector suffered a full-blown crisis and the most important banks in the region went under: the Descaus, the D'Olivella, the Pasqual y Esquerit, the Medir, and the Gari. Things went from bad to worse and in 1427 and 1454 there were severe monetary collapses and then, to cap it all, in 1462 civil war broke out.

In 1337 a conflict broke out between England and France. Referred to by historians as the Hundred Years' War, this conflict, with various interruptions, in fact lasted rather more than 100 years, ending in 1453. Most of the fighting took place on French territory and the devastation done to French society and the economy were indescribable: entire villages laid waste, vineyards devastated, livestock destroyed, whole populations massacred. The scars left by such havoc were still clearly visible decades after the war had come to an end.

The 150 years that followed the beginning of the fourteenth century were thus a time of wrack and ruin across Tuscany, Flanders, France, Castiglia, and Catalonia. And it was followed by a pandemic of plague that between 1348 and 1351 killed roughly 25 million people from a population of about 80 million. The plague caused a shortage of labour, thereby strengthening the position of labor. It is not surprising therefore that in the period following the epidemics there were peasants' and artisans' rebellions: the French Jacquerie of 1358, the uprising of the Ciompi in 1378 in Florence, the Catalan peasants' rebellion in 1380 and the English peasants' revolt in 1381, and the riots led by van Artevelde in Flanders in 1382. Jean d'Outre Meuse wrote that "in these times every part of the population in all the world is in a state of revolt." It should come as no surprise that most historians have always described the 1300–1450 period as one of the bleakest periods in European economic history, and that they contrast it with the preceding period of growth from 1000 to 1300. It is perfectly true that the two periods stand in stark contrast: the earlier one was a period of optimism and of the *Cantico delle Creature*; the later period was a time of pessimism and of the *Danse Macabre*.[12] Yet it is wrong to view the 1300–1500 period as a time of unmitigated disaster.

In a number of areas, development undoubtedly did occur. It was, after all, during the fourteenth and fifteenth centuries that the Hanseatic League reached the height of its power. In Lombardy, the period following the death of Gian Galeazzo Visconti was strewn with wars, famines, plague, and pillage that devastated the country from 1405 to 1430 (*pestifera stimula ac totius quasi patriae consumptio*) and the period following the death of Duke Filippo Maria (d. 1447) was scarcely less calamitous. Yet overall 1350 to 1500 was a period of undeniable growth for Lombardy. For Portugal too, the beginning of the fifteenth century marked a new phase of both economic and geographical expansion that culminated in the creation of an extraordinary empire of global dimensions (see map on p. 207).

There is no doubt that the areas that prospered between 1300 and 1450 were fewer and smaller than those that suffered devastation and economic ruin. But throughout this period there was an upturn in the social and economic conditions of sections of the population that during the preceding period had been exploited without mercy. The underlying reality of the 1300–1500 period is that the recurrent outbreaks of plague had the effect of dissipating the demographic pressure that had been building up in Europe and that had made itself increasingly felt from the second half of the fourteenth century onward. The 1348–51 pandemic and the subsequent series of epidemics were an enormous human tragedy, but in economic terms their effects were not necessarily all bad. In the agricultural sector, land that was barely productive but had been cultivated during the previous period of demographic pressure was abandoned when the population shrank. It was this process that created the German *Wüstungen* and the English Lost Villages but it fed through to an increase in the productivity of agricultural labor and a redistribution of income. Between 1350 and 1500 salaries increased steadily (see Figures 8.1 and 8.2) while return on capital tended to stagnate or decline.

Similar developments occurred in the manufacturing sector. One has only to read the last will and testament of the Flemish draper Jehan Boinebrooke (d. 1285), who was clearly anxious to make posthumous amends for the misdeeds of his life, to form an idea of the almost incredible bullying to which artisans and workers were subject in those times. The simple fact is that capital was in short supply whereas labor was relatively plentiful. The plague pandemic that erupted in 1348 reversed the situation. Suddenly workers rediscovered they had a voice and that it did not have to assume silken tones. In 1356 the managers of the Florence mint reported to the city Commune that

> the four workers employed at the mint do not want to work except when it suits them. And if one remonstrates with them, they reply with vulgar and arrogant curse words saying that they only want to work when it is convenient to them and provided there are increases

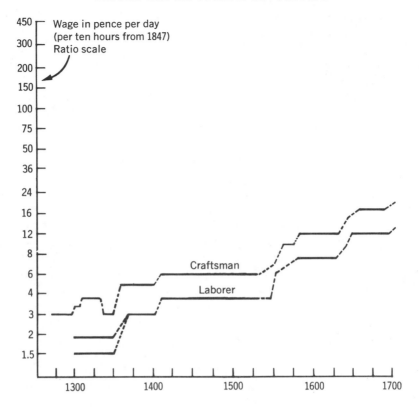

Figure 8.1 Monetary wages of a building craftsman and a laborer in southern England, 1264–1700.

Source: E.H. Phelps Brown and Sheila V. Hopkins, "Wage-rates and Prices: Evidence for Population Pressure in the Sixteenth Century."

in salary. And although they have many times been made offers of reasonable salaries, none the less, rising in their arrogance, they behave themselves worse and worse and insist that no one other than they may come to work in the mint and indeed threaten anyone who would dare to infringe their obstructionism. And thus they form a sect within the mint.

In the new situation, real salaries increased and the living conditions of working people improved quite markedly. Matteo Villani bears witness to the fact that in the aftermath of the plague "the little people, men and women, given the superabundance of things, no longer wished to labor at their former trades." Prior to the plague people had actually volunteered for demeaning and back-breaking work as galley oarsmen. After the plague, no

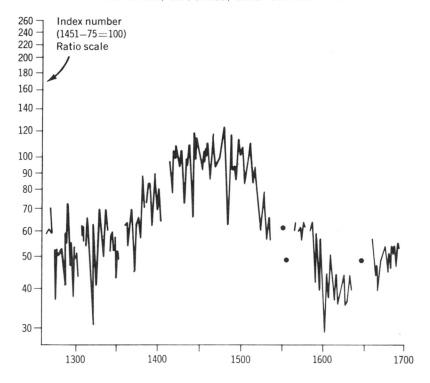

Figure 8.2 Real wage-rate of a building craftsman expressed as a composite physical
unit of consumable goods in southern England, 1264–1700.

Source: See Figure 8.1.

one could be found who was prepared to do that job and it became an
occupation reserved for slaves and convicts. Matteo Villani of Florence also
opined that in the second half of the fourteenth century,

> everyone was wealthy from their own work, earning greedily and the
> more ready they were to purchase and live off the best things the more
> they were willing to pay in order to have them before the most ancient
> and wealthiest citizens. Though this is a unseemly and a wondrous
> fact to relate it is so continuously observed that we can bear clear
> witness to it.... And so the little people feasted and dressed and dined
> as if they had vast wealth and abundance of every possible good.

Far-reaching investigations undertaken by de la Roncière and by R.A.
Goldthwaite have provided quantitative data that support Matteo Villani's
assertions. In Professor Goldthwaite's view, after 1348 in Florence there was
"a dramatic rise" in real wages and by 1360 real wages were approximately

50 percent higher than pre-1348 levels. This upturn in real wages in Florence seems to have lasted until 1470, after which real wages seem to have embarked upon a long-term decline.[13] Writing in Piacenza towards the end of the fourteenth century, Giovanni De Mussis commented that:

> The people of Piacenza live at present in a clean and opulent way and in the houses they now possess implements and tableware of a much better quality than seventy years ago (i.e. roughly 1320). The houses are more beautiful than they then were because they now have beautiful rooms with fireplaces, porticoes, courtyards, wells, gardens and attics. Each house now has several chimneys whereas once there used to be no chimney at all and one had simply to make a fire in the middle of one of the rooms and then everyone in the house would gather around that one fire and it was there that food was cooked. In general the people of Piacenza now drink better wines than their parents did.[14]

De Mussis's comments recall those cited above from Dante, Ricobaldo da Ferrara and fra Galvano Flamma. De Mussis, however, is referring not to the powerful oligarchies but rather to the lower social classes at the end of the fourteenth century. De Mussis himself makes this explicit when he states that his comments "apply not only to nobles and merchants but also to those who exercise manual occupations." As regards England, E.H. Phelps Brown and S.V. Hopkins several years ago worked out an index of real wages for the 1264–1700 period. Calculations of this type leave a lot to be desired when they refer to periods prior to the nineteenth century – because of the dearth of data. However, the conclusions of Phelps Brown and Hopkins seem to be fairly acceptable: from 1350 onward the real wages of English workers followed a clear upward trend (see Figure 8.2) which led to a clear improvement in the general standard of living of the labouring classes. More recently, Christopher Dyer, drawing on broad-based research and a considerable amount of documentary evidence, was able to confirm that:

> the changes of the fourteenth and fifteenth centuries offered the underprivileged sections of society a range of uses for new wealth. Wage earners could either raise their level of consumption of food, clothing and housing or they could escape the drudgery of continuous labor by taking more frequent holidays. All these changes shook the structure of society but did not turn it upside-down, as upper-class contemporaries believed.[15]

Even the most pessimistic of economic historians, who see nothing but unrelieved gloom descending on Europe after the end of the thirteenth century, tend to agree that the series of disasters and calamities that befell almost the entire continent began to abate towards the middle of the

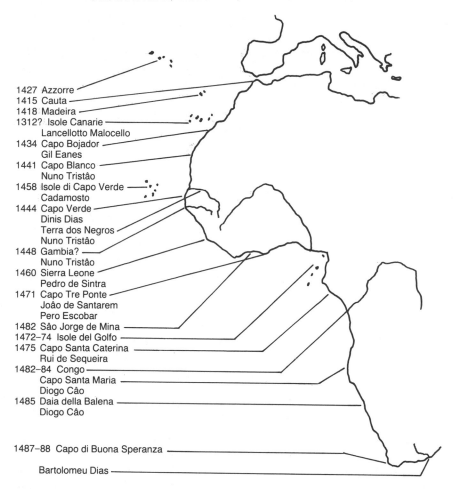

1427 Azzorre
1415 Cauta
1418 Madeira
1312? Isole Canarie
Lancellotto Malocello
1434 Capo Bojador
Gil Eanes
1441 Capo Blanco
Nuno Tristâo
1458 Isole di Capo Verde
Cadamosto
1444 Capo Verde
Dinis Dias
Terra dos Negros
Nuno Tristâo
1448 Gambia?
Nuno Tristâo
1460 Sierra Leone
Pedro de Sintra
1471 Capo Tre Ponte
Joâo de Santarem
Pero Escobar
1482 Sâo Jorge de Mina
1472–74 Isole del Golfo
1475 Capo Santa Caterina
Rui de Sequeira
1482–84 Congo
Capo Santa Maria
Diogo Câo
1485 Daia della Balena
Diogo Câo

1487–88 Capo di Buona Speranza

Bartolomeu Dias

The Portuguese advance along the African coast in a quest for a passage to
the Indies.

fifteenth century. The Hundred Years' War ended in 1453 and during
succeeding decades France set to work to rebuild its economy with hard
effort but also with efficiency. By 1494 King Charles VIII was already in a
position to launch a lightning attack on the Italian peninsula that demonstrated the military fragility of the Italian statelets. Prior to the attack
launched on it by Charles VII, Italy reclined in a state of extraordinary
cultural and economic well-being. During the 1470s, the marriage between
Isabel of Castile and Ferdinand of Aragon had united the crowns of their
two countries and laid the basis for future Spanish power. With striking
success, the Portuguese continued to push further and further south along
the western coast of Africa in their quest for a sea route to the Indies, and in

1497–98 Vasco de Gama at last rounded the Cape of Good Hope and sailed on to the East Indies. At the same time, southern Germany was also embarking on a period of unparalleled development, founded on the discoveries of rich deposits of silver and copper in the Tyrol and in the Saxon-Bohemian area. Nor was this all. Powerful endogenous forces had also developed in Germany through constant contact between southern Germany and more developed countries such as northern Italy. In the second half of the fifteenth century the powerhouses in this development were the cities of Nuremberg, Augsburg, Ravensburg, Basel and St Gall. The most enterprising and successful companies included the Fugger, the Imhof, the Welser, the Baumgartner, and the Grosse Ravensburger-handelsgesellschaft. The large quantities of silver that were available locally enabled these companies to act not only as commercial and industrial enterprises but also as banks. The Fugger, for instance, became personal bankers to Charles V and lent him the large sums he needed in order to buy the votes of the grand Electors and thereby to secure the crown of the Holy Roman Emperor. There is no doubt that for a while the Fugger were the most powerful bankers in Europe.

Technically, however, especially in terms of banking expertise, the large German companies remained somewhat backward as compared to their Italian counterparts. German accounting systems, for example, remained relatively primitive and the head accountant of the Fugger eventually had to travel to Italy in order to learn the latest in accounting techniques. Despite this, the mass of energy that had been released in Nuremberg, Augsburg, Ravensburg, and St Gall made up for any other deficiencies and turned these towns into the nerve centres of a world economic system. The most important markets with which they operated were Antwerp in the Low Countries and Milan and Venice in northern Italy. In Antwerp, German merchants could purchase English products (wool, woollen cloths, and tin) as well as products from the Baltic. They also came into direct contact with Portuguese traders from whom they could purchase black pepper, gold, and spices. In Milan they found woollen and silk fabrics and by this time great quantities of arms and armor also. In Venice they could purchase cotton, spices, and a range of other oriental products. For their part, the Germans brought to all these markets copper, silver, top quality bronze cannons, clocks, and special fabrics such as fustian. The Fugger also launched themselves into the pharmaceutical business, acquiring a temporary monopoly over trade in guaiacum (*lignum vitae*), a form of bark or cortex imported from the recently discovered American continent and which according to doctors was a good cure for syphilis.

9

THE EMERGENCE OF THE MODERN AGE

UNDERDEVELOPED EUROPE OR DEVELOPED EUROPE?

In the years that immediately followed the Second World War, it became fashionable among economists to discuss economic development and to distinguish between developed and underdeveloped societies. An underdeveloped society is normally defined as a society in which the economy is characterized by the underemployment of human and material resources; low real income per capita in comparison with that of the United States, Canada, and western Europe; and the prevalence of malnutrition, illiteracy, and disease. This definition makes development synonymous with industrialization and underdevelopment with preindustrial society. On this reckoning, every society anywhere in the world prior to 1750 was underdeveloped: not only the Tuaregs in Africa but also the Florentines at the time of the Medicis. Once the shortcomings of a definition have been acknowledged, its usefulness depends on the amount of assistance it can provide in one's inquiries. Clearly, the notion that the whole world was underdeveloped until 1750 is not useful. The term *underdeveloped* has however acquired a certain resonance and it is worth preserving, not as shorthand for "per capita incomes lower than in the United States" but redefined, albeit vaguely, as "performance" levels lower than in the advanced societies of the period in question.

On this basis, there is no doubt that from the fall of the Roman Empire to the beginning of the thirteenth century Europe was an underdeveloped area in relation to the major centers of civilization at the time, whether China of the T'ang or Sung Dynasties, the Byzantine Empire under the Macedonian dynasty, or the Arab Empire under the Ommayads or the Abbasids. To the Arabs it was an area of so little interest that, while their geographical knowledge continually improved between AD 700 and 1000, their "knowledge of Europe did not increase at all." If Arabian geographers did not bother with Europe, it was not because of a hostile attitude, but rather because Europe at the time "had little to offer" of any interest.[1] The accounts by Liutprando of Cremona of his voyage to Constantinople, or centuries later, those by Marco Polo of his journey to China reflect wonder and admiration for societies far more refined and developed than their own.

However, from about the year 1000, the European economy "took off" and gradually gained ground. One cannot say precisely when the balance first began to right itself and then to move in Europe's favor: among other difficulties, one has to remember that in matters of this kind, not all sectors of a society move at the same pace. We have to make do with a few vague clues.

During the thirteenth century, Venetian merchants proved they had developed business techniques more advanced than those used in the Byzantine Empire and Byzantine merchants had to submit to their new and aggressive competitors.[2] In addition, the make-up of international trade between East and West seems to point to the thirteenth and fourteenth centuries as the period when Europe gained the upper hand. In the twelfth century the West still exported to the East mostly raw materials (iron, timber, pitch) and slaves, and imported manufactured goods and raw materials. The Near East had, at the time, flourishing paper, soap, and textile industries. By the fourteenth century the situation had completely changed. In the second half of the thirteenth century the court of Byzantium, which had until then used paper imported from Arab countries, began to buy paper from Italy; by the middle of the fourteenth century the textiles and soaps of Syria and Egypt were no longer a match for the products of the West. Soap, paper, and especially textiles were now exported in increasing quantities from West to East.[3]

One of the main reasons for European success, at least in the paper and textile industry, was the mechanization of the productive process by the adoption of the water mill – a step that the Arabs failed to accomplish. According to Al-Makrīzī, imported European textiles were often of a coarser sort than traditional oriental ones, but they cost much less and even the upper classes soon began to dress in garments made of western materials.

By the fifteenth century, western glass too was widely exported to the Near East and a telling symptom of the European "capitalist" spirit, unhampered by religious considerations, was the fact that the Venetians manufactured mosque lamps for the Near Eastern market and decorated them with both western floral designs and pious koranic inscriptions.[4]

In the summer of 1338 the cargo of a galley which set sail from Venice for the East included a mechanical clock,[5] symbolic beginning of the export of machinery reflecting the incipient technological supremacy of the West. At the end of the fifteenth century, some Byzantine writers, such as Demetrius Cydone, admitted for the first time that the West was not after all the land of primitive barbarians that the Byzantines had always thought it to be.[6] A few decades later the Byzantine Cardinal Bessarion wrote to Constantine Paleologus, urging him to send young Greeks to Italy to learn western techniques in mechanics, iron metallurgy, and the manufacture of arms.[7] Soon after the arrival of Portuguese ships in Canton in 1517, the scholar-official Wang Hong wrote that "the westerners are extremely dangerous because of their artillery. No weapon ever made since memorable antiquity is superior to their cannon."[8]

By the beginning of the sixteenth century, the situation which had prevailed five centuries earlier was completely reversed: western Europe had become the most developed area. As Lynn White wrote, "The Europe which rose to global dominance about 1500 had an industrial capacity and skill vastly greater than that of any of the cultures of Asia – not to mention Africa or America – which it challenged."[9]

EUROPEAN EXPANSION

The most spectacular consequences of the technological supremacy acquired by Europe were the geographic explorations and the subsequent economic, military, and political expansion of Europe. Between the eleventh and fifteenth centuries, although Europe was startlingly aggressive in the economic sphere, it remained at the political and military mercy of potential invaders. The Crusades should not mislead us. The success of the initial stages of the European onslaught was due in large part to an element of surprise and to the temporary weakness and disorganization of the Arab world. As Grousset said, it was "the victory of the Frankish monarchy over Muslim anarchy." But the forces of Islam reorganized themselves, and the Europeans were compelled to beat a retreat.

The disaster of Wahlstatt (1241) showed dramatically that Europe was militarily incapable of standing up to the Mongol menace. That Europe was not invaded was due to the death of the Mongol chief Ogödäi (December 1241) and to the fact that the Khans were more strongly attracted to the East than to the West. In the following century the Christian defeat at Nicopolis (1396) showed yet again the military weakness of the Europeans in the face of the oriental invaders. Europe was saved once more by chance circumstances. Bayazed, the conqueror, became embroiled with the Mongols of Timur Lenk (Tamerlane), and one potential danger luckily and unexpectedly cancelled out the other.

If, however, exceptional circumstances saved Europe from complete destruction, its chronic weakness was demonstrated by the steady loss of its oriental territories. The Turkish advance continued inexorably, conquering one European outpost after another. On 28 May 1454, Constantinople fell. "A terrible thing to describe and utterly deplorable for those who still have in them a glimmer of humanity and Christianity," wrote Cardinal Bessarion to the Doge of Venice.

After the fall of Constantinople the European position gradually deteriorated. Northern Serbia was lost in 1459; Bosnia-Herzegovina in 1463–66; the Negroponte and Albania in 1470. "I see nothing good on the horizon," wrote Pope Pius II.

Yet, at the very time when the Turks seemed poised to strike at the very heart of Europe, a sudden and revolutionary change took place. Outflanking the Turkish blockade, some European countries launched a wave of attacks over the oceans. Their advance was as rapid as it was unexpected. In little more than a century, first the Portuguese and the Spaniards, then the Dutch and the English, laid the basis of worldwide European predominance.

It was the gun-carrying ocean-going sailing ship developed by Atlantic Europe during the fifteenth, sixteenth, and seventeenth centuries that made the European saga possible. The ships of Atlantic Europe carried all before them. In 1513 the great Portuguese navigator Albuquerque proudly wrote to his king that "at the rumor of our coming, the native ships all vanished, and even the birds ceased to skim over the water." The prose was rhetorical, but the substance of the statement reflected truth. Within fifteen years of their first arrival in Indian waters, the Portuguese had completely destroyed Arab navigation.[10]

While Atlantic Europe expanded overseas, European Russia launched its expansion to the east across the steppes and to the south against the Turks. Russian expansion also was the result of European technological superiority. As G.F. Hudson wrote of the Russian attack against the Hordes of the Kasaks,

> The collapse of the power of the nomads with so slight a resistance after they had again and again turned the course of history with their military powers, is to be attributed not to any degeneracy of the nomads themselves but to the evolution of the art of war beyond their capacity of adaptation. The Tartars in the seventeenth and eighteenth centuries had lost none of the qualities which had made so terrible the armies of Attila and Baian, of Genghis Khan and Tamerlane. But the increasing use in war of artillery and musketry was fatal to a power which depended on cavalry and had not the economic resources for the new equipment.[11]

The European eastward expansion did not occur with the dramatic speed of the overseas expansion of Atlantic Europe, essentially because the technological superiority of the Europeans was not as marked on land as it was on the sea. On the open sea, a small band of men exploiting wind and gunpowder in combination were practically invulnerable. But on land the Asians could compensate for their technological inferiority with weight of numbers. The eastward advance became inexorable only after the middle of the seventeenth century, when European technology succeeded in developing more mobile and rapid-firing guns. In the face of a technological gap which constantly widened, numbers counted less and less, and the oriental masses suffered one defeat after another.

The lightning overseas expansion of Europe had immense economic effects.

212

One of the major consequences was the discovery in Mexico and Peru of rich deposits of gold and especially silver. For over a century, the legendary Spanish *Flotas de Indias* brought fabulous treasures to Europe. The figures calculated by E.J. Hamilton are not as reliable as was once thought, but they do give a rough idea (see Table 9.1).

A proportion of the metals, probably more than 20 percent, was transferred to the mother country as income of the Crown,[12] and with sovereigns such as the Spanish who were obsessed with the idea of a Catholic Crusade, that part of the treasure was immediately transformed into effective demand for military services and for arms and provisions. Some of the remaining 80 percent of the treasure was brought back to Spain by returning *Conquistadores*; most of it, however, came to Europe as effective demand for consumer and capital goods – textiles, wine, weapons, furniture, various implements, jewels, and so forth – and for the commercial and transport services necessary for the transportation of the goods in question to the Americas.

This demand, with its multiplier effects (this being the sequence of expenditure set off by the original increase in spending), happened to coincide with a general increase in the population of Europe throughout the sixteenth century. Since supply was elastic, the rise in demand tended to increase production, but since certain bottlenecks in the productive apparatus – especially in the agricultural sector – put a brake on the

Table 9.1 Kilograms of gold and silver allegedly imported into Spain from the Americas, 1503–1650[1]

Period	Silver	Gold
1503–10		4,965
1511–20		9,153
1521–30	149	4,889
1531–40	86,194	14,466
1541–50	177,573	24,957
1551–60	303,121	42,620
1561–70	942,859	11,531
1571–80	1,118,592	9,429
1581–90	2,103,028	12,102
1591–1600	2,707,627	19,451
1601–10	2,213,631	11,764
1611–20	2,192,256	8,856
1621–30	2,145,339	3,890
1631–40	1,396,760	1,240
1641–50	1,056,431	1,549

Source: Hamilton, *American Treasure*, p. 42.
[1]One kilogram = 2.2046 pounds.

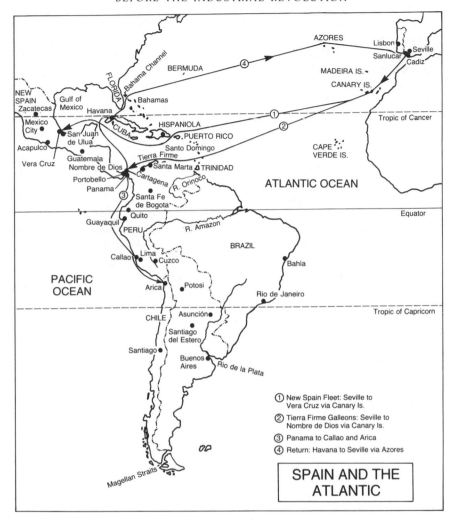

The routes followed by the Spanish fleets transporting a variety of goods to the Americas and, above all, silver back from the Americas to Spain.

In 1545 rich deposits of silver were discovered in Potosí, vice-royalty of Peru (today in Bolivia) and in 1546 further rich deposits of silver were discovered in Zacatecas, Mexico. In 1571, deposits of mercury were found at Huencavelica (also in Peru) and the more efficient method of extracting and refining silver using an amalgam of mercury was soon introduced in Potosí. The production of silver in the Spanish colonies in America reached levels that for Europe represented a dramatic shock. The famine of precious metals that had strangled the European economy during the Middle Ages was over. For half a century Europe was now flooded by masses of silver that, by the final quarter of the sixteenth century, came two-thirds from Peru and one-third from Mexico.

The silver arrived in Europe at Seville's port of San Lucar, which enjoyed the monopoly of American trade. A system of convoys was used to transport the expansion of production, the rise in demand resulted in rising prices. The period 1500 to 1620 has been labeled by economic historians – with a bit of exaggeration – the age of the "Price Revolution." It is generally thought that between 1500 and 1620, the average level of prices in the various European countries increased by 300 to 400 percent. Statements of this kind look more or less impressive, but they are scarcely significant. The "average general level of prices" is an extremely ambiguous statistical abstraction; the average general index of prices varies according to the prices considered and the weightings one adopts. Table 9.2 provides a clear example of the fact that, in the same market, prices of various products moved in different ways. The different behaviors of the different sets of prices can be attributed either

Table 9.2 Percentage rise in prices of selected groups of commodities at Pavia (Italy), 1548–80

Commodities	(a) Raw materials and semi-finished goods	(b) Finished goods	Weighted average of (a) and (b)
Clothing and textiles	31	58	50
Foodstuffs			86
Metallurgical, mineral, and chemical products	87	57	81
Hides and leather goods			18
Spices, drugs, and dyes			43
Miscellaneous			16
Total	45	58	65

Source: Zanetti, "Rivoluzione dei prezzi," p. 13.

treasures. Two fleets left San Lucar each year under heavy escort. The *flota* left in May bound for Vera Cruz in Mexico and the *galeones* left in August on a more southerly course for Nombre de Dios (Portobello) on the isthmus of Panama. After offloading the commodities shipped from Spain for the colonists, the *galeones* retired to the more sheltered harbour of Cartagena.

Both fleets wintered in the Indies. The Mexican *flota* generally left Vera Cruz in February on a three- to four-week voyage against the winds to Havana (Cuba). Meanwhile, in Peru, the silver mined at Potosi was carried down from the mountains to the port of Arica. From there it was shipped to Callao, the port of Lima, and loaded on to the ships of the *armada del sur*, which then took some twenty days to reach Panama. At Panama the silver was loaded on to mules and carried across the isthmus to Nombre de Dios, where the *galeones* were lying at anchor. Once the silver was aboard, the galeones set sail for Havana to join the Mexican *flota*. By the time the hurrican season began, the combined fleets had left for Seville, which they reached, assuming all went well, by the late summer or early autumn.

Source: Elliott, *Spain and its World*, map p. 6.

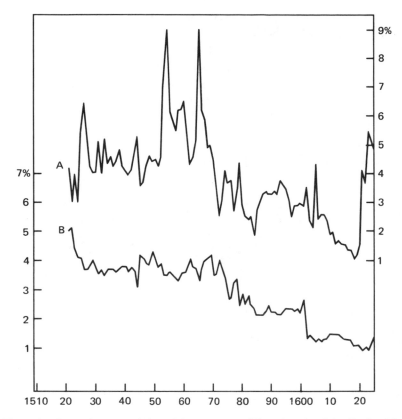

Figure 9.1 Rate of interest (A) and discount rate (B) on bonds of the Bank of St George, Genoa (Italy), 1522–1620

to changes in the structure of demand or to the presence (or absence) of bottlenecks in the various productive sectors, or both.

The increase in liquidity brought down the interest rate in at least some major financial centers. At the beginning of the seventeenth century in Genoa, interest rates on safe government securities were down to 1.5 percent, and in Amsterdam in the second half of the seventeenth century it was possible to borrow capital at the rate of 3 percent.[13] Table 9.3 and Figure 9.1 show the downward trend of interest rates in Genoa. It was perhaps the first time in the history of the world that capital was offered at such low rates.

Gold and silver were accepted all over the world as means of payment for international transactions. The increased supply of precious metals meant greater international liquidity and favored the development of international exchanges. This effect was particularly notable in trade with the East.

American silver enabled western Europe to overcome its traditional

Table 9.3 Rate of interest (A) and discount rate (B) on bonds of the
Bank of St George, Genoa (Italy), 1522–1620

Year	A %	B %	Year	A %	B %	Year	A %	B %
1522	4.2	5.0	1555	9.0	3.5	1588	3.3	2.2
1523	3.0	5.1	1556	6.2	3.6	1589	3.4	2.3
1524	4.0	4.4	1557	5.9	3.5	1590	3.3	2.5
1525	2.9	4.1	1558	5.5	3.4	1591	3.3	2.3
1526	5.5	4.1	1559	6.2	3.3	1592	3.4	2.3
1527	6.5	3.7	1560	6.2	3.6	1593	3.3	2.2
1528	5.2	3.7	1561	6.5	3.6	1594	3.8	2.2
1529	4.2	3.8	1562	5.6	3.6	1595	3.7	2.3
1530	4.0	4.0	1563	4.3	4.1	1596	3.5	2.4
1531	4.0	3.8	1564	4.6	3.8	1597	3.1	2.4
1532	5.1	3.5	1565	7.3	3.8	1598	2.5	2.4
1533	4.0	3.7	1566	9.0	3.3	1599	2.9	2.3
1534	5.2	3.5	1567	6.2	3.8	1600	2.9	2.4
1535	4.3	3.7	1568	5.9	4.0	1601	3.0	2.3
1536	4.6	3.7	1569	4.9	4.1	1602	2.9	2.7
1537	4.2	3.7	1570	5.0	4.2	1603	3.6	1.4
1538	4.4	3.6	1571	4.4	3.5	1604	2.4	1.5
1539	4.8	3.7	1572	3.6	3.6	1605	2.1	1.4
1540	4.2	3.8	1573	2.5	4.1	1606	4.4	1.3
1541	4.0	3.8	1574	3.0	3.8	1607	2.4	1.4
1542	3.9	3.6	1575	4.2	3.5	1608	2.6	1.3
1543	4.1	3.8	1576	3.7	2.7	1609	2.6	1.4
1544	4.6	3.7	1577	3.8	2.7	1610	2.4	1.4
1545	5.3	3.1	1578	2.7	3.3	1611	1.9	1.6
1546	3.5	4.2	1579	3.3	3.4	1612	2.0	1.6
1547	3.7	4.1	1580	4.4	2.5	1613	1.6	1.6
1548	4.3	3.9	1581	2.9	2.9	1614	1.7	1.6
1549	4.6	3.8	1582	2.5	2.5	1615	1.6	1.5
1550	4.4	4.3	1583	2.4	2.9	1616	1.6	1.4
1551	4.5	4.1	1584	2.5	2.5	1617	1.4	1.4
1552	4.3	3.8	1585	1.9	2.4	1618	1.4	1.4
1553	4.6	3.9	1586	2.7	2.2	1619	1.1	1.2
1554	7.3	3.5	1587	3.0	2.2	1620	1.2	1.2

Source: Cipolla, "Note sulla storia del saggio di interesse."

trading deficit with the Baltic area. It has been calculated that between
approximately 1600 and 1650, of the total value of goods transported
through the Sund straits, an average of 70 percent was leaving the Baltic for
the West, whereas 30 percent was going the other way. This trade gap was
offset by exports of American silver.[14] Similar problems, with similar
solutions, developed in the trade relations between Europe and Asia.

Once Europe had established direct relations with the Far East, it faced
an economic problem of considerable difficulty. Europeans found products

Table 9.4 Analysis of silver and gold received in Batavia from the Netherlands, 1677/78–1684/85

	1677/78	1678/79	1679/80	1680/81	1681/82	1682/83	1683/84	1684/85
				(thousands of florins)				
Silver								
Reales of eight	—	—	—	—	—	—	10	—
Mark reales	786	407	503	889	1,182	337	91	316
Ducatoons	101	60	110	36	63	68	—	39
Rixdollars	357	26	44	23	—	—	—	—
Leeuwendaalders	240	109	254	205	108	331	254	53
Silver in bullion	102	93	500	332	236	1,020	649	532
Payment	472	134	58	339	46	183	45	192
Gold								
Ducats	—	—	20	—	—	—	—	—
Gold in bullion	165	222	89	—	13	209	305	—
Total	2,223	1,051	1,578	1,824	1,648	2,148	1,354	1,132

Source: Glamann, Dutch-Asiatic Trade, p. 61.

in the East which sold very well in Europe,[15] but no European product succeeded in finding similar outlets in the East.

With their powerful galleons, the Europeans destroyed most of the Muslim shipping trade in the Indian Ocean and established themselves as masters of the high seas. They replaced the traditional merchants and captured a large share of the intra-Asian trade. By bringing Japanese copper to China and India, Spice Islands cloves to India and China, Indian cotton textiles to Southeast Asia, and Persian carpets to India, the Europeans made good profits and used them to pay for some of their imports from Asia. The Dutch, who were allowed to continue to trade in Japan, there obtained silver and, later, gold which they used to pay for their imports from other parts of Asia. Between 1640 and 1699 the Dutch exports of silver and gold from Japan were as follows:[16]

	Silver (florins)	Gold (florins)
1640–49	15,188,713	
1650–59	13,151,211	
1660–69	10,488,214	4,060,919
1670–79		11,541,481
1680–89		2,983,830
1690–99		2,289,520

All this, however, was not enough to make up for the huge deficit in the balance of trade between Europe and the Far East. To settle that deficit Europe used American silver in the form of Mexican dollars, *reales*, or pieces of eight minted in Spain; ducatoons minted in Italy; rixdollars minted in Holland (see Tables 9.4, 9.5, and 9.6). Leaving aside the relatively small-scale direct trade between the Spanish Colonies in America and the Philippines, one can say that intercontinental trade in the sixteenth and seventeenth centuries consisted essentially of a large flow of silver which moved eastward from the Americas to Europe and from Europe to the Far East, and a flow of commodities which moved in the opposite direction: Asian products bound for Europe and European products bound for the Americas.

J.H. Van Linschoten, observing the East Indiamen leaving for the East, wrote:

> When they go out they are but lightly laden, only with certain pipes of wine and oil, and some small quantity of merchandise; other things they have not in, but balast and victuals for the company, for that the most and greatest ware that is commonly sent into India are reales of eight.[17]

At the end of the sixteenth century, the Florentine merchant and traveler Francesco Carletti estimated that the Chinese extracted from these two nations [Portugal and Spain] in silver more than a million and a half écus a year, selling their goods and never buying anything, so that, once the silver gets into their hands it never leaves them.[18]

It is difficult to say what value can be attributed to Carletti's estimate of the Portuguese and Spanish deficit to China, but for England there are the account books of the East India Company, and the figures which emerge from them are significant: the value of the gold and silver exported was never less than two-thirds of total exports (goods plus precious metals) and in the decade 1680–89 it was as much as 87 percent (Table 9.5). For Holland there are the account books of the Dutch East India Company and they tell substantially the same story (see Table 9.6)

The chronic trade deficit obviously caused much anxiety in mercantilistic Europe. After unsuccessfully attempting to export all sorts of things, ranging from English textiles to religious as well as pornographic paintings, Europeans found a solution to their problems after the end of the eighteenth century in Indian opium – which eventually triggered a tragic conflict and severely poisoned relations between China and Europe.

Geographic exploration and overseas expansion brought new and unusual products to Europe. Europeans were especially fascinated by the new drugs and medicaments that they encountered. The Spaniards, for instance, did not show any particular interest in or respect for the civilization of the American Indians, but the interest and respect which they accorded to the pharmacopeia of the Indians of Mexico was remarkable. In 1570 Philip II of Spain appointed Francisco Hernandes (1517–78) head physician (proto-physician) of the West Indies and charged him especially with the task of collecting information on the drugs and medicines of the natives. Dr Hernandes eventually produced his monumental and classic *Treasure of Medical Matters of New Spain*.[19] The subject became very popular. Two

Table 9.5 Exports of the English East India Company to the Far East, 1660–99

Year	Metals	Commodities	Total	Metals as percentage of total
	(thousands of the current £)			
1660–69	879	446	1,325	66
1670–79	2,546	883	3,429	74
1680–89	3,443	505	3,948	87
1690–99	2,100	787	2,887	73

Source: Chaudhuri, "Treasure and Trade Balances," pp. 497–98.

Table 9.6 Exports of silver to Asia by the Dutch East India Company (Verenigde Oostindische Compagnie), in annual averages of *gulden* and kilograms of fine silver, 1602–1795

Decade (or years)	Gulden (guilders)	Kilograms of fine silver
1602–1609	647,375	6,959.7
1610–1619	965,800	10,382.9
1620–1629	1,247,900	12,610.8
1630–1639	890,000	8,994.0
1640–1649	880,000	8,892.9
1650–1659	840,000	8,488.7
1660–1669	1,190,000	11,563.1
1670–1679	1,220,000	11,854.6
1680–1689	1,972,000	18,847.0
1690–1699	2,900,000	27,720.9
1700–1709	3,912,500	37,392.9
1710–1719	3,882,700	37,108.1
1720–1729	6,602,700	63,104.0
1730–1739	4,254,000	40,656.8
1740–1749	3,994,000	38,171.9
1750–1759	5,502,000	52,584.3
1760–1769	5,458,800	52,171.4
1770–1779	4,772,600	45,613.2
1780–1789	4,804,200	45,915.2
1790–1795	3,233,600	30,904.5

1 *gulden* = (a) 1606–1620 = 10.7506 g fine silver
(b) 1621–1659 = 10.105 g
(c) 1659–1681 = 9.7169 g
(d) 1681–1795 = 9.5573 g

Source: F.S. Gaastra, "The exports of precious metal from Europe to Asia by the Dutch East India Company, 1602–1795."

Iberian doctors, Garcia d'Orta and Nicolas Monardes, became deservedly famous for writing on *The Simple Aromats and Other Things Pertaining to the Use of Medicine Which are Brought From the East Indies and the West Indies.* From America, they said,

three things [are brought into Europe] which are praised all over the world and which allow the achievement in medicine of results which have never been achieved with any other drug known up to now. These are the wood called guaiacum, the cinchona, and sarsaparillo.[20]

Other drugs contributed to European medicine by South American Indians included curare and ipecac. The Mayas used capsicum, chenopodium, guaiacum, and vanilla. From the Americas the Europeans also learned to use

221

tomatoes, maize, and beans. The potato, discovered in 1538 by a Spanish soldier, Pedro de Cieza de Leon, in the Cauca Valley (Colombia), was introduced as a curiosity into Europe in 1588. The introduction and subsequent spread of maize and potato cultivation in Europe helped to solve Europe's food problem and to reduce the danger of famines when Europe entered a period of accelerated population growth from the eighteenth century onward.[21] Tobacco was brought into England by Ralph Lane and popularized by Sir Walter Raleigh. Between 1537 and 1559 fourteen books mentioning medicinal tobacco appeared in Europe. In 1560, Jean Nicot, the French ambassador to Portugal, began to experiment with the medicinal herb and to spread the news of his successful results. Between 1560 and 1570 numerous other books important to the development of tobacco therapeutics came out, and by the end of the century the doctrine that tobacco was the panacea of panaceas had been fully elaborated. In 1602 an author who wrote a booklet exposing the harmful effects of tobacco found it prudent to write anonymously. However, in 1602 King James of England wrote a booklet entitled *A Counterblaste to Tobacco*. In Russia Tsar Michael punished his soldiers with the rack and knout for smoking. The Puritans condemned it. But many people used smoking as a preventive against epidemic disease and in 1665 the boys at Eton were made to smoke pipes to ward off the plague. As time went on the consumption of tobacco spread among large strata of the European population. In the early days tobacco was taken either in a pipe or in the form of snuff, while cigars became popular in Regency days; the cigarette was allegedly a South American invention of the 1750s. Imports into London of tobacco from Virginia and Maryland between 1619 and 1701 showed the following trend (in pounds weight):

1619:	20,000
1635:	1,000,000
1662–63:	7,000,000
1668–69:	9,000,000
1689–92:	12,000,000
1699–1701:	22,000,000

Cocoa was another product that reached Europe from America. The natives made considerable use of the substance in both solid form and also diluted in water. But its extreme bitterness was not to European taste. Fra Gerolamo Benzoni in 1572 referred to cocoa as a "drink fit for pigs." The Spanish, however, soon took steps to make cocoa acceptable to European palates, by adding white sugar, vanilla and a whole series of spices ranging from cinnamon, cloves, aniseed, almonds, musk and whatever else was to hand. Cocoa consumption among the Spaniards of America rocketed. B. Marradon wrote in 1616 that in Latin America roughly 13 million pounds of sugar were used annually in the manufacture of chocolate.

From Latin America chocolate consumption spread first to Spain and thence to the rest of Europe. Antonia Colmenero de Ledesma, a doctor and surgeon from the city of Ecija, wrote in 1631 that chocolate consumption had reached Italy and Flanders. At about the same date chocolate could also be found in England, Holland, and France. From Holland and from England the consumption of the new exotic product then spread to Germany and in 1661 to Bohemia. Indeed, it earned a mention in Elizabetta Ludmilla de Lisov's cookbook.

Chocolate, however, was a costly product and its consumption remained for a long time confined to aristocratic and rather snobbish circles. Spain strove hard to maintain its monopoly on cocoa sales but their efforts were undermined by the rapid emergence of smuggling on an enormous scale centered on Amsterdam. According to R. Delcher, towards the end of the seventeenth century, of 65,000 quintals of cocoa harvested in Venezuela, only 20,000 were exported legally, and between 1706 and 1722 not a single cargo of cocoa arrived in Spain.

Europe acquired markedly fewer new products from the East than from the Americas since, by way of a variety of intermediaries, Europe and the East had always been in contact. During the thirteenth century in particular, thanks to the rise of the Yüan dynasty in China and the founding of the Mongol Empire – the largest land Empire in human history – communications by caravan across Asia became much safer than ever before or after, and this helped to boost the flow of goods and people between East and West. Throughout the whole of the Middle Ages, Europe imported spices and silk from the Orient. With the dawn of the modern age, the list of imported goods grew longer with the addition of three products that were to become very popular throughout Europe: coffee, tea, and porcelain.

Coffee – as a beverage – seems to have originated in Ethiopia. Towards the end of the fifteenth century, coffee spread to Mecca and there is no doubt that by 1511 it was commonly drunk there. By the first half of the sixteenth century coffee had reached Hijaz and Cairo. By the middle of the sixteenth century coffee was being drunk in Constantinople, and in the second half of the seventeenth century it spread into Europe. At the beginning of the eighteenth century, the Dutch began growing coffee in their Asian territories, especially in Java and Surinam. The French followed the Dutch example, growing coffee in their American possessions, especially in Guyana, Martinique, San Domingo, and Guadaloupe. Finally, the English too began to plant coffee in their American colonies. Coffee accordingly flowed into Europe from both east and west. Eastern coffee, however, was always more prized by Europeans than western coffee. Of the western coffee available, however, Europeans preferred Martinican coffee.

Tea arrived on the markets of London and Amsterdam in the 1650s but failed to arouse any enthusiasm. It was not until 1664 that the decisive event took place. King Charles II had a passion for exotic birds and the East India

Company was continually requested to contribute new specimens to the king's collection. In 1664, however, the Company did not manage to bring to Europe any bird worthy of the royal collection and, not knowing what else to do, the directors of the Company decided to present the king with a packet of exotic herbs – a packet weighing 2 pounds, 2 ounces, and valued at £4.5s.0d. of the time. It must have been a success, because the gift was repeated the following year. As usual, the example set by the Court proved contagious. First the aristocracy and then other classes took to drinking tea, though it remained almost until the end of the eighteenth century a beverage reserved for the rich and well-off. After all, owing to the high price caused by the prohibitive duty imposed on the importation of the raw material, tea remained a luxury. In 1703, an agent of the Company in Chusan still bemoaned the fact that the Chinese compelled him to buy tea instead of supplying him with the silks he asked for, but in London, it was remarked that "tea is becoming popular with people of all classes" and in the 1720s tea toppled silk as the principal import of the company.[22]

Among the aristocracy, the upper bourgeoisie, and the intellectuals the spread of the consumption of tea, as of coffee, chocolate, and tobacco, was facilitated by the fact that considerable medicinal properties were attributed to all these products. Of tea in particular wonders were told and, noting that in Europe tea did not perform the therapeutic miracles it was claimed to perform in China, the great physician Lionardo di Capua observed:

> The tea herb is commonly used by us now, although we do not see from it those wonderful effects which it allegedly shows in China – it may be that, during the journey of such long duration, it loses for the most part its volatile alkali and with it, little less than the whole of its virtue – or some other reason.[23]

Other doctors were less critical, and the medical profession as a whole largely favored the consumption of tea, coffee, and chocolate. One may quote as an example the *Tractaat* by the Dutch physician Cornelis Bontekoe on the excellence of tea, coffee, and chocolate (The Hague, 1685) and the book by the French Nicolas de Blégny (Paris, 1687) on *The proper use of tea, coffee and chocolate for the prevention and for the cure of illnesses.* Early in the eighteenth century Dr Daniel Duncan reversed the trend and wrote a book on the bad effects of the excessive use of these drinks and a number of physicians followed his example,[24] but their recommendations had little impact.

The rapid expansion in tea, coffee, and chocolate imports into Europe was an eighteenth-century phenomenon. It is not however possible to give any precise figures on this since, owing to the high duties charged on these three products and their consequent high prices, smuggling – by definition impossible to evaluate with any precision – was widespread. According to one well-informed accountant at the East India Company, during the decade from 1773 to 1782, an average of 7½ million pounds of tea were smuggled into England each year.[25]

Sugar had been known to Europeans since antiquity but had always been a very scarce commodity. In fact, it was so scarce that in the Middle Ages it was mostly sold in pharmacies in the form of pills (which is the origin of our candies). To sweeten their daily foods and beverages, Europeans of the time of Chaucer and Leonardo used honey, and in 1500 sugar was still expensive. Cultivation of the rare sugar cane centered on Cyprus, Sicily, and Madeira. By the end of the fifteenth century Madeira had become the most important center of production and seventy thousand *arrobas* (each equivalent to about 25 pounds) were produced there in 1508, and 200,000 in 1570. This, however, was the apogee. In the 1580s production fell to between 30,000 and 40,000 *arrobas* and died away completely in the seventeenth century. Madeira's sugar was killed off by cheap and plentiful supplies from Brazil. In the 1560s about 180,000 *arrobas* were exported annually from the colony, rising to 350,000 in the early years of the seventeenth century. Production reached 2 million *arrobas* a year (more than 22 tons) by 1650. In 1662, a contemporary wrote: "Whoever says Brazil says sugar and more sugar." Sugar shipments from the West Indies to London grew from about 15 million pounds per year during the period 1663–69 to about 37 million pounds per year in 1699–1701. Between 1650 and 1700 the price of sugar in London fell by about 50 percent, and sugar progressively became an object of daily and popular consumption.

But the sugar business was not all sweetness. The growth of the plantations created a strong demand for black slaves. Slaves were bought by Europeans on the coast of West Africa in exchange for textiles (about 60 percent of the slaves purchased), guns and gunpowder (about 20 percent), spirits (about 10 percent), and other goods (about 10 percent). Table 9.7 gives some very rough estimates of the number of people forcibly transported in wretched conditions across the Atlantic to the New World.

The influx of precious metals and of exotic products are facts which easily appeal to the imagination, but the overseas expansion of Europe had other effects at least as important, if not more so. For ease of presentation, one can consider separately (a) technology, (b) economics, and (c) demography.

Ocean navigation was very different from coastal navigation. Its development called forth, and in turn depended upon, the creation and development of new instruments and new techniques. Worthy of mention are the invention of the marine chronometer and the new developments in nautical mapmaking, naval artillery, naval construction, and the use of sail. These developments, though primarily technical, of course had economic implications: the invention of the marine chronometer ushered in new developments in clockmaking; the evolution of naval artillery brought about developments in the metallurgical industry; innovations in naval construction led to developments in the shipbuilding industry. No less important

Table 9.7 Estimated slave imports by importing region, 1451–1700

	1451–1600	1601–1700
Importing region	*(thousands of slaves)*	
British North America	—	—
Spanish America	75	300
Caribbean	—	450
Brazil	50	550
Europe	50	—
São Thomé and Atlantic Isl.	100	25
Total	275	1,325
Annual average	2	13

Source: Curtin, *The Atlantic Slave Trade*, p. 77. Figures have been rounded to indicate a large margin of error.

were the innovations in business techniques. The emergence of large companies such as the English East India Company or the Dutch East India Company; the appearance of the "supercargo" or traveling agent, who represented the interests of the company on board the ships and at overseas ports; the development of maritime insurance companies (like Lloyds of London) – all these and other innovations were essentially the result of overseas expansion. Many of the economic effects are implicit in what has already been said with regard to the inflow of precious metals and new products, and the development of clockmaking, mapmaking, shipbuilding, maritime insurance, and so on. One could add to the list such an item as the rise and rapid spread of coffeehouses, first in London and then over the whole of Europe. Overseas trade entailed great risks and great losses but, above all, much greater profits than any other business venture. In London as in Amsterdam trade in imports and re-exports and all the subsidiary activities which this trade set in motion made possible a notable accumulation of capital. There is much talk nowadays of the early accumulation of capital as a necessary precondition for growth. Things are not as simple as certain theorists would have one believe, but it cannot be denied that England was able to do what she did in the early stages of the Industrial Revolution partly because the previous Commercial Revolution had allowed for a considerable (for those days) accumulation of capital: profits from overseas trade overflowed into agriculture, mining, and manufacturing.

In marked contrast with the technological and economic effects, the demographic consequences of the transoceanic expansion were altogether negligible until the end of the nineteenth century. About the middle of the seventeenth century in all the Portuguese, Spanish, English, and French overseas possessions taken together, there were fewer than one million whites, including those born locally but of European parents. The fact is that those who left Europe were few, not all reached their destination, and a great many of those who survived the exertions and dangers of the voyage and of life overseas returned to Europe as soon as they could. Until the nineteenth century European expansion remained essentially a commercial venture.

As far as society was concerned, however, the profound significance of overseas expansion can be understood only if seen in human terms. Overseas trade was a great practical school of entrepreneurship – not only for those who, like ships' captains, the supercargo, and the merchants, actually went overseas, but also for the merchants, insurance agents, shipbuilders, re-exporters, victuallers, employees of companies who, although remaining in Europe, took part in overseas trade in different capacities and degrees. It was also a good school for those savers who learned how to invest their savings in trading companies or in insurance ventures. One of the most significant economic consequences of the commercial development of the sixteenth and seventeenth centuries was the unusual accumulation of wealth it made possible in some European countries. But an even more important consequence was the accumulation of a precious and rich "human capital," that is, of people endowed with sturdy standards of business honesty, adventurous attitudes to risk-taking, and an attitude of mind that was open to the world. It is time now to look more closely at the cultural developments of the period.

THE SCIENTIFIC REVOLUTION

Events such as the discovery of new worlds and new products, the proof of the roundness of the earth, the invention of printing, the perfecting of firearms, the development of shipbuilding and navigation were at the root of a cultural revolution.[26]

In many seventeenth-century texts one encounters the refrain that since the ancients did not know the world in which they lived, they could not be regarded as the source of all knowledge. The blind and absolute faith in the authors of antiquity which had prevailed throughout the Middle Ages entered a period of crisis. Instead of continuing to regard the past as a long-lost golden age, an increasing number of Europeans began to look optimistically ahead, dreaming of progress and of what the future might have in store.

The seventeenth century saw an acrid, violent intellectual battle develop between the "ancients" and the "moderns," between those who upheld the dogma of authority and the omniscience of the classics and those who used reason and experiment to oppose dogma and who subjected the errors and absurdities of the classics to the harsh light shed by recent discoveries. The age of Galileo, Newton, Huygens, Leeuwenhoek, Harvey, Descartes,

Copernicus, and Leibnitz saw the victory of the "moderns," of the experimental method, and of the application of mathematics in the explanation of reality. Physics, and in particular mechanics, in which, by the very nature of the subject, the application of mathematical logic was bound to yield the best results, made spectacular progress, and fascination with this progress was such that gradually a mechanical conception of the universe came to prevail.[27] It was then that God himself was described as "the perfect clockmaker."

One of the by-products of the revolution in human thought of that period was the growth of the statistical approach. The writers and the experimenters of the seventeenth century endlessly recorded, catalogued, and counted. William Letwin wrote that:

> The best minds of England squandered their talents in minutely recording temperature, wind and the look of the skies hour by hour, in various corners of the land. Their efforts produced nothing more than unusable records. This impassioned energy was turned also to the measurement of economic and social dimensions of various sorts.[28]

The judgment is ungenerous. To the educated layman as well as to the government clerk, numbers began to take on an aura of reality. The new approach was particularly noticeable in the treatment of the problems of international trade[29] and population.

It was in this cultural climate that the school of "arithmetic politicians" rose and developed; Graunt, Petty, and Halley put forward their demographic estimates and constructed their first survival tables; and Gregory King calculated the English National Income. Even today in books and articles on the history of population, historical statistics of world population always begin with 1650 (see Table 9.8). The reason is that just after the middle of the seventeenth century Europeans started making estimates of the population of the world or of parts of it (see Table 9.9).

However, the use of figures did mean that the figures used were scientifically handled. In 1589, the work of Giovan Maria Bonardo, *The Size, Width, and Distance of All Spheres Reduced to Our Miles,* was reprinted in Venice. It maintained, among other things, that "Hell is 3,758¼ miles away from us" and has "a width of 2,505½ miles," while "the Empire of Heaven ... where the blessed rest in the greatest happiness ... is 1,799,995,500 miles away from us." The figures compiled in Table 9.9 show that some of the estimates put forward in the second half of the seventeenth century about the world population had no greater merit than those of Giovan Maria Bonardo regarding the distance of Heaven and Hell from the earth. The two things, however, cannot be put on the same plane. One of the fundamental characteristics of the Scientific Revolution of the seventeenth century was, in fact, that it turned human speculation away from such insoluble and absurd

Table 9.8 Present mini-max estimates of world population, 1650–1900 (in millions)

Years	Africa	North America	Latin America	Asia (excl. Russia)	Europe and Russia	Oceania	World
1650	100(?)	1	7–12	257–327	103–105	2	470–545
1750	95–106	1–2	10–16	437–498	144–167	2	695–790
1800	90–107	6–7	19–24	595–630	192–208	2	905–980
1850	95–111	26	33–38	656–801	274–285	2	1090–1260
1900	120–141	81–82	63–74	857–925	423–430	6	1570–1650

Sources: United Nations, *The Determinants and Consequences of Population Trends*, p. 11, Table 2; Durand, *The Modern Expansion of World Population*, p. 109.

Table 9.9 Estimates of world population by writers of the seventeenth and eighteenth centuries (in millions)

Year	Author	World	Europe	Asia	Africa	America	Oceania
1661	Riccioli	1,000	100	500	100	200	100
1682	Petty	320					
1685	Vossius	500	30	300			
1696	King	700	100	340	95	65	100
1696	Nicholls	960					
1702	Whiston	4,000					
1740	Struyck	500	100	250	100	50	
1741	Süssmilch	950	150	500	150	150	

problems as the distance between Hell and earth or the number of angels that could stand on the head of a pin, and directed it instead toward problems which were capable of solution. The estimate of the distance of Hell given by Giovan Maria Bonardo and the estimate of Riccioli on world population are both improbable, but the first answers an absurd question while the second is merely an imperfect measurement of a rationally valid problem. Once a question is correctly formulated an answer will inevitably follow.

Modern statistics was practically born in those decades, and quantitative information about population, production, trade, and money became increasingly more abundant and more reliable. On the other hand, the new set of problems was the outcome of a new mental attitude which gave greater emphasis to the rational than to the irrational, placed pragmatism before idealism, stressed reality rather than eschatology. At the level of human relations, the ground was prepared for the tolerance of the Enlightenment. At the technological level, the emphasis on experimentation paved the way to the solution of concrete problems of production.

This whole grandiose movement of ideas had particular importance in another way. In the Middle Ages, according to a tradition inherited from the ancient world, science and technology had remained separate and distinct. As the masterbuilders of the Duomo in Milan emphatically stated in 1392, *"scientia est unum et ars est aliud,"*[30] that is, science is one thing and technology is quite another. Science was philosophy; technology was the *ars* of the artisan. Official "science" had no interest in, or inclination toward, technological affairs, and technological developments were mostly the results of the toil of unlettered artisans. The Renaissance, with its unquestioning cult of the values of classical antiquity, accentuated this dichotomy, which in Italy, from the middle of the fifteenth century onward, was further intensified by the progressive accentuation and hardening of class distinctions. It is in this context that we must see Leonardo's admission of being a "man without letters," Tartaglia's warning that his doctrine was "not taken from Plato nor from Plotino" and the efforts of the physicians who, considering themselves scientists and therefore philosophers,[31] dissociated themselves from the surgeons, who were regarded as technicians and therefore simple artisans.

The "moderns" of the seventeenth century, in their reaction against traditional values and in their effort to impose the experimental method, set themselves doggedly to reappraise the work of craftsmen. Francis Bacon repeatedly emphasized the need for collaboration among scientists and artisans. Galileo, in his famous "Dialogue," made the imaginary Sagredo assert that conversation with the artisans of the Venetian Arsenal had helped him considerably in the study of several difficult problems. The Royal Society of London charged some of its members with the compiling of a history of artisan trades and techniques; an idea to be fully adopted later by the editors of the *Encyclopédie*.

While all this was happening in the field of "science," developments in technology were proceeding in the same direction. First, one must take into account the fact that different sections of society, however divided or distinct, still react to common cultural stimuli. Moreover, the spread of the press and, especially in the Protestant countries, the spread of literacy signaled the victory of the book over the proverb, of the text over the icon, of reasoned information over slavish reiteration, and all this, in turn, meant the progressive abandonment of customary and traditional attitudes in favor of more rational and experimental attitudes. The same printing presses that made it possible for men to educate themselves also afforded those with special talents and unconventional interests a means of conveying their ideas to others. Last but not least, developments in ocean navigation, in the watch and clock industry, and in experimental science prompted the emergence of an increasing number of makers of precision instruments. These grew to represent a type of superior technician, capable of conversing with contemporary scientists. It is no accident that the steam engine was at the root of the Industrial Revolution and that the inventor of the steam engine was one of these makers of precision instruments.

By the time of Galileo, those sciences that were concerned with utilitarian technology had found spokesmen capable of gaining attention and commanding respect. Galileo himself entitled his pamphlet on mechanics "On the utilities to be drawn from mechanical science and its instruments." Admittedly, until the end of the eighteenth century, the contributions that "science" made to "technology" remained occasional and of little note. But cultural developments during the seventeenth century brought the two branches closer together, creating the conditions for cooperation that in the course of time formed the basis for modern industrial development.

AN ENERGY CRISIS

In historical description, it is inevitable that the historian should be influenced by the fact that he observes human phenomena *ex post* – that is, with the benefit of hindsight. In the selection of the factors at play, as well as in the interpretation of their role, the historian is inevitably influenced by the fact that he knows how events later unfolded. When attempting to explain what he may describe as a failure, he is prone to stress the "negative" circumstances and factors that foreshadowed it. Similarly when the historian describes a success, he will inevitably stress the "positive" circumstances and factors which preceded it. History, however, is never as simple and straightforward as it is told. Disasters are not necessarily preceded by dire circumstances, and success does not emerge only from promising situations. Moreover, many factors or circumstances can be defined as "positive" or "negative" only after the outcome has been given a positive or negative reading by us. Another way of expressing this is to say that, seeing things *ex post*, we accord the events of a period weights and meanings very different from those attributed to them by their contemporaries. Atkinson has shown that, of all the books printed in France between 1480 and 1700, more than twice as many dealt with the Turkish Empire as with the Americas.[32]

In the sixteenth and seventeenth centuries, some of the circumstances which paved the way to the Industrial Revolution appear to us in a decidedly positive light. But mingled with them there were also circumstances of more doubtful character, circumstances which must certainly have appeared to the people of the times to be etched in black, even though we tend to color them pink because we know *ex post* that things ended well.

The timber crisis provides a clear case in point. Since the dawn of time, timber had been the fuel *par excellence*, as well as the basic material for construction, shipbuilding, and the manufacture of furniture, tools, and machines. After the twelfth and thirteenth centuries, in the Mediterranean area, timber became scarce and, in building, was increasingly replaced by bricks, stone, and marble. But it remained practically the only fuel in everyday use and continued to be the basic material for making furniture, ships, tools, and machines.

In 1492, in central Italy, a chronicler reported that the area had begun to suffer from "a great shortage of timber": it was impossible to find oak timber any more, and people had begun to cut "domestic trees" and "as these do not suffice, people have now begun to cut even olive trees and entire olive groves have been destroyed."[33] This was a foretaste of what was to happen on a much larger-scale all over Europe in the following decades. During the sixteenth century, population growth, the expansion of ocean navigation and shipbuilding, the development of metallurgy, and the consequent increase in the consumption of charcoal for the smelting of metals, caused a considerable increase in the consumption of timber. By the middle of the sixteenth century, approximately 2.1 million cubic feet of wood were used each year in the silver mines at Freiburg. About the same amount was consumed in the Hüttenberg and Joachimstal mines. In the districts of Schlaggenwald and Schönfeld, over 2.6 million cubic feet of wood were used each year. Woods and forests literally disappeared and in many places timber crises erupted. In England in 1548–49, the government ordered an inquiry into timber wastage and deforestation. About 1560, the foundries of State Hory and Harmanec in Slovakia were compelled to reduce drastically their activities or to close altogether because of the shortage of wood. The movements in timber and charcoal prices provide a measure of the timing and gravity of the crisis. In Genoa, the price of oak used in shipbuilding grew from a base index of one hundred in 1463–68 to three hundred in 1546–55, to twelve hundred in 1577–81.[34] In the seventeenth century Italy embarked upon a period of severe economic decline, the demand for fuel and construction materials consequently stagnated, and the price of timber stopped rising.[35] But in the north, where economic activity was expanding, the price of timber soared. In some parts of England, the price index for timber (1450–1650 = 100) rose as follows:[36]

1490–1509:   88
1510–29:   98
1530–49:   108
1550–69:   176
1570–89:   227
1590–1609: 312
1610–29:   424
1630–49:   500

The price of charcoal was also rising (see Table 10.9, p. 270). According to the data collected in Table 10.9 the price of charcoal rose rapidly especially following the first decades of the seventeenth century at a time when the general level of prices showed a tendency towards stability. It must be borne in mind that the rise in the price of charcoal would have been considerably sharper if coal had not been increasingly used as a substitute for timber and charcoal. The scissor movement of prices seems to indicate that the country was experiencing a growing relative scarcity of vegetable fuel. The statistical evidence available is undeniably inadequate, but it does seem to indicate that the energy crisis exploded in its full gravity towards 1630.[37]

It has become fashionable in England over the last few years to deny that there was any timber crisis at all during the seventeenth century, in spite of the fact that a great number of English sources – as we shall see in the section on England in Chapter 10 – complained bitterly about the growing scarcity of timber. To undermine such evidence, English historians drew attention to the number of large forests still intact in remote corners of the kingdom, overlooking the fact that, given the high cost of transporting charcoal, what mattered was the extent of deforestation in and close to the industrial areas of the country. That there was plenty of wood available at some distance was economically irrelevant. What is more, English economic historians, though in the main very talented, make a habit of ignoring non-English sources. The French minister Colbert kept a close eye on developments in the iron and armaments industry in England, and wishing to gain precise first-hand information he dispatched to England his own son the Marquis de Seignelay. In the early 1670s the Marquis was able to inform his father in quite unambiguous terms that the English "not having enough wood to produce the artillery that they need, are obtaining cannons from Sweden even though they consider Swedish iron to be of a quality that bears no comparison with English iron." It is typical that English historians never cite this authoritative and plain-speaking French source.

Considering the important role that timber played in the contemporary economy both as a source of energy and as a raw material, any severe shortage of timber could obviously have led to bottlenecks that might have had disastrous consequences for the subsequent development of Europe. As it turned out, the energy crisis helped instead to push England down the road towards industrialization. For that to happen, however, other factors had to come into play.

10

THE CHANGING BALANCE OF ECONOMIC POWER IN EUROPE

ECONOMIC TRENDS: 1500–1700

In current historical and economic literature, the sixteenth and seventeenth centuries are painted in black and white. The sixteenth century is painted as *"el siglo de oro,"* a sort of golden age, not only for Spain, which received substantial quantities of gold and silver from her American colonies, but also for the rest of Europe. In contrast, the seventeenth century is painted gloomily, and it has become fashionable to write of the "crisis of the seventeenth century."[1]

Fashions and descriptions in black and white should always be regarded with suspicion, for while there is some truth in stereotyped narratives, there is also much that is superficial and erroneous. For a considerable section of northern Italy, which was one of the leading areas of the European economy, the first half of the sixteenth century was neither a golden age nor even a silver one. It was an age of iron and fire, of destruction and misery. The second half of the century was definitely not a golden age for the southern Low Countries.

As for Germany, the sixteenth century saw a complex mix of successes and calamities. Between 1524 and 1526 the Peasants' Revolt left 100,000 people dead while also destroying a massive quantity of fixed capital. In Augsburg, between 1556 and 1584, approximately seventy large companies declared themselves bankrupt. The German Hanse suffered a disastrous decline that lasted throughout the whole of the sixteenth century. Southern Germany, on the other hand, enjoyed considerable prosperity during the first half of the century thanks to the activity of its merchant-bankers. But after about 1550, southern Germany too was shaken by depression and economic decline. In northern Germany, Hamburg was a shining exception, owing above all to the entrepreneurial skill of immigrants from many parts of Europe. Hamburg became home to the beer industry, to shipbuilding, to large-scale trade, and to banking. The Bank of Hamburg, modeled on the Bank of Amsterdam, was founded in 1619, and the *Dictionnaire* compiled by J. Savary de Bruslons recorded the excellent reputation that it had earned through "the faithfulness and exactitude with which everything is handled there."

The information at our disposal on trends in French domestic trade is wholly inadequate but there is a fair abundance of evidence on French foreign trade. During the sixteenth century, trading relations with England were difficult and very limited. There was instead a marked expansion in trade with Spain and trade with Italy also remained good. But the most dynamic sector of the French economy in the sixteenth century was trade with the Levant, in which France assumed a dominant position. Also during the sixteenth century, the artisan sector showed clear signs of prosperity even if the development of manufacturing in rural areas

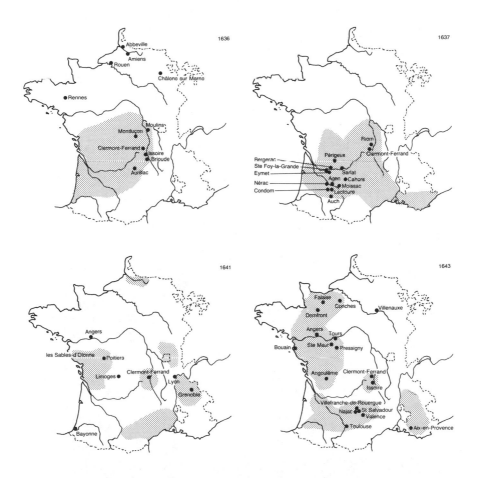

Popular revolts in France in the seventeenth century.

Source: **Braudel**, *L'identité de la France.*

235

was more sluggish than in England or Holland. The Crown and the nobility provided considerable stimulus to the manufacture of luxury products. In the farming sector there were no particular breakthroughs. Overall it may be said that the 1500–70 period was one of prosperity and development for the French economy. The wars of religion broke the spell. The 1570–1600 period ushered in a very deep crisis which did not ease until the beginning of the eighteenth century.

As already been said, the seventeenth century is generally referred to as a century of crisis for the European economy. It was indeed a grim century for much of Germany, where the Thirty Years' War brought wrack and ruin to vast parts of the country. It was a bad century for Turkey also and, as we shall see, for Spain and Italy. The French economy was not in good shape in the first part of the seventeenth century but it recovered in the 1660s and for about thirty years, between 1660 and 1690, it enjoyed great prosperity. The fastest expanding sector was colonial trade with French possessions in the Americas and, once again, trade with the Levant. For Holland, England, and Sweden, the seventeenth century was, apart from a few brief periods, a century of success and prosperity. Figure 10.1 is also the result of simplification and suffers from the defects inherent in all simplifications, but however superficial and simplistic, it serves at least to indicate how much more so are the descriptions which make of the sixteenth and seven-

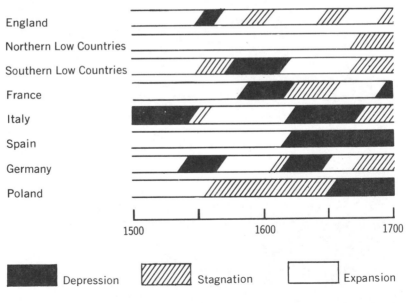

Figure 10.1 Economic trends in selected European countries, 1500–1700.

236

teenth centuries, respectively, *"el siglo de oro"* and "the age of depression.

The most serious drawback to considering the sixteenth century indiscriminately as a period of general prosperity and the seventeenth as a period of general depression or stagnation is that such a view prevents one from understanding the most important aspect of European history at the beginning of the modern era; that is, the upsetting of the traditional balance of economic power within Europe. At the end of the fifteenth century, the most highly developed area in western Europe was the Mediterranean area, and in particular central and northern Italy. During the sixteenth century, because of the influx of American treasure, Spain enjoyed a period of splendor which enabled the Mediterranean to maintain its position of economic superiority. By the end of the seventeenth century, however, the Mediterranean was clearly a backward area. The center of gravity of the European economy had shifted to the North Sea. To account for this dramatic turnaround with the tired refrain about "geographical discoveries" and the consequent change in "trade routes" is superficial and naïve. The problem is so complex and intricate that to treat it adequately would require many volumes. We shall deal here only with certain aspects of it.

THE DECLINE OF SPAIN

Half way through the fifteenth century, Spain did not yet exist. The Iberian peninsula was still divided into four kingdoms: the Crown of Castile, the Crown of Aragon, the Kingdom of Portugal, and the Kingdom of Navarre. Towards the second half of the sixteenth century, these four states had roughly the following surface areas and populations:

	km²	*Population*
Crown of Castile	378,000	8,300,000
Crown of Aragon	100,000	1,400,000
Kingdom of Portugal	90,000	1,500,000
Kingdom of Navarre	17,000	185,000

Mother Nature had not been generous with these territories. Most of the peninsula consisted of a rather infertile plateau called the *Meseta*. About 38 percent of the country was, strictly speaking, cultivable but no more than 10 percent was really fertile; 47 percent of the land was fit for grazing, 10 percent was wooded, and 6 percent was unusable. The natural poverty of the country was exacerbated by the shortcomings of the human capital.

At the beginning of the sixteenth century, Francesco Guicciardini, in his *Relazione di Spagna*, wrote:

> poverty is great here, and I believe it is due not so much to the quality
> of the country as to the nature of the Spaniards, who do not exert

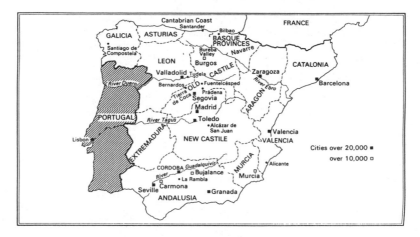

Spain in 1590.

themselves; they rather send to other nations the raw materials which grow in their kingdom only to buy them back manufactured by others, as in the case of wool and silk which they sell to others in order to buy them back from them as cloths of silk and wool.[2]

In 1557, the Venetian Ambassador Badoer reiterated, "I do not believe there is another country less well provided with skilled workers than Spain."[3]

The massive inflow of gold and silver from the Americas and the consequent expansion of effective demand might have been expected to stimulate the economic development of the country. But sixteenth-century Spain provides a classic illustration of the fact that, though demand is a necessary element to stimulate development, it is not a sufficient one.

Spain as a whole (that is, irrespective of income distribution between regions and between social classes) became considerably richer during the sixteenth century, and her importance in the European economy increased dramatically because silver and gold were internationally accepted liquid assets. By 1569 the theologian Tomás de Mercado could justifiably write that Seville and the Atlantic provinces of Spain "from being the far edge of the world had become the center of it." Spanish failure was due to bottlenecks in the productive system, in particular the lack of skilled labor, popular prejudice against craft and trade, and the guilds with their restrictive practices. Increased demand did stimulate some growth: between 1570 and 1590 the annual production of woollen cloth rose to 13,000 pieces in Segovia and to 15,000 pieces in Cordoba. Textile production grew in Toledo and Cuenca also. Building activity also expanded. Yet production failed to grow fast enough to satisfy the expanding demand. As a result, prices rose and excess demand attracted foreign goods and services.

In 1545 it was estimated that Spanish manufacturers had a six-year backlog of orders from the merchants of Cartagena, Porto Belo, and Vera Cruz.[4] Under these circumstances, to satisfy the demand from the American colonies the merchants were soon compelled to turn to foreign producers to whom they lent their name in order to evade the law that prohibited the colonies from trading with non-Spaniards. As Luzzatto put it, "All this gave way to the greatest system of contraband in the history of commerce until the Napoleonic blockade."

The prevalent *hidalgo* mentality looked upon imports more as a source of pride than as a latent danger for the country's economy. In 1675 Alfonso Nuñez de Castro wrote:

> Let London manufacture those fabrics of hers to her heart's content; Holland her chambrays; Florence her cloth; the Indies their beaver and vicuña; Milan her brocades; Italy and Flanders their linens, so long as our capital can enjoy them; the only thing it proves is that all nations train journeymen for Madrid and that Madrid is the queen of Parliaments, for all the world serves her and she serves nobody.

With such ideas prevailing in the country, it is not surprising that, in 1659, in the Peace of the Pyrenees, France obtained the right to introduce into Catalonia all kinds of duty-free products, and that a few years later, in 1667, the Spanish frontiers were opened to English goods. From then on, there was no longer any need for contraband. "Spain supplies itself from other countries with almost all things which are manufactured for common use and which consist in the industry and toil of man" wrote a well-informed contemporary observer, and the Venetian Ambassador Vendramin commented:

> about this precious metal which comes to Spain from the Indies, the Spaniards say not without reason that it falls on Spain as does rain on a roof – it pours on her and then flows away.

Through both legal and smuggled imports, effective Spanish demand, sustained by American silver, promoted the economic development of Holland, England, and other European countries. As the 1588–93 Cortes observed:

> although our kingdoms could be the richest in the world for the abundance of gold and silver that have come into them and continue to come in from the Indies, they end up as the poorest because they serve as a bridge across which gold and silver pass to other kingdoms that are our enemies.

That was not all. Bogged down in interminable wars, the Spanish administration spent its tax revenues and the riches it gained from the Indies long before it ever set eyes on them. As a result, the administration was constantly at the mercy of bankers who advanced the sums it needed and then transferred them to the geographical areas where they were required. Until roughly 1555 it was German bankers and especially the Fuggers who had the whip hand. Following the bankruptcy of the Spanish administration in 1557, the Germans withdrew in good order, surrendering their place to the Genoese who displayed extraordinary skill both in handling advances (for which they charged high rates of interest) and transfers (gaining on the exchange rate) thus maximizing the profits that could be made from such operations. Philip II detested them but could not do without them, and in February 1580 admitted to one of his counsellors that "esto de cambios y intereses nunca me ha podido entrar en la cabeza" (I have never managed to get matters of exchange and interest into my head). The supremacy of the Genoese lasted until approximately 1630 when, after the umpteenth Spanish bankruptcy, they were superseded by Portuguese Jewish bankers.

By the end of the sixteenth century, Spain was much richer than a century earlier, but she was not more developed – "like an heiress endowed by the accident of an eccentric will."[5] As I have said already above, the riches of the Americas provided Spain with purchasing power but ultimately they stimulated the development of Holland, England, France, and other European countries. With typical perceptiveness, a Venetian ambassador remarked, "Spain cannot exist unless relieved by others, nor can the rest of the world exist without the money of Spain."

In the course of the seventeenth century, however, the influx of precious metals from America fell drastically, largely because of successful French, English, and Dutch smuggling. It has been estimated that about two-thirds of the treasure that left America between 1620 and 1648 was not recorded on the official Spanish records and did not reach Spain.[6] These are bold and wild

Table 10.1 State income and debt in Castile, 1515–1667

Year	Revenue	Debt	Interest on debt
		(in millions of ducats)	
1515	1.5	12	0.8
1560	5.3	35	2.0
1575	6.0	50	3.8
1598	9.7	85	4.6
1623	15.0	112	5.6
1667	36.0	130	9.1

Source: Wilson and Parker, An Introduction to the Sources, p. 49.

estimates but are not absurd. Thus, the main source of Spanish euphoria dried up. In the meanwhile, however, a century of artificial prosperity had led the government to engage in continuous warfare, with disastrous consequences for the treasury. Moreover, this artificial prosperity had induced many to abandon the land; schools had multiplied, but they had served mostly to produce a half-educated intellectual proletariat who scorned productive industry and manual labor and found positions in the clergy and in the bloated state bureaucracy, both of which served above all to disguise unemployment.[7] Spain in the seventeenth century was heavily in debt (see Table 10.1) and lacked entrepreneurs and artisans but had an overabundance of bureaucrats, lawyers, priests, beggars, and bandits. And the country sank into a dispirited decline.

THE DECLINE OF ITALY

The economic decline of Italy was more complex than that of Spain. Starting in the fourteenth century, the decline of communes and the establishment of the *Signorie* led to a sharp deterioration in social life. People began to regard craft and mercantile activities as menial occupations that barred their practitioners from the upper classes. Yet, however potentially dangerous, these trends had not appreciably affected Italian economic efficiency and wealth.

At the end of the fifteenth century, with good reason and in full knowledge of the facts, Francesco Guicciardini could still write:

> Italy had never known such prosperity, nor experienced such a desirable state as that in which she securely rested in the year of Christian grace 1490, and the years linked to that before and after. The reason was that, because she had been brought wholly to peace and tranquility, tilled no less in the more mountainous and barren places than in the plains and in the most fertile regions, not only did she have an abundance of people and riches, but also, ennobled by the magnificence of many Princes, by the splendor of numerous and very noble cities, by the seat and majesty of the religion, she flowered with eminent men, in the administration of public affairs, in all the sciences, and in every distinguished industry and art.

This was the rosy picture at the end of the fifteenth century. Then suddenly, between 1494 and 1538, the Horsemen of the Apocalypse descended upon Italy. The country became the battle-ground for an international conflict involving Spain, France, and what we would today call Germany. With the war came famines, epidemics, destruction of capital and disruption of trade.

Brescia, which produced 8,000 pieces of woollen cloth a year at the beginning of the century, was producing no more than 1,000 by about 1540. In Como industry and commerce went from bad to worse. Pavia, which had

had about 16,000 inhabitants at the end of the fifteenth century, was reduced to fewer than 7,000 in 1529.[8] In that same year the English ambassadors attending the coronation of Charles V in Bologna reported:

> It is, Sire, the most pitie to see this contree, as we suppose, that ever was in Christendom; in some places nother horsmet nor mans mete to be found, the goodly towns destroyed and desolate.
>
> Betwexte Verceilles, belongyng to the Duke of Savoye, and Pavye, the space of 50 miles, the moost goodly contree for corne and vynes that maye be seen, is so desolate, in all that weye we sawe oon man or woman laborers in the fylde, nor yett creatour stering, but in great villaiges five or six myserable personnes; sawying in all this waye we saw thre women in oone place, gathering of grapis yett uppon the vynes, for there are nother vynes orderyd and kepte, nor corne sawed in all the weye, nor personnes to gather the grapes that growith upon the vynes, but the vynes growyth wyld, great contreys, and hangyng full of clusters of grapes. In this mydde waye is a towne, the which hath been oone of the goodly townes of Italye, callyed Vegeva; there is a strong hold, the towne is all destroyed and in maner desolate. Pavye is in lyke maner, and great pitie; the chyldryn kreyeng abowt the streates for bred, and ye dying for hungre. They seye that all the hole peuple of that contrey and dyvers other places in Italya, as the Pope also shewyd us, with many other, with warre famine and pestilence are utterly deadde and goone; so that there is no hope many yeres that Italya shalbe any thing well restored, for wante of people; and this distruction hath been as well by Frenche men as the Emperours, for they sey that Monsr de Lautreyght destroyed much where as he passyd.[9]

A few years later, in 1533, the Venetian ambassador Basadonna reported:

> The State of Milan is totally ruined; such poverty and ruin cannot be remedied in a short time because the factories are ruined and the people have died out, which is why industry is lacking.[10]

In Florence things were no better. Between the end of the fifteenth century and 1530–40, the population fell from 72,000 to about 60,000, the number of the woollen workshops fell from about 270 to little more than 60, and the annual production of woollens fell accordingly.[11]

Peace finally returned about the middle of the century, and the prediction that "poverty and ruin cannot be remedied in a short time" proved wrong. A centuries-old tradition of industriousness and enterprise had created a human capital of remarkable potential. The recovery was amazingly rapid. Bergamo, which had produced some 7,000 to 8,000 pieces of cloth a year about 1540, produced about 26,500 in 1596. In Florence, wool production increased from 14,700 pieces of cloth in 1553 to 33,000 in 1561 as indicated in Table 10.2. Wool production in Venice suffered badly from the development

Table 10.2 Woollens production in Florence, 1537–1644

Year	No. workshops	No. pieces of cloth produced annually
1537	63	
1553		14,700
1560		30,000
1561		33,000
1571		28,490
1572		33,210
1586	114	
1596	100	
1602		14,000
1606	98	
1616	84	
1626	47	
1629		10,700
1636	41	
1644		5,650

Source: Romano, "A Florence," pp. 509–11; Sella; "Venetian Woollen Industry," p. 115; Diaz, *Il Granducato di Toscana*, p. 356.

of wool production in other centers,[12] but the expansion in the other sectors of the Venetian economy more than offset the losses of the woollens manufactures.[13]

The second half of the sixteenth century was the "Indian summer" of the Italian economy. In that Indian summer, however, were sown the seeds of future difficulties. Reconstruction there was, but it was restoration of old structures, and recovery took place along traditional lines. The guild organization was strengthened, but all the guilds achieved was to prevent competition and innovation.

Italy became progressively less competitive in international markets – at a moment when Italy could ill afford the luxury of becoming less competitive.

Italy had a relatively limited internal market and poor natural endowments. Her economic prosperity was traditionally dependent on her capacity to export a higher percentage of the manufactures and services she produced. During the sixteenth century, other countries, particularly the northern Low Countries and England, developed their production along new scales and with new methods, and their products did well in the international market. As a Milanese official gloomily remarked in 1650, "Of late, man's ingenuity has sharpened everywhere."[14]

Until the end of the sixteenth century demand boomed in the international markets and this sustained efficient, less efficient, and marginal producers. Behind a cheerful façade, however, Italy was sliding imperceptibly from a leading position into a marginal one.

Between the second and third decades of the seventeenth century, a series of weighty factors upset the international economic situation. Imports of precious metals from the Americas entered into a long period of sharp decline and Spain embarked upon its painful decline. In central Europe, a disastrous war broke out in 1618 and, for more than thirty years, brought devastation and endless misery to large areas of the German states. From Turkey in 1611 the Venetian ambassador warned of a marked deterioration of the local market as a consequence of turbulent internal conditions which contributed to declines in both population and income. Between 1623 and 1638, the Turko-Persian War further aggravated an already precarious economic situation. The combined collapse of the Spanish, German, and Turkish markets, added to the contraction in international liquidity, had immediate repercussions on the international economic scene. There was no longer a place for marginal producers, and Italy, by this time, had become a marginal producer.

The documents of the time give an accurate enough idea of the collapse of Italian exports in the course of the seventeenth century. Toward the end of the sixteenth century Genoa exported annually about 360,000 pounds of silk cloth worth some 2.1 million lire; one century later the relevant figures were only 50,000 pounds and half a million lire (see Table 10.4). At the beginning of the seventeenth century Venice exported some 25,000 woollen cloths a year to the Near East. A century later, according to the Venetian ambassador at Constantinople, Venice exported no more than 100 cloths a year, that is, about 50 to Constantinople and the same number to Smyrna. The volume of Venetian business in the two centers had been reduced to an average of 600,000 ducats a year, while that of the French was about 4 million and that of the English not much less than that of the French.[15] As for Florence, in 1668 Count Priorato Gualdo sadly remarked, "We used to have great success with our woollen cloths, but the Dutch have considerably spoiled our sales with their draperies."[16]

Dutch, English, and French products ousted Italian products not only from foreign markets, but even from the Italian one. The combined loss of foreign and internal markets brought about a drastic collapse of production and a massive disinvestment in the manufacturing and service sectors. Data in Tables 10.2 and 10.3 show the collapse in the volume of woollens production in selected major cities. A number of other data relating to other centers or to other sectors confirm the generality of the decline. In Cremona in 1615 there were one hundred and eighty-seven firms producing woollens, and their tax bill was 742 lire. By 1648 the number of firms was down to twenty-three, and the bill was down to 97 lire. By 1749 only two firms were in business. In Cremona again there were ninety-one firms producing fustian cloth in 1615. By 1648 their number had fallen to forty-one.[17] In Como at the beginning of the seventeenth century there were more than thirty looms in operation in the silk manufactures. By 1650 there were only two, one of which worked only six months of the year. By the beginning of the eighteenth century there were no longer any looms operating in Como.[18] The silk industry in Genoa numbered about ten thousand looms in 1565, about four thousand in 1630 and about twenty-five hundred in 1675.[19] Venice produced annually about 800,000 yards of silk cloths at the beginning of the seventeenth century. By 1623 it produced about 600,000 yards and by 1695 only about 250,000 (although this decline was partly compensated by an increase in the proportion of more valuable cloth produced).[20] In the early years of the seventeenth century, Verona and its territory produced up to 150,000 pounds of silk annually. After 1620 production was reduced to less than 90,000 pounds, and by 1713 only 83 silk looms were still in operation in the whole territory.[21]

In Milan the silk looms numbered about 3,000 in 1600, some 600 in 1635 and about 350 in 1711. The economic decline of the state of Milan is borne out by the sums at which the general excise tax was farmed out between 1619 and 1648. The course of the state revenue from the tax was as follows:[22]

    1619–21: 2.1 million lire
    1622–24: 1.8
    1625–27: 1.6
    1628–30: 1.7
    1631–32: 1.2
    1634–36: 1.3
    1637–39: 1.2
    1640–42: 1.1
    1643–45: 1.2
    1646–48: 0.9

In Florence, the annual average production of fabrics (*tele macchiate*) fell from about 13,000 pieces at the beginning of the seventeenth century to about 6,000 pieces around 1650.[23]

The fundamental reason for the replacement of Italian goods and services by foreign ones was always the same: English, Dutch, and French commodities and services were offered at lower prices. But why this disparity in prices? Generally Italian products were of a higher quality. Italian manufacturers, partly because of their proud tradition, but mainly because they were constrained by guild regulations, used traditional methods to produce excellent but outmoded products. In the field of textiles, for example, the English and the Dutch swamped the international market with lighter and less durable products in brighter colors. In qualitative terms the Dutch and English products were inferior to the Italian products, but they cost a good deal less.

Italian products, however, were more expensive not only because they were of better quality, but also because production costs – other things

245

Table 10.3 Production of woollen cloth in selected Italian cities, 1600–99

Decade	Average number of pieces of woollen cloth produced per year		
	Venice	Milan	Como
1600–09	22,430	15,000	10,000
1610–19	18,700		
1620–29	17,270		
1630–39	12,520		
1640–49	11,450	3,000	
1650–59	9,930		400
1660–69	7,480		
1670–79	5,420	445	
1680–89	3,050	489	
1690–99	2,640	400	

Sources: Sella, "Venetian Woollen Industry"; Sella, *Crisis and Continuity*; Cipolla, "The Decline of Italy."

Table 10.4 Exports of silk textiles from Genoa, 1578–1703

Years	Velvets Bolts	Tapestries and damasks Palms	Silk cloths Pounds	Cases	Small frescos Pounds	Total Weight (pounds)	Value (lire)
1578	3,056	45,735	12,561	7	116	359,028	2,131,733
1621	1,745	28,227	11,912	251	9,292	135,109	702,266
1622	5,249	66,920	20,137	171	12,191	198,502	1,320,933
1623	5,181	58,251	15,627	329	4,985	232,158	1,751,200
1624	5,270	57,000	20,596	395	5,182	258,905	1,146,660
1625	4,139	24,337	6,806	228	3,923	167,738	1,031,466
1626	5,024	39,986	8,103	365	6,888	232,770	1,352,933
1627	4,047	50,165	21,177	274	9,480	201,326	1,400,000
1628	3,715	61,084	20,667	259	12,790	193,442	1,475,066
1629	3,834	66,096	20,844	210	8,142	177,090	1,153,333
1630	3,429	66,738	20,936	210	6,471	167,051	908,000
1639	4,798	130,494	28,784	70	6,704	166,608	1,111,333
1693	513	77,805	34,385		20,703	71,264	553,200
1694	518	70,013	29,390		28,626	73,756	609,066
1695	728	83,591	34,461		25,194	80,748	608,266
1696	730	49,264	17,774		5,241	41,766	260,800
1697	746	38,679	25,842		6,578	50,772	356,533
1700	404	75,680	20,010		30,357	64,107	533,866
1703	496	71,200	21,176		12,705	49,241	487,066

Source: Sivori, "Il tramonto dell'industria serica genovese," p. 937.

being equal – were higher in Italy than in Holland, England and France. This was essentially due to three circumstances:

a. Excessive control by the guilds compelled Italian manufacturers to continue using obsolete methods of production and organization. The guilds had become associations primarily directed at preventing competition among associates, and they constituted a formidable obstacle to technological and organizational innovations.
b. The pressure of taxation in Italian states was too high and badly designed.
c. Labor costs in Italy were too high in relation to the wage levels in competing countries. During the so-called price revolution of the sixteenth century, nominal wages outside Italy did not keep pace with prices. In Italy, because of a stronger guild organization, workers managed to obtain wage increases proportionate to the rise in prices. While in England the level of real wages at the beginning of the seventeenth century was noticeably lower than a hundred years earlier, in Italy real wages did not show any substantial decrease in the course of the sixteenth century.[24] Everything points to the fact that, at the beginning of the seventeenth century, Italian wages were out of step with wages in other countries. If these higher wage levels had been balanced by higher productivity, Italy would not have suffered, but for the reasons indicated above, labor productivity was lower in Italy than in England, Holland, or France.

The effects of all these developments on the Italian economy were as follows: (a) a drastic decline in exports which lasted for decades and continually worsened; (b) a prolonged process of disinvestment in manufacturing and shipping.

Outside Italy too there was a flight of manufacturing activity from the cities to the countryside. North of the Alps, economic historians have given this phenomenon a positive gloss, seeing in it the symptoms of a process of proto-industrialization. There indeed, when manufacturing shifted from city to countryside it actually escaped from the controls of the city guilds and its innovating efforts generally gained the benevolent support of the Crown. In Italy, on the other hand, the city's overweening power over the surrounding countryside sustained the city guilds' ability to interfere. This spelled ruin for the few paltry attempts by enterprising operators to introduce innovations. As a result, Italian manufacturing firms remained prisoners of the past.

Against the background of these purely economic factors, other social and cultural forces were at work. The social structures of the country had grown rigid, as had the prevailing mindset. Italians at the time of Dante and Marco Polo had displayed mental openness and acute curiosity but success generates conceitedness which in turn feeds ignorance. Commenting on the attitude of the Italians at the beginning of the seventeenth century, Fynes Moryson wrote:

> Italians are so convinced that they know and understand everything ... so that they never travel abroad unless forced to by necessity. The opinion that Italy is well stocked with everything that may be seen or known makes Italians provincial and presumptuous.[25]

This state of mind went hand in hand with technological and organizational backwardness. This is well illustrated by the following episode. As already mentioned, in the course of the sixteenth and seventeenth centuries those large trading companies that managed to obtain from their respective governments a trading monopoly over a particular geopolitical area enjoyed both fame and fortune. Of these colossi the two biggest were the English Company of the East Indies, authorized in December 1600 by Queen Elizabeth and given the name "The Governor and Merchants of London trading into the East Indies" and the Dutch Company founded in 1602 under the name Vereinigde Ostindische Compagnie. Attracted by the enormous profits that these new companies managed to earn, similar companies were established in other European countries, including France and Denmark.

In Italy a number of Genoese entrepreneurs combined to make a similar attempt and so in 1647 the "Compagnia Genovese delle Indie Orientali" was founded with a capital of 100,000 *scudi*. However, once the company existed on paper, the entrepreneurs found that local conditions were too under-developed for their venture to take off properly. To start with, there were no shipyards in Genoa able to construct ocean-going ships of the type used by the English and Dutch companies. This meant that the Genoese had to order two ships from the Texel shipyards in Holland. This order, however, had to remain shrouded in secrecy since it was strictly prohibited in Holland to build ships of the Dutch type for foreign powers. Having taken delivery of the ships, the Genoese then realized that there were no sailors in Genoa with the requisite experience in sailing such ships on difficult ocean voyages. They therefore had to engage a Dutch crew. Once they had over-come these hitches – which in themselves demonstrated the extent of Italy's backwardness as compared with the other main European powers – the ships weighed anchor in Genoa on 3 March 1648. However, the Portuguese and the Dutch – normally arch enemies – joined to nip in the bud this nascent competitor, and on 26 April 1649 a small Dutch fleet seized the Genoese ships and forced them to sail to Batavia.

In 1630 central-northern Italy was devastated by the plague. In less than two years, about 1.1 million people died out of a population of four million. If one concedes that it would have been impossible for Italy to keep her traditional sources of income or to find new ones, then a slow, protracted decline in population might have been a solution to her economic diffi-culties. But a drastic and rapid fall in population like that caused by the plague of 1630 had the effect of raising wages and putting Italian exports in an even more difficult position. Moreover, in the long run, after the plague, population expanded again. In 1600 the entire population of the Italian peninsula must have been around 12 million. In 1700 it was around 13 million.[26] However, in 1700 Italy had few manufactures left and had lost her position of commercial and banking supremacy.

By the end of the seventeenth century Italy imported large quantities of manufactured goods from England, France, and Holland. At this stage she exported mostly agricultural and semi-finished goods, namely, oil, wheat, wine, wool, and especially raw and thrown silk. In the area of maritime services, Italy was reduced to playing a passive role and the great expansion of the free port of Leghorn in the seventeenth century was the result of the triumph of English and Dutch shipping in the Mediterranean.

What happened to Italy provides a good illustration of the ambivalence of foreign trade. From the eleventh to the sixteenth centuries foreign trade had been indeed an "engine of growth" for Italy because (a) it provided the country with raw materials and commodities for re-export and (b) it boosted demand for manufactured goods, thus stimulating the growth of craft skills and manufacturing production. From the beginning of the seventeenth century, however, the structure of Italian foreign trade changed completely. Foreign manufactures were brought in and drove Italian products and producers out of the market. At the same time foreign demand promoted the production of oil, wine, and raw silk. One may argue that in the short run Italy derived from this new arrangement some comparative advantages of the kind illustrated by the Ricardian theory. In the long run, however, foreign trade acted as an "engine of decline": it helped to shift both capital and labor from the secondary and tertiary sectors to agriculture. In regard to labor this shift meant, in the long run, (a) the reduction in number of both literate craftsmen and enterprising merchants, (b) the expansion of the illiterate peasantry, and (c) the rise in power of the landed nobility. The nobility asserted its pre-eminence economically as well as politically, socially, and administratively. The cities lost their previous vitality. The great universities of Padua and Bologna slipped into oblivion. Venice sent her best gun-founder, Alberghetti, to London to learn the most modern techniques for working metals. The few remaining Italian clockmakers copied the style and the mechanisms of the numerous and skilful London clockmakers. Italy had begun her career as an underdeveloped area within Europe.

THE RISE OF THE NORTHERN NETHERLANDS

Traditionally, the Netherlands can be divided into the southern Netherlands and the northern Netherlands.[27] In the mid-sixteenth century the southern Netherlands included the counties of Flanders, Namur, Hainault and Artois, the duchies of Brabant, Luxembourg and Limburg, the lordship of Malines, and the bishoprics of Liège and Cambrai. The northern Netherlands included the provinces of Holland, Zealand, Frisia, Utrecht, Groningen, Gelderland, Drente, and Overijssel.

From the eleventh to the fifteenth centuries the southern Netherlands were at the forefront of unprecedented economic and urban development. The southern Netherlands became one of Europe's major centers of development, second only to Italy. The most important international business center in northern Europe in the thirteenth and fourteenth centuries was Bruges, in the county of Flanders, and in the fifteenth century and first half of the sixteenth century it was Antwerp, in the duchy of Brabant.[28] The textile manufacturers of Flanders largely supplied northern and central Europe with the best woollen cloths. And the Flemish painters translated the vitality of their people into masterpieces of color.

The northern Netherlands did not keep pace with the southern provinces: their development was slower and less brilliant. But development there was, and it was consistent. It was based particularly on agriculture and stock-raising, and on two other sectors, both linked to sailing: fishing and trade with the Baltic lands. During the Middle Ages various towns in the northern Netherlands had joined the Hanseatic League. From the beginning of the fifteenth century, with the growth of their strength and their commercial aggressiveness, the League sought to bar these towns from access to the Baltic. The Dutch left the League and after a tough struggle (1438–71) managed to have that sea kept open to their ships. The Baltic always remained the most important area of the foreign trade of the northern Netherlands. Even when centuries later the United Provinces launched themselves successfully into the trade with the Americas and the Far East, trade with the Baltic remained so paramount that it was always referred to as the "mother trade." The relative importance of Baltic trade for the Netherlands as a whole (that is both northern and southern Low Countries) at the middle of the sixteenth century is indicated in Table 10.5.

Initially, trade with the Baltic consisted mainly of exports of non-bulky high unit value goods such as salt, fabrics, spices, and wine traveling from west to east and of furs, wax, honey, and potash from east to west. It was unusual for ships to sail around the Jutland peninsula. Goods from the west were taken by sea to Hamburg where they were offloaded and transported overland to Lübeck. At Lübeck they were then reloaded on ships and transported by sea to their destination. Goods traveling from east to west went through the same process in reverse. This complicated system of loading, offloading, and reloading was very advantageous to Hamburg and Lübeck which both profited from the transit trade and the activities of offloading and transportation. During the fourteenth century, however, shipbuilding techniques and navigation improved to the point where it became feasible for ships to sail round the Jutland peninsula as a matter of course. Having eliminated costly loading operations at Hamburg and Lübeck, it now made

Table 10.5 Estimated value of yearly imports into the Low Countries (northern and southern) about the middle of the sixteenth century

Country or area of origin	Value of imports (guilders)
England	4,150,000
Baltic	4,500,000
German principalities	2,000,000
France	2,700,000
Spain and Portugal	4,650,000
Italy	4,300,000
Total	22,300,000

Source: Brulez, "The Balance of Trade," pp. 20–48.

economic sense to transport from the eastern Baltic countries quite bulky and low cost goods as flax, hemp, and particularly grain and timber.

The effects of such changes were soon felt in the competition between the Hanseatics and the Dutch. Initially, the Baltic rich trades remained securely in the hands of the merchants of Lübeck and to a lesser extent of Hamburg. Things changed during the 1580s and 1590s. As J.I. Israel has remarked, there was nothing gradual about the emergence of the Dutch as the masters of the northern trade. The Hansa towns lost their age-old struggle with the Hollanders in the Baltic bulk trade essentially because they proved unable to cope with its growing scale and complexity. The 1590s saw the entry of the Dutch into valuable commerce with northern Russia. By 1604, 70 percent of the pepper and much of the cloth entering Muscovy from the West was being dispatched from Holland and by 1609 the Dutch dominated the Russian trade. By the first decades of the seventeenth century, Amsterdam· was the hub of the European world economy, the great emporium that both reflected and dictated the pace of European trade. By that time the economy of the northern Netherlands had reached a high degree of differentiation. Foreign trade had been systematically integrated with manufacturing. The situation is brought out well in the report of an acute Italian observer, Ludovico Guicciardini, who in 1567 wrote:

> This country produces little wheat and not even rye because of the low ground and wateriness, yet enjoys so much plenty that it supplies other countries as much grain is imported, especially from Denmark and from Ostarlante [countries of the Baltic]. It does not make wine, and there is more wine and more of it is drunk than in any other part where it is made, and it is brought from a number of places, particularly Rhine wine. It has no flax, yet it makes finer textiles than any

other region of the world [and it still imports such textiles] from Flanders and from the area of Liège.... It has no wool, and it makes countless woollens [and even imports some] from England, Scotland, Spain, and a few from Brabant. It has no wood and makes more furniture and more stacks of wood and other things than does the whole of the rest of Europe.[29]

With these words Guicciardini highlighted both the importance of international trade for the northern Netherlands and the close relationship between international trade and the manufacturing sector. Behind developed trading and manufacturing activities was also an agriculture which, thanks to a tradition going back centuries, was among the most developed of the age.

The foregoing gives only a rough indication of some of the more distant causes of the Dutch "miracle" of the seventeenth century. The fact of the matter is that the country that in the second half of the sixteenth century rebelled against Spanish imperialism and then rose to become Europe's economically most dynamic nation, was anything but an underdeveloped country from the outset.

With the revolt against Spain and the ensuing long war came the ruin of the southern Netherlands. In 1571 the fulling mills of Ninove and Ath were reduced to ashes. In 1584 the only fulling mills left standing anywhere in Flanders were those of Blendesques. Hondschote, Bailleul, Nieuwkerke, Weert, Zichem, and other centers of textile production were also seriously damaged in the war. In 1585 Antwerp was sacked. The Dutch remained masters of the seas, and the ruin of the southern provinces gave them a free hand in the commercial penetration of the southern seas and the oceans. Not only did they take advantage of the situation, but they gave events a helping hand. Since the southern Low Countries were now under Spanish domination and the war dragged on, the Dutch blockaded the southern ports and did their best to delay the recovery of the southern provinces.

After the peace of 1609, the Northern United Provinces emerged with political independence and religious freedom. An even more startling fact was that the economy of the new state was far more vital than ever – in fact, it was the most dynamic, the best developed, and the most competitive economy in Europe, despite forty years of war against the Spanish giant and despite the fact that the country was poorly endowed with natural resources.[30] In 1611, only two years after the end of the war, the Venetian ambassador Foscarini reported from London:

It is generally thought that in a very short time the trade of the United Provinces with all parts of the world will multiply, for the Dutch are content with moderate gains and are richly equipped with excellent seamen, ships, money, everything which used to be the specialties of Venice when her trade was flourishing.

and a few years later, in 1618, another Venetian diplomat described Amsterdam as "the image of Venice in the days when Venice was thriving."[31]

Attempting to explain this "miracle," Charles Wilson[32] stressed the importance of the "old Burgundian tradition" – in other words, as already noted, the country which rose against Spain, fought for forty years and emerged victorious, was not an underdeveloped country but an advanced and civilized country of old tradition. What Charles Wilson wrote with regard to the political and military aspects of the "miracle" can be repeated about the economic aspects – with an important addition.

The most damaging blow which Spanish fanaticism and intolerance dealt to the southern Netherlands was not perhaps the destruction of wealth and physical capital, however great such destruction was, but the flight of "human capital." Involuntarily, Spain enriched her own enemy with the most precious of all capital. The fugitives from the southern provinces – known throughout northern Europe as Walloons – went here, there, and everywhere: to England, to Germany, to Sweden, but, naturally, mostly to the northern Netherlands. Among them were craftsmen, sailors, merchants, financiers, and professionals who brought to their elected country artisanship, commercial know-how, entrepreneurial spirit and, often, hard cash. Admissions to the freedom of Amsterdam rose from 344 in 1575–79 to 2,768 in 1615–19.[33] For the southern provinces it proved to be a frightening bloodletting; for the northern ones, a powerful tonic. The most famous merchant of the time, the founder and administrator of a great economic empire with headquarters in Amsterdam, Luis de Geer (1587–1652), was a Walloon.[34] By the beginning of the seventeenth century the Walloons were one of the most powerful groups of shareholders within the Dutch East India Company. In 1609–11 Walloons held half of the largest bank deposits in Amsterdam and represented about 30 percent of the citizens in the highest tax brackets.[35] It was Walloon exiles who introduced new mills for the fulling of woollen cloth at Leyden in 1585 and Rotterdam in 1591.[36]

Vigorous in their own right, strengthened by the injection of a powerful new dose of vitality and galvanized by the opening of countless new opportunities in ocean trade, the Northern United Provinces entered their golden age. Amsterdam became an international market where one could find goods from all over the world – Japanese copper, Swedish copper, Baltic grain, Italian silk, French wines, Chinese porcelain, Brazilian coffee, oriental tea, Indonesian spices, Mexican silver. Amsterdam, in fact, became the main world market for a variety of products – from guns to diamonds, from sugar to porcelain – and the price quotations on the Amsterdam market dictated the prices on the other European markets.[37] The business techniques inherited from the Italians were refined and developed. The stock exchange was born, and what Werner Sombart described as "Früh Kapitalismus" was replaced by incipient modern capitalism.

253

As always in such cases, the vigor of a people is by its nature diasporic. What a pope had said of Florentines in the Middle Ages can be applied to the Dutch of the seventeenth century: they were the fifth element in the world. They were to be found everywhere – acting as consultants to the Grand Duchy of Tuscany, reclaiming the Maremma; establishing the first smelting plants for iron cannon in Russia; expanding sugar plantations in Brazil; buying tea, porcelain, and silk in China; founding New Amsterdam (later to be called New York) in North America, and, in the Adriatic in 1616–19, protecting with their galleons the once-greatest naval power, Venice, from possible Spanish attacks. The economic development of Sweden in the seventeenth century was the by-product of Dutch activity. When Japan closed its doors to the West and embarked upon centuries of isolation, an exception was made for the Dutch, who were permitted to maintain a base in Nagasaki.

Just as the vitality of a people knows no geographic frontiers, neither does it know professional boundaries. When between the thirteenth and fourteenth centuries Tuscany gave Europe her most active merchants and craftsmen, she also produced exceptional poets, writers, and doctors. The northern Netherlands in the seventeenth century were pre-eminent in shipping as well as in painting, in commercial as well as in philosophical speculation, and in scientific observation. The annual cloth production in Leyden grew from about 30,000 pieces in 1585 to over 140,000 pieces around 1665.[38] At the same time, the University of Leyden became known as the most important center for the study of medicine in Europe. While de Keyster, van de Welde, and Frans Hals painted their superb masterpieces, while Huygens made important contributions to both technology and science, in the field of international law Grotius elaborated a theory of international and territorial waters which still rules international relations today.

It is no accident that Grotius appeared when and where he did. The life and prosperity of the northern Netherlands in their golden age continued to depend upon the freedom of the seas and upon the strength of their fleets. Impressed by Dutch naval power, contemporaries made the most fantastic estimates about it. Sir Walter Raleigh maintained that the Dutch built a thousand ships a year and that their navy and merchant marine consisted of about twenty thousand units. Colbert estimated in 1669 that "the maritime trade of all Europe is carried out by twenty thousand ships, of which fifteen to sixteen thousand are Dutch, three to four thousand are English, and five to six hundred are French."[39] However, it was a question not only of quantity but also of quality. In 1596 the town council of Amsterdam could write to the States-General of the Dutch Republic that "this country in merchant marine and shipbuilding is so much more advanced than the kingdoms of France and England that it is impossible to make a comparison."[40] As R.W. Unger remarked, "Over the following two centuries it was the task of other European shipbuilders to try to equal the technical progress made by Dutch shipcarpenters."[41]

The most dynamic and glamorous sector of the Dutch economy was undoubtedly foreign trade. As Daniel Defoe put it:

> The Dutch must be understood as they really are, the Middle Persons in Trade, the Factors and Brokers of Europe.... They buy to sell again, take in to send out, and the greatest part of their vast commerce consists in being supply'd from all parts of the world that they may supply all the world again.[42]

It is convenient to divide the Dutch commerce of the sixteenth and seventeenth centuries into two fairly distinct areas, each characterized in general by different techniques of trading, shipping, and finance. On the one hand, there was the long-distance trade overseas – in the East and West Indies, in Brazil, at Canton and Nagasaki. On the other hand there was the trade in the home waters of western Europe. Within both areas it was the Baltic trade which for the Dutch retained absolute pre-eminence. The composition of Baltic trade and the overwhelming importance of the Dutch in it is well known because the Danes were able to levy tolls on almost all international shipping which passed through the only navigable passage from the Baltic to the North Sea. The records of the tolls at the Sound have survived in great detail from the end of the fifteenth century, and, making due allowance for omissions, smuggling, errors of interpretation, and the like, one can derive from them a fairly reliable picture of Baltic trade patterns. Of the ships which passed through the Sound from 1550 to 1650, the Dutch share fluctuated between 55 and 85 percent. The Dutch share of the imports into the Baltic fluctuated around 50 percent for salt, 60 to 80 percent for herring, more than 80 percent for Rhine wines. Among exports from the Baltic to the West, grains were a major commodity (about 65 percent of total exports around 1565 and some 55 percent in 1635). The Dutch share of the grain trade fluctuated around a long-term average of about 75 percent.[43] Dutch prosperity however did not rest on mercantile success alone. Agriculture and manufactured goods developed remarkably in seventeenth-century Holland. As has been said, the Netherlands became the Mecca of European agricultural experts, and it is possible that the Low Countries reached relatively advanced technical levels with yields two or three times above those of the rest of Europe. Manufacturing also developed noticeably and on a broad front.

A number of manufacturing activities in the Netherlands were closely linked with international trade insofar as they were concerned with finishing or refining commodities imported in a crude or partly manufactured state.[44] Thus, there were in the northern Low Countries numerous and important concerns for the cutting and wrapping of imported tobacco, for the weaving of imported silk, for the refining of imported sugar. There were three sugar refineries in Amsterdam in 1605 and sixty in 1660. Using copper from Japan and Sweden, the foundries of Amsterdam, Rotterdam, and other towns produced guns which were mostly sold to foreign countries – even to the arch-enemy, Spain. Of French wine, according to Colbert, the Dutch consumed only a third. Two-thirds they re-exported after much manipulation, processing, and blending. As Roger Dion wrote,

> Merchants *par excellence*, the Dutch lacked respect for the integrity of the "cru" which was one of the fundamental principles of high-quality viticulture in France. Even good wines did not escape their manipulations.[45]

The development of shipping and overseas trade stimulated the growth of related activities such as shipbuilding, the making of precision instruments, cartography and map production.

In horology seventeenth-century Holland may justly claim two most important contributions, namely the development of the pendulum and the balance spring. The Dutch makers as a whole failed to take full advantage of Huygens's discoveries and in general they did not carry the art to the stage of refinement and accuracy which characterized English production, but they produced watches, bracket clocks, and long-case clocks in considerable number. As to other precision instruments, early in the eighteenth century it was reported that "there is a greater choice of astronomical, geometrical, and other mathematical instruments in Holland than anywhere else in the world."

In cartography the Italians had traditionally dominated the field, but the year 1570 marks a clear turning point, for in that year Ortelius produced the first edition of his celebrated atlas in Antwerp. Ortelius was closely followed by Mercator and Hondius and pre-eminence in map production passed from Italy to the Low Countries. The centers of production, at first in Antwerp and Duisberg, soon shifted to Amsterdam, and it can be said that for roughly a century, from 1570 to 1670, the Low Countries produced in some respects the greatest map makers of the world. For accuracy (according to the knowledge of their time), magnificence of presentation and richness of decoration, the Dutch maps of the seventeenth century have never been surpassed.[46]

Any attempt to explain Dutch success in such varied sectors as agriculture, trade, and industry would be incomplete if it did not take account of the fact that the Dutch managed to break through the bottleneck of the energy constraint by large-scale exploitation of two inanimate energy sources, namely peat and the wind.

The Netherlands were poor in trees but rich in peat deposits. Large-scale exploitation of this energy source began in the sixteenth century. Dr de Zeeuw has calculated that in the mid-seventeenth century the Netherlands were burning peat equivalent to 6,000 million kilocalories per year. This enormous quantity of energy was used not only for home heating but also for industrial purposes such as producing brick, glass, and beer.

The Dutch also exploited wind energy on a very large scale. At sea they did so through the ever more massive and rationalized use of sail; on land through the massing of windmills. De Zeeuw has calculated that in the mid-seventeenth century some 3,000 windmills were in operation in the northern Low Countries, with a potential energy output of some 45,000 million kilowatt hours per year, equivalent to the use of some 50,000 horses. Windmills were used in many different ways. About 1630 in the province of Holland there were 222 industrial windmills, plus an unknown number of grain mills and drainage mills. Most of these mills were located in the area of Noorder-Kwartier, an area just north of Amsterdam. In this area (approximately 148,000 acres and 85,000 people), the operational distribution of the windmills was as follows:[47]

Operation	Number of mills
Saw milling	60
Oil pressing	57
Grain milling	53
Paper production	9
Hemp working	5
Cloth fulling	2
Shell crushing	1
Tanning	1
Buckwheat milling	1
Paint production	1
Dye production	1
Drainage	?

Whether one looks at the agricultural, commercial, or manufacturing sector, one finds that the Dutch had a genius, if not an obsession, for reducing costs. They succeeded in selling anything to anybody anywhere in the world because they sold it more cheaply than anybody else, and their prices were competitively low because their costs of production were more compressed than elsewhere.

Wages were notoriously high in the United Provinces, where heavy excise taxes burdened all articles of general consumption. But the productivity of Dutch labor more than offset this comparative disadvantage. "The thrifty and neat disposition" of the Dutch craftsmen praised by Nicolaes Witsen (see above, p. 159) was admiringly recognized also by Colbert, who wrote of "l'économie et l'application continuelle au travail" of the Dutch workers.[48] The Dutch relied on cheap money.[49] Moreover, they made extensive use of labor-saving devices. We have already discussed the extensive exploitation of the energy of the wind both on land and at sea. In the field of maritime transport, their greatest achievement was the production of the *fluitship* (*fluyt*).

The design of the *fluyt* grew out of experience with the flyboat. As has been aptly said, "the fluyt was the outstanding achievement of Dutch ship-building in the era of full-rigged ships, the fulfilment of a long period of improvement in Dutch ship design,"[50] and it became the great cargo carrier of northern Europe in the seventeenth century. Sail area was kept small and masts short relative to carrying capacity; although these features meant a slower ship, such a ship, more importantly, needed a smaller crew, and consequently incurred lower costs. The excellent handling qualities of the ship further helped to reduce the size of the crew, as did the extensive use of pulleys and blocks in controlling the yards and sails. Cheap, light pine was generally used, except for the hull, where oak was needed to withstand exposure to salt water. The lightly built *fluyt* was almost defenseless, and when it carried guns the complement was small; but this too was a calcu-lated risk[51] which further lowered operating costs.

When the Dutch could not reduce costs in any other way, they reduced the quality of the product. In the woollens sector, they produced brightly colored cloths of inferior quality – known as "cloths in the fashion of Holland" – and used them to corner a large part of the international market to the detriment of those who continued to produce "cloths of the good old standard."[52] In the wine trade, they dealt in the "*petits vins*" (inferior wines) which had never before been considered in international trade.[53]

The *fluyt*. This was the masterpiece of the Dutch shipbuilders of the seventeenth century.

In sacrificing quality for the sake of reducing price, the Dutch departed from a tradition that had prevailed in the Middle Ages and the early Renaissance and heralded a principle which was to prevail in modern times. The medieval merchant had normally tried to maximize profit per unit of production – thus his insistence on high quality. The Dutch, however, made a decisive move toward mass production. In an increasing number of activities they endeavoured to maximize their profit by maximizing the volume of sales. As the Venetian ambassador Foscarini reported in 1611 "the Dutch are content with moderate gains." Even Dutch painters produced their masterpieces at low prices and in prolific quantities. The average price of, say, a Salomon Ruisdael landscape or a Steen genre picture was about a quarter of the weekly wage of a Leyden textile worker.[54] The new attitude of the Dutch was prompted by – and their success was linked to – the fact that new, larger social groups were ascending the economic ladder in Europe, and price elasticity of demand was growing for an increasing number of commodities.

Dutch success evoked admiration among some, envy among others, and great interest everywhere. Holland held all Europe fascinated, but more than anyone else their neighbors across the Channel, the English.

THE RISE OF ENGLAND

At the end of the fifteenth century, England was still an "underdeveloped country" – underdeveloped not only in comparison with modern industrialized countries, but also in relation to the standards of the "developed" countries of that time, such as Italy, the Low Countries, France, and southern Germany.

There were fewer than 4 million inhabitants in England and Wales, while France numbered over 15 million, Italy about 11 million, and Spain between 6 and 7 million. The small size of the English population was not offset by greater wealth. On the contrary, from both the technological and economic points of view, England was backward compared with most of the continent.

As D.C. Coleman put it,

England was still a country on the near fringes of the European world, economically and culturally as well as geographically. The dominant economies were in the Mediterranean lands, especially in Italy; in South Germany; in the commercial and industrial cities of Flanders; and the north German towns of the commercial empire of the Hanseatic League. Indeed Hansards and other aliens, mainly Italians, still controlled about 40 per cent of English overseas trade. The English mercantile marine, though showing healthy signs of expansion, was of small significance. England's one substantial commercial city, London, was overshadowed in wealth and size as well as in political and cultural consequence by the great cities of continental Europe. It was about the same rank as Verona or Zurich; it did not compare with the greatest seaport in Europe, Venice; and nothing in England even began to match such a manifestation of wealth and power as the Medici family controlling the biggest financial organization in Europe, with its base in Florence.[55]

England, however, produced the best wool in Europe, and from the fourteenth century onward she moved more and more into the production of woollen cloth. Wool and woollen cloth represented the bulk of English exports in the last centuries of the Middle Ages and the rise in the proportion of woollen cloth to raw wool in export figures can be taken as an index of the increasing weight of manufacturing in the economy. (See Table 10.6 and Figure 10.2.) The transition from a stage characterized by massive exports of indigenous raw materials to a stage increasingly characterized by manufactured goods made from such raw materials is a typical step on the road to economic development.

English products were traditionally exported to markets in the southern Netherlands – first Bruges, then Antwerp – whence they were distributed to various parts of the continent.

Table 10.6 Average yearly English exports of raw wool and woollen cloth, 1361–1500

Years	Raw wool (bags)	Woollen cloths (as equivalent to bags of raw wool)
1361–70	28,302	3,024
1371–80	23,241	3,432
1381–90	17,988	5,521
1391–1400	17,679	8,967
1401–10	13,922	7,651
1411–20	13,487	6,364
1421–30	13,696	9,309
1431–40	7,377	10,051
1441–50	9,398	11,803
1471–80	9,299	10,125
1481–90	8,858	12,230
1491–1500	8,149	13,891

Source: Bridbury, *Economic Growth*, p. 32. Data are derived from customs records and account must therefore be taken of possible underregistration. As it appears that underregistration was more widespread during the Civil War years, the figures for the two decades 1451–70 have been omitted.

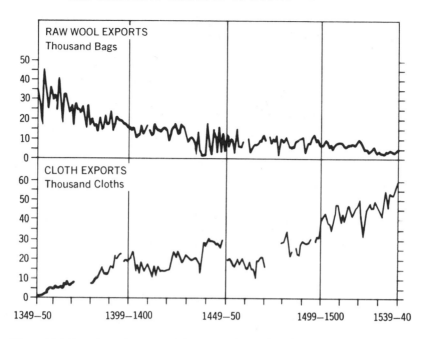

Figure 10.2 Trends in the export of raw wool and cloth from England, 1349–1540.

Source: H.C. Darby (ed.), *A New Historical Geography of England*, p. 219.

In the course of the fifteenth century, the merchants of Nuremburg, Augsburg, Ravensburg, and other cities of southern Germany established closer contacts with Bruges and Antwerp, using as intermediaries the merchants of the Rhineland towns and, in the second half of the century, these contacts became more frequent and direct. The development of Portuguese trade in Antwerp was the catalyst; the Portuguese sold ivory, gold, and pepper from West Africa and sugar from Madeira, and were active purchasers of those products that the Germans could sell in large quantities, namely, silver, mercury, copper, and weapons.[56] The period 1490–1525 marked the apogee of the southern German merchants' success on the Antwerp market where, among others, economic giants such as the Imhofs, the Welsers, and the Fuggers were very active.[57] On the Antwerp market, south German merchants found not only the commodities brought there by the Portuguese, but also English textiles.

Traditionally, the merchants of southern Germany obtained their supplies of woollen cloth on the markets of northern Italy (especially Milan, Como, Brescia, and Bergamo)[58] and then redistributed them throughout central and eastern Europe. However, as we have seen above, in the first half of the sixteenth century Italian production collapsed because of the war

261

and the ensuing disasters. As Italian suppliers were no longer in a position to satisfy German demand, German merchants availed themselves of cloth that was made in England and available in Antwerp.

A golden age thus began for English exports, later boosted between 1522 and 1550 by the chaotic devaluations of the pound which Henry VIII debased to finance his extravagant military expenditure.

The textile manufacturing sector in England was the first to show the effects of the boom in exports. But in economics waves travel far, and what happens in one sector never fails to make ripples in others – especially when the expanding sector is a key one in the economy. Professor F.J. Fisher has elicited evidence to show that English shortcloth exports tripled between 1500 and 1550 and that as a result "arable land was turned over to pasture, the textile industry spread throughout the countryside, the number of merchants swelled ... there was a considerable rise in the standard of living, as demonstrated by the proliferation of sumptuary laws." But Professor J.D. Gould has shown that, on close examination, Fisher's assertion that there was an increase of 300 percent in exports of woollen goods is invalidated by mistakes in his interpretation of sources.[59]

Nobody, however, contests the fact that English exports did grow substantially even if not by as much as Fisher has maintained. It is none the less undeniable that English economic development in that half century was based on the creation and on the prosperity of the London–Antwerp axis. This fact explains the tendency during that period for southern and especially southeastern England to be the richer and more active area of the economy, sucking in people, goods, and trade. Many provincial traders found themselves unable to compete against the increasingly rich and powerful London merchants. The commerce of the old and important port of Bristol declined and a similar fate befell such ports as Hull, Boston, and Sandwich – although some developed other types of trade, for example the coastal trade of coal and cereals to supply the rapidly growing population of London.

By the middle of the sixteenth century, the value of England's total exports in normal years stood perhaps at some £75,000 per annum. Woollens of one sort or another still accounted for over 80 percent of all exports, with raw wool down to a mere 6 percent. Most of the English trade was still limited to Europe. The English mercantile marine was as yet of small consequence, perhaps about 50,000 tons, and much of the country's foreign trade, even when handled by English merchants, was carried by foreign vessels.

The elements of continuity were numerous and significant, and yet in more than one sense by the middle of the sixteenth century England looked very different from what she had been a century earlier. Literacy – to take one indicator – was rapidly spreading among the population and society as well as the economy was undergoing a process of substantial change.

England was rapidly lining up with the most advanced countries of the continent.[60]

At this juncture a severe and prolonged crisis interrupted the expansionist trend which had characterized the English economy for about two-thirds of a century. Following the remarkable increase in the 1500–50 period, exports of shortcloths from the port of London fell sharply between 1550 and 1564, stabilizing towards the end of the century at around 100,000 cloths per year.[61] The recovery of the Italian textile industry, the stagnation of southern Germany, the war in the southern Low Countries, the revaluation of the currency, all contributed to the difficulties of the English exporters. As a text of the time reported, the English "Merchants perceived the commodities and wares of England to be in small request with the contrys and people about and near England, and the price thereof abated, and certain grave citizens of London and men of great wisdom and careful for the good of their country began to thinke with themselves how this mischiefe might be remedied."

The "mischiefe" was "remedied." Relying on the evidence of shortcloths export figures relating to London, Professor Fisher advanced the hypothesis that "the maladjustments of the fifties" opened the way to a "great depression" which lasted until the end of the century.[62] This is an exaggeration. As another economic historian pointed out, we must "modify the picture of stagnation and depression given by the London cloth statistics."[63] The fact of the matter is that the period 1550–1650 was characterized by England's entry into a new stage in her economic development – a stage in which other manufactures besides woollens began to play a major role in the economy.

Obviously the shift from one type of economy to another occurred gradually. Woollen textiles still accounted for about 48 percent of exports (see Table 10.7) at the end of the seventeenth century. But from the middle of the sixteenth century, new sectors began to expand and to achieve a

Table 10.7 Commodity composition of English foreign trade, 1699–1701

	Exports %	Imports %
Wool manufactures	47.5	31.7
Other manufactures	8.4	
Foodstuffs	7.6	33.6
Raw materials	5.6	34.7
Re-exports	30.9	
Total	100.0	100.0

Source: Davis, "English Foreign Trade 1660–1700," p. 109.

steadily increasing importance in the economy. The generations of the second half of the sixteenth century were not melancholic generations, gloomily bemoaning the stagnating exports of shortcloth from the harbor of London. They were bold and adventurous generations which, if they encountered some difficulties, looked to new horizons, searched for opportunities, and redirected English development. The production of iron, lead, armament, new types of cloth, glass, silk, grew remarkably in the second half of the sixteenth century. The blast furnaces of England and Wales produced some 5,000 tons of iron per annum around 1550 and 18,000 tons per annum around 1600 (see Table 10.8). The output of lead reached 3,200 tons in about 1580. And that was not all. Joshua Gee mentions that

the manufacture of Linnen was settlled in several parts of the Kingdom.... Also the manufacture of Copper and Brass were set on Foot, which are brought to great Perfection and now in a great Measuere supply the Nation with Coppers, Kettles and all Sorts of Copper and Brass ware. The making of Sail cloth was began and carried on to great Perfection; also Sword Blades, Sciffars and a great many Toys made of Steel which formerly we used to have from France.[64]

Table 10.8 Occupied blast-furnace sites, average furnace output, and total output, by decades, England and Wales, 1530–1709

Date	Furnaces	Average output (tons)	Total output (000 tons)
1530–9	6	200	1.2
1540–9	22	200	4.4
1550–9	26	200	5.2
1560–9	44	200	8.8
1570–9	67	200	13.4
1580–9	76	200	15.2
1590–9	82	200	16.4
1600–9	89	200	17.8
1610–19	79	215	17.0
1620–9	82	230	19.0
1630–9	79	250	20.0
1640–9	82	260	21.0
1650–9	86	270	23.0
1660–9	81	270	22.0
1670–9	71	270	19.0
1680–9	68	300	21.0
1690–9	78	300	23.0
1700–9	76	315	24.0

Source: Hammersley, "The Charcoal Iron Industry," and Riden, "The Output of the British Iron Industry."

As usual, the vitality of a people did not manifest itself in one sector only. To this dynamism in trade corresponded an equal dynamism in the field of navigation, technology, culture, and art. At Florence, on the walls of Palazzo Vecchio in the room of the maps, an inscription of the second half of the sixteenth century on England recalls that "the people of this Island, which was described by the ancients as having neither letters nor music, are now seen to be great in both fields." And a Venetian gun founder of good repute, Gentilini, wrote "The English, to say the truth, are judicious people and of great intelligence, and are very ingenious in their inventions."

In order to understand adequately what happened then in England, one must take into account the growth of privateering, the economic policy of the English government, and the contribution of immigrants.

By the middle of the sixteenth century, overseas trade had experienced an enormous expansion in both value and volume. It had started with the discovery of rich deposits of silver in Mexico and Peru (see Chapter 9). Precious metals in vast quantities were shipped across the Atlantic to Europe and then on to the Orient via the Baltic or, alternatively, the circum-navigation of Africa and the Indian Ocean. In the opposite direction, precious commodities from the Far East reached Europe and the Americas. To a nation of seafarers like the English, all this coming and going of galleons and carracks laden with precious cargoes represented an irresis-tible temptation. By the 1560s commerce-raiding had become an important form of capital accumulation in England. Indeed, according to Ronald Hope, in the three years following the defeat of the Spanish Armada (1588), at least 236 English vessels were involved in privateering, most of which were specially converted merchantmen.[65] In this period at least 299 prizes were captured. In 1573 Francis Drake returned to England with captured goods worth upwards of £40,000 and in 1580 landed the immense booty won during the circumnavigation of the world, possibly amounting to £600,000. The capital accumulated through privateering by such London merchants as Sir John Watts, Sir Thomas Myddelton, and Paul Bayning played no small part in the subsequent launching of the East India Company and the foundation of England's first American colonies.

The second point to be considered is the contribution made by the economic policy of the government. This policy was strictly mercantilistic, that is protectionist, and given the conditions of the times it turned out to be successful. Local manufactures were protected by savage duties on foreign products. So, for instance, duties of the order of 50 percent were imposed on French linen cloth and of 70 percent on other French manufactures. Particu-larly important were those measures known as the Navigation Acts.

Charles I was executed in 1649. Two years later the Commonwealth government provoked the first war between the English and Dutch of 1652–54 by passing a Navigation Act. Although this Act marked no major change of policy, it was more comprehensive than anything that had gone before and most of its basic decrees were to remain in force for nearly 200 years.

The Navigation Act of 1651 ordered that English imports should be brought direct from the country of production or the first port from which they were normally shipped either in English ships or in ships of the country of origin or first shipment. From outside Europe all goods were to be brought to England in English ships.

In 1660, very shortly after the restoration of Charles II, a still more detailed Act was passed. The coasting trade was completely reserved to English ships and, to be considered English, ships had to have an English master and crews three-quarters English. Nearly all the principal products of the Mediterranean and the Baltic, and all Turkish and Russian products, were to be imported either in English ships or in ships of the country of origin or place of first shipment. Imports from places outside Europe were to be carried in English, Welsh or Irish ships or in ships belonging to the country of origin. Exports to the colonies were to be sent only on English, Welsh, Irish or colonial ships.

In 1662 a new Act was designed to limit the use of foreign-built ships other than prizes of war, as well as of foreign-owned ships, and bounties for large ships were revived though the definition of large ships was changed.[66] Partly as a result of the Navigation Acts the size of the English merchant marine increased from 130 ships in 1652 to 173 ships in 1688.

The third point to be considered is the contribution of immigrants to English economic development. As noted previously, religious and political persecution in France, devastation and persecution by the Spaniards in the southern Low Countries, and economic difficulties in other areas, drove many people to seek peace, tranquility, and employment in more hospitable countries. Walloons and French Huguenots poured into England in increasing numbers after the middle of the century. The development of the "new drapery" was above all the result of "Walloon" immigration. The development of the glass industry, of horology, and of the silk industry was essentially due to French immigrants. Contemporaries were aware of this contribution. Early in the seventeenth century, John Stow wrote:

> The making of Spanish needles was first taught in England by Elias Crowse a Germane about the eighth year of Queen Elizabeth.... The first making of Venice glasses in England began at the Crotched Fryers in London, about the beginning of the Reign of Queen Elizabeth, by one Jacob Venaline, an Italian.... The cutting of iron bars in a mill for the ready use of smiths to make long rods and all sorts of nayles was brought first into England in the year 1590 by Godfrey Box of the province of Liege.... Upon the Dartford River not long before was set up a mill to make white paper by master John Spilman, a German, who was long after knighted by King James; this was the first mill in England wherein fine white paper was made.[67]

A few decades later, T. Violet wrote:

> It cannot be denied that most of these men [the refugees] have brought
> many industrious manufactures into this land, by which means this
> nation hath been enriched with the merchant strangers, witness
> Colchester, Norwich, Canterbury and the sea port towns wherein they
> live. I have ever esteemed a good Dutch merchant as beneficial to us
> and our nation as they in Holland esteem of their Dutch cows.[68]

W. Cunningham wrote a classic little book on the subject at the end of the
last century.[69] It is a pity that the subject has been neglected since then, and
that the contribution of immigrants to English economic development
between 1550 and 1650 is usually mentioned only in passing and as a factor
of secondary importance. The fact that a great deal was owed to immigrants
does not detract anything from the English. Admittedly the refugees were
frequently harassed by those English craftsmen who saw in them potential
and dangerous competitors.[70] But the Crown and public opinion protected
the immigrants, and local craftsmen, even when hostile, learned from the
refugees the more advanced techniques and in most cases managed to
perfect them.

In fact, two features of English society of that time strike even the most
casual observer: an extraordinary cultural receptiveness and an equally
extraordinary ability to react decisively to the difficulties of the moment,
making such difficulties the starting-points of new developments and new
comparative advantages.

Cultural receptiveness was probably sharpened by the fact that, for
centuries, the English had lived in close contact with far more highly
evolved areas and had, therefore, developed a strong spirit of emulation.
While there was no shortage of conservatives, fully satisfied with local
culture and traditions, many looked beyond parochial horizons with intense
curiosity. The taste for foreign travel and the educational importance
attributed to the "Grand Tour," the notion of sending young men to study at
foreign universities in Padua or Paris or, later, in Leyden, were aspects of a
general cultural phenomenon which acquired great vigor between the
middle of the sixteenth century and the middle of the seventeenth century.[71]

The Elizabethans were fond of traveling abroad and were accustomed to
commend it as a facet of education. "He cannot be a perfect man, not being
tried or tutored in the world," says Antonio in *The Two Gentlemen of Verona*.
While the craftsmen learned the techniques and trades practiced by the
immigrants, travelers imported new ideas.[72] In a number of instances the
newly adopted ideas and techniques were actually developed with superior
skills. Early in the seventeenth century John Stow wrote, "At this day the
best and finest knives in the world are made in London.... The Englishmen

began to make all sorts of pinnes and at this day they excell all nations."[73] When Henry VIII decided to have work done on the great clock in Nonesuch Palace, he had to invite French clockmakers; Nicholas Cratzer, "deviser of the King's horloges," was a Bavarian; Nicholas Urseau, clockmaker to Queen Elizabeth, was of French origin but by 1680 "England [had] secured an un-challenged preeminence in the horological field, a preeminence which she was to enjoy for about a century."[74]

As Eric Hoffer wrote, "The vigor of a society shows itself partly in the ability to borrow copiously without ill-effects and without impairing its identity."

Not only was there open-mindedness in England at that time, the very fiber of contemporary English society was exceptional. In Toynbian terms, one can say that to the numerous and serious "challenges" which she had to face at that time, England was always able to give positive and innovative "responses" in the same way as a healthy organism reacts to natural abuses and emerges strengthened from them. The destruction of the Spanish Armada is a classic example of the way in which the English took advantage of a few factors favorable to them, and turned an essentially unfavorable situation into a triumph. We saw that in the sector of woollen exports after 1550 the English were faced with increasing competition and difficulties. Instead of admitting defeat, with the aid of the immigrants they swiftly adopted new Dutch methods of production and, abandoning the tradition of having foreign merchants to come to England to buy wool and woollens, they aggressively launched themselves into the conquest of North African and Middle Eastern markets.

In the armaments sector, England found herself at a disadvantage when, with the royal finances in ruin, it became increasingly difficult for her to buy the artillery she needed from the continental cannon merchants. The artillery of the time was mostly made of bronze, and England lacked copper. Between 1543 and 1545, under the pressure of necessity, a few English tech-nicians, assisted by foreign ones, turned to the raw material which was available locally and successfully developled new techniques for the casting of iron guns. By 1575 England was producing over 500 tons of iron artillery, and, by the end of the century, about 1,000 tons a year. Iron guns were much cheaper than bronze ones and, although inferior to the latter in quality, were more than adequate, especially for the arming of merchant ships and for privateering. In one generation an adverse situation had been turned into an advantageous one.

A similar story is that of energy. England was never a heavily wooded country. What forest there was dwindled rapidly during the course of the sixteenth century, because of a combined expansion of population; building activity and timber consumption for domestic heating; shipbuilding; and production of charcoal, which was the only known fuel for a number of industrial processes. During the sixteenth century a number of Acts of

Parliament tried to suppress the cutting of timber for industrial purposes. As has already been observed, English historians tend to deny that there was any timber crisis at the beginning of the seventeenth century. But what was happening on the continent combined with a range of contemporary English evidence demonstrate that there certainly was quite a severe crisis. In 1548–49 the English government ordered an inquiry into the consumption of timber by the iron foundries in Sussex.[75] Government action was to little or no avail. English timber reserves were rapidly depleted. About 1580 William Harrison pointed to the fact that a man could often ride ten or twenty miles and find very little wood or even none at all "except where the inhabitants have planted a few elms, oaks, hazels or ashes about their dwellings." In 1611 Arthur Standish pointed to the destruction that had taken place during the preceding twenty or thirty years and urged that trees be replanted. Early in the seventeenth century Edmund Howes wrote:[76]

> Such hath been the plenty of wood in England for all bless that, within man's memory, it was held impossible to have any want of wood in England. But contrary to former imaginations such hath beene the great expence of timber for navigation, with infinite increase of building of houses, with the great expence of wood to make household furniture, caskes, and othes vessels not to be numbered, and of carts, wagons and coaches, besides the extreme waste of wood in making iron, burning of brick and tile, that at this present, through the great consuming of wood as aforesaid, and the neglect of planting of woods, there is so great a scarcitie of wood through the whole kingdom....

In 1637 the clothmakers of the town of Cranbrook, in Kent, complained to the Privy Council against John Browne on the ground that he had caused a rise in the price of wood by burning large quantities in his furnace.[77]

According to the data in Table 10.9 the price of charcoal increased by a factor of four between the 1530s and the 1620s. This was more or less in line with the movement of the general level of prices. From the 1620s to the 1690s, however, the price of charcoal doubled while most prices remained stagnant or even showed a tendency to a mild decline.[78] It has already been pointed out that the movement of relative prices seems therefore to indicate that in England the fuel crisis exploded in the 1630s.[79] The consequences of this crisis can be clearly observed in the armaments industry. Since the middle of the sixteenth century England had become a manufacturer and exporter of cast-iron ordnance. According to a report in 1573, there were "above 400 tonnes cast yearly and all this will not be sold nor bought to remain within the Realme," according to a report in 1607, between 1596 and 1603 about 2,270 tons of iron ordnance were exported yearly, under license, as well as an unknown quantity that was exported illegally.[80] By 1630, however, the production of cast-iron ordnance was severely hit by the

Table 10.9 Charcoal prices in England, 1530–1699

Decade	Shillings per load
1530–39	3
1570–79	3.4
1580–89	9.5
1590–99	10
1610–19	10
1620–29	14.4
1650–59	18
1690–99	30

Source: Hammersley, "The Charcoal Iron Industry."

shortage of fuel, and England was then unable to produce enough guns for her own needs. In 1632 one hears of iron guns made in Sweden shipped to England and, as already noted above, by the early 1670s the Marquis de Seignelay reported to Colbert, his father, that the English "not having enough timber for casting all the ordnance they need, import cannon from Sweden, although they esteem that the Swedish iron is not as good as that of England."[81]

England reacted to the energy crisis in two ways. First of all, she strengthened shipping and trade with Scandinavian countries, where timber was in ample supply. Second, England increasingly resorted to the kind of fuel which was abundantly available in the British Isles. As one Englishman remarked in 1577, "of coalmines we have such plentie in the north and western parts of our Island."

Coal was well known in London in 1228, for in that year there is a definite record of the existence of a "sea-coal lane" which, it is suggested, was then used as a landing place for sea-coal from boats. In the same year coal fumes allegedly drove Queen Eleanor from Nottingham Castle. In 1257 mention is made of shiploads of coal imported into London. Throughout the Middle Ages, however, the English – like all other Europeans – remained very reluctant to use coal extensively, instinctively regarding its fumes as toxic. Early in the seventeenth century, however, the English were forced to put aside all their reservations, and after 1500 they resorted extensively to coal not only for domestic heating but also in industrial processes such as the oven-drying of bricks and tiles and of malt for beer, the refining of sugar, the production of glass and soap, and iron-smelting. As early as 1631 Edmund Howes wrote:

> There is so great a scarcitie of wood through the whole Kingdom, that not only the Citie of London, all haven-towns [ports] and in very

many parts within the land, the inhabitants in generall are constrained to make their fires of sea-coal or pit-coal, even in the chambers of honourable personages, and through necessitie, which is the mother of all arts, they have of very late years devised the making of iron, the making of all sorts of glasse and burning of bricke with sea-coal or pit-coal.[82]

From the late sixteenth century onward coal production expanded remarkably as the market, both domestic and industrial, grew and as supplies of wood fuel declined.

British annual total coal production was about 210,000 tons in about 1550; in 1630 it was about 1.5 million tons.[83] In 1650, John Cleveland wrote:

> England's a perfect world
> hath Indies too;
> Correct your maps,
> Newcastle is Peru.

British coal production was to reach 11 million tons in 1800 and about 60 million tons in about 1850. Development was greater where there was access to water transport. The transport of coal by sea from Newcastle to London increased as follows:

1549–50:   35,000 tons
1579–80:   141,000 tons
1633–40:   409,000 tons
1679–80:   560,000 tons

This development in turn stimulated shipping and shipbuilding. It was said in seventeenth-century England that the coal trade was "if not the only, yet the special nursery and school of seamen" and "the chiefest in employment of seamen." By 1738 a French traveler wrote that coal was "the soul of all English Industries."

Reacting to serious shortages, England ingeniously developed new techniques which allowed her to utilize those natural resources locally available in relatively ample quantities. Concentrating on iron and coal, England set herself on the road that led directly to the Industrial Revolution. Iron and coal much more than cotton played a role of critical importance in the origins of the Industrial Revolution. The development of early textile machinery was a major episode in European economic history, but as has been aptly said:

[Early cotton machinery] fits better as an appendage to the evolution of the old industry than in the way it is usually presented as the beginning of the new.... Would it have been impossible, if capital could have been raised and if the regular water power of Lancashire had been available, for something very like it to have occurred, say in

271

fifteenth-century Florence? There is continuity between the eighteenth-century development of Lancashire and the West Riding and the pre-Industrial Revolution world. There might have been no Crompton and Arkwright, and still there could have been an Industrial Revolution.[84]

If the increasing use of and reliance on coal and iron were, perhaps, the major development leading to the Industrial Revolution in the form and shape it took, other concomitant factors and developments should not be overlooked. Another process which led directly to the Industrial Revolution was the increase in the size of plants and the concurrent concentration of labor and capital in technical units of production. At iron foundries fixed capital was substantial, but the labor force remained small.[85] In other sectors, however, such as in the production of alum, shipbuilding, and textile manufacture, there was an increasingly large concentration of both capital and labor; plants were worth several million pounds sterling, and hundreds of workers were employed.[86]

Much of what happened in the manufacturing and shipping sectors cannot be understood without taking due account of what was happening at the same time in the commercial sector. In 1706 the Venetian Ambassador in London, Alvise Mocenigo, wrote: "there is no corner of the known world which is accessible by sea, where numerous ships of England are not to be found," and, "with sad memory," he commented that England was now what "this same city [Venice] had been in former times." The important role of immigrants stressed above in relation to the development of England's manufactures between 1550 and 1650 was equally in evidence in the development of English foreign trade in the course of the seventeenth and early eighteenth centuries. As Ashton remarked, "Of the 810 merchants who kissed the hand of George III, at least 250 must have been of alien origin. It was one of the merits of the English at this time that they opened their doors to capital and enterprise from all quarters." Table 1.14 shows that between the early seventeenth and the early eighteenth century total exports (exports plus re-exports) increased about six-fold. While these figures, like all statistics of the time, require caution, there is no doubt that English foreign trade underwent a most remarkable expansion. In this expansion, extra-European trade and the re-export trade grew steadily in importance (see Table 10.10). Around 1640 re-exports accounted for *circa* 18 percent of total exports (see Table 1.14, p. 51). At the end of the century they were about 31 percent (see Table 10.7), and in 1773, about 37 percent.[87] This re-export trade consisted mainly of goods from the East and West Indies. As Phyllis Deane wrote:[88]

The immense importance of the tropical commodities lay in the fact that they increased British purchasing power on the continent of Europe. Britain needed her European imports for vital productive purposes and not merely to meet the upper class demand for wine and

Table 10.10 Geographical distribution of English foreign trade, 1700–50

	1700–01 %	1750–51 %
Total imports from		
Europe	66	55
North America	6	11
West Indies	14	19
East Indies and Africa	14	15
Total	100	100
Re-export to		
Europe	85	79
North America	5	11
West Indies	6	5
East Indies and Africa	4	5
Total	100	100
Domestic exports to		
Europe	85	77
North America	6	11
West Indies	5	5
East Indies and Africa	4	7
Total	100	100

Source: Deane, *The First Industrial Revolution*, p. 56.

brandy. She needed foreign timber, pitch and hemp for her ships and buildings, high-grade bar iron for her metal trade, raw and thrown silk for her textile trades. Her industrial expansion along traditional lines was severely restricted by the fact that the demand for woollen products was inelastic and already near saturation point in traditional markets. Had it not been for the tropical products with their elastic demand and growing markets in temperate regions, it would have been difficult to expand British trade with Europe.

Trade in tropical products also allowed the development of altogether new industries, such as sugar refining. The pivotal point of the wide, intricate, multilateral network of world trade that developed during the eighteenth century was London with its wide sheltered anchorages, its vast wharves and warehouses, its rich city banks, its specialists in marine insurance and its world-wide mercantile contacts.[89] As shown in Table A.1 in the Appendix, the population of London grew from about 70,000 people in 1500 to some 450,000 in 1650, to over 500,000 by the end of the seventeenth century. London had become the largest, busiest, and wealthiest metropolis in the world and Samuel Johnson wrote, "When a man is tired of London he is tired of life, for there is in London all that life can afford."

The sort of trade on a world-wide scale that England had managed to develop between 1550 and 1700 demanded a degree of skill, sophistication, and international dealing totally different from that required by the simple exchange pattern of the early sixteenth-century London–Antwerp axis. The resources that enabled the English to develop their world-wide commercial network were mainly (a) a relatively abundant stock of good sailors and able merchants; (b) a relatively abundant supply of both physical capital (see Table 10.11) and financial capital; (c) a well-developed organizational structure of credit, commerce, and insurance; (d) a government deeply aware of and intelligently favorable to the aspirations of the merchant class; and (e) the extension of diplomatic offices and the strength of the Royal Navy. For its part, international trade contributed considerably to general economic development. It is not easy to define this contribution in precise terms since quite apart from those direct effects that can be detected if not always measured, there were also important indirect effects, especially on economic organization, training, value systems and the like, which are difficult to identify. By way of rough classification one can say, however, that the vigorous development of international trade:

a. contributed to the expansion of demand for the products of British industry
b. gave access to raw materials which both widened the range and lowered the price of the products of British industry
c. provided underdeveloped countries with the purchasing power to buy English goods
d. favored an accumulation of capital which helped to finance industrial expansion and agricultural improvement

Table 10.11 Size of the English merchant navy, 1572–1686

		Number of ships	
Years	Total tonnage	100–199 tons	200 tons and over
1572	50,000	72	14
1577		120	15
1582	67,000	155	18
1629	115,000	>178	>145
1686	340,000		

Source: Davis, *The Rise of the English Shipping Industry*, pp. 7, 15, 25, 27.

e. stimulated the development of insurance and transport activities
f. helped to create an institutional structure and a business ethic which was to prove effective in promoting both internal activity and foreign trade
g. proved to a great school of entrepreneurship for all those who, directly or indirectly, participated in international trade
h. was the prime cause of growth of large towns and industrial centers[90]

In addition to all that precedes, one has to emphasize another development which affected the delicate relationship between trade and manufacture. In Britain as a whole, there is no doubt that the economic importance of guilds declined in the course of the sixteenth and seventeenth centuries. This was partly related to the action of the Crown, which did not approve of the restrictive practices of the crafts guilds. But it was related above all to the growth of trade. In London, crafts guilds came under the domination of mercantile guilds, whose rich and economically powerful members controlled either the market or the raw material of the craftsmen. That was the situation which had prevailed in northern Italy in her golden age. But in Italy during the fifteenth, sixteenth, and seventeenth centuries, the crafts guilds had managed to free themselves from the tutelage and predominance of the mercantile guilds and had succeeded in enforcing, with increasing determination, their restrictive and conservative practices, with severe consequences on the costs of production. In seventeenth-century England the opposite took place.

It would be difficult to overestimate the importance of the various factors mentioned so far. Ultimately, however, human events can be understood only in human terms. I referred above to the presence on the English scene of a large class of capable merchants and to the intelligent action of government in relation to trade. But one should go farther than that. Admittedly, most of the human qualities which ultimately determine the success or the failure of a society can scarcely be defined and certainly not measured. But this fact does not detract from their relevance. When one reads the writings of Samuel Pepys, John Graunt, William Petty, Isaac Newton; when one observes their endeavors and the activity of the Royal Society, one distinctly perceives pervasive traits of systematic, enlightened, logical rationalism which seems to have characterized increasingly broad strata of English society in the seventeenth century and was perhaps its most valuable asset.

During the seventeenth century the English came to a full realization of their power. And in vigor lies the seed of aggression. The English brought forward their theory of *Mare Clausum* in opposition to the Dutch theory of *Mare Liberum*. A Swedish diplomat who attempted to mediate between the two nations wrote from London to Queen Christine of Sweden in June 1653 that the English were "intolerably arrogant and it may be that God will punish them for their pride." But God was busy with other things.

EPILOGUE

Between 1780 and 1850 an unprecedented and far-reaching revolution changed the face of England. From then on the world was no longer the same. Historians have often used and abused the word "revolution" to mean a radical change, but no revolution has been as dramatically revolutionary as the Industrial Revolution.[1] The Industrial Revolution opened the door to a completely new world, a world of new and untapped sources of energy such as coal, oil, electricity, and the atom; a world in which man found himself able to handle huge masses of energy to an extent inconceivable in the preceding rural world. From a narrowly technological and economic point of view, the Industrial Revolution can be defined as the process by which a society acquired control over vast sources of inanimate energy. But such a definition does not do justice to the phenomenon, in terms of either its distant origins or its economic, cultural, social, and political implications.

Crescenzi in the thirteenth century and the agronomists of the fifteenth and sixteenth centuries could still usefully refer to the agricultural treatises of the ancient Romans. The ideas of Hippocrates and Galen continued to form the basis of official medicine well into the eighteenth century – two centuries after the revolt of Paracelsus. It did not seem absurd to Machiavelli to refer to Roman military arrangements when he planned an army for his times. At the end of the eighteenth century Catherine II of Russia had transported an enormous stone from Finland to St Petersburg, to set it at the base of the monument dedicated to Peter the Great. The method of transporting the colossal stone was much the same as that used thousands of years earlier by the ancient Egyptians when they built their pyramids. As Cederna wrote,

> From the Pharaohs to Baron Hausmann certain things in the architecture of the past have remained constant and immutable even through a thousand stylistic variations: the materials – stone, lime, bricks – and certain fundamental relations between supporting and supported, wall and roof, column and arch, pillar and vault, and so on. It is easy to give examples of monuments literally born out of existing

ones. The travertine of the Colosseum served excellently in the building of St Peter's in the Vatican in the 16th century.[2]

A basic fundamental continuity characterized the preindustrial world, even through grandiose changes, such as the rise and fall of Rome, the triumph and decline of Islam, the Chinese dynastic cycles. As C.H. Waddington has observed:

> If a Roman of the Empire could be transported some eighteen centuries forward in time, he would have found himself in a society which he could, without too great difficulty, have learned to comprehend. Horace would have felt himself reasonably at home as a guest of Horace Walpole and Catullus would soon have learned his way among the sedan chairs, the patched-up beauties and the flaring torches of London streets at night.[3]

This continuity was broken between 1780 and 1850. If, at the middle of the nineteenth century, a general studied the organization of the Roman army, if a physician concerned himself with the ideas of Hippocrates and Galen, if an agronomist read Columella, they did it purely out of historical interest or as an academic exercise. Even in far-away, unchanging China, it was becoming painfully evident to the most enlightened among the scholar-officials of the Celestial Empire that the ancient classical texts and values which had given continuity to Chinese history through invasions and dynastic cycles were no longer valid for survival in the contemporary world. By 1850 the past was not merely past – it was dead.

Yet, if in the course of three generations the Industrial Revolution had become a dramatic watershed in the course of history, its roots nevertheless reached deep into the preceding century. In Chapter 4 I tried to show that the origins of the Industrial Revolution reach back to that profound change in ideas, social structures, and value systems that accompanied the rise of the urban communes in the eleventh and thirteenth centuries. In Chapter 6 I stressed that the technological changes that we identify with the Industrial Revolution were the extrapolation of the technological innovations of the western Middle Ages. The Industrial Revolution occurred in England because it was there that a series of historical circumstances brought about – as W.S. Jevons once wrote – "the union of certain happy mental qualities with material resources of an altogether peculiar character." From England the Industrial Revolution soon spread to the rest of Europe. To date the beginning of the Industrial Revolution in any country is as arbitrary as to date the beginning of the Middle Ages or the modern age. Within the same country geographical areas, social groups, and economic sectors move at different paces; new activities and new forms of life develop while a number of traditional activities and old institutions manage to survive. In broad terms, however, one can say that by 1850 the Industrial Revolution had penetrated Belgium, France, Germany, and Switzerland. By 1900 it had extended to northern Italy, Russia and Sweden.

That the Industrial Revolution was essentially and primarily a socio-cultural phenomenon and not a purely technological one, becomes patently obvious when one considers that the first countries to industrialize were those which had the greatest cultural and social similarities with England.

The Industrial Revolution gave Europe a tremendous technological and economic advantage over the rest of the world, and the nineteenth century saw Europe proudly asserting this global predominance.

If one pauses to ponder on all that Europe accomplished in the nine centuries of her ascent, one cannot help being filled with amazement and admiration. Undoubtedly there were dark and bloody pages, but there was, above all, an endless series of superb accomplishments in all fields of human activity. The medieval cathedrals; the paintings of the Renaissance; the music of Mozart, Beethoven, and Bach; the poetry of Dante; the prose of Boccaccio and Chaucer; the tragedies of Shakespeare; the philosophy of Aquinas, Descartes, and Kant; the wit of Montaigne and Voltaire; the medieval clocks; the drawings of Leonardo da Vinci; the innumerable techno-logical innovations of the Middle Ages and the Renaissance; the steam engine; the microscope; the discoveries of microbiology, the miracles of chemistry; the Suez canal; the business techniques, from the check to the stock exchange; the condemnation of torture; the assertion of the principle of human freedom and rights; the parliamentary system – there is no end to the list of Europe's accomplishments in the period AD 1000–1900. Moreover, technology and the Industrial Revolution in Europe irrevocably changed the course of history, not only in Europe's own territories, but throughout the world. The history of any remote corner of the world after 1500 cannot be properly understood without taking into account the impact of European culture, economy, and technology. Henri Pirenne once wrote that *Sans Mahomet Charlemagne est inconcevable*. We can paraphrase him by saying that *Sans l'Europe l'histoire moderne est inconcevable*.

"La Belle Epoque" was the apogee of the European saga. The great International Exhibitions in London, Paris, and Vienna were the proud and optimistic celebrations of Europe's success. The Eiffel Tower was the monument to her economic and technological achievements. But deep within, the germ of decay was already at work. The reaction against rationalism had been voiced already by Rousseau, and it gained ground in the course of the nineteenth century, favoring nationalism and a whole series of other "isms." The latent crisis eventually exploded in the brutal form of a war which westerners labeled the "First World War," but which to a perceptive Asian historian looked more like "the European Civil War." It was the beginning of a rapid end. Within less than half a century a major economic crisis and a second major war gave Europe the *coup de grâce*. The Spenglerian vision of the Decline of the West came into sharper focus day by day. The dawn of the twentieth century had seen Britannia ruling the waves and both England and continental Europe ruling the world. "At the beginning of the twentieth century there were six world powers and they were all located in Europe. If one mentioned the United States or Japan it was merely to make a show of geographical knowledge." At the end of the twentieth century Europe seems to be struggling for survival.

Paradoxically, Europe is on the retreat at a moment when the industrial way of life, which was originally developed by Europe, is taking over the whole world. The agony of Europe finds many echoes around the globe. After the optimism of the 1950s and the early 1960s ample evidence of anxiety is to be found in most nations. A sense of unease and foreboding is blanketing mankind. As the future of Europe looks more uncertain than ever, a question plagues an increasing number of people: is there any hope for the kind of civilization which Europe developed and then spread all over the world?

APPENDIX TABLES

Table A.1 Approximate population of selected European cities, 1300–1700
(thousands)

Country	City	c. 1300	c. 1400	c. 1500	c. 1550	c. 1600	c. 1650	c. 1700
Italy	Asti					9		10
	Bergamo				18	24		25
	Bologna			55	55	63	58	63
	Brescia			50	40	50	40	35
	Como		10			11	9	
	Cremona				37	40	17	
	Ferrara					33	25	27
	Florence	95	55	70	60	80	70	80
	Genoa					63	70	
	Lucca					25	25	
	Mantua			27	35	31	15	20
	Milan			100	50	110	95	100
	Modena			18	20	18		18
	Naples				210	250		215
	Padua	30		27	32	35	25	
	Palermo			50	80	100		100
	Parma			16	20	25	20	30
	Pavia			18	13	18	19	20
	Perugia					20	16	16
	Piacenza				27	30		
	Pistoia	11	4		8	8		8
	Rome			50	45	110	126	135
	San Gimignano		3		5			3
	Siena			15	10	19	16	16
	Turin		4		14	20		42
	Venice			115	160	150	120	140
	Verona		20	40	46	55	25	
	Vicenza					35	25	26
Germany	Augsburg				18		20	
	Cologne		30		35			
	Frankfurt		10			25	15	25
	Hamburg	5	10	20		20	50	
	Leipzig				7	15	15	22
	Nuremberg		20	50				
	Vienna		20			60		
France	Angers					25	32	27
	Besançon				8	11		17
	Lyon				70			90
	Paris	100				300		500
	Rouen		40			80		65
	Strasbourg					25		27
	Toulouse		23	35			42	43

Table A.1 continued

Country	City	c. 1300	c. 1400	c. 1500	c. 1550	c. 1600	c. 1650	c. 1700
Low Countries	Amsterdam			15	35	100	135	180
	Antwerp						57	
	Bruges	35					34	
	Leyden						66	
	Liège						50	55
	Ypres		11	8				12
England	London		35	70	80	250	450	600
Switzerland	Geneva		5	13				17
	Zürich			5		7		
Sweden	Stockholm							50
Spain	Barcelona						64	
	Madrid						75	
	Seville				100	150	125	
Russia	Novgorod		6					

Table A.2 Rough birth and death rates in selected European cities, 1551–1699

City	Years	Births	Deaths
		(per thousand inhabitants)	
Antwerp	1696–99	30	
Bologna	1581	38	
	1587	38	
	1595	36	
	1600	35	18
	1605		46
	1606	36	43
	1615		11
	1617	35	
	1619		46
	1620		49
Florence	1551	41	
	1559	36	
	1561	47	
	1562	42	
	1622	39	
	1630	45	
	1632	43	
	1633	44	
	1642	48	
	1657	48	
	1660	49	
	1661	48	
	1668	50	
London	1696–99	38	37
Louvain	1635–44	44	
Pavia	1640–49	46	30
	1650–59	40	41
	1690–99	52	44
Parma	1505–9	41	
	1545–49	45	
	1590–94	42	
	1650–54	42	
Venice	1581	34	33
	1624	31	35
	1642	37	30
	1696	31	32
Verona	1641–50		38
	1651–60		37
	1661–70		49
	1671–80		54
	1681–90		42
	1691–1700		43
Zürich	1631–50	37	36

Table A.3 Infant mortality rate (died in first year of life, per thousand christened) in Fiesole (Tuscany), 1621–99

Years	Deaths	Years	Deaths
1621	141	1661	303
1622	238	1662	167
1623	119	1663	230
1624	258	1664	358
1625	177	1665	199
1626	278	1666	388
1627	216	1667	377
1628	148	1668	383
1629	186	1669	212
1630	164	1670	245
1631	140	1671	277
1632	228	1672	301
1633	224	1673	183
1634	243	1674	115
1635	213	1675	339
1636	257	1676	145
1637	319	1677	364
1638	193	1678	423
1639	315	1679	515
1640	322	1680	184
1641	205	1681	302
1642	192	1682	362
1643	287	1683	492
1644	224	1684	565
1645	369	1685	459
1646	234	1686	430
1647	118	1687	360
1648	363	1688	567
1649	514	1689	393
1650	296	1690	259
1651	223	1691	341
1652	236	1692	298
1653	222	1693	396
1654	355	1694	392
1655	273	1695	277
1656	411	1696	468
1657	310	1697	252
1658	496	1698	370
1659	736	1699	229
1660	162		

Table A.4 Characteristics of a typical preindustrial population: Sweden, 1778–82

Phenomenon	Value
Total population	2,104,000 inhabitants
Population under 15 years of age	31.9 percent
Population between 15 and 64 years	63.2 percent
Population 65 years and over	4.9 percent
Dependency ratio	58.3 percent
Crude birth rate	34.5 per thousand
Crude death rate	25.9 per thousand
Crude rate of natural increase	8.6 per thousand
Intrinsic birth rate (females)	31.2 per thousand
Intrinsic death rate (females)	25.3 per thousand
Intrinsic rate of natural increase (females)	5.9 per thousand
Infant mortality	211.6 per thousand
Age-specific death rates:	
Age 1–4 (males)	45.9 per thousand
Age 1–4 (females)	44.3 per thousand
Age 50–54 (males)	20.8 per thousand
Age 50–54 (females)	16.1 per thousand
Life table values:	
Probability of dying in first year	
Males	0.1974
Females	0.1768
Survivors to the age of 50 per 100 births:	
Males	41
Females	45
Life expectancy at birth:	
Males	36 years
Females	39 years
Life expectancy at 1 year:	
Males	44 years
Females	46 years
Life expectancy at 50 years:	
Males	19 years
Females	20 years
Average age of women at procreation	32 years
General fertility rate	145.2 children per 1,000 women
Gross reproduction rate	2.2 female children per woman

Source: Keyfitz and Flieger, *Population*, pp. 100–03.

NOTES

1 DEMAND

1 Drummond and Wilbraham, *The Englishman's Food*, pp. 68, 69, 124, 125.
2 The distribution of income affects the level and the structure of demand because elasticities of demand vary at different levels of income.
3 Dallington, *The View of France*, p. T3 v.
4 Boutruche, *Bordeaux*, p. 504.
5 Strauss, *Nuremberg*, p. 201.
6 Fanfani, *Storia del lavoro*, pp. 421–22.
7 See Herlihy, *Pistoia*, p. 188 and Fiumi, "Popolazione," p. 94.
8 Vauban, *Project de dîme royale*, pp. 2–4 (p. 6 in the edition by Coornaert).
9 Inequality of wealth distribution is normally greater than inequality of income distribution; in other words, holdings of wealth are more concentrated than incomes earned annually. To what degree the distribution of wealth differed from the distribution of income in preindustrial Europe is difficult to say, but one would have thought that the discrepancy was greater in those days than today because of the tremendous concentration of land and other property in the hands of the nobility and the Church.
10 Samuelson, "A Fallacy in the Introduction of Pareto's Law of Alleged Constancy of Income Distribution," p. 246.
11 Guicciardini, "Relatione," p. 131.
12 Gee, *The Trade and Navigation*, Chapter 23, p. 57.
13 Reinhard, Armengaud, Dupaquier, *Histoire générale de la population*, pp. 192–93.
14 Beloch, *Bevölkerungsgeschichte*, vol. 3, p. 259.
15 Wilson, *England's Apprenticeship*, p. 231.
16 Tadino, *Raguaglio*, p. 11.
17 Gascon, *Grand commerce*, vol. 1, p. 404.
18 Villani, *Cronica*, Book 10, Chapter 162. In fact, if six denari a head were given out and 430 pounds were spent, the total of beneficiaries was 17,200. Florence counted then about 900,000 inhabitants within the city walls.
19 Priuli, "Diarii," p. 179.
20 Mollat, "La Mortalité," p. 505.
21 Carabellese, *La peste del 1348*, pp. 51 and 65.
22 Passerini, *Stabilimenti di beneficenza*, pp. 344–35. In pp. 873 *et seq.*, Appendix L, Passerini provides the list of names of benefactors of the hospital.
23 Paschetti, *Lettera*, p. 26.
24 Gnoli, "Roma e i Papi," p. 123. See also Fanfani, *Storia del lavoro in Italia*, pp. 430 *et seq.*

25 Pullan, *Rich and Poor in Renaissance Venice*, p. 632.
26 Elton, "An early Tudor Poor Law"; Leonard, *Early History of English Poor Relief*; Marshall, "The Old Poor Law"; Jordan, *Philanthropy in England*.
27 In the Protestant countries, the Reformation modified substantially the pattern described above. While in Catholic areas a substantial proportion of charity continued to flow to the church, in Protestant countries religion lost much ground as an object of private philanthropy. Jordan (*Philanthropy in England*) studied the records of ten English counties; he calculated that while about 54 percent of funds given to charity went to the Church between 1480 and 1540, this dropped to less than 15 percent after the Reformation.
28 In 1970 all forty-five Christian churches in the United States contributed a total of $764 million in benevolences, or 0.08 percent of GNP, while they spent much more than that amount on new construction and four times as much on congregational expenses (Kohler, *Economics*, p. 220).
29 Snape, *English Monastic Finances,* pp. 112 *et seq.* and Coulton, *Medieval Panorama,* p. 168.
30 Coulton, *Medieval Panorama*, p. 168.
31 Pullan, *Rich and Poor in Renaissance Venice*, pp. 180–84.
32 Jordan, *Philanthropy in England*.
33 Dati, *Libro segreto*, p. 57. See also pp. 113, 114, and 116.
34 Pitti, *Cronica*, pp. 40–41.
35 Grierson, "Commerce in the Dark Ages," p. 131.
36 Sclafert, *Cultures en Haute-Provence*, pp. 11, 37.
37 Wolff, *Toulouse*, p. 61, n. 189.
38 For these and other ·examples, compare F. Redlich, "De Praeda Militari," pp. 54ff.
39 For this and other examples see Grierson, *Commerce in the Dark Ages*, p. 135.
40 Mignet, *Rivalité de François I et de Charles-Quint*, vol. 2, pp. 452–61.
41 Grierson, *Commerce in the Dark Ages*, p. 140.
42 Duby, *Guerriers et paysans*, p. 60.
43 All studies of family living expenditures have confirmed Engels's law: outlays for food increase proportionately and outlays for other goods and services decline as the level of total expenditure declines. According to H. Working, ". . . the relation between expenditure on food and total expenditure, presents a marked uniformity and comes close to this type of relation:
$$F/T = a - b \log T$$
where F represents expenditure on food and T total expenditure" (Working, "Statistical Law," p. 45).
44 The ultimate reason for which grains are the food of the poor must be sought in the ecological chain of energy. The wheat plant transforms solar energy directly into chemical energy. Animal meat, on the other hand, is the product of a double transformation process in which are added the "losses" of the primary process, connected with the growth of forage, and the "losses" of the secondary process, connected with the development and growth of the animal.
45 Cipolla, *Prezzi e salari in Lombardia*, p. 15.
46 Van der Wee, *Antwerp Market*, vol. 2, p. 391.
47 Fourastié, *Machinisme et bien-être*, p. 61.
48 See the *Ordinationi per il buon governo di tutti li Hospitali del Contado di Perugia*, Perugia, 1582, p. 3.
49 Cipolla, *Cristofano*, pp. 117–18.
50 Lebarge, *A Baronial Household*, p. 141.
51 Beltrami, *Popolazione di Venezia*, p. 222.

52 Rondinelli, *Relazione*, p. 59.
53 Fiochetto, *Trattato*, p. 19.
54 Besta, *Vera narratione*, p. 31.
55 Archivio di Stato di Cremona, Arch. Comunale, Inv. 4, t. 3.
56 Archivio di Stato di Milano, Fondo Sanità, Parte Antica, b. 278.
57 Presotto, "Genova," p. 385.
58 Cipolla, *Cristofano*, pp. 156ff.
59 Piponnier, *Costume*, p. 95.
60 Strachey, *Portraits*, p. 111.
61 De Muinck, "A Regent's Family Budget," p. 229. Each servant consumed, on an average, 187 pounds of meat and 77 pounds of butter a year.
62 Ramazzini, *Le malattie dei lavoratori*, p. 27.
63 Cipolla, *Cristofano*, p. 31, n. 1.
64 Mira, *Vicende economiche*, p. 208.
65 On Ambrogio di Negro see Doria, "Mezzo secolo," p. 773, n. 9; on the Riccardi family see Malanima, *I Riccardi di Firenze*, pp. 127–29; on Cornelis de Jonge van Ellemeet see De Muinck, "A Regent's Family Budget," p. 224.
66 Gould, *Economic Growth*, p. 154.
67 Paolo di Messere Pace da Certaldo, *Il libro di buoni costumi*, p. CLVI, n. 356.
68 Aleati, "Una dinastia di magnati medievali, p. 753.
69 On the significance of the episode, see Grierson, *Numismatics*.
70 Raoul Glaber, *Les cinq livres*, Book 2, par. 5.
71 Violante, "I Vescovi dell'Italia Centro-settentrionale," p. 201.
72 Herlihy, "Treasure Hoards in the Italian Economy," p. 5.
73 Duby, *Guerriers et paysans*, p. 183.
74 See Postan, "Investment in Medieval Agriculture," pp. 579 and 581.
75 Rey, *Finances royales*, p. 608.
76 Ashton, "Deficit Finance," pp. 15–16.
77 Fiumi, "Fioritura e decadenza," p. 455.
78 Lane, *Venice*, p. 426.
79 Partner, "The Budget of the Roman Church," pp. 263–66.
80 Vicens Vives, *Manual de historia economica de España*, Chapter 30.
81 Dietz, "English Government Finance," p. 190.
82 Clamageran, *Histoire de l'impôt*, vols 1 and 2.
83 In a statement made to the Commons in 1467, King Edward IV of England declared, "I purpose to live upon my own and not to charge my subjects but in great and urgent causes concerning more, the weal of themselves and also the defence of them and of this realm rather than my own pleasure." The phrase "to live of his own" meant strictly that the king should live on what was lawfully his, namely on the rents from the Crown lands and on the income from his rights as feudal suzerain.
84 Porisini, *La proprietà terriera nel Comune di Ravenna*, pp. 31, 75–76.
85 At the middle of the nineteenth century in most European states, public expenditure still represented only 2 to 6 percent of national income.
86 Feasts and days of rejoicing were the occasion for distributions of charity, processions, tournaments, and – at least by our standards – less cheerful kinds of shows. In Spain, the marriage in 1680 of Charles II to Marie-Louise was celebrated by the public execution of accused persons – some of them sentenced to perish in the flames.
87 For the above, compare Cipolla, *Public Health*, Chapter 1.
88 Fiumi, "Fioritura e decadenza," vol. 117, p. 467.
89 Carabellese, *La peste del 1348*, pp. 7 *et seq.*

90 Wolff, "Prix et marché," p. 465.
91 Lombardini, *Pane e denaro a Bassano,* pp. 29 *et seq.*
92 Basini, *L'Uomo e il pane,* p. 39.
93 Catellacci, "Ricordi," pp. 384–85.
94 *Bilanci della Repubblica di Venezia,* vol. 1, book I, pp. ccix–ccxv.
95 Romano, "Economic aspects," p. 80.
96 Formentini, *Il Ducato di Milano,* pp. 618 *et seq.*
97 Bean, *War,* p. 216.
98 Supposing the public revenues amounted to 5 percent of national income; if
    military expenditures were as high as 50 percent of the public budget, they still
    amounted to only 2.5 percent of national income. In 1961, 1965, and 1970,
    military spending as a percent of GNP at factor cost was:

	1961	*1965*	*1970*		*1961*	*1965*	*1970*
Argentina	3	2	2	Israel	7	12	25
Australia	5	3	4	Jordan	16	13	21
Canada	4	3	2	Saudi Arabia	12	7	13
Cuba	8	7	6	Sweden	4	4	4
Czechoslovakia	6	6	5	Switzerland	3	3	2
Egypt	6	7	9	UK	6	6	5
France	6	6	4	US	9	8	8
Iran	4	4	8	USSR	6–10	6–10	6–10

99 For what precedes, see Latouche, *The Birth of Western Economy,* p. 55.
100 For the Republic of Venice, see Stella, "La proprietà ecclesiastica"; for Pistoia,
    see Fioravanti, *Memorie storiche di Pistoia,* p. 444; for Ravenna, see Porisini, *La
    proprietà terriera,* p. 19; for the Kingdom of the Two Sicilies, see De Gennaro,
    L'abate Minervini, pp. 64–65.
101 Woodward, *The Dissolution,* p. 122; Cooper, "The Social Distribution of Land,"
    pp. 108–9; Youings, *The Dissolution, passim.*
102 Woodward, *The Dissolution,* p. 130.
103 Cipolla, "Propriété ecclésiastique," p. 326. In a vast area (about 115,000 acres) of
    the irrigated plain, the church held more than 25 percent of the land while the
    nobility held about 60 percent. See Coppola, "L'Agricoltura," p. 218.
104 Romani, *La gente e i redditi del Piacentino,* p. 88; Vaini, *La distribuzione della
    proprietà terriera,* p. 7.
105 For the Republic of Venice, see Stella, "La proprietà ecclesiastica." For the Grand
    Duchy of Tuscany, see Galluzzi, *Istoria del Granducato,* vol. 3, p. 266. For Pistoia,
    see Fioravaniti, *Memorie storiche di Pistoia,* p. 44.
106 Monter, *Calvin's Geneva,* p. 156. On secularization in Berne see Feller, *Geschichte
    Berns,* pp. 314–21.
107 The comparison was made even in the period in question. Cf. Woodward, *The
    Dissolution,* p. 4.
108 Conti, *La formazione della struttura agraria,* vol. 1, pp. 215–16.
109 Porisini, *Proprietà terriera,* p. 20.
110 Anselmi, *Insediamenti,* pp. 34 and 51.
111 Desaive, "Clergé rural," pp. 924ff.
112 Derlange, "Cannes," p. 30.
113 On this important point see Gould, *Economic Growth,* Chapter 4.

2 THE FACTORS OF PRODUCTION

1 If we assume conventionally that age 15 separates children from adults and age 65 separates the labor force from the old, then the children are designated as $_{15}P_0$, the labor force as $_{50}P_{15}$ and the old as $_\infty P_{65}$ (in this typical notation the beginning age interval is shown by the subscript on the lower right of the letter P and the length of the interval by a subscript on the lower left). Thus: the dependency ratio may be written:

$$\frac{_{15}P_0 + {}_\infty P_{65}}{_{50}P_{15}} \times 100$$

2 Beltrami, *Popolazione di Venezia*, p. 143, n. 17.
3 For the figures above, compare Battara, *Popolazione di Firenze*, p. 34, and Cipolla, *Cristofano*, pp. 35 and 44. It must be noted that, out of the total number of foundlings, females often exceeded males by a long way. Even in faraway China, females were predominantly the victims of infanticide.
4 Beltrami, *Popolazione di Venezia*, p. 143, n. 17.
5 Between 1680 and 1715 the population of Milan and its suburbs was about 120,000. In one large parish the birth rate was about 30 per thousand. Adopting this rate for the whole city, one may assume that in the city and its suburbs the births numbered approximately 3,600 per year. See Sella, "Popolazione di Milano," pp. 471 and 478.
6 Archivio Mensa Vescovile di Pavia, b. 123, decree of 22 March 1590.
7 Frank, *Medizinischen Polizey*, vol. 1, p. 16.
8 See below, p. 64.
9 Archivio Stato Firenze, *Sanità*, Negozi, b. 161, c. 40 2 September 1631.
10 Wolff, *Toulouse*, p. 441.
11 Beltrami, *Popolazione di Venezia*, p. 201.
12 Coleman, *The Economy of England*, p. 73.
13 The census does not, however, include the town of Bristol.
14 Parenti, *Popolazione della Toscana*, pp. 73 and 126.
15 Beloch, *Bevölkerungsgeschichte Italiens*, vol. 1, pp. 73–79.
16 Ruiz Martin, "Demografia ecclesiastica," p. 685.
17 Reinhard, Armengaud, Dupaquier, *Histoire générale de la population*, pp. 192–93.
18 For the data for 1377 see Russell, "The Clerical Population," pp. 177–212. For the data relating to the first decades of the sixteenth century see Woodward, *The Dissolution of the Monasteries*, p. 2. See also Knowles, *Religious Orders*, vol. 2, pp. 256–57.
19 Kjoczowski, "La Population ecclésiastique," *passim*.
20 Cipolla, *Public Health*, Chapter 2.
21 Cipolla, "The Professions," pp. 37–52.
22 Gade, *Hanseatic Control*, p. 16.
23 Coryat, *Crudities*, vol. 2, p. 38.
24 Montaigne, *Journal*, p. 142.
25 Dallington, *Survey of Tuscany*, p. 48.
26 Battara, *Popolazione di Firenze*, pp. 58 and 66.
27 Graf, *Il Cinquecento*, p. 265.
28 For the catalogue see Bloch, *Die Prostitution*, vol. 2, part I, p. 123. On the estimates of the number of official prostitutes see Beloch, *Bevölkerungsgeschichte*, vol. 3, p. 101.
29 Bloch, *Die Prostitution*, vol. 2, part I, p. 254; and Delumeau, *Rome*, p. 420.
30 Coryat, *Crudities*, vol. 2, p. 46.

31 Dallington, *Survey of Tuscany*, p. 48.
32 D'Ancona, in Montaigne, *Journal*, pp. 303 n.
33 Scavizzi, "Attività edilizia," p. 175, n. 7.
34 Cipolla, "Storia delle epidemie," pp. 117–18.
35 Cipolla, "Popolazione Lombarda," p. 152.
36 Coleman, *The Economy of England*, p. 73.
37 Allison, "Elizabethan Village," pp. 91–103.
38 Noel, "Paroisse de Laguiole," pp. 199–223.
39 For all above, see Mazzaoui, "Veronese Textile Artisans."
40 Cipolla, *Prezzi, salari*, p. 14.
41 For Venice see Sella, *Commerci e industrie a Venezia*, p. 124; for Florence and Prato see Di Agresti, *Aspetti di vita*, p. 93.
42 Hill, *Puritanism*, p. 43.
43 Gould, *Economic Growth*, pp. 75 *et seq.*
44 Villermé, *Tableau*, vol. 2, p. 245.
45 Villani, *Cronica*, book 11.
46 For above, see Cipolla, *Literacy*, pp. 45–47.
47 Cipolla, *Literacy*, pp. 60–61.
48 Unwin, *Economic History*, pp. 92–99.
49 Hicks, *A Theory*, pp. 141–42.
50 See for all Pollard, "Fixed Capital."
51 Duby, *The Early Growth*, p. 26.
52 Duby, *L'Economie rurale*, vol. I, p. 74.
53 According to Hodgen ("Domesday Water Mills") one gets from the Domesday Book the figure of 5,624 water mills for England at the end of the eleventh century. According to Lennard (*Rural England*, p. 278), however, "the figure of 5,624 given by Miss Hodgen as the total number of Domesday mills is almost certainly too low."
54 Muendel, "The Horizontal Mills."
55 Horn and Born, *The Barns*.
56 Duby, *The Early Growth*, p. 196.
57 ibid., p. 193.
58 Rotelli, *Economia agraria*, p. 20.
59 Slicher Van Bath, *Agrarian History*, pp. 180–81.
60 Beretta, *Pagine*, p. 84.
61 Galassi, *Campagna Imolese*, p. 112.
62 Sclafert, *Cultures en Haute-Provence*, pp. 140–48.
63 Finberg, *Agrarian History*, vol. 4, p. 413.
64 Petty, "Verbum sapienti," p. 106.
65 Sclafert, *Cultures en Haute-Provence*, p. 148.
66 On the history of epizootics, see the works cited in Haeser, *Bibliotheca epidemiographica*, p. 17.
67 *Annales Laurissenses vel Einhardi*, a. 791.
68 Stow, *Annales*, p. 200.
69 Faber, "Cattle-plague."
70 Doria, *Uomini e terre*, p. 52.
71 ibid.
72 Braudel, *Civilisation matérielle*, p. 267.
73 Aleati and Bianchi, *Farmacie pavesi*, p. 31.
74 Poni, "Archéologie," p. 2.
75 Felloni, *Gli Investimenti Finanziari*, p. 49.
76 Contamine, "Consommation et demande militaires," p. 8.

77 Zanetti, *Problemi alimentari*, pp. 56–71.
78 Spengler, "Population Problem," p. 196.
79 Gould, *Economic Growth*, pp. 39, 81, 82.
80 Pugliese, *Condizioni economiche*, Table 2.
81 Devèze, *Histoire des forêts*, pp. 52–53.
82 Coleman, "Naval Dockyards," p. 160.
83 Communication by H. Soly at the ninth week of the Instituto Datini at Prato.
84 Barbour, *Capitalism in Amsterdam*, p. 68.
85 Poni, "All'origine del sistema di fabbrica," p. 466.
86 Cipolla, "Storia del lavoro," pp. 12–13.

3 PRODUCTIVITY AND PRODUCTION

1   Schumpeter, "The Creative Response," p. 150.
2   *Chronique de Robert de Torigny*, p. 238.
3   *Epistole Hugonis*, pp. 318–19.
4   Leo Di Ostia, *Cronica*, III, p. 26.
5   On the influence of sources of energy upon human history, see Cipolla, *Economic History of World Population*, Chapter 2.
6   For wheat only, in England, yields were:

        1200–49: 2.9
        1250–99: 4.2
        1300–49: 3.9
        1350–99: 5.2
        1400–49: 4.1
        1450–99: 4.9

    Slicher van Bath, "Accounts and Diaries," p. 22. The discrepancy between Slicher van Bath's data in Table 3.2 and those of the same author in Table 3.1 arises from the fact that data in Table 3.1 are averages of the yields of wheat, rye, barley, and oats, while those of Table 3.2 are yields of wheat only.
7   E. LeRoy Ladurie, in a moment of polemical skepticism, has defined such figures above as a "*mirage chiffré* (numerical mirage)." See LeRoy Ladurie, *Paysans de Languedoc*, and Morineau, *Les Faux-semblants*.
8   Pini, "La Viticultura," p. 74.
9   Duby, *The Early Growth*, pp. 27 and 189.
10 Slicher van Bath, *Agrarian History*, pp. 182, 334, 335.
11 Slicher van Bath, pp. 334–35; and Benassar, *L'Alimentation d'une Capitale*, p. 53.
12 Lastri, *L'Osservatore*, pp. 163–67.
13 According to a document published by Carmona, "Sull'economia Toscana," p. 43, among the weavers, besides the 878 men and 1,457 women, there were also 358 children.
14 A "piece" was about 35 yards in length.
15 The figures reveal that, during the decline of the industry in the period 1604–27 (a) the larger firms survived, and (b) among the weavers employment of males diminished far more than employment of females.
16 Weavers were not necessarily concentrated in the workshops, that is, in the firms. They usually worked at home, on commission from the "merchants." See above, p. 95.
17 Edler de Roover, "Andrea Bianchi," p. 248.
18 Massa, *Un'impresa serica genovese*, pp. 109–10.
19 Archivio di Stato di Milano, *Commercio*, P.A., b, 228.

20 Sella, *Commerci e Industrie a Venezia*, p. 127.
21 Coleman, *The Economy of England*, p. 78.
22 Blanchard, "Labour productivity," p. 3.
23 Hammersley, "The Charcoal Iron Industry."
24 Cipolla, *Guns and Sails*, p. 154.
25 Scavia, *Industria della Carta*, p. 10.
26 Schubert, *British Iron Industry*, p. 345.
27 See for instance Sclafert, *Culture en Haute-Provence*, p. 9.
28 Darby, *A New Historical Geography*, p. 61.
29 Fourquin, *Histoire économique*, p. 335.
30 Sclafert, *Culture en Haute-Provence*, p. 88.
31 Forquin, *Histoire économique*, p. 348.
32 Gould, *Economic Growth*, p. 9.
33 Ramazzini, *Le malattie dei lavoratori*, Chapter IV.
34 Dallington, *Survey of Tuscany*, pp. 15–16.
35 Barrow, *Travels in China*, p. 67.
36 Garosi, *Siena*, p. 11.
37 Ramazzini, *Le malattie*, pp. 6, 11, 20.

4 THE URBAN REVOLUTION: THE COMMUNES

1 Pirenne, *Medieval Cities*.
2 Ennen, "Different Types," pp. 399–411.
3 Sestan, "Città comunale italiana," pp. 75–95.
4 *Gesta Federici*, 2, 12, RRGGSS 54.

5 POPULATION: TRENDS AND PLAGUES

1 The evidence for this growth is discussed in Genicot, "On the Evidence of Growth of Population," pp. 14–23.
2 Hajnal, "European Marriage Patterns," pp. 101–40.
3 The Italian missionary, Father Matteo Ricci, reported from China in the sixteenth century that "celibacy is not approved of and polygamy is permitted" (Gallagher, *The Journals*, p. 97). At the end of the eighteenth century, the Englishman John Barrow reported from China, "Public opinion considers celibacy as disgraceful and a sort of infamy is attached to a man who continues unmarried beyond a certain time of life" (Barrow, *Travels*, pp. 398–99).
4 Moryson, *Itinerary*, pp. 156 and 409.
5 ibid., p. 296.
6 Wrigley, *Population and History*, pp. 86–87.
7 ibid., p. 119.
8 ibid., p. 124.
9 Boase, *Death in the Middle Ages*.
10 Infant mortality relates infant deaths (number of children dying at less than one year of age) to live births in the same year. The infant mortality rate is thus obtained by dividing the number of deaths of infants during a calendar year by the number of live births in the same period and by multiplying the result by 1,000. Adolescent mortality relates the number of deaths of children one to nine years old during a calendar year to the population of the same age group.
11 On what precedes, see Rosen, *From Medical Police*, p. 44, and Cipolla, *The Bills of Mortality of Florence*.

12 For the statement by the Mayor of Padua see Ferrari, *L'ufficio della Sanità*, p. 86, n. 2. For the statement by Ramazzini, see Ramazzini, *Malattie dei Lavoratori*, Chapter XL.

13 Le Roy Ladurie, "L'Histoire immobile," p. 682.

14 Zinsser, *Rats, Lice and History*, pp. 111ff.

15 Benaglio, "Relazione della carestia," pp. 422–23.

16 Pullan, *Rich and Poor*, pp. 243ff.

17 For Poland, see Hoffmann, *Warfare, Weather and a Rural Economy*, p. 285; for Venice, Sanuto, *Diarii*, XLVI, col. 380 and 612; for Bergamo, Benaglio, "Relazione della carestia," pp. 419–21.

18 Segni, *Trattato*, p. 55.

19 Johnsson, *Storia della peste di Busto Arsizio*, p. 15.

20 As has been said, "War and famine have probably always taken their toll of human life more through the intermediary of the microbe than by starvation and the sword" (Burnett White, *Natural History of Infectious Disease*, p. 12).

21 Allix, *L'Oisans*, p. 32.

22 Fiumi, "La popolazione del territorio volterrano-sangimignanese," p. 283.

23 For England see Shrewsbury, *Bubonic Plague*, p. 231; for Venice see Carbone, *Provveditori*, p. 8; for Paris see Franklin, *Vie privée*, vol. 14, pp. 18–75; for Barcelona see Nadal, *Población española*, p. 596.

24 Hull, *The Economic Writings*, vol. 2, p. 347.

25 ibid., vol. 1, p. 109.

26 ibid., vol. 2, pp. 369–70.

27 Mols, *Introduction*, vol. 2, p. 334.

28 Helleiner, "The Vital Revolution," p. 85.

6 TECHNOLOGY

1 Lilley, "Technological Progress," p. 188. See also Gould, *Economic Growth*, pp. 327ff.

2 Compare Finley, "Technical Innovation," pp. 29–45; Kiechle, "Probleme der Stagnation;" and Pleket, "Technology and Society," pp. 1–24.

3 On the windmills of antiquity, see Moritz, *Grain-mills*.

4 The episode is recounted by Suetonius in Chapter 18 of his *Life of Vespasian*.

5 See the observations by Landes, *Engineering in the Ancient World*.

6 Lilley, "Technological Progress," p. 188.

7 White, "Expansion of Technology," p. 143.

8 White, "Cultural Climates," p. 172.

9 White, "Expansion of Technology," p. 147.

10 Leighton, *Transport and Communication*, p. 105.

11 Needham, *Science and Civilization*, vol. 4, pp. 303–27.

12 White, "Expansion of Technology," p. 153.

13 For all that precedes, see Duby, *The Early Growth*, pp. 15, 75–76, 194–95.

14 On all that precedes, see Bautier, "Les plus anciennes mentions de moulins," pp. 569ff. and Carus-Wilson, *An Industrial Revolution*.

15 White, "Expansion of Technology," p. 157.

16 Honig, "De Molens," p. 79.

17 See Cipolla, *The Economic History of World Population*, Chapter 2.

18 Compare Lane, "The Economic Meaning of the Invention of the Compass." Compare also Taylor, "Mathematics and the Navigator."

19 Narducci, "Tre prediche," pp. 125–26, and Rosen, "The Invention of the Eyeglasses," pp. 13–46 and 183–218.

20 We know, for example, that at the beginning of the fourteenth century the normal size of a Hanseatic ship was about 75 tons. Around 1400, the traditional "Kogge" was replaced by larger vessels of the "Holk" type. Around 1440 the average size of the Hanseatic vessels was about 150 tons. Thirty years later, when the carvel-type vessels were introduced in the Hanseatic fleet, the average tonnage was about 300 tons. For the French–English wine trade it has been observed that early in the fifteenth century few ships can have carried more than 100 tuns of wine. But by the middle of the century ships from Bordeaux brought an average of 150 tuns, and there were a few ships which could carry as many as 500 tuns of wine. For Portuguese ships, it has been suggested that between 1450 and 1550 the average tonnage at least doubled. In Venice about 1450, anything over 200 tons was considered big. Later, 400 tons became a normal size for most cogs, and by the mid-sixteenth century there were numerous Venetian carracks of 600 to 700 tons.

21 White, *The Flavor of Early Renaissance Technology.*

22 Cipolla, *Money, Prices and Civilization,* p. 61.

23 Walker, "The Origins of the Machine Age," pp. 591–92.

24 *Annali,* vol. 1, p. 248.

25 The pages which follow are partially derived from an article by the author which appeared under the title "The Diffusion of Innovations in Early Modern Europe," *Comparative Studies in Society and History,* 14, 1972. I should like to express my thanks to the journal and to the Cambridge University Press for kindly giving me permission to reproduce here several pages of the article in question.

26 On the whole story, consult W.H. Chaloner, "Sir Thomas Lombe."

27 Oakeshott, *Political Education,* p. 15.

28 Britten, *Old Clocks and Their Makers,* p. 272.

29 Archivio di Stato di Milano, *Commercio,* P.A., b, 264/fasc. 2.

30 Casoni, "Note sull'artiglieria veneta," pp. 177–80.

31 Cipolla, *Guns and Sails,* p. 54, n. 1.

32 Ullyett, *British Clocks and Clockmakers,* p. 18.

33 Amburger, *Die Familie Marselis.*

34 Smith, *Old Scottish Clockmakers,* p. 323.

35 Luzzatto, *Studi di Storia Economica,* pp. 42–43.

36 Fanfani, *Storia del lavoro in Italia,* pp. 147–48.

37 See above, p. 84.

38 Cipolla, *L'Economia Milanese,* p. 353.

39 Cipolla, *Guns and Sails,* p. 69, n. 2.

40 *Svenskt Biografiskt Lexicon* ad vocem *De Besche.*

41 Cipolla, *Clocks and Culture,* pp. 65ff.; Kenyon, *The Glass Industry of the Weald;* Cunningham, *Alien Immigrants;* Bodmer, *Der Einfluss der Refugianten.*

42 Frankel, *The Economic Impact on Underdeveloped Societies,* pp. 22–24.

43 Quoted and translated by Barbour, *Dutch and English Merchant Shipping,* p. 234.

7 ENTERPRISE, CREDIT, AND MONEY

1 It is possible that double-entry bookkeeping developed in Tuscany in the thirteenth century. In the fourteenth and fifteenth centuries this type of accounting spread to other Italian cities. See De Roover, "Aux Origines d'une Technique," and Melis, *Storia della Ragioneria.* Prototypes of marine insurance may have emerged in the thirteenth century, but the earliest extant documents which undoubtedly refer to insurance contracts go back to the fourteenth

century. Genoa long remained the major center for this type of business. See Edler De Roover, "Marine Insurance." From the seventeenth century on, the major center of insurance in Europe was London.

2   Postan, "Credit in Medieval Trade," pp. 65–71.
3   The original document, in Latin, is preserved in the Archive of Genoa. The English translation is by Lopez and Raymond, *Medieval Trade*, pp. 182–83.
4   Ferretto, "Giovanni Mauro di Carignano," pp. 43–44.
5   Kedar, *Merchants in Crisis*, pp. 25ff. One form of participation in maritime trade was the *sea loan*. Its main peculiarity was that the borrower pledged the return of the loan only on condition that the ship carrying the borrowed money or the goods purchased with it safely completed its voyage. Sea loans lost their popularity at the same time that the *commenda* did, in the second half of the thirteenth century.
6   Among the many who have written on the subject, see Sapori, "Le Compagnie Mercantili Toscane," pp. 803–05.
7   De Roover, *Lettres de Change*.
8   In the *sendeve* a master entrusted an agent with goods. In the *vera societas* only one of the parties provided capital. The other carried out the commercial operation and profit and losses were usually shared equally. In the *contrapositio* each partner brought his share of capital and profits were shared in proportion to the capital invested. In the *complete partnership* partners pledged in common all or the greater part of their fortunes. For more details see Dollinger, *The German Hansa*, pp. 166–67.

8 PRODUCTION, INCOMES, AND CONSUMPTION: 1000–1500

1   For a more detailed account of all that precedes, see Smith, *An Historical Geography* and for the *Drang nach Osten*, see also Dollinger, *The German Hansa*.
2   Giovanni Villani, *Cronica*, book 11, Chapter 94. The English translation is by Lopez and Raymond, *Medieval Trade*, pp. 71–74.
3   The *moggio* was a dry measure equal to 16.59 bushels.
4   Bonvesin della Riva, *De Magnalibus Urbis Mediolani*, pp. 67–114. For an English translation of the relevant passages see Lopez and Raymond, *Medieval Trade*, pp. 61–69.
5   Dante, *Comedy*, Paradise 15, translation by L. Binyon.
6   Ricobaldus, *Historia Universalis*, in R.R. II S.S., vol. 9, col. 128. On the relation between Ricolbaldo's text and the successive texts of Flamma and of De Mussis, as well as on contemporary ideas of economic progress, cf. Rubinstein, "Some Ideas on Municipal Progress," pp. 165–83, and Herlihy, *Pistoia*, pp. 1–5.
7   Flamma, "Opusculum" in R.R. II S.S., vol. 12, cols 1033–4.
8   In Piacenza, the first fireplaces appeared after 1320. In Rome they were still rare in 1368.
9   The Emperor Charles V had a dozen forks among his possessions, but the courtiers of Henry III of France were still laughed at for the amount of food they lost on the way to their mouths. As to handkerchiefs, one must keep in mind that the height of good manners in the Middle Ages was to use only the left hand to blow one's nose at the table. In the sixteenth century the middle class had begun to use the sleeve, rather than the fingers. Then the handkerchief slowly came to be adopted. Henry IV of France allegedly possessed five handkerchiefs and this was thought worthy of note.

10 On the famine of 1317 see Lucas, "The Great European Famine"; on that of 1346–47 see Pinto, "Firenze e la carestia."
11 Israel, *Dutch Primacy*, p. 4.
12 Concerning the effects of the plague on the collective psychology, and on the art forms, consult, among others, Langer, "Next Assignment," pp. 283–304; Meiss, *Painting*; Brossolet, "L'Influence de la peste."
13 Goldthwaite, *The Building of Renaissance Florence*, p. 354.
14 De Mussis, "Chronic Placentium," in RR.II S.S., vol. XVI, cols 582–84.
15 Dyer, *Standards of Living in the Later Middle-Ages*, pp. 276–77.

9 THE EMERGENCE OF THE MODERN AGE

1 Ashtor, "Che cosa sapevano i geografi arabi dell'Europa occidentale?"
2 Andreades, "The Economic Life of the Byzantine Empire."
3 On all that precedes, see Ashtor, "Observations on Venetian Trade"; Ashtor, "Levantine Sugar Industry", Ashtor, "Aspetti della espansione italiana"; Irigoin, "Les Débuts de l'emploi du papier à Byzance."
4 Charleston, "The Import of Venetian Glass into the Near East."
5 Lopez, "Venezia," pp. 53–59.
6 Sevcenko, "The Decline of Byzantium," pp. 176ff., and Geanakoplos, "A Byzantine Look at the Renaissance," pp. 157–162.
7 Lambros, "Ipomnina tou Kardinaliou Vissarionos," pp. 15–27, and Keller, "A Byzantine Admirer of Western Progress," pp. 343–48.
8 Cipolla, *Guns and Sails*, p. 89. For an analysis of the "relative decline" of China compared to Europe on the technological plane from the fourteenth century onward, see Elvin, *The Patterns of the Chinese Past*, pp. 177–78 and Chapter 14.
9 White, "Expansion of Technology," p. 157.
10 On the preceding, cf. Cipolla, *Guns and Sails*, pp. 15–18 and 137.
11 Hudson, *Europe and China*, p. 268.
12 Brading and Cross, "Colonial silver mining," pp. 560ff.
13 Cipolla, "Saggio di Interesse"; Barbour, *Capitalism in Amsterdam*, pp. 85ff.; Homer, *Interest Rates*, p. 128.
14 Attmann, *The Russian and Polish Markets*, pp. 119ff.
15 Throughout the sixteenth century and at the beginning of the seventeenth, nearly 80 percent of European imports from the East consisted of pepper, other spices, and dyes. During the seventeenth century, textiles acquired greater importance and toward the end of the century made up about 60 percent of imports into Europe by the English and Dutch East India Companies. Compare Glamann, *Dutch-Asiatic Trade*, pp. 13, 14; and Pach, "The Role of East-Central Europe," pp. 220–22.
16 Glamman, *Dutch-Asiatic Trade*, p. 58.
17 Van Linschoten, *The Voyage to the East Indies*, vol. 1, p. 10. Western Europe's trade with the Baltic also showed a deficit. It has been estimated that, at the end of the sixteenth century and the beginning of the seventeenth, of the total value of the goods in transit through the Sound, 70 percent went from the Baltic toward the West as against 30 percent which went in the opposite direction. The deficit was settled with western exports of silver. Compare Attman, *The Russian and Polish Markets*, pp. 119ff.
18 Carletti, *Ragionamenti*, p. 189.
19 Hernandes, *Rerum Medicarum*.
20 D'Orta and Monardes, *Dell'Historia de i semplici aromati*, part II, p. 19. On Garcia

d'Orta and Nicolas Monardes, see Boxer, *Two Pioneers of Tropical Medicine.*

21 In the Low Countries, in the period 1557–1710, per capita consumption of grain was about one liter a day. In the decade 1781–91, consumption fell to 0.6 liters because, in the interval, the potato had in part replaced grain in daily food consumption. In Ireland, the rate of substitution was very much higher. For what precedes, see Vandenbroeke, "Cultivation and Consumption of the Potato," pp. 28–29.

With reference to the classic case of Ireland, see Connell, *The Population of Ireland*, Chapter 5, and Davidson, "The History of the Potato and Its Progress in Ireland". In general, see Salaman, *History and Social Influence of the Potato.* Barrow, *Travels in China*, p. 398n., wrote at the end of the eighteenth century, "The great advantage of a potato crop is the certainty of its success. Were a general failure of this root to take place, as sometimes happens to crops of rice, Ireland, in its present state, would experience all the horrors that attend a famine in some of the provinces of China." In this brief, inconspicuous footnote Barrow was amazingly prophetic. Less than five decades after he wrote these words the potato crops failed in Ireland and the country experienced "all the horrors that attend a famine in some of the provinces of China."

22 Morse, *The Chronicles of the East India Company*, vol. 1, pp. 9, 125, and 158.

23 Lionardo di Capua, *Parere*, p. 110.

24 Duncan, *Avis salutaire.* Among his followers see Tissot, *Santé des gens de lettres*, pp. 189ff.

25 Cole, *Trends in Eighteenth Century Smuggling*, p. 396.

26 On this point consult in particular the erudite work of Jones, *Ancients and Moderns.*

27 Dijksterhuis, *The Mechanization of the World Picture.*

28 Letwin, *The Origins of Scientific Economics*, pp. 99–100.

29 Stone, "Elizabethan Overseas Trade," p. 30.

30 *Annali della fabbrica del Duomo*, vol. 1, pp. 209–10.

31 As the Milanese doctor G.B. Silvatico asserted in 1607, paraphrasing a sentence of Galen, *"qui medicus esse vult optimus, is prius philosophus sit necesse est."* See Cipolla, *Public Health.*

32 Atkinson, *Les nouveaux horizons*, p. 10.

33 Matarazzo, "Cronaca della città di Perugia," p. 3.

34 Calegari, "Legname e costruzioni navali," p. 94.

35 Calegari, ibid., and Sella, *Salari e lavoro*, Appendix, Table IX.

36 Coleman, *The Economy of England*, p. 23.

37 See pp. 269–70 of this book.

10 THE CHANGING BALANCE OF ECONOMIC POWER IN EUROPE

1 For a salutary reaction to this fashion, see Schöffer, "Holland's Golden Age," pp. 82–107.

2 Guicciardini, "Relazione di Spagna," p. 131.

3 Cited in Luzzatto, *Storia economica*, vol. 1, p. 139.

4 On the importance of exports to the American colonies see Vilar, *Oro e moneta*, pp. 107ff. Exports consisted mainly of oil, wine, vinegar, flour, silks, velvets, shoes, hats, textiles, glass, soap, weapons of all kinds, and so on.

5 The simile is by Tawney, *Business and Politics*, p. 28.

6 Sevrano Mangas, *Armadas y flotas de la Plata*, p. 316.

7   Trevor-Davies, *Spain in Decline*, pp. 92–93 and Kagan, *Students and Society in Early Modern Spain.*
8   For the above, see Sella, "Venetian Woollen Industry," pp. 113–15.
9   State Papers, Henry VIII, edition of 1830–52, volume VII (1849), p. 226 (Sir Nicholas Carew and Richard Sampson to Henry VIII from Bologna, 12 December 1529).
10 *Relazione del Ducato di Milano di G. Basadonna*, p. 333.
11 Sella, "Venetian Woollen Industry," p. 114.
12 ibid., p. 116.
13 Pullan, *Crisis and Change*, pp. 8–9.
14 Quoted in Sella, "Industrial Production," p. 247.
15 For all that precedes, compare Cipolla, "The Decline of Italy: The Case of a Fully Matured Economy," p. 203.
16 Gualdo, *Relatione*, p. 87.
17 Meroni, *Cremona fedelissima*, vol. 2, pp. 19–21.
18 Cipolla, "The Decline of Italy," p. 197.
19 Sivori, *Il tramonto dell'industria serica*, p. 896.
20 Sella, *Commerci e industrie*, p. 126.
21 Borelli, *Un Patriziato della Terraferma Veneta*, p. 26.
22 Sella, *Crisis and Continuity*, p. 59.
23 Romano, "A Florence," pp. 508–11.
24 Parenti, *Prime Ricerche*, Chapter III, and Pullan, "Wage Earners," pp. 146–74.
25 Moryson, *Itinerary*, p. 419.
26 Cipolla, "Four Centuries of Italian Demographic Development," p. 573.
27 On the economic history of Holland, consult Baasch, *Holländische Wirtschaftsgeschichte*, which is methodical and complete. Decidedly more brilliant is Barbour, *Capitalism in Amsterdam*; see also Van Houtte, *Economische en Sociale Geschiedenis*; Boxer, *The Dutch Seaborne Empire*; and Israel, *Dutch Primacy.*
28 On the development of the southern Low Countries in the Middle Ages, consult the classic work by Pirenne, *Histoire de Belgique*, and the brief outline of Doehaerd, "L'expansion économique belge au Moyen Age." On the development of Antwerp and the decline of Bruges, see the brilliant and classic article by Van Houtte, "La genèse du grand marché international d'Anvers à la fin du Moyen Age," and more recently Van Der Wee, *Antwerp Market.*
29 Guicciardini, *Descrittione*, p. 176.
30 With reference to Holland's poor endowment in natural resources, a seventeenth-century Englishman described the country as "such a spot as if God had reserved it as a place only to dig turf out of."
31 Burke, *Venice and Amsterdam.*
32 Wilson, *The Dutch Republic*, pp. 15–18.
33 In admitting foreign craftsmen, Amsterdam compromised with guild opposition, found housing for newcomers, and offered incentives to masters deemed capable of starting new industries or improving techniques in those already established. The status of citizen could be acquired at a cost of 8 florins until 1622, when it was raised to 14 florins. Barbour, *Capitalism in Amsterdam*, pp. 15–16.
34 On this famous personage, consult Dahlgren, *Louis de Geer.*
35 Jeannin, *L'Europe du Nord-Ouest*, pp. 70–71.
36 Van Uytven, "The Fulling Mill," p. 12.
37 Bulletins of prices quoted on the Amsterdam Commodities Exchange were published from 1585 and circulated throughout Europe. In 1634 these bulletins gave the prices of 359 commodities. In 1686 the list increased to 550 commodities.

38 Jeannin, *L'Europe du Nord-Ouest*, p. 75.
39 Clément, *Lettres*, vol. 6, p. 264. For modern estimates of the size of the Dutch fleet, consult Vogel, "Handelsflotten," pp. 268–334; and Boxer, *The Dutch in Brazil*, pp. 204–05. According to Christensen, *Dutch Trade to the Baltic*, p. 94, a "most reliable calculation from the Dutch States Provincial" of 1636 estimated the size of the Dutch merchant navy trading to the Baltic, Norway, and France at 1,050 ships.
40 Elias, *Het Voorspel*, p. 60.
41 Unger, "Dutch Ship Design," p. 409.
42 Defoe, *A Plan of the English Commerce*, p. 192.
43 Christensen, *Dutch Trade to the Baltic, passim*.
44 In some cases, Dutch entrepreneurs found it more convenient to transform raw materials into finished products at the source where the raw materials were available. De Geer and the Tripps operated iron foundries in Sweden. The product, in the shape of iron bars and iron cannon, was imported into the United Provinces: a good deal of it was re-exported, but the profits of course were retained in Amsterdam.
45 Dion, *Histoire de la vigne*, pp. 426–27.
46 On Dutch horology see Britten, *Old Clocks*, pp. 246ff.; on precision instruments see Barbour, *Capitalism in Amsterdam*, p. 63n; on cartography and map production, see Tooley, *Maps and Map Makers*, pp. 21 and 29.
47 Van der Woude, "Het Noorderkwartier," vol. 2, p. 320, Table 5.11.
48 Barbour, *Dutch and English Merchant Shipping*, p. 239.
49 The average rate of interest in Amsterdam was about 3 percent when it was 6 percent in London, and Josiah Child in 1665 considered this as the "causa causans of all the other causes of riches in that people." Compare Wilson, *The Dutch Republic*, pp. 33–34, and Homer, *A History of Interest Rates*, p. 128.
50 Unger, "Dutch Ship Design," p. 405. In accordance with the character of technological development before the Industrial Revolution, Dutch shipbuilding was "exclusively based on tradition and experience: there was no question of scientific shipbuilding." Compare Van Kampen, *Scheepsbouw*, p. 240.
51 Defensibility and speed were sacrificed by private shipowners since in most cases their ships could count on the protection of the Dutch navy. For all that precedes, see Unger, "Dutch Ship Design," pp. 406–08.
52 See above, p. 244.
53 Dion, *Histoire de la vigne*, p. 427.
54 Price, *Culture and Society in the Dutch Republic*.
55 Coleman, *The Economy of England*, p. 49.
56 For the preceding, see Van Houtte, "Anvers au XVᵉ et XVIᵉ siècles," p. 251.
57 Van der Wee, *Antwerp*, vol. 2, p. 131.
58 For all this, consult Schulte, *Geschichte des Mittelalterlichen Handels*.
59 Fisher, "Commercial Trends and Policy," pp. 154–55; Gould, *The Great Debasement*, pp. 126ff.
60 For all that precedes, see Coleman, *The Economy of England*, pp. 61ff.
61 Fisher, "Commercial Trends and Policy," pp. 153ff.
62 ibid., pp. 160, 169, 172.
63 Coleman, *The Economy of England*, p. 64.
64 J. Gee, *The Trade and Navigation of Great Britain*, London, 1738, Chapter 1, p. 7.
65 See Hope, *A New History*, p. 172, and Challis, "Spanish Bullion," p. 384.
66 Hope, *A New History*, p. 189.
67 Stow, *Annales*, pp. 1038–40.
68 Violet, *Mysteries and Secrets of Trade*, pp. 17–18.

69 Cunningham, *Alien Immigrants*.
70 See the documents reproduced by Thirsk and Cooper, *Seventeenth-Century Economic Documents*, pp. 713 and 737.
71 Stoye, *English Travelers*, pp. 22 and ff.
72 Henry VIII's quarantine regulations, the "Plague Orders" of Elizabeth, and the College of Physicians at London were all instituted on Italian models. Copeman, *Doctors and Disease*, p. 169; and Clark, *Royal College of Physicians*, vol. 1, pp. 58ff.
73 Stow, *Annales*, p. 1038.
74 Britten, *Old Clocks*, p. 77.
75 Tawney and Power, *Tudor Economic Documents*, vol. 1, pp. 231–38.
76 Stow, *Annales*, p. 1025.
77 Nef, *British Coal Industry*, vol. 1, p. 214.
78 For the movement of prices, see Coleman, *The Economy of England*, pp. 100–02.
79 For additional information, see Cipolla, *Guns and Sails*, pp. 62–64.
80 ibid., p. 44, n. 2.
81 ibid., p. 64.
82 Stow, *Annales*, p. 1025.
83 Nef, *British Coal Industry*, vol. 1, pp. 19–20, 36, 208.
84 Hicks, *A Theory of Economic History*, p. 147.
85 Nef, *The Conquest of the Material World*, p. 125, talks of two hundred workers employed in the cannon foundries of John Browne at the beginning of the seventeenth century. But in all likelihood the number includes charcoal burners and transport workers. (Cipolla, *Guns and Sails*, p. 153). Attendants to the furnaces were always relatively few throughout the seventeenth century.
86 Nef, "The Conquest of the Material World," pp. 124ff.; Davis, *The Rise of the English Shipping Industry*, p. 389; Coleman, "Naval Dockyards," pp. 189ff.
87 Davis, "English Foreign Trade 1700–1774," p. 109. Compare also Davis, "English Foreign Trade 1660–1700," pp. 78–98.
88 Deane, *The First Industrial Revolution*, p. 53.
89 ibid., p. 57.
90 ibid., pp. 66–68.

EPILOGUE

1 On the origins and history of the term "Industrial Revolution," consult Bezançon, "The Early Use of the Term Industrial Revolution." On the Industrial Revolution see, among many others, apart from the classic works of Mantoux and Ashton, the volumes of Beales, *The Industrial Revolution*; Deane, *The First Industrial Revolution*; Mathias, *The First Industrial Nation*; Fohlen, *Qu'est-ce que la Révolution Industrielle*; Crouzet, *Capital Formation in the Industrial Revolution*; Musson, *Science, Technology and Economic Growth*; Drake, *Population in Industrialization*.
2 Cederna, *I Vandali*, p. 8.
3 Waddington, *The Ethical Animal*, p. 15.

BIBLIOGRAPHY

The existing bibliography of the economic and social history of preindustrial Europe has reached colossal proportions and is still expanding rapidly, so that it is increasingly difficult to keep up with what is written and published. As in every other sector of industrial society, quality does not always go hand in hand with quantity. Learned contributions, however, are not lacking, and our knowledge has progressed considerably in recent decades.

This list that follows does not claim to be and must not be taken as a complete bibliographical repertoire. An entire volume of considerable dimensions would be necessary for the purpose. Essentially, the list that follows aims to provide the full titles of works cited in shortened version in the preceding pages, although it also contains a few additional titles. Readers who wish to obtain further bibliographical information may consult the bibliographies published in the *Cambridge Economic History of Europe* and the *Fontana Economic History of Europe*. I also recommend the classic works by W. Sombart, *Der Moderne Kapitalismus*, Munich/Leipzig, 1924; and by J. Kulischer, *Allgemeine Wirtschaftsgeschichte des Mittelalters und der Neuzeit*, Munich/Berlin, 1928, which are irreplaceable mines of historical and bibliographical information. Such works suffer from the fact that they were written over half a century ago, but if today they are seldom quoted and even less often read, this is due to fashion and not to their obsolescence. No subsequent author has produced anything even remotely comparable to works so powerful in erudition, sharpness of perception, and originality of thought.

Abel, W., *Die Wüstungen des ausgehenden Mittelalters*, Jena, 1943.

Abel, W., *Agrarkrisen und Agrarkonjunktur in Mitteleuropa vom 13. bis zum 19. Jahrhundert*, Berlin, 1966.

Abel, W., *Massenarmut und Hungerkrisen in vorindustriellen Deutschland*, Göttingen, 1972.

Abulafia, D., *The Two Italies: Economic Relations between the Norman Kingdom of Sicily and the Northern Communes*, Cambridge, 1977.

Alberi, E. (ed.), *Relazioni degli Ambasciatori veneti al Senato*, Florence, 1840.

Albion, R.G., *Forests and Sea Power*, Cambridge, Mass., 1926.

Aleati, G., "Una dinastia di magnati medievali: gli Eustachi di Pavia," *Studi in onore di A. Sapori*, vol. 2, Milan, 1957.

Allison, K.J., "An Elizabethan Village Census," *Bulletin of the London University Institute of Historical Research*, vol. 36 (1963).

Allix, A., *L'Oisans au Moyen Age. Étude de géographie historique en haute montagne*, Paris, 1929.

Amburger, E., *Die Familie Marselis. Studien zur russischen Wirtschaftsgeschichte*, Giessen, 1967.

Amodeo, D., *A proposito di un antico bilancio di previsione del Vicereame di Napoli*, Naples, 1953.

Andreades, A.M., "The Economic Life of the Byzantine Empire," in N.H. Baynes and H.L.B. Moss (eds), *Byzantium*, Oxford, 1948.

Annali della Fabbrica del Duomo di Milano, Milan, 1877.

Anselmi, S., *Insediamenti, agricoltura, proprietà nel Ducato Roverasco*, Urbino, 1975.

Antero, Maria di S. Bonaventura, *Li Lazzaretti della Città e Riviere di Genova del 1657*, Genoa, 1658.

Arnould, M.A., *Les dénombrements des foyers dans le comté de Hainaut (XIV–XVI siècles)*, Brussels, 1956.

Ashton, R., "Deficit Finance in the Reign of James I," *The Economic History Review*, ser. 2, vol. 10 (1957).

Ashton, T.S., *The Industrial Revolution*, London, 1948.

Ashtor, E., "Che cosa sapevano i geografi arabi dell'Europa occidentale?," in *Rivista storica italiana*, vol. 81 (1969).

Ashtor, E., *Les métaux précieux et la balance des payements du Proche-Orient à la Basse Époque*, Paris, 1971.

Ashtor, E., "Observations on the Venetian Trade in the Levant in the XIVth Century," *The Journal of European Economic History*, vol. 5 (1976).

Ashtor, E., "Levantine Sugar Industry in the Later Middle Ages," *Israel Oriental Studies*, vol. 7 (1977).

Ashtor, E., "Aspetti della espansione italiana nel Basso Medioevo," *Rivista storica italiana*, vol. 90 (1978).

Atkinson, G., *Les nouveaux horizons de la Renaissance française*, Paris, 1935.

Attman, A., *The Russian and Polish Markets in International Trade 1500–1650*, Göteborg, 1973.

Baasch, E., *Holländische Wirtschaftsgeschichte*, Jena, 1927.

Balbi, E., *L'Austria e le primarie potenze*, Milan, 1846.

Ball, J.N., *Merchants and Merchandise: The Expansion of Trade in Europe, 1500–1630*, London, 1977.

Barbour, V., "Dutch and English Merchant Shipping to the Seventeenth Century," *The Economic History Review*, vol. 2 (1930).

Barbour, V., *Capitalism in Amsterdam in the Seventeenth Century*, Ann Arbor, 1963.

Barrow, J., *Travels in China*, Philadelphia, 1805.

Basini, G.L., *L'uomo e il pane*, Milan, 1970.

Battara, P., *La popolazione di Firenze alla metà del Cinquecento*, Florence, 1935.

Bautier, R.H., "Les foires de Champagne," in *Recueil Jean Bodin*, vol. 5, Brussels, 1953.

Bautier, R.H., "Les plus anciennes mentions de moulins hydrauliques industriels et de moulins à vent," *Bulletin Philologique et Historique*, vol. 2 (1960).

Beales, H.L., *The Industrial Revolution, 1752–1850*, London, 1958.

Bean, J.M.W., "Plague, Population and Economic Decline in the Later Middle Ages," *The Economic History Review*, ser. 2, vol. 15 (1963).

Beloch, K.J., *Bevölkerungsgeschichte Italiens*, Berlin, 1937–1961.

Beltrami, D., "La composizione economica e professionale della popolazione di Venezia nei secoli XVII e XVIII," *Giornale degli economisti*, n.s., vol. 10 (1951).

Beltrami, D., *Storia della popolazione di Venezia dalla fine del secolo XVI alla caduta della Repubblica*, Padua, 1954.

Beltrami, D., *Saggio di storia dell'agricoltura nella Repubblica di Venezia durante l'età moderna*, Venice/Rome, 1955.

Benaglio, M.A., "Relazione della carestia e della peste di Bergamo," *Miscellanea di Storia Italiana*, vol. 6 (1865).

Bennassar, B., "L'alimentation d'une ville espagnole au XVIᶜ siècle. Quelques données sur les approvisionnements et la consommation de Valladolid," *Annales E.S.C.*, vol. 16 (1961).

Berengo, M., *Nobili e mercanti nella Lucca del Cinquecento*, Turin, 1965.

Beretta, R., *Pagine di storia briantina*, Como, 1972.

Bergier, J.F., *Problèmes de l'histoire économique de la Suisse*, Berne, 1968.

Bergier, J.F., *Naissance et croissance de la Suisse industrielle*, Berne, 1974.

Bergier, J.F., *Histoire économique de la Suisse*, Lausanne, 1984.

Bergier, J.F. and Solari, L., "Histoire et élaboration statisque. L'exemple de la population de Genève au XVᶜ siècle," in *Mélanges Antony Babel*, Geneva, 1963.

Besta, G.F., *Vera narratione del successo della peste*, Milan, 1578.

Beveridge, W., *Prices and Wages in England from the Twelfth to the Nineteenth Century*, London, 1939.

Bezançon, A., "The Early Use of the Term Industrial Revolution," *The Quarterly Journal of Economics*, vol. 36 (1922).

Bianchini, L., *Della Storia delle Finanze del Regno di Napoli*, Palermo, 1839.

Bilanci generali della Repubblica di Venezia, Venice, 1912–72.

Blanchard, I., "Labour productivity and work psychology in the English Mining Industry," *The Economic History Review*, ser. 2, vol. 31 (1978).

Bloch, I., *Die Prostitution*, Berlin, 1912–25.

Bloch, M., *Les caractères originaux de l'histoire rurale française*, Paris, 1931.

Boas, M., *The Scientific Renaissance: 1450–1630*, New York, 1966.

Boase, T.S.R., *Death in the Middle Ages*, New York, 1972.

Bodmer, W., *Der Einfluss der Refugianten-einwanderung von 1500–1700 auf die Schweizerische Wirtschaft*, Zürich, n.d.

Borelli, G., *Un Patriziato della Terraferma Veneta*, Milan, 1974.

Boutruche, R., *La crise d'une société; seigneurs et paysans du Bordelais pendant la Guerre de Cent Ans*, Paris, 1947.

Boutruche, R., "La dévastation des campagnes pendant la guerre de Cent Ans et la reconstruction agricole de la France," *Publications de la Faculté des Lettres de l'Université de Strasbourg*, vol. 3, Paris, 1947.

Boutruche, R. (ed.), *Bordeaux de 1453 à 1715*, Bordeaux, 1966.

Boutruche, R., *Signoria e feudalesimo*, Bologna, 1971.

Bowden, P.J., *The Wool Trade in Tudor and Stuart England*, London, 1962.

Boxer, C.R., *The Dutch in Brazil*, Oxford, 1957.

Boxer, C.R., *Two Pioneers of Tropical Medicine: Garcia d'Orta and Nicolás Monardes*, London, 1963.

Boxer, C.R., *The Dutch Seaborne Empire, 1600–1800*, London, 1965.

Boyd, A., *The Monks of Durham*, Cambridge, 1975.

Brading, D.A. and Cross, H.E., "Colonial silver mining: Mexico and Peru," *The Hispanic American Historical Review*, vol. 52 (1972).

Braudel, F., *Civilisation matérielle et capitalisme*, Paris, 1967.

Braudel, F., *L'identité de la France*, Paris, 1986.

Bridbury, A.R., *Economic Growth: England in the Later Middle Ages*, London, 1962.

Britten, F.J., *Old Clocks and Watches and Their Makers*, ed. G.H. Baille, C. Clutton, and C.A. Ilbert, New York, 1956.

Brossolet, J., "L'influence de la peste du Moyen Age sur le thème de la danse macabre," *Pagine di storia della medicina*, vol. 13 (1969).

Brown, M., *On the Theory and Measurement of Technological Change*, Cambridge, 1966.

Brucker, G.A., *Florentine Politics and Society, 1343–1378*, Princeton, 1967.

Brucker, G. (ed.), *Two Memoirs of Renaissance Florence: The Diaries of Buonaccorso Pitti and Gregorio Dati*, New York, 1967.

Brütil, C.R. and Violante, C., *Die Honorantie Civitatis Papie*, Köln, 1983.

Brulez, W., "The Balance of Trade in the Netherlands in the Middle of the 16th Century," *Acta Historiae Neerlandica*, vol. 4 (1970).

Bücher, K., *Die Bevölkerung von Frankfurt am Main im 14. und 15. Jahrhundert*, Tübingen, 1886.

Buffini, A., *Ragionamenti intorno all'ospizio dei trovatelli*, Milan, 1844.

Burke, P., *Economy and Society in Early Modern Europe*, New York, 1972.

Burke, P., *Venice and Amsterdam: A Study of Seventeenth-century Elites*, London, 1974.

Caizzi, B., *Il Comasco sotto il dominio spagnolo*, Como, 1955.

Calegari, M., "Legname e costruzioni navali nel Cinquecento," in VV.AA. *Guerra e Commercio nell'evoluzione della marina genovese*, vol. 2, Genoa, 1973.

Capmany y de Montpalau, *Memorias históricas sobre la marina, commercio y artes de Barcelona*, Madrid, 1779.

Carabellese, F., *La peste del 1348 e le condizioni della Sanità Pubblica in Toscana*, Rocca San Casciano, 1897.

Carande, R., *Carlos V y sus banqueros*, Madrid, 1964.

Carbone, S., *Provveditori e Sopraprovveditori alla Sanità della Repubblica di Venezia*, Rome, 1962.

Carletti, F., "Ragionamenti del mio viaggio intorno al mondo (1594–1606)," in M. Guglielminetti (ed.), *Viaggiatori del Seicento*, Turin, 1967.

Carmona, M., "Sull'economia toscana del Cinquecento e del Seicento," *Archivio storico italiano*, vol. 120 (1962).

Carpentier, E., "Famines et épidemies dans l'histoire du XIVe siècle, *Annales E.S.C.*, n.s., vol. 6 (1962).

Carus-Wilson, E.M., "An Industrial Revolution of the Thirteenth Century," in E.M. Carus-Wilson (ed.), *Essays in Economic History*, vol. 1, London, 1954.

Carus-Wilson, E.M. (ed.), *Essays in Economic History*, vol. 1, London, 1954.

Carus-Wilson, E.M. *The Merchant Adventurers of Bristol in the XVth Century*, Bristol, 1962.

Carus-Wilson, E.M. and Coleman, O., *England's Export Trade 1275–1547*, Oxford, 1963.

Casoni, G., "Note sull'artiglieria veneta," in *Veneziae le sue lagune*, vol. 1, part 2, Venice, 1847.

Catellacci, D., "Ricordi del Contagio di Firenze del 1630," *Archivio storico italiano*, ser. 5, vol. 20 (1897).

Cavaciocchi, S. (ed.), *Metodi, risultati e prospettive della storia economica secoli XIII–XVIII*, Florence, n.d.

Cavaciocchi, S. (ed.), *Produzione commercio della carta e del libro, secoli XIII and XVIII*, Florence, 1992.

Cederna, A., *I vandali in casa*, Bari, 1956.

Cernovodeanu, P., *England's Trade Policy in the Levant (1660–1714)*, Bucharest, 1972.

Challis, C.E., "Spanish Bullion and Monetary Inflation in England in the Later Sixteenth Century," *Journal of European Economic History*, vol. 4 (1975).

Challis, C.E., *The Tudor Coinage*, Manchester, 1978.

Chaloner, C.W., "Sir Thomas Lombe and the British Silk Industry," in *People and Industries*, London, 1963.

Chambers, J.D. and Mingay, G.E., *The Agricultural Revolution (1750–1880)*, London, 1966.

Chandaman, C.D., *The English Public Revenue 1660–1688*, Oxford, 1975.

Charleston, R.J., "The Import of Venetian Glass into the Near East," *Annales du III Congrès International d'études historiques du verre* (Damascus, 1964), Liège, 1968.

Chaudhuri, K.N., "Treasure and Trade Balances: The East India Company's Export Trade 1660–1720," *The Economic History Review*, ser. 2, vol. 21 (1968).

Chaudhuri, K.N., *Trade and Civilization in the Indian Ocean*, London, 1987.

Cherubini, G., *Agricoltura e società rurale nel Medioevo*, Florence, 1972.

Cherubini, G., "La proprietà fondiaria di un mercante toscano del Trecento," *Rivista di storia dell'agricoltura*, vol. 5 (1965).

Christensen, A.E., "Der handelsgeschichte Wert der Sundzollregister," *Hansische Geschichtblätter*, vol. 59 (1934).

Christensen, A.E., *Dutch Trade to the Baltic about 1600*, Copenhagen/The Hague, 1941.

Cipolla, C.M., "Per una storia del lavoro," *Bollettino Storico Pavese*, vol. 5 (1944).

Cipolla, C.M., "Comment s'est perdue la propriété ecclésiastique dans l'Italie du Nord," *Annales E.S.C.*, n.s., vol. 2 (1947).

Cipolla, C.M., "Per la storia della popolazione lombarda nel secolo XVI," in *Studi in onore di G. Luzzatto*, Milan, 1949.

Cipolla, C.M., "The Decline of Italy: the Case of a Fully Matured Economy," *The Economic History Review*, ser. 2, vol. 5 (1952).

Cipolla, C.M., "Note sulla storia del saggio di interesse," *Economia internazionale*, vol. 5 (1952).

Cipolla, C.M., *Money, Prices and Civilization*, Princeton, N.J., 1956.

Cipolla, C.M., *Prezzi, salari e teoria dei salari in Lombardia alla fine del Cinquecento*, Rome, 1956.

Cipolla, C.M., "Per la storia delle epidemie in Italia," *Rivista storica italiana*, vol. 75 (1963).

Cipolla, C.M., "Currency Depreciation in Medieval Europe," *The Economic History Review*, ser. 2, vol. 15 (1963).

Cipolla, C.M., "Four Centuries of Italian Demographic Development," in D.V. Glass and D.E.C. Eversley (eds), *Population in History*, London, 1965.

Cipolla, C.M., *Guns and Sails in the early Phase of European Expansion*, London, 1965.

Cipolla, C.M., *Clocks and Culture*, London, 1967.

Cipolla, C.M., *Literacy and Development in the West*, Harmondsworth, 1969.

Cipolla, C.M., *Cristofano and the Plague*, London, 1973.

Cipolla, C.M., "The Professions – the Long View," *The Journal of European Economic History*, vol. 2 (1973).

Cipolla, C.M., *The Economic History of World Population*, 6th edn, Harmondsworth, 1974.

Cipolla, C.M., "The Plague and the pre-Malthus Malthusians," *The Journal of European Economic History*, vol. 3 (1974).

Cipolla, C.M., *Public Health and the Medical Profession in the Renaissance*, Cambridge, 1975.

Cipolla, C.M., *Il governo della moneta a Firenze e a Milano nei secoli XIV–XVI*, Bologna, 1990.

Cipolla, C.M., *Between History and Economics: An Introduction to Economic History*, London/New York, 1991.

Cipolla, C.M. (ed.), *The Economic Decline of Empires*, London, 1970.

Clamageran, J.J., *Histoire de l'impôt en France*, Paris, 1867–68.

Clark, G.N., *A History of the Royal College of Physicians of London*, Oxford, 1964.

Clément, P. (ed.), *Lettres, instructions et mémoires de Colbert*, Paris, 1859–82.

Coleman, D.C., "Naval Dockyards," *The Economic History Review*, ser. 2, vol. 6 (1953).

Coleman, D.C., *The Economy of England, 1450–1750*, Oxford, 1977.

Coniglio, G., *Il Viceregno di Napoli nel secolo XVII*, Rome, 1955.

Connell, K.H., *The Population of Ireland: 1750–1845*, Oxford, 1950.

Connell, K.H., "The Potato in Ireland," *Past and Present*, vol. 23 (1962).

Contamine, P., "Consommation et demande militaires en France et en Angleterre, XIII–XV siècles," in Istituto Intern. di Storia Economica F. Datini, *Sesta Settimana di Studio*, Prato, 1974.

Conti, E., *La formazione della struttura agraria moderna nel contado fiorentino*, Rome, 1965.

Conti, E., *L' imposta diretta a Firenze nel Quattrocento*, Rome, 1984.

Cooper, J.P., "The Social Distribution of Land and Men in England, 1436–1700," in R. Floud (ed.), *Essays in Quantitative Economic History*, Oxford, 1974.

Copeman, W.C.S., *Doctors and Disease in Tudor Times*, London, 1960.

Coppola, G., "L'agricoltura di alcune pievi della pianura irrigua milanese nei dati catastali della metà del secolo XVI," *Contributi dell'Isituto di storia economica e sociale* (dell'Università Cattolica di Milano), Milan, 1973.

Corradi, A., *Annali delle epidemie occorse in Italia dalle prime memorie fino al 1850*, Bologna, 1867–92.

Coryat, T., *Crudities*, London, 1786.

Coulton, G.C., *The Black Death*, London, 1929.

Coulton, G.C., *Medieval Panorama*, New York, 1958.

Craeybeckx, J., *Un grand commerce d'importation: les vins de France aux anciens Pays-Bas*, Paris, 1958.

Creighton, C., *A History of Epidemics in Britain*, Cambridge, 1891–94.

Croix, A., "La Démographie du pays nantais au XVI siècle," in *Annales de Demographie historique* (1967).

Crosby, A.W., *The Columbian Exchange: Biological and Cultural Consequences of 1492*, Westport, Conn., 1973.

Crouzet, F. (ed.), *Capital Formation in the Industrial Revolution*, London, 1972.

Cunningham, W., *Alien Immigrants to England*, London, 1897.

Curschmann, H.W.F., *Hungersnöte im Mittelalter*, Leipzig, 1900.

Curtin, P.D., *The Atlantic Slave Trade: a Census*, Madison, Wis., 1969.

Dahlgren, E.W., *Louis de Geer*, Uppsala, 1923.

Dallington, R., *Survey of Tuscany*, London, 1605.

Darby, H.C. (ed.), *A New Historical Geography of England*, Cambridge, 1973.

Davidson, R., *Storia di Firenze*, Florence, 1956.

Davidson, W.D., "The History of the Potato and Its Progress in Ireland," *Journal of the Department of Agriculture*, 34.

Davis, J.C., *The Decline of the Venetian Nobility as a Ruling Class*, Baltimore, 1962.

Davis, R., "England and the Mediterranean 1570–1670," in F.J. Fisher (ed.), *Essays in the Economic and Social History of Tudor and Stuart England*, Cambridge, 1961.

Davis, R., *The Rise of the English Shipping Industry*, London, 1962.

Davis, R., *A Commercial Revolution: English Overseas Trade in the Seventeenth and Eighteenth Centuries*, London, 1967.

Davis, R., "English Foreign Trade 1660–1700," in W.E. Minchinton (ed.), *The Growth of English Overseas Trade in the Seventeenth and Eighteenth Centuries*, London, 1969.

Davis, R., "English Foreign Trade 1700–1774," in W.E. Minchinton (ed.), *The Growth of English Overseas Trade in the Seventeenth and Eighteenth Centuries*, London, 1969.

Davis, R., *The Rise of the Atlantic Economies*, London, 1973.

Daviso di Charvensod, M.C., *I pedaggi delle Alpi occidentali nel Medio Evo*, Turin, 1961.

Deane, P., "The Implications of Early National Income Estimates for the Measurement of Long-term Economic Growth in the United Kingdom," *Economic Development and Cultural Change* (1955).

Deane, P., *The First Industrial Revolution*, Cambridge, 1967.

Deane, P., "Capital Formation in Britain before the Railway Age," in F. Crouzet (ed.),

Capital Formation in the Industrial Revolution, London, 1972.

Deane, P. and Cole, W.A., *British Economic Growth (1688–1959)*, Cambridge, 1967.

Defoe, D., *A Plan of the English Commerce*, London, 1728.

De Gennaro, G., *L'abate Ciro Saverio Minervini*, Naples, 1975.

Del Panta, L., *Una traccia di storia demografica della Toscana nei secoli XVI–XVIII*, Florence, 1974.

Delumeau, J., *Vie économique et sociale de Rome dans la seconde moitié du XVI^c siècle*, Paris, 1957.

De Maddalena, A., "Il mondo rurale italiano nel Cinque e nel Seicento," *Rivista storica italiana*, vol. 76 (1964).

De Muinck, B.W., "A Regent's Family Budget about the Year 1700," *Acta Historiae Neerlandica*, vol. 2 (1967).

De Mussis, J., "Chronicon Placentinum," *Rerum Italicarum Scriptores*, vol. 16.

Derlange, M., "Cannes," *Cahiers de la Méditerranée*, vol. 5 (1972).

De Roover, R., "Aux origines d'une technique intellectuelle: la formation et l'expansion de la compatibilité à partie double," *Annales d'histoire économique et sociale*, vol. 9 (1937).

De Roover, R., *L'évolution de la lettre de change*, Paris, 1953.

De Roover, R., "The Development of Accounting prior to Luca Pacioli," in *Studies in the History of Accounting*, London, n.d.

De Roover, R., *The Rise and Decline of the Medici Bank 1397–1494*, New York, 1966.

Desaive, J.P., "Clergé rural et documents fiscaux," *Revue d'histoire moderne et contemporaine*, vol. 17 (1970).

Devèze, M., *La vie de la forêt française au XVI^c siècle*, Paris, 1961.

Devèze, M., *Histoire des forêts*, Paris, 1965.

Devèze, M., *L'Europe et le monde à la fin du XVIII^c siècle*, Paris, 1970.

De Vries, J., *The Dutch Rural Economy in the Golden Age, 1500–1700*, New Haven, Conn., 1974.

De Vries, J., *Barges and Capitalism: Passenger Transportation in the Dutch (1632–1839)*, Utrecht, 1981.

De Vries, J., *The Decline and Rise of the Dutch Economy 1675–1900. Essays in honor of W.N. Parker*, ed. G. Saxonhouse and G. Wright, Greenwich, 1984.

Deyon, P., *Amiens, capitale provinciale*, Paris, 1967.

De Zeeuw, J.W., "Peat and the Dutch Golden Age: The Historical Meaning of Energy Attainability," in *AGG Bijdragen* 21 (1978).

Di Agresti, D.G.M., *Aspetti di vita Pratese*, Florence, 1976.

Diaz, F., *Il Granducato di Toscana*, Turin, 1976.

Di Capua, L., *Parere divisato in otto Ragionamenti*, Naples, 1689.

Dietz, F.C., "English Government Finance 1485–1558," *University of Illinois Studies in the Social Sciences*, vol. 9 (1920).

Dietz, F.C., *English Public Finance, 1558–1641*, New York, 1932.

Dijksterhuis, E.J., *The Mechanisation of the World Picture*, Oxford, 1961.

Dion, R., *Histoire de la vigne et du vin en France dès origines au XIX^c siècle*, Paris, 1959.

Di Simplicio, O., "Due secoli di produzione agraria in una fattoria del Senese, 1550–1751," *Quaderni storici*, vol. 21 (1972).

Doehaerd, R., *L'expansion économique belge au Moyen Age*, Brussels, 1946.

Dollinger, P., *La Hanse, XII^c–XVII^c siècles*, Paris, 1964.

Dollinger, P., *The German Hansa*, London, 1970.

Doren, A., *Storia economica dell'Italia nel Medio Evo*, Padua, 1937.

Doria, G., *Uomini e terre di un borgo collinare del XVI al XVIII secolo*, Milan, 1968.

Doria, G., "Mezzo secolo di attività finanziarie de un doge di Genova," in *Beitrage zur Wirtschaftsgeschichte*, vol. 4 (1978).

D'Orta, G. and Monardes, N., *Dell'Historia de i semplici aromati et altre cose che vengono portate dall'Indie pertinenti all'uso della medicina*, Venice, 1582.

Drake, M. (ed.), *Population in Industrialization*, London, 1969.

Drummond, J.C. and Wilbraham, A., *The Englishman's Food. A History of Five Centuries of English Diet*, London, 1939.

Dublin, L., Lotka, A., and Spiegelman, M., *Length of Life. A Study of the Life Table*, New York, 1949.

Duby, G., *L'économie rurale et la vie des campagnes dans l'Occident médiéval*, Paris, 1962.

Duby, G., *Guerriers et paysans*, Paris, 1973.

Duby, G., *The Early Growth of the European Economy*, London, 1974.

Duby, G. and Wallon, A. (eds), *Histoire de la France rurale*, Paris, 1975.

Duncan, D., *Avis salutaire contre l'abus des choses chaudes et particulièrement du café, du chocolat et du thé*, Rotterdam, 1705.

Dupaquier, J., *Introduction à la démographie historique*, Paris, 1974.

Durand, J.D., *The Modern Expansion of World Population*, in C.B. Nam (ed.), *Population and Society*, Boston, 1968.

Dyer, C., *Standards of Living in the Later Middle Ages: Social Change in England, c. 1200–1520*, Cambridge, 1989.

East, G., *Géographie historique de l'Europe*, Paris, 1939.

Eden, F.M., *The State of the Poor*, London, 1797.

Edler de Roover, F., "Early Example of Marine Insurance," *Journal of Economic History*, vol. 5 (1945).

Edler de Roover, F., "Andrea Bianchi, Florentine Silkmanufacturer and Merchant in the Fifteenth Century," *Studies in Medieval and Renaissance History*, vol. 3 (1966).

Ehrman, J., *The Navy in the War of William III*, Cambridge, 1952.

Elias, J.E., *Het Voorspel van den Eersten Engelschen Oorlog*, The Hague, 1920.

Elliott, J.H., *Imperial Spain 1469–1716*, New York, 1963.

Elliott, J.H., "Self-perception and Decline in Early Seventeenth-century Spain," *Past and Present*, vol. 74 (1977).

Elliott, J.H., *Spain and its World 1500–1700*, New Haven/London, 1989.

Elsas, M.J., *Umriss einer Geschichte der Preise und Löhne in Deutschland*, Leiden, 1949.

Elton, G.R., "An early Tudor Poor Law," *The Economic History Review*, ser. 2, vol. 6 (1953).

Elvin, M., *The Patterns of the Chinese Past*, London, 1973.

Endres, R., "Zur Einwohnerzahl und Bevölkerungsstruktur Nürnbergs im 15/16. Jahrhundert," *Mitteilungen des Vereins für Geschichte der Stadt Nürnberg*, vol. 57 (1970).

Ennen, E., *Frühgeschichte der Europäischen Stadt*, Bonn, 1953.

Ennen, E., "Les différents types de formation des villes européennes," *Le Moyen Age*, ser. 4, vol. 11 (1956).

Ennen, E., "The Different Types of Formation of European Towns," in S.L. Thrupp (ed.), *Early Medieval Society*, New York, 1967.

Espinas, G., *Deux fondations de villes dans l'Artois et la Flandre Française (X–XV siècles): Saint Omer et Lannoy-du-Nord*, Lille/Paris, 1948.

Eulenberg, P., "Städtische Berufs und Gewerbestatistik im 16. Jahrhundert," *Zeitschrift für die Geschichte des Oberrheis*, n.s., vol. 11 (1896).

Faber, J.A., "Cattle-plague in the Netherlands during the Eighteenth Century," *Medelingen van de Landbouwhogeschool te Wegeningen*, vol. 62 (1962).

Fanfani, A., *Storia del lavoro in Italia dalla fine del secolo XV agli inizi del XVIII*, Milan, 1943.

Fasoli, G. and Bocchi, F., *La città medievale italiana*, Florence, 1973.

Feller, G., *Geschichte Berns*, Berne, 1953.

Felloni, G., *Gli investimenti finanziari genovesi in Europa tra il Seicento e la Restaurazione*, Milan, 1971.

Ferrari, C., *L'Ufficio della Sanità di Padova*, Venice, 1909.

Ferrario, G., *Statistica medica di Milano*, Milan, 1838–40.

Ferretto, A., "Giovanni Mauro di Carignano," *Archivio della Società Ligure di Storia Patria*, vol. 52 (1924).

Finberg, H.P.R. (ed.), *The Agrarian History of England and Wales*, Cambridge, 1967.

Finch, M.E., *The Wealth of Five Northamptonshire Families 1540–1640*, Northamptonshire Record Society, vol. 19 (1956).

Finley, M.I., "Technical Innovation and Economic Progress in the Ancient World," *The Economic History Review*, ser. 2, vol. 18 (1965).

Fiochetto, G.F., *Trattato della peste*, Turin, 1720.

Fioravanti, J.M., *Memorie storiche della città di Pistoia*, Lucca, 1758.

Fisher, F.J., "Commercial Trends and Policy in Sixteenth-Century England," in E.M. Carus-Wilson (ed.), *Essays in Economic History*, vol. 1, London, 1961.

Fisher, H.E.S., *The Portuguese Trade*, London, 1971.

Fiumi, E., "Fioritura e decadenza dell'economia fiorentina," *Archivio storico italiano*, vols 115–17 (1960).

Fiumi, E., "La popolazione del territorio volterrano-sangimignanese ed il problema demografico dell'età comunale," in *Studi in onore di A. Fanfani*, vol. 1, Milan, 1962.

Fiumi, E., "Popolazione, società ed economia volterrana dal catasto del 1428–29," *Rassegna volterrana*, vols 36–39 (1972).

Flamma, G., "Opusculum," *Rerum Italicarum Scriptores*, vol. 12.

Flinn, M.W., *The European Demographic System, 1500–1820*, Baltimore, 1981.

Fohlen, C., *Qu'est-ce que la Révolution industrielle*, Paris, 1971.

Formentini, M., *Il Ducato di Milano*, Milan, 1877.

Forster, E.R. (ed.), *European Diet from Pre-Industrial to Modern Times*, New York, 1975.

Foss, M., *The Art of Patronage: The Arts in Society 1660–1750*, London, 1972.

Fourquin, G., *Les Campagnes de la région parisienne à la fin du Moyen Age*, Paris, 1964.

Fourquin, G., *Histoire économique de l'Occident médiéval*, Paris, 1969.

Frank, J.P., *System einer vollständingen medizinischen Polizey*, Vienna, 1786.

Frankel, S.H., *The Economic Impact on Underdeveloped Societies*, Oxford, 1953.

Franklin, A., "La vie privée d'autrefois," vol. 14: *L'hygiène*, Paris, 1890.

Franz, G., *Der Dreissigjährige Krieg und das deutsche Volk*, Jena, 1943.

Frumento, A., *Imprese lombarde nella storia della siderurgia italiana*, Milan, 1963.

Fumagalli, V., *L'alba del Medioevo*, Bologna, 1993.

Gaastra, F.S., "The exports of precious metal from Europe to Asia by the Dutch East India Company, 1692–1795," in *Proceedings on Pre-modern Monetary History*, University of Wisconsin, August 1977.

Gade, J.A., *The Hanseatic Control of Norwegian Commerce during the Late Middle Ages*, Leyden, 1951.

Galassi, N., *I rapporti sociali nella campagna imolese dal sec. XVI al sec. XIX*, Imola, n.d.

Gallagher, L.J. (ed.), *The Journals of Matthew Ricci*, New York, 1953.

Galluzzi, R., *Istoria del Granducato di Toscana*, Florence, 1781.

Ganshof, F.L., *Etude sur le développement des villes entre Loire et Rhin au Moyen Age*, Paris/Brussels, 1943.

Ganshof, F.L., *Qu'est-ce que la Féodalité?*, Brussels, 1947.

Ganshof, F.L., *Recherches sur les Capitulaires*, Paris, 1958.

Garcia-Baquero Gonzales, A., *Cadiz y el Atlantico 1717–1748*, Seville, 1976.
Garcia Sanz, A., *Desarrollo y crisis del antiguo Regimen en Castilla la Vieja*, Madrid, 1977.
Garosi, A., *Siena nella storia della medicina (1240–1555)*, Florence, 1958.
Gascon, R., *Grand commerce et vie urbaine au XVIe siècle – Lyon et ses marchands*, Paris, 1971.
Geanakoplos, D.J., "A Byzantine Look at the Renaissance," *Greek and Byzantine Studies*, vol. 1 (1958).
Gee, J., *The Trade and Navigation of Great Britain*, London, 1738.
Genicot, L., "On the Evidence of Growth of Population from the 11th to the 13th Century," in S.L. Thrupp (ed.), *Change in Medieval Society*, New York, 1964.
Gilbert, M. and ass., *Comparative National Products and Price Levels*, Paris, 1958.
Gilli, G.A., *Origini dell'eguaglianza. Ricerche sociologiche sull'antica Grecia*, Turin, 1988.
Glamann, K., *Dutch-Asiatic Trade, 1620–1740*, The Hague, 1958.
Glass, D.V., "Graunt's Life Table," *Journal of the Institute of Actuaries*, vol. 76 (1950).
Glass, D.V., "Two Papers on Gregory King," in D.V. Glass and D.E.C. Eversley (eds), *Population in History*, London/Chicago, 1965.
Glass, D.V. and Eversley, D.E.C. (eds), *Population in History*, London, 1965.
Gnoli, D., "Roma e i Papi nel Seicento," in *La vita italiana nel Seicento*, Milan, 1895.
Godinho Magalhães, V., *A Expansão Quatrocentista Portuguesa*, Lisbon, 1945.
Goldthwaite, R.A., *The Building of Renaissance Florence*, Baltimore/London, 1980.
Göller, E., *Die Einnahmen der Apostolischen Kammer unter Johann XXII*, Paderborn, 1910.
Goubert, P., *Beauvais et le Beauvaisis de 1600 à 1730*, Paris, 1960.
Gould, J.D., *Economic Growth in History*, London, 1972.
Graf, A., *Attraverso il Cinquecento*, Turin, 1888.
Grasby, R., "The Rate of Profit in Seventeenth-Century England," *The English Historical Review*, vol. 84 (1962).
Grendi, E., *La Repubblica aristocratica dei genovesi*, Bologna, 1987.
Grierson, P., "Commerce in the Dark Ages: a Critique of the Evidence," in *Transactions of the Royal Historical Society*, ser. 5, vol. 9 (1959).
Gualdo Priorato, G., *Relatione della città di Firenze e del Gran Ducato di Toscana*, Cologne, 1668.
Guarducci, A. (ed.), *Gerarchie Economiche e Gerarchie Sociali secc. XII–XVIII*, Florence, 1990.
Guicciardini, F., "Relazione di Spagna (1512–13)," in *Opere*, ed. R. Palmarocchi, Bari, 1936.
Guicciardini, L., *Descrittione di tutti i Paesi Bassi*, Antwerp, 1567.
Guillaume, P. and Poussou, J.P., *Démographie historique*, Paris, 1970.

Haeser, H., *Bibliotheca epidemiographica*, Greifswald, 1969.
Hajnal, J., "European Marriage Patterns in Perspective," in D.V. Glass and D.E.C. Eversley (eds), *Population in History*, London, 1965.
Hall, A.R., *The Scientific Revolution*, Boston, 1956.
Halley, E., *Degrees of Mortality of Mankind (1693)*, Baltimore, 1942.
Hamilton, E.J., *American Treasure and the Price Revolution in Spain, 1501–1650*, Cambridge, Mass., 1934.
Hammersley, G., "The Charcoal Iron Industry and Its Fuel, 1540–1750," *The Economic History Review*, ser. 2, vol. 26 (1973).
Hare, R., *Pomp and Pestilence*, London, 1954.
Harrison, M. and Royston, O.M., *How They Lived*, Oxford, 1965.
Hart, S., "Historisch-demografishe notitie," *Maandblad Amstelodamum*, vol. 55 (1968).

Hart, S., "Amsterdam Shipping and Trade to Northern Russia in the Seventeenth Century," *Mededelingen van de Nederlandse Vereniging voor Zeegeschiedenis*, vol. 26 (1973).

Hartwell, R.M. (ed.), *The Causes of the Industrial Revolution*, London, 1967.

Haudricourt, A.G., "De l'origine de l'attelage moderne," *Annales d'histoire économique et sociale*, vol. 8 (1936).

Haudricourt, A.G. and Hédin, L., *L'homme et les plantes cultivées*, Paris, 1944.

Haudricourt, A.G. and Bruhnes Delamarre, M.J., *L'homme et la charrue*, Paris, 1955.

Hauser, H., *La pensée et l'action economique du Cardinal de Richelieu*, Paris, 1944.

Headrick, D.R., *The Tools of the Empire. Technology and European Imperialism in the Nineteenth Century*, New York/Oxford, 1981.

Heaton, H., "Financing the Industrial Revolution," in F. Crouzet (ed.), *Capital Formation in the Industrial Revolution*, London, 1972.

Hecksher, E.F., *An Economic History of Sweden*, Cambridge, Mass., 1954.

Heidemann, H., "Bevölkerungszahl und Beruflische Gliederung Münster in Westfalia am Ende des 17. Jahrhundert," *Münsterische Beitrage zur Geschichtsforschung*, vol. 37, Münster, 1917.

Helleiner, K.F., "The Vital Revolution reconsidered," in D.V. Glass and D.E.C. Eversley (eds), *Population in History*, London, 1965.

Hémardinquer, J.J. (ed.), *Pour une histoire de l'alimentation*, Paris, 1970.

Henning, F.W., "Der Ochshandel aus den Gebieten nördlich der Karpaten im 16 Jahrhundert," *Scripta Mercaturae*, 1973.

Henry, L., *Anciennes familles genevoises*, Paris, 1956.

Herlihy, D., "Treasure Hoards in the Italian Economy, 960–1139," *The Economic History Review*, ser. 2, vol. 10 (1957).

Herlihy, D., *Medieval and Renaissance Pistoia*, New Haven, Conn., 1967.

Herlihy, D., "Family and Property in Renaissance Florence," in *The Medieval City*, ed. H.A. Miskimin, D. Herlihy, and A.L. Udovitch, New Haven, 1977.

Herlihy, D. and Klapish, C., *Les Toscans et leur familles, Une étude du Catasto Florentin de 1427*, Paris, 1978.

Hernandez, F., *Rerum medicarum Novae Hispaniae Thesaurus*, Rome, 1651.

Hicks, J., *A Theory of Economic History*, Oxford, 1969.

Hilf, R.B., *Der Wald*, Potsdam, 1938.

Hill, C., *Puritanism and Revolution*, London, 1965.

Hobsbawm, E.J., "The Crisis of the Seventeenth Century," *Past and Present*, vols 5–6 (1954).

Hodgen, M.T., "Domesday Water Mills," *Antiquity*, vol. 13 (1939).

Hollingsworth, T.H., *A Demographic Study of British Ducal Families*, in D.V. Glass and D.E.C. Eversley (eds), *Population in History*, London, 1965.

Homer, S., *A History of Interest Rates*, New Brunswick, N.J., 1963.

Honig, G.J., "De Molens van Amsterdam," *Jaarboek van het Genootschap Amstelodamum*, vol. 27 (1930).

Hope, R., *A New History of British Shipping*, London, 1990.

Horn, W. and Born, E., *The Barns of the Abbey of Beaulieu*, Berkeley/Los Angeles, 1965.

"Household Book of Edward Stafford, Duke of Buckingham", *Archaeologia*, vol. 25 (1834).

"Household and Privy Purse Accounts of the Lestranges (1519–78)," *Archaeologia*, vol. 25 (1834).

Hovinden, M.A. (ed.), *Households and Farm Inventories in Oxfordshire, 1500–1590*, Oxford, 1965.

Howes, E. (ed.), *see* Stow, J.

Hudson, G.F., *Europe and China*, London, 1961.

313

Hull, C.H. (ed.), *The Economic Writings of Sir William Petty together with the Observations upon the Bills of Mortality by John Graunt,* New York, 1963.

Imberciadori, I., "Spedale scuole e chiesa in popolazioni rurali dei secoli XVI–XVII," *Economia e storia,* vol. 6 (1959).
Irigoin, J., "Les débuts de l'emploi du papier à Byzance," *Byzantinische Zeitschrift,* vol. 46 (1953).
Israel, J.I., *Dutch Primacy in World Trade, 1585–1740,* Oxford, 1989.

Jack, S.M., *Trade and Industry in Tudor and Stuart England,* London, 1977.
James, M.K., *Studies in the Medieval Wine Trade,* ed. E.M. Veale, Oxford, 1971.
Jeannin, P., *L'Europe du Nord-ouest et du Nord aux XVIIe et XVIIIe siècles,* Paris, 1969.
Johnsson, J.W.S., *Storia della peste avvenuta nel borgo di Busto Arsizio 1630,* Copenhagen, 1924.
Jones, E.L. (ed.), *Agriculture and Economic Growth in England 1650–1815,* London, 1967.
Jones, R.F., *Ancients and Moderns: Study of the Rise of the Scientific Movement in Seventeenth-Century England,* St Louis, 1961.
Jordan, W.K., *Philanthropy in England 1480–1660,* London, 1959.

Kagan, R.L., *Students and Society in Early Modern Spain,* Baltimore, 1974.
Karmin, O., *Vier Thesen zur Lehre von der Wirtschaftskrisen,* Heidelberg, 1905.
Kedar, B.Z., *Merchants in Crisis,* New Haven/London, 1976.
Kedar, B.Z., Meyer, H.E., and Smail, R.C. (eds), *Outremer: Studies in the History of the Crusading Kingdom of Jerusalem,* Jerusalem, 1982.
Kellenenz, H., *The Rise of the European Economy,* London, 1976.
Keller, A.G., "A Byzantine Admirer of Western Progress: Cardinal Bessarion," *Cambridge Historical Journal,* vol. 11 (1953–55).
Kennedy, C. and Thirlwall, A.P., "Technical Progress: A Survey," *Economic Journal,* vol. 82 (1972).
Kenyon, G.H., *The Glass Industry of the Weald,* Leicester, 1968.
Kerridge, E., *Agrarian Problems in the Sixteenth Century and After,* London/New York, 1969.
Keyfitz, N. and Flieger, W., *Population,* San Francisco, 1971.
Kiechle, F., "Probleme der Stagnation des technischen Fortschritts im Altertum," *Geschichte in Wissenschaft und Unterricht,* vol. 16 (1965).
King, G., "Natural and Political Observations," in G.E. Barnett (ed.), *Two Tracts by Gregory King,* Baltimore, 1936.
Kirchner, W., *Commercial Relations between Russia and Europe 1400 to 1800,* Bloomington, Indiana, 1966.
Kirsten, E., Buchholz, E.W., and Köllmann, W., *Raum und Bevölkerung in der Weltgeschichte,* Würzburg, 1956.
Kjoczowski, J., "La Population ecclésiastique des villes du Bas Moyen Age," in Istitutò Internaz. di Storia Economica F. Datini, *Sesta Settimana di Studio,* Prato, 1974.
Knoop, D. and Jones, G.P., *The Medieval Mason,* Manchester, 1967.
Knowles, D., *The Religious Orders in England,* Cambridge, 1948–59.
Kohler, H., *Economics and Urban Problems,* Lexington, 1973.
Kuznets, S., *National Income. A Summary of Findings,* New York, 1946.
Kuznets, S., *Economic Growth,* Glencoe, Ill., 1959.

Labarge, M. Wade, *A Baronial Household of the Thirteenth Century,* New York, 1965.

Labrousse, C.E., *La crise de l'économie française à la fin de l'ancien régime*, Paris, 1944.
Lambros, S.P., "Ipomnina tou Kardinaliou Vissarionos," *Neos Hellenomnemon*, vol. 3 (1906).
Landes, J., *Engineering in the Ancient World*, Cambridge, 1977.
Landry, A., *Traité de démographie*, Paris, 1945.
Lane, F.C., "The Economic Meaning of the Invention of the Compass," *American Historical Review*, vol. 68 (1963).
Lane, F.C., *Venice, a Maritime Republic*, Baltimore, 1973.
Langer, W.L., "The Next Assignment," *American Historical Review*, vol. 63 (1958).
Lantbertus, "Vita Heriberti," *Monumenta Germaniae Historica, Scriptores*, vol. 4.
Lastri, M., *L'osservatore fiorentino sugli edifizi della sua patria*, ed. G. Del Rosso, Florence, 1821.
Latouche, R., *The Birth of Western Economy: Economic Aspects of the Dark Ages*, London, 1961.
Le Comte, L., *Empire of China*, London, 1737.
Le Goff, J., *La Civilisation de l'Occident médiéval*, Paris, 1964.
Leighton, A.C., *Transport and Communication in Early Medieval Europe*, Newton Abbott, 1972.
Lennard, R., *Rural England, 1086–1135*, Oxford, 1959.
Leonard, F.M., *Early History of English Poor Relief*, Cambridge, 1910.
Leonardo di Capua, *see* Di Capua.
Le Roy Ladurie, E., *Les Paysans de Languedoc*, Paris, 1966.
Le Roy Ladurie, E., *Histoire du climat depuis l'an Mil*, Paris, 1967.
Le Roy Ladurie, E., "L'Histoire immobile," *Annales E.S.C.*, vol. 29 (1974).
Letwin, W., *The Origins of Scientific Economics*, London, 1963.
Lilley, S., *Men, Machines and History*, London, 1965.
Lilley, S., "Technological Progress and the Industrial Revolution," in *The Fontana Economic History of Europe*, vol. 3, London, 1973.
Lloyd, C., *English Corsairs on the Barbary Coast*, London, 1981.
Lloyd, T.H., *The English Wool Trade in the Middle Ages*, Cambridge, 1977.
Lombardini, G., *Pane e denaro a Bassano tra il 1501 e il 1799*, Vicenza, 1963.
Lopez, R.S., "Venezia e le grandi linee dell'espansione commerciale nel secolo XIII," in *La civiltà veneziana del secolo di Marco Polo*, Venice, 1955.
Lopez, R.S., *The Commercial Revolution*, Englewood Cliffs, N.J., 1971.
Lopez, R.S. and Raymond, I.W. (eds), *Medieval Trade in the Mediterranean World: Illustrative Documents*, New York, 1955.
Lucas, H.S., "The Great European Famine of 1315, 1316 and 1317," in E.M. Carus-Wilson (ed.), *Essays in Economic History*, vol. 2, London, 1962.
Lütge, F., *Deutsche Sozial- und Wirtschaftsgeschichte*, Berlin, 1960.
Luzzatto, G., "Sull'attendibilità di alcune statistiche economiche medievali," *Giornale degli Economisti*, ser. 4, vol. 69 (1929).
Luzzatto, G., *Storia economica dell'età moderna e contemporanea*, Padua, 1938.
Luzzatto, G., *Studi di storia economica veneziana*, Padua, 1954.
Luzzatto, G., *Storia economica di Venezia dall'XI al XVI secolo*, Venice, 1961.

McEvedy, C. and Jones, R., *Atlas of World Population History*, Harmondsworth, 1978.
MacKay, A., *Spain in the Middle Ages: from Frontier to Empire*, London, 1977.
Malanima, P., *I Riccardi di Firenze*, Florence, 1977.
Malanima, P., *I piedi di legno. Una macchina alle origini dell'industria medievale*, Milan, 1988.
Malassis, L., *Economie agro-alimentaire*, Paris, 1973.
Malfatti, C.V. (ed.), *Two Italian Accounts of Tudor England*, Barcelona, 1953.

Malowist, M., "Poland, Russia and Western Trade, in the 15th and 16th Centuries," *Past and Present*, vol. 13 (1958).

Malowist, M., *Croissance et regression en Europe XVIe–XVIIe siècles*, Paris, 1972.

Marshall, D., "The Old Poor Law, 1662–1795," in E.M. Carus-Wilson (ed.), *Essays in Economic History*, vol. 1, London, 1954.

Massa, P., *Un'impresa serica genovese della prima metà del Cinquecento*, Milan, 1974.

Matarazzo, F., "Cronaca della Città di Perugia dal 1492 al 1503", ed. A. Fabretti, *Archivio Storico Italiano*, vol. 16, part 2 (1851).

Mathias, P., *The First Industrial Nation*, London, 1969.

Mazzaoui, M.F., "The Emigration of Veronese Textile Artisans to Bologna in the XIIIth Century," *Atti e Memorie dell'Accademia di Agricoltura, Scienze e Lettere di Verona*, vol. 149 (1967–68).

Mazzaoui, M.F., *The Italian Cotton Industry in the Later Middle Ages*, Cambridge, 1981.

Meiss, M., *Painting in Florence and Siena after the Black Death*, Princeton, N.J., 1951.

Melis, F., *Storia della ragioneria*, Bologna, 1950.

Melis, F., *Aspetti della vita economica medievale*, Siena, 1962.

Melis, F. (ed.), *Guida alla Mostra internazionale della storia della banca*, Siena, 1972.

Meroni, U., *Cremona fedelissima*, Cremona, 1951–57.

Mignet, M., *Rivalité de François I et de Charles-Quint*, Paris, 1886.

Miller, E. and Hatcher, J., *Medieval England: Rural Society and Economic Change, 1086–1348*, London, 1978.

Minchinton, W.E. (ed.), *The Growth of English Overseas Trade in the Seventeenth and Eighteenth Centuries*, London, 1969.

Mira, G., *Aspetti dell'economia comasca all'inizio dell'età moderna*, Como, 1939.

Mira, G., *Vicende economiche di una famiglia italiana dal XIV al XVII secolo*, Milan, 1940.

Mira, G., "Le entrate patrimoniali del Comune di Perugia," in *Annali della Facoltà di economia e commercio dell'Università di Cagliari*, 1959–60.

Mokyr, J., *The Lever of Riches: Technological Creativity and Economic Progress*, Oxford, 1990.

Mollat, M., "La Mortalité à Paris," in *Le Moyen Age*, vol. 69 (1963).

Mollat, M., *Le rôle du sel dans l'histoire*, Paris, 1968.

Mollat, M., *Etudes sur l'histoire de la pauvreté*, Paris, 1974.

Mollat, M. (ed.), *Les pauvres dans la société médiévale*, Paris, 1973.

Mols, R., *Introduction à la démographie historique des villes d'Europe du XIVe au XVIIIe siècle*, Louvain, 1954.

Montaigne, M. de, *Journal de voyage en Italie, 1580–81*, ed. A. D'Ancona, Città di Castello, 1859.

Monter, W., *Calvin's Geneva*, New York, 1967.

Moritz, L.A., *Grain-mills and Flour in Classical Antiquity*, Oxford, 1958.

Morris, C., "The Plague in Britain," *The Historical Journal*, vol. 14 (1971).

Morse, H.B., *The Chronicles of the East India Company Trading to China, 1615–1834*, Cambridge, Mass., 1926.

Moryson, F., *Itinerary* (ed. C. Hughes), London, 1903.

Muendel, J., "The Horizontal Mills of Medieval Pistoia," *Technology and Culture*, vol. 15 (1974).

Mullet, C.F., *The Bubonic Plague and England*, Lexington, Ky., 1956.

Munro, J.H., "The Central European Silver Mining Boom: Mint Outputs and Prices in the Low Countries and England 1450–1550," in E.H. van Cauwenberghe (ed.), *Money, Coins and Commerce: Essays in the Monetary History of Asia and Europe*, Louvain, 1991.

Muratori, L.A., *Della carità cristiana*, Modena, 1723.

Musson, A.E. (ed.), *Science, Technology and Economic Growth in the Eighteenth Century*, London, 1972.

Nadal, J., *Historia de la población española*, Barcelona, 1966.

Narducci, E. (ed.), "Tre prediche inedite del B. Giordano da Rivalto," *Giornale Arcadico di scienze, lettere ed arti*, vol. 146 (1857).

Needham, J., *Science and Civilisation in China*, Cambridge, 1954–1973.

Needham, J., *The Grand Tritation. Science and Society in East and West*, London, 1969.

Nef, J.U., *Rise of the British Coal Industry*, London, 1932.

Nef, J.U., *The Conquest of the Material World*, Chicago/London, 1964.

Noel, R., "La population de la paroisse de Laguiole d'après un recensement de 1691," *Annales de démographie historique*, 1967.

Oakeshott, M., *Political Education*, Cambridge, 1951.

Ozanam, J.A.F., *Histoire médicale générale et particulière des maladies épidémiques contagieuses et épizootiques qui ont régné en Europe*, Paris, 1817.

Pach, Z.P., "The Role of East-Central Europe in International Trade (16th and 17th Centuries)," *Etudes Historiques*, Budapest, 1970.

Pagano de Divitiis, G. *Mercanti Inglesi nell'Italia del Seicento*, Venice, 1990.

Palmieri, M., *Ricordi Fiscali (1427–1474)*, ed. E. Conti, Rome, 1983.

Paolo di Messer Pace da Certaldo, *Il Libro di Buoni Costumi*, ed. S. Morpurgo, Florence, 1921.

Parenti, G., *La popolazione della Toscana sotto la Reggenza lorenese*, Florence, 1937.

Parenti, G., *Prime ricerche sulla rivoluzione dei prezzi in Firenze*, Florence, 1939.

Parenti, G., *Prezzo e mercato del grano a Siena (1546–1765)*, Florence, 1942.

Partner, P., "The Budget of the Roman Church in the Renaissance Period," in E.F.Jacob (ed.), *Italian Renaissance Studies*, London, 1960.

Paschetti, B., *Lettera*, Genoa, 1580.

Passerini, L., *Storia degli stabilimenti di beneficenza*, Florence, 1853.

Patzelt, E., *Karolingische Renaissance*, Vienna, 1924.

Pazzagli, C., *L'agricoltura toscana nella prima metà dell'800*, Florence, 1973.

Pernoud, R., *Les origines de la bourgeoisie*, Paris, 1947.

Petty, W., "Verbum Sapienti," in *The Economic Writings*, ed. C.M. Hull, vol. 1, New York, 1963.

Phelps Brown, E.H. and Hopkins, S.V., "Wage-rates and Prices: Evidence for Population Pressure in the Sixteenth Century," *Economica*, vol. 24 (1957).

Phelps Brown, E.H. and Hopkins, S.V., "Seven Centuries of Building Wages," in E.M. Carus-Wilson (ed.), *Essays in Economic History*, vol. 2, London, 1962.

Phelps Brown, E.H. and Hopkins, S.V., "Seven Centuries of the Prices of Consumables Compared with Builders' Wage-rates," in E.M. Carus-Wilson (ed.), *Essays in Economic History*, vol. 2, London, 1962.

Pini, A.I., "Problemi demografici bolognesi del Duecento," *Atti e Memorie della Deputazione di Storia Patria per le Provincie di Romagna*, n.s., vols 16–17 (1969).

Pini, A.I., "La Viticultura Italiana nel Medioevo," *Studi Medievali*, ser. 3, vol. 15 (1974).

Pinto, G., "Firenze e la carestia del 1346–7," *Archivio Storico Italiano*, vol. 130 (1972).

Pipponier, F., *Costume et vie sociale. La Cour d'Anjou, XIVe–XVe siècle*, Paris, 1970.

Pirenne, H., *Histoire de Belgique*, Brussels, 1900–32.

Pirenne, H., *A History of Europe*, New York, 1936.

Pirenne, H., *Medieval Cities*, Princeton, N.J., 1952.

Pirenne, H., *Histoire économique et sociale du Moyen Age*, ed. H. van Wervecke, Paris, 1963.

Pitti, B., *Cronica*, ed. A. Bacchi della Lega, Bologna, 1905 (*see also* Brucker).

Planitz, H., *Die Deutsche Stadt im Mittelalter*, Cologne, 1965.

Pleket, H.M., "Technology and Society in the Greco-Roman World," *Acta Historiae Neerlandica*, vol. 2 (1967).

Pollard, J., "Fixed Capital in the Industrial Revolution in Britain," *Journal of Economic History*, vol. 24 (1964) (reprinted in F. Crouzet (ed.), *Capital Formation in the Industrial Revolution*, London, 1972).

Poni, C., "Archéologie de la fabrique: la diffusion des moulins à soie 'alla bolognese' dans les Etats vénitiens du XVI^c au XVIII^c siècle," *Annales E.S.C.*, vol. 27 (1972).

Poni, C., "All'origine del sistema di fabbrica," *Rivista storica italiana*, vol. 88 (1976).

Porisini, G., *La proprietà terriera nel Comune di Ravenna dalla metà del secolo XVI ai giorni nostri*, Milan, 1963.

Postan, M.M., "Credit in Medieval Trade," in E.M. Carus-Wilson (ed.), *Essays in Economic History*, vol. 1, London, 1954.

Postan, M.M., "Investment in Medieval Agriculture," *The Journal of Economic History*, vol. 27 (1967).

Posthumus, N.W., *Geschiedenis der Leidsche Lakenindustrie*, La Haje, 1908–39.

Power, E., *The Wool Trade in English Medieval History*, Oxford, 1941.

Presotto, D., "Genova 1656 – Cronache di una pestilenza," in *Atti della Società Ligure di Storia Patria*, vol. 79 (1965).

Preto, P., *Venezia e i Turchi*, Florence, 1975.

Price, J.L., *Culture and Society in the Dutch Republic during the Seventeenth Century*, London, 1974.

Priuli, G., "Diarii," *Rerum Italicarum Scriptores*, vol. 24.

Pullan, B., "Wage-earners and the Venetian Economy: 1550–1630," in B. Pullan (ed.), *Crisis and Change in the Venetian Economy*, London, 1968.

Pullan, B., *Rich and Poor in Renaissance Venice*, Oxford, 1971.

Pullan, B. (ed.), *Crisis and Change in the Venetian Economy*, London, 1968.

Ramazzini, B., *Le malattie dei lavoratori*, ed. O. Rossi, Turin, 1933 (English translation by W.C. Wright, New York, 1940).

Ramsay, J.H., *A History of the Revenue of the Kings of England, 1066–1399*, Oxford, 1925.

Redlich, F., "An Eighteenth-Century German Guide for Investors," *Bulletin of the Business Historical Society*, vol. 26 (1952).

Redlich, F., "De Praeda Militari," *Vierteljahrschrift für Sozial- und Wirtschaftsgeschichte*, vol. 39 (1956).

Reinhard, M.R., Armengaud, A., and Dupaquier, J., *Histoire générale de la population mondiale*, Paris, 1968.

Renouard, Y., *Etudes d'histoire médiévale*, Paris, 1968.

Renouard, Y., *Les Villes d'Italie*, Paris, 1969.

Rey, M., *Les finances royales sous Charles VI – Les causes du déficit 1388–1413*, Paris, 1965.

Richards, J.F. (ed.), *Precious Metals in the Later Medieval and Early Modern Period*, Durham, N.C., 1983.

Richet, D., "Croissance et blocage en France du XV and XVIII siècle," *Annales E.S.C.*, vol. 23 (1968).

Riden, P., "The Output of the British Iron Industry before 1870," in *The Economic History Review*, 2nd ser., vol. 30 (1977).

Rodenwalt, E., "Untersuchungen über die Biologie der Venetianischen Adels," *Homo*, vol. 8 (1957).

Romani, M.A., *La gente, le occupazioni e i redditi del Piacentino*, Parma, 1969.

Romani, M.A., *Aspetti dell'evoluzione demografica parmense nei secoli XVI e XVII*, Parma, 1970.

Romani, M.A., *Nella spirale di una crisi*, Milan, 1975.

Romano, R., "A Florence au XVII^c siècle. Industries textiles et conjoncture," *Annales E.S.C.*, vol. 7 (1952).

Romano, R., "Economic Aspects of the Construction of Warships in Venice in the Sixteenth Century," in B. Pullan (ed.), *Crisis and Change in the Venetian Economy*, London, 1968.

Rondinelli, F., *Relazione del Contagio stato in Firenze l'anno 1630 e 1633*, Florence, 1634.

Rörig, F., *The Medieval Town*, Berkeley, 1967.

Rosen, E., "The Invention of Eyeglasses," *Journal of the History of Medicine*, vol. 11 (1956).

Rosen, G., *From Medical Police to Social Medicine*, New York, 1974.

Rossi, P., *I filosofi e le macchine*, Milan, 1962.

Rotelli, C., "Rendimenti e produzione agricola nell'Imolese dal XVI al XIX secolo," *Rivista storica italiana*, vol. 79 (1967).

Rotelli, C., *L'economia agraria di Chieri attraverso i catasti dei secoli XIV–XVI*, Milan, 1967.

Rubinstein, N., "Some Ideas on Municipal Progress and Decline in the Italy of the Communes," in *Fritz Saxel*, ed. D.J. Gordon, London, 1957.

Ruiz Martin, F., "Demografia eclesiástica hasta el siglo XIX," in *Dictionario de Historia Eclesiástica de España*, vol. 2, Madrid, 1972.

Russell, J.C., "The Clerical Population of Medieval England," *Traditio*, vol. 2 (1944).

Russell, J.C., *British Medieval Population*, Albuquerque, N.M., 1948.

Salaman, R.N., *History and Social Influence of the Potato*, Cambridge, 1949.

Samuelson, P.A., "A Fallacy in the Introduction of Pareto's Law of Alleged Constancy of Income Distribution," *Rivista Internazionale di Scienze Economiche*, vol. 12 (1965).

Saraceno, P., *La produzione industriale*, Venice, 1965.

Sapori, A., "L'attendibilità di alcune testimonianze cronistiche dell'economia medievale," *Archivio storico italiano*, ser. 7, vol. 12 (1929).

Sapori, A., *Le marchand italien au Moyen Age*, Paris, 1952.

Sapori, A., "Le compagnie mercantili toscane del Dugento," in *Studi di storia economica*, vol. 2, Florence, 1955.

Savary de Brusolons, *Dictionnaire*, Copenhagen, 1750–56.

Sayous, A., "Les débuts du commerce de l'Espagne avec l'Amerique," in *Révue Historique*, vol. 2 (1934).

Scavia, M., *L'industria della carta in Italia*, Turin, 1903.

Scavizzi, P., "Considerazioni sul'attività edilizia a Roma nella prima metà del Seicento," *Studi storici*, vol. 9 (1968).

Schaube, A., *Handelsgeschichte der romanischen Völker des Mittelmeergebiets bis zum Ende der Kreuzzügge*, Munich/Berlin, 1906.

Schiavoni, C., "Introduzione allo studio delle fonti archivistiche per la storia demografica di Roma," *Genus*, vol. 27 (1971).

Schmitz, H.J., *Faktoren der Preisbildung für Getreide und Wein in der Zeit von 800 bis 1350*, Stuttgart, 1968.

Schöffer, I., "Did Holland's Golden Age Coincide with a Period of Crisis?," *Acta Historiae Neerlandica*, vol. 1 (1966).

Schollier, E., *De Levensstandaard in de 15 en 16 Eeuw te Antwerpen*, Antwerp, 1960.

Schubert, H.R., *History of the British Iron and Steel Industry*, London, 1957.

Schulte, A., *Geschichte des mittelalterlichen Handels und Verkehrs zwischen Westdeutschland und Italien mit Auschluss von Venedig*, Leipzig, 1900.

Schumpeter, E.B., *English Overseas Trade Statistics 1697–1808*, Oxford, 1960.

319

Schumpeter, J.A., "The Creative Response in Economic History," *The Journal of Economic History*, vol. 7 (1947).

Sclafert, T., *Cultures en Haute-Provence*, Paris, 1959.

Scott Thompson, G., *Life in a Noble Household: 1614–1700*, Ann Arbor, Mich., 1959.

See, H., *Histoire économique de la France*, Paris, 1939.

Segni, G.B., *Trattato sopra la carestia e fame*, Bologna, 1602.

Sella, D., "La popolazione di Milano nei secoli XVI e XVII," in *Storia di Milano*, vol. 12 (1959).

Sella, D., *Commerci e industrie a Venezia nel secolo XVII*, Venice/Rome, 1961.

Sella, D., "The Rise and Fall of the Venetian Woollen Industry," in B. Pullan (ed.), *Crisis and Change in the Venetian Economy*, London, 1968.

Sella, D., *Salari e lavoro nell'edilizia lombarda durante il sec. XVII*, Pavia, 1968.

Sella, D., "Industrial Production in 17th-century Italy," in *Explorations in Entrepreneurial History*, vol. 6 (1969).

Sella, D., *Crisis and Continuity: The Economy of Spanish Lombardy in the Seventeenth Century*, Cambridge, Mass., 1979.

Serrano Mangas, F., *Armadas y flotas de la Plata*, Madrid, 1989.

Sestan, E., "La città comunale italiana dei secoli X–XII," *XI Congrés International des Sciences Historiques*, vol. 3, Stockholm, 1960.

Sevcenko, I., "The Decline of Byzantium Seen through the Eyes of Its Intellectuals," *Dumbarton Oaks Papers*, vol. 15 (1961).

Shrewsbury, J.F.D., *A History of Bubonic Plague in the British Isles*, Cambridge, 1970.

Siegfried, A., *Itinéraires de contagions: épidémies et idéologies*, Paris, 1960.

Simons, F.J., *Eat not This Flesh*, Madison, Wis., 1961.

Sivori, G., "Il tramonto dell'industria serica genovese," *Rivista storica italiana*, vol. 84 (1972).

Slicher van Bath, B.H., "Accounts and Diaries of Farmers before 1800," *Afdeling Agrarische Geschiedenis Bijdragen*, vol. 8 (1962).

Slicher van Bath, B.H., "Yield Ratios 810–1820," *Afdeling Agrarische Geschiedenis Bijdragen*, vol. 10 (1963).

Slicher van Bath, B.H., *The Agrarian History of Western Europe 500–1850*, London, 1963.

Smith, C.T., *An Historical Geography of Western Europe before 1800*, New York/Washington, 1967.

Smith, J., *Old Scottish Clockmakers*, Edinburgh, 1921.

Smith, R.A., *Canterbury Cathedral Priory; A Study in Monastic Administration*, Cambridge, 1969.

Snape, R.H., *English Monastic Finances in the Late Middle Ages*, London, 1968.

Soltow, L., "Long-run changes in British income inequality," *The Economic History Review*, ser. 2, vol. 21 (1968).

Spengler, J.J., "The Population Problem," *The Southern Economic Journal*, vol. 27 (1961).

Sprandel, R., *Das Eisengewerbe im Mitellalter*, Stuttgart, 1968.

Spufford, P., *Money and Its Use*, London, 1989.

Stella, A., "La proprietà ecclesiastica nella Repubblica di Venezia dal secolo XV al secolo XVII," *Nuova rivista storica*, vol. 42 (1958).

Stephenson, C., *Borough and Town: A Study of Urban Origins in England*, Cambridge, Mass., 1933.

Stone, L., "Elizabethan Overseas Trade," *The Economic History Review*, ser. 2, vol. 2 (1949).

Stone, L., *La crisis dell'aristocrazia*, Turin, 1972.

Stouff, L., *Ravitaillement et alimentation en Provence au XIVe et XVe siècles*, Paris/The Hague, 1970.

Stow, J., *Annales*, continued and augmented by E. Howes, London, 1631.
Stoye, J.W., *English Travellers Abroad*, London, 1952.
Strachey, L., *Portraits in Miniature*, New York, 1962.
Strauss, G., *Nuremberg in the 16th Century*, New York, 1966.
Supple, B.E., *Commercial Crisis and Change in England 1600–1642*, Cambridge, 1959.
Sutherland, I., "John Graunt: A Tercentenary Tribute," *Journal of the Royal Statistical Society*, ser. A, vol. 126 (1963).
Svenskt Biografiskt Lexikon, Stockholm, 1918.

Tadino, A., *Raguaglio dell'origine et giornali successi della gran peste*, Milan, 1648.
Tagliaferri, A., *L'economia veronese secondo gli estimi dal 1409 al 1635*, Milan, 1966.
Tagliaferri, A., *Consumi e tenore di vita di una famiglia borghese del 1600*, Milan, 1968.
Tagliaferri, A. (ed.), *Relazioni dei Rettori Veneti in Terraferma*, Milan, 1973–79.
Talbot, C.H., *Medicine in Medieval England*, London, 1967.
Tawney, A.J. and Tawney, R.H., "An Occupational Census of the Seventeenth Century," *The Economic History Review*, vol. 5 (1934–35).
Tawney, R.H., *Business and Politics under James I*, Cambridge, 1958.
Tawney, R.H. and Power, E. (eds), *Tudor Economic Documents*, London/New York/Toronto, 1953.
Taylor, E.G.R., "Mathematics and the Navigator in the 13th Century," *Journal of the Institute of Navigation*, vol. 13 (1960).
Thirsk, J., *Economic Policy and Projects. The Development of a Consumer Society in Early Modern England*, London/Oxford, 1978.
Thirsk, J. and Cooper, J.P., *Seventeenth-Century Economic Documents*, Oxford, 1972.
Tissot, S.A., *De la santé des gens de Lettres*, Lausanne, 1768.
Titow, J.Z., *English Rural Society 1200–1350*, London, 1969.
Titow, J.Z., *Winchester Yields. A Study in Medieval Agricultural Productivity*, Cambridge, 1972.
Toderi, G., Toderi, F., and Paolozzi Strozzi, B., *Le monete della Repubblica Senese*, Siena, 1992.
Tooley, R.V., *Maps and Map Makers*, New York, 1962.
Trenard, L., "Le charbon avant l'ère industrielle," in *Charbon et Sciences Humaines* (col. Université de Lille), Paris/The Hague, 1966.
Trevor-Davies, R., *Spain in Decline, 1621–1700*, London/New York, 1965.
Trexler, R.C., "Une table florentine d'espérance de vie," *Annales E.S.C.*, vol. 26 (1971).
Trow-Smith, R., *A History of British Livestock Husbandry to 1700*, London, 1957.
Tucci, U., "L'industria del ferro nel Settecento in Val Trompia," in *Ricerche storiche ed economiche in memoria di C. Barbagallo*, Naples, 1970.

Ullyet, K., *British Clocks and Clockmakers*, London, 1947.
Unger, R.W., "Dutch ship design in the 15th and 16th Centuries," *Viator*, vol. 4 (1973).
Unger, R.W., *Dutch Shipbuilding before 1800*, Assen, 1978.
Unger, R.W., *The Ship in the Medieval Economy (600–1600)*, London/Montreal, 1980.
United Nations, *The Determinants and Consequences of Population Trends*, New York, 1953.
Unwin, G., *Studies in Economic History*, London, 1927.
Urlanis, T.S., *Rost naselenija v Evropi*, Moscow, 1941.
Usher, A.P., *The Early History of Deposit Banking in Mediterranean Europe*, Cambridge, Mass., 1943.
Usher, A.P., *A History of Mechanical Inventions*, Boston, 1959.

Valentinitsch, H., "Der ungarische und innerösterreichische Viehhandel nach Venedig," *Carinthia*, vol. 1 (1973).

Vandenbroeke, C., "Cultivation and Consumption of the Potato in the 17th and 18th Century," in *Acta Historiae Neerlandica*, vol. 5 (1971).

Van der Wee, H., *The Growth of the Antwerp Market and the European Economy*, The Hague, 1963.

Van der Wee, H., "Anvers et les innovations de la technique financière aux XVIᶜ– XVIIᶜ siècles," *Annales E.S.C.*, vol. 22 (1967).

Van der Wee, H., "The Economy as a Factor in the Start of the Revolt in the Southern Netherlands," *Acta Historiae Neerlandica*, vol. 5 (1971).

Van der Woude, A.M., "Het Noorderkwartier," in *Afdeling Agrarische Geschiedenis Bijdragen*, vol. 16 (1972).

Van Houtte, J.A., "La genèse du grand marché international d'Anvers à la fin du Moyen Age," *Revue belge de philologie et d'histoire*, vol. 19 (1940).

Van Houtte, J.A., "Anvers aux XVᶜ et XVIᶜ siècles. Expansion et apogée," *Annales E.S.C.*, vol. 16 (1961).

Van Houtte, J.A., *Economische en Sociale Geschiedenis van de Lage Landen*, Antwerp, 1964.

Van Houtte, J.A., *An Economic History of the Low Countries, 800–1800*, London, 1977.

Van Kampen, S.C. *De Rotterdamse particuliere Sheepsbouw in de tijd van de Republiek*, Assen, 1953.

Van Linschoten, J.H., *The Voyage to the East Indies*, ed. A.C. Burnell and P.A. Tiele, London, 1885.

Van Uytven, R., "The Fulling Mill: Dynamics of the Revolution in Industrial Attitudes," *Acta Historiae Neerlandica*, vol. 5 (1971).

Vauban, S. La Preste de, *Project de dîme royale*, Paris, 1707.

Ventura, A., *Nobilità e popolo nella società veneta del '400 e '500*, Bari, 1965.

Verdenius, W.J., "Science grecque et science moderne," *Revue philosophique*, vol. 152 (1962).

Vicens Vives, J., *Manual de historia economica de España*, Barcelona, 1959.

Vilar, P., *Crecimiento y desarrollo. Economia e historia: reflexiones sobre el caso espanol*, Barcelona, 1964.

Vilar, P., *Catalunya dins l'Espanya moderna*, Barcelona, 1964–68.

Vilar, P., *Oro e moneta nella storia*, Bari, 1971.

Villermé, L.R., *Tableau de l'état physique et moral des ouvriers*, Paris, 1840.

Violante, C., "I Vescovi dell'Italia centro-settentrionale e lo sviluppo dell'economia monetaria," in *Vescovi e Diocesi in Italia nel Medio-Evo*, Padua, 1964.

Violet, T., *Mysteries and Secrets of Trade and Mint Affairs*, London, 1653.

Vogel, W., "Zur Grosse der Europäischen Handelsflotten im 15., 16. und 17. Jahrhundert," *Festschrift Dietrich Schäfer*, Jena, 1915.

Waddington, C.H., *The Ethical Animal*, Chicago, 1960.

Walford, C., "The Famines of the World, Past and Present," *Journal of the Statistical Society*, vols 41–42 (1878–79).

Walker, P.G., "The Origins of the Machine Age," *History Today*, vol. 16 (1966).

Waters, D.W., *The Art of Navigation in England in Elizabethen and Early Stuart Times*, London/New Haven, Conn., 1958.

Wertime, T., *The Coming of the Age of Steel*, Leyden, 1961.

Westermann, E., "Zum Handel mit Ochsen aus Osteuropa in 16 Jahrhundert," *Zeitschrift für Ortforschung*, vol. 22 (1973).

Westermann, E., "Zur Erforschung des nordmitteleuropäischen Ochshandels," *Zeitschrift für Agrargeschichte und Agrarsoziologie*, vol. 23 (1975).

White, L., *Medieval Technology and Social Change*, Oxford, 1962.
White, L., "What Accelerated Technological Progress in the Western Middle Ages," in A.C. Crombie (ed.), *Scientific Change*, New York, 1963.
White, L., "Cultural Climates and Technological Advance in the Middle Ages," *Viator*, vol. 2 (1971).
White, L., "The Expansion of Technology 500–1500," in *The Fontana Economic History of Europe*, vol. 1, London, 1972.
Williams, N.J., *The Maritime Trade of the East Anglian Ports 1550–1590*, Oxford, 1988.
Wilson, C., *England's Apprenticeship, 1603–1763*, Oxford, 1965.
Wilson, C., *The Dutch Republic*, London, 1968.
Wilson, C. and Parker, G. (eds), *An Introduction to the Sources of European Economic History, 1500–1800*, Ithaca, 1977.
Wolff, P., *Commerce et marchands de Toulouse (1350–1450)*, Toulouse, 1954.
Wolff, P., "Prix et marché," *Méthodologie de l'histoire et des sciences humaines*, Toulouse, 1973.
Woodward, G.W.O., *The Dissolution of the Monasteries*, London, 1966.
Working, H., "Statistical Laws of Family Expenditure," *Journal of the American Statistical Association*, vol. 38 (1943).
Wrigley, E.A., *Population and History*, New York, 1969.
Wrigley, E.A. and Schofield, R.S., *The Population History of England 1541–1871*, Cambridge, 1981.

Youings, Y., *The Dissolution of the Monasteries*, London, 1971.
Young, A., *Political Arithmetic*, London, 1774.
Young, A., *Travels in France during the Years 1787, 1788, 1789*, London, 1912.

Zanetti, D., *Problemi alimentari di una economia preindustriale*, Turin, 1964.
Zanetti, D., "Note sulla Rivoluzione dei prezzi," *Rivista storica italiana*, vol. 77 (1965).
Zanetti, D., *La demografia del patriziato milanese*, Pavia, 1973.
Ziegler, P., *The Black Death*, London, 1969.
Zinsser, H., *Rats, Lice and History*, New York, 1935.

HISTORICAL ATLASES

Atlas Historique Belfram, ed. F. Michel, B. Anglivel and A. Rigade, Paris, 1969.
Atlas of World History, ed. R.R. Palmer, Chicago, 1965.
British History Atlas, ed. M. Gilbert, London, 1968.
Historical Atlas, ed. W.R. Shepherd, New York, 1980.
Historical Atlas of the Muslim Peoples, ed. H.A.R. Gibb, Cambridge, Mass., 1957.
Historischer Atlas der Schweiz, ed. H. Amman and K. Schib, Aarau, 1958.
Nouvel Atlas historique, ed. P. Serryn and R. Plasselle, n.d.
Russian History Atlas, ed. M. Gilbert, London, 1972.
Westermanns Grosser Atlas zur Weltgeschichte, ed. H.E. Stier and Associates, Berlin, 1956.

INDEX